Reading STREET

Program Authors

Peter Afflerbach   P. David Pearson

Camille Blachowicz   Sam Sebesta

Candy Dawson Boyd   Deborah Simmons

Elena Izquierdo   Alfred Tatum

Connie Juel   Sharon Vaughn

Edward Kame'enui   Susan Watts Taffe

Donald Leu   Karen Kring Wixson

Jeanne R. Paratore

PEARSON

Glenview, Illinois • Boston, Massachusetts
Chandler, Arizona • Upper Saddle River, New Jersey

We dedicate Reading Street to
Peter Jovanovich.

His wisdom, courage,
and passion for education
are an inspiration to us all.

Accelerated Reader

PEARSON

ISBN-13: 978-0-328-46999-4
ISBN-10: 0-328-46999-8
2 3 4 5 6 7 8 9 10 V064 14 13 12 11 10
CC1

Any Path, Any Pace

Reading STREET

CALLE de la Lectura

"Welcome to
Reading Street!
Bienvenidos too."

PEARSON

Find Your Place on Reading Street!

Who said so?

The Leading Researchers,

Practitioners, and Authors.

Consultant

Sharroky Hollie, Ph.D.
Assistant Professor
California State University
Dominguez Hills, CA

Teacher Reviewers

Dr. Bettyann Brugger
*Educational Support Coordinator–
Reading Office*
Milwaukee Public Schools
Milwaukee, WI

Kathleen Burke
K–12 Reading Coordinator
Peoria Public Schools, Peoria, IL

Darci Burns, M.S.Ed.
University of Oregon

Bridget Cantrell
District Intervention Specialist
Blackburn Elementary School
Independence, MO

**Tahira DuPree Chase,
M.A., M.S.Ed.**
*Administrator of Elementary
English Language Arts*
Mount Vernon City School District
Mount Vernon, NY

Michele Conner
Director, Elementary Education
Aiken County School District
Aiken, SC

Georgia Coulombe
*K–6 Regional Trainer/
Literacy Specialist*
Regional Center for Training and
Learning (RCTL), Reno, NV

Kelly Dalmas
Third Grade Teacher
Avery's Creek Elementary, Arden, NC

Seely Dillard
First Grade Teacher
Laurel Hill Primary School
Mt. Pleasant, SC

Jodi Dodds-Kinner
Director of Elementary Reading
Chicago Public Schools, Chicago, IL

Dr. Ann Wild Evenson
District Instructional Coach
Osseo Area Schools, Maple Grove, MN

Stephanie Fascitelli
Principal
Apache Elementary, Albuquerque
Public Schools, Albuquerque, NM

Alice Franklin
*Elementary Coordinator, Language
Arts & Reading*
Spokane Public Schools, Spokane, WA

Laureen Fromberg
Assistant Principal
PS 100 Queens, NY

Kimberly Gibson
First Grade Teacher
Edgar B. Davis Community School
Brockton, MA

Kristen Gray
Lead Teacher
A.T. Allen Elementary School
Concord, NC

Mary Ellen Hazen
State Pre-K Teacher
Rockford Public Schools #205
Rockford, IL

Patrick M. Johnson
Elementary Instructional Director
Seattle Public Schools, Seattle, WA

Theresa Jaramillo Jones
Principal
Highland Elementary School
Las Cruces, NM

Sophie Kowzun
*Program Supervisor, Reading/
Language Arts, PreK-5*
Montgomery County Public Schools
Rockville, MD

David W. Matthews
Sixth Grade Teacher
Easton Area Middle School
Easton, PA

Ana Nuncio
Editor and Independent Publisher
Salem, MA

Joseph Peila
Principal
Chappell Elementary School
Chicago, IL

Ivana Reimer
Literacy Coordinator
PS 100 Queens, NY

Sally Riley
Curriculum Coordinator
Rochester Public Schools
Rochester, NH

Dyan M. Smiley
Independent Educational Consultant

Michael J. Swiatowiec
Lead Literacy Teacher
Graham Elementary School
Chicago, IL

Dr. Helen Taylor
Director of English Education
Portsmouth City Public Schools
Portsmouth, VA

Carol Thompson
Teaching and Learning Coach
Independence School District
Independence, MO

Erinn Zeitlin
Kindergarten Teacher
Carderock Springs Elementary School
Bethesda, MD

Any Path, Any Pace

UNIT 3

Changes

In this Teacher's Edition Unit 3, Volume 1

Table of Contents...vi–xiii
Unit 3 Skills Overview ....xiv–xv
Unit 3 Monitor Progress ....xvi–xvii
Assessment and Grouping ....xviii–xix
Unit 3 Concept Launch ....xx–xxi
Flexible Pacing Plans..xxii

WEEK 1 · A Place to Play Realistic Fiction....12a–43l
My Neighborhood, Then and Now Autobiography

Differentiated Instruction **SI** **OL** **A** **ELL** ....DI•1–DI•21

WEEK 2 · Ruby in Her Own Time
Animal Fantasy..44a–83l
The Ugly Duckling Fairy Tale

Differentiated Instruction **SI** **OL** **A** **ELL** ....DI•22–DI•42

WEEK 3 · The Class Pet Expository Text 84a–117l
Belling the Cat Fable

Differentiated Instruction **SI** **OL** **A** **ELL** ....DI•43–DI•63

Customize Writing ....CW•1–CW•10
Customize Literacy...CL•1–CL•47
Let's Learn Amazing Words ....OV•1–OV•3

In the **First Stop** on Reading Street

- **Dear First Grade Teacher**

- **Research into Practice on Reading Street**

- **Guide to Reading Street**

- **Assessment on Reading Street**

- **Customize Writing on Reading Street**

- **Differentiated Instruction on Reading Street**

- **ELL on Reading Street**

- **Customize Literacy on Reading Street**

- **Digital Products on Reading Street**

- **Teacher Resources for Grade 1**

- **Index**

 GO Digital!

See It!

- **Big Question Video**
- **Concept Talk Video**
- **Interactive Sound-Spelling Cards**
- **Envision It! Animations**
- **Sing with Me Animations**

Hear It!

- **Sing with Me Animations**
- **eSelections**
- **Grammar Jammer**
- **eReaders**
- **Leveled Reader Database**

Do It!

- **Vocabulary Activities**
- **Story Sort**
- **21st Century Skills Activities**
- **Online Assessment**
- **Letter Tile Drag and Drop**

UNIT R

My World

Table of Contents...vi–xiii
Unit R Skills Overview..xiv–xv
Unit R Monitor Progress ....xvi–xvii
Assessment and Grouping ....xviii–xix
Unit R Concept Launch.. xx–xxi
Flexible Pacing Plans xxii

Volume 1

WEEK 1 • **Sam** Realistic Fiction...............................12a–35f

Rip Van Winkle Folk Tale

Differentiated Instruction SI OL A ELL ....DI•1–DI•21

WEEK 2 • **Snap!** Realistic Fiction..............................36a–61f

Families Photo Essay

Differentiated Instruction SI OL A ELL ....DI•22–DI•42

WEEK 3 • **Tip and Tam** Realistic Fiction.........................62a–87f

Yards Photo Essay

Differentiated Instruction SI OL A ELL ....DI•43–DI•63

Volume 2

WEEK 4 • **The Big Top** Realistic Fiction.........................88a–113f

Around the Block Procedural Text

Differentiated Instruction SI OL A ELL ....DI•64–DI•84

WEEK 5 • **School Day** Realistic Fiction.........................114a–139f

How Do You Get to School? Photo Essay

Differentiated Instruction SI OL A ELL ....DI•85–DI•105

WEEK 6 • **Farmers Market**
Realistic Fiction...140a–165h
The Maid and the Milk Pail Fable

Differentiated Instruction SI OL A ELL ....DI•106–DI•126

Customize Literacy...CL•1–CL•47
Let's Learn Amazing Words ....OV•1–OV•3

Animals, Tame and Wild

Table of Contents..vi–xiii
Unit 1 Skills Overview ....xiv–xv
Unit 1 Monitor Progress ....xvi–xvii
Assessment and Grouping ....xviii–xix
Unit 1 Concept Launch ....xx–xxi
Flexible Pacing Plans... xxii

Volume 1

WEEK 1 • Sam, Come Back! Realistic Fiction.............12a–37l

"Puppy Games" Sing-Along

Differentiated Instruction SI OL A ELL ....DI•1–DI•21

WEEK 2 • Pig in a Wig Animal Fantasy 38a–65l

"We Are Vets" Sing-Along

Differentiated Instruction SI OL A ELL ....DI•22–DI•42

WEEK 3 • The Big Blue Ox Animal Fantasy..................66a–93l

They Can Help Photo Essay

Differentiated Instruction SI OL A ELL ....DI•43–DI•63

Volume 2

WEEK 4 • A Fox and a Kit Literary Nonfiction............94a–119l

The Fox and the Grapes Fable

Differentiated Instruction SI OL A ELL ....DI•64–DI•84

WEEK 5 • Get the Egg! Realistic Fiction 120a–145l

Help the Birds How-to Article

Differentiated Instruction SI OL A ELL ....DI•85–DI•105

WEEK 6 • Animal Park Literary Nonfiction....................146a–l71n

Poetry Collection Poetry

Differentiated Instruction SI OL A ELL ....DI•106–DI•126

Customize Writing ....CW•1–CW•20
Customize Literacy..CL•1–CL•47
Let's Learn Amazing Words ....OV•1–OV•3

UNIT 2

Communities

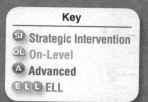

Table of Contents..vi–xiii
Unit 2 Skills Overview ....xiv–xv
Unit 2 Monitor Progress ....xvi–xvii
Assessment and Grouping ....xviii–xix
Unit 2 Concept Launch ....xx–xxi
Flexible Pacing Plans xxii

Volume 1

WEEK 1 • A Big Fish for Max Animal Fantasy...........12a–43l

At Home Literary Nonfiction

Differentiated Instruction SI OL A ELL ....DI•1–DI•21

WEEK 2 • The Farmer in the Hat Realistic Fiction 44a–77l

Helping Hands at 4-H Expository Text

Differentiated Instruction SI OL A ELL ....DI•22–DI•42

WEEK 3 • Who Works Here? Expository Text..........78a–103l

Neighborhood Map Procedural Text

Differentiated Instruction SI OL A ELL ....DI•43–DI•63

Volume 2

WEEK 4 • The Big Circle Fiction....................................104a–137l

We Are Safe Together Literary Nonfiction

Differentiated Instruction SI OL A ELL ....DI•64–DI•84

WEEK 5 • Life in the Forest Expository Text............138a–169l

A Mangrove Forest Magazine Article

Differentiated Instruction SI OL A ELL ....DI•85–DI•105

WEEK 6 • Honey Bees Expository Text.........................170a–201n

Poetry Collection Poetry

Differentiated Instruction SI OL A ELL ....DI•106–DI•126

Customize Writing ....CW•1–CW•20
Customize Literacy..CL•1–CL•47
Let's Learn Amazing Words ....OV•1–OV•3

Changes

Table of Contents..vi–xiii
Unit 3 Skills Overview ....xiv–xv
Unit 3 Monitor Progress ....xvi–xvii
Assessment and Grouping ....xviii–xix
Unit 3 Concept Launch ....xx–xxi
Flexible Pacing Plans xxii

Volume 1

WEEK 1 • **A Place to Play** Realistic Fiction....................12a–43l

My Neighborhood, Then and Now Autobiography

Differentiated Instruction SI OL A ELL ....DI•1–DI•21

WEEK 2 • **Ruby in Her Own Time**
Animal Fantasy..44a–83l
The Ugly Duckling Fairy Tale

Differentiated Instruction SI OL A ELL ....DI•22–DI•42

WEEK 3 • **The Class Pet** Expository Text 84a–117l

Belling the Cat Fable

Differentiated Instruction SI OL A ELL ....DI•43–DI•63

Volume 2

WEEK 4 • **Frog and Toad Together**
Animal Fantasy..118a–149l
Growing Plants How-to Article

Differentiated Instruction SI OL A ELL ....DI•64–DI•84

WEEK 5 • **I'm a Caterpillar** Literary Nonfiction.........150a–181l

My Computer 21st Century Skills

Differentiated Instruction SI OL A ELL ....DI•85–DI•105

WEEK 6 • **Where Are My Animal Friends?** Drama................................182a–217n
Poetry Collection Poetry

Differentiated Instruction SI OL A ELL ....DI•106–DI•126

Customize Writing ....CW•1–CW•20
Customize Literacy..CL•1–CL•47
Let's Learn Amazing Words ....OV•1–OV•3

UNIT 4

Treasures

Table of Contents...vi–xiii
Unit 4 Skills Overview ....xiv–xv
Unit 4 Monitor Progress ....xvi–xvii
Assessment and Grouping ....xviii–xix
Unit 4 Concept Launch ....xx–xxi
Flexible Pacing Plans...xxii

Volume 1

WEEK 1 • Mama's Birthday Present
Realistic Fiction 12a–51l
Limonada Recipe Recipe
Differentiated Instruction **SI OL A ELL** .... DI•1–DI•21

WEEK 2 • Cinderella Fairy Tale........................52a–87l
Anarosa Fairy Tale
Differentiated Instruction **SI OL A ELL** .... DI•22–DI•42

WEEK 3 • A Trip to Washington, D.C.
Expository Text..88a–119l
My 4th of July Autobiography
Differentiated Instruction **SI OL A ELL** .... DI•43–DI•63

Volume 2

WEEK 4 • A Southern Ranch Expository Text.........120a–153l
On the Way to a Ranch Procedural Text
Differentiated Instruction **SI OL A ELL** .... DI•64–DI•84

WEEK 5 • Peter's Chair Realistic Fiction 154a–189l
Peter's Baby Sister 21st Century Skills
Differentiated Instruction **SI OL A ELL** .... DI•85–DI•105

WEEK 6 • Henry and Mudge and Mrs. Hopper's House Realistic Fiction.............190a–227n
Poetry Collection Poetry
Differentiated Instruction **SI OL A ELL** .... DI•106–DI•126

Customize Writing ....CW•1–CW•20
Customize Literacy..CL•1–CL•47
Let's Learn Amazing Words ....OV•1–OV•3

UNIT 5

Great Ideas

Table of Contents.. vi–xiii
Unit 5 Skills Overview ....xiv–xv
Unit 5 Monitor Progress .... xvi–xvii
Assessment and Grouping .... xviii–xix
Unit 5 Concept Launch .... xx–xxi
Flexible Pacing Plans xxii

Volume 1

WEEK 1 • Tippy-Toe Chick, Go! Animal Fantasy...... 12a–51l

Little Red Hen Folk Tale

Differentiated Instruction **SI** **OL** **A** **ELL** .... DI•1–DI•21

WEEK 2 • Mole and the Baby Bird
Animal Fantasy...52a–89l

Brave Little Cuckoo Folk Tale

Differentiated Instruction **SI** **OL** **A** **ELL** .... DI•22–DI•42

WEEK 3 • Dot & Jabber Informational Fiction................ 90a–129l

Water Expository Text

Differentiated Instruction **SI** **OL** **A** **ELL** .... DI•43–DI•63

Volume 2

WEEK 4 • Simple Machines Expository Text............. 130a–165l

Roy's Wheelchair Literary Nonfiction

Differentiated Instruction **SI** **OL** **A** **ELL** .... DI•64–DI•84

WEEK 5 • Alexander Graham Bell:
A Great Inventor Biography 166a–201l

Inventions 21st Century Skills

Differentiated Instruction **SI** **OL** **A** **ELL** .... DI•85–DI•105

WEEK 6 • The Stone Garden Realistic Fiction 202a–241n

Poetry Collection Poetry

Differentiated Instruction **SI** **OL** **A** **ELL** .... DI•106–DI•126

Customize Writing .... CW•1–CW•20
Customize Literacy...CL•1–CL•47
Let's Learn Amazing Words .... OV•1–OV•3

Skills Overview

Key

T	Tested Skill
⟳	Target Skill

	WEEK 1 	**WEEK 2** 
	A Place to Play Realistic Fiction pp. 20–33 **My Neighborhood, Then and Now** Autobiography pp. 38–41	**Ruby in Her Own Time** Animal Fantasy pp. 52–73 **The Ugly Duckling** Fairy Tale pp. 78–81

Get Ready to Read

Question of the Week	How do places change?	What do we learn as we grow and change?
Amazing Words	*growth, population, public, teeter, shuffle, crooked, makeshift, spindly*	*attempt, event, time line, famous, flatter, correct, lovely, common*
Phonemic Awareness	Segment and Blend Phonemes, Add Initial Phonemes	Segment and Blend Phonemes, Add Initial and Final Phonemes
Phonics	T ⟳ Vowel Sounds of *y* T ⟳ Syllable Pattern CV **Review** Long *e: e, ee*; Syllables VC/CV	T ⟳ Consonant Patterns *ng, nk* T ⟳ Compound Words **Review** Vowel Sounds of *y*, Syllable Pattern CV
Spelling	Vowel Sounds of *y*	Words with *ng, nk*

Read and Comprehend

Comprehension	T ⟳ **Skill** Sequence ⟳ **Strategy** Summarize **Review Skill** Author's Purpose	T ⟳ **Skill** Compare and Contrast ⟳ **Strategy** Inferring **Review Skill** Sequence
High-Frequency Words	T *things, always, day, become, nothing, stays, everything*	T *ever, sure, were, enough, every, any, own*
Vocabulary	Antonyms	Synonyms
Fluency	Accuracy and Rate	Appropriate Phrasing

Language Arts

Writing	Realistic Story Trait: Organization	Comments About a Story Trait: Voice
Conventions	T Action Verbs	T Verbs that Add -*s*
Speaking/Listening	Relate an Experience in Sequence	Respect
Research Skills	Interview	Glossary

The Big Question
What is changing in our world?

WEEK 3	WEEK 4	WEEK 5	WEEK 6
The Class Pet Expository Text pp. 92–105 **Belling the Cat** Fable pp. 110–115	**Frog and Toad Together** Animal Fantasy pp. 126–141 **Growing Plants** How-to Article pp. 146–147	**I'm a Caterpillar** Literary Nonfiction pp. 158–173 **My Computer** 21st Century Skills pp. 178–179	**Where Are My Animal Friends?** Drama pp. 190–207 **Poetry Collection** Poetry pp. 212–215
What can we learn about animals as they grow and change?	What changes happen in a garden?	What changes can be seen in nature?	What do animals do when the seasons change?
mature, natural, features, tumble, swoop, crumple, nudges, nibble, wriggle	*gardener, sprout, nature, dim, shade, sprinkling, destroy, humongous*	*insect, develop, cycle, rearrange, flurries, emerge, fragile, vessel*	*hibernate, migrate, temperature, autumn, freeze, bitterly, weary*
Segment and Blend Phonemes, Add Initial and Final Phonemes	Isolate Phonemes, Add Phonemes	Isolate Phonemes, Add Phonemes	Segment and Blend, Change Initial Phonemes
T Ending -es, Plural -es **T** Vowels: *r*-Controlled *or, ore* **Review** Consonant Patterns *ng, nk;* Compound Words	**T** Inflected Endings **T** Vowel: *r*-Controlled *ar* **Review** Ending -es, Plural -es; *r*-Controlled *or, ore*	**T** Vowels: *r*-Controlled *er, ir, ur* **T** Contractions *'s, 've, 're* **Review** Inflected Endings -ed, -ing; *r*-Controlled *ar*	**T** Comparative Endings **T** Consonant Pattern -dge **Review** *r*-Controlled *er, ir, ur;* Contractions
Words with -es	Words with -ed	Words with er, ir, ur	Words with -er, -est
T **Skill** Fact and Opinion **Strategy** Monitor and Clarify **Review Skill** Compare and Contrast	**Skill** Author's Purpose **Strategy** Visualize **Review Skill** Plot	**T** **Skill** Fact and Opinion **Strategy** Text Structure **Review Skill** Sequence	**T** **Skill** Draw Conclusions **Strategy** Background Knowledge **Review Skill** Compare and Contrast
T *very, car, away, our, house, school, friends*	**T** *few, afraid, read, soon, how, again*	**T** *know, push, done, wait, visit*	**T** *does, good-bye, before, won't, oh, right*
Descriptive Words	Dictionary/Glossary	Dictionary/Glossary	Context Clues
Appropriate Phrasing	Expression and Intonation	Expression and Intonation	Expression and Intonation
Writing for Tests Summary	Lists Trait: Sentences	Captions and Pictures Trait: Focus/Ideas	Play Scene Trait: Sentences
T Verbs That Do Not Add -s	**T** Verbs for Past and Future	**T** Verbs *Am, Is, Are, Was, Were*	**T** Contractions with *Not*
Give Descriptions	Poetry Presentation	Share Information and Ideas	Give Announcements
Classifying and Categorizing	Diagram	Technology: My Computer	Picture Graph

UNIT 3

Monitor Progress
Make Data-Driven Decisions

Data Management
- Assess
- Diagnose
- Prescribe
- Disaggregate

Classroom Management
- Monitor Progress
- Group
- Differentiate Instruction
- Inform Parents

Don't Wait Until Friday

SUCCESS PREDICTORS	WEEK 1	WEEK 2	WEEK 3	WEEK 4
Phonics *(Word Reading)*	T Vowel Sounds of *y* T Syllable Pattern CV	T Consonant Patterns *ng, nk* T Compound Words	T Ending *-es*, Plural *-es* T Vowels: *r*-Controlled *or, ore*	T Inflected Endings T Vowel: *r*-Controlled *ar*
Fluency *(WCPM)*	Read with Accuracy and Rate 20–30 WCPM	Read with Appropriate Phrasing 20–30 WCPM	Read with Appropriate Phrasing 20–30 WCPM	Read with Expression and Intonation 25–35 WCPM
High-Frequency Words *(Vocabulary)*	T things T always T day T become T nothing T stays T everything	T ever T sure T were T enough T every T any T own	T very T car T away T our T house T school T friends	T few T afraid T read T soon T how T again
Oral Vocabulary/ Concept Development (assessed informally) *(Vocabulary)*	growth population public teeter shuffle crooked makeshift spindly	attempt event time line famous flatter correct lovely common	mature wriggle natural features tumble swoop crumple nudges nibble	gardener sprout nature dim shade sprinkling destroy humongous
Text Comprehension *(Retelling)*	T **Skill** Sequence **Strategy** Summarize	T **Skill** Compare and Contrast **Strategy** Inferring	T **Skill** Fact and Opinion **Strategy** Monitor and Clarify	T **Skill** Author's Purpose **Strategy** Visualize

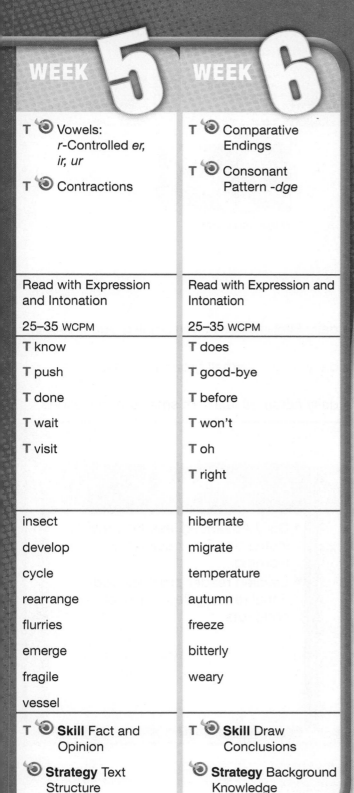

Key

T Tested Skill

🎯 Target Skill

WEEK 5

T 🎯 **Vowels:**
r-Controlled *er*, *ir*, *ur*

T 🎯 **Contractions**

Read with Expression and Intonation
25–35 WCPM

T know

T push

T done

T wait

T visit

insect

develop

cycle

rearrange

flurries

emerge

fragile

vessel

T 🎯 **Skill** Fact and Opinion

🎯 **Strategy** Text Structure

WEEK 6

T 🎯 **Comparative Endings**

T 🎯 **Consonant Pattern** *-dge*

Read with Expression and Intonation
25–35 WCPM

T does

T good-bye

T before

T won't

T oh

T right

hibernate

migrate

temperature

autumn

freeze

bitterly

weary

T 🎯 **Skill** Draw Conclusions

🎯 **Strategy** Background Knowledge

Online ASSESSMENT
ReadingStreet.com

Online Classroom

Manage Data

- Assign the Unit 3 Benchmark Test for students to take online.

- Online Assessment records results and generates reports by school, grade, classroom, or student.

- Use reports to disaggregate and aggregate Unit 3 skills and standards data to monitor progress.

- Based on class lists created to support the categories important for AYP (gender, ethnicity, migrant education, English proficiency, disabilities, economic status), reports let you track adequate yearly progress every six weeks.

Group

- Use results from Unit 3 Benchmark Tests taken online through Online Assessment to measure whether students have mastered the English-Language Arts Content Standards taught in this unit.

- Reports in Online Assessment suggest whether students need Extra Support or Intervention.

Individualized Instruction

- Tests are correlated to Unit 3 tested skills and standards so that prescriptions for individual teaching and learning plans can be created.

- Individualized prescriptions target instruction and accelerate student progress toward learning outcome goals.

- Prescriptions include remediation activities and resources to reteach Unit 3 skills and standards.

UNIT 3

Assessment and Grouping
for Data-Driven Instruction

4-Step Plan for Assessment
1 Diagnose and Differentiate
2 Monitor Progress
3 Assess and Regroup
4 Summative Assessment

STEP 1 Diagnose and Differentiate

Baseline Group Tests

Diagnose

To make initial grouping decisions, use the Baseline Group Test, the Texas Primary Reading Inventory (TPRI), or another initial placement test. Depending on children's ability levels, you may have more than one of each group.

Differentiate

If... student performance is **SI** **then...** use the regular instruction and the daily **Strategic Intervention** small group lessons.

If... student performance is **OL** **then...** use the regular instruction and the daily **On-Level** small group lessons.

If... student performance is **A** **then...** use the regular instruction and the daily **Advanced** learners small group lessons.

Small Group Time

SI Strategic Intervention

- Daily small group lessons provide more intensive instruction, more scaffolding, more practice, and more opportunities to respond.
- Reteach lessons in the *First Stop on Reading Street* provide additional instructional opportunities with target skills.
- Leveled readers build background and provide practice for target skills and vocabulary.

OL On-Level

- Explicit instructional routines teach core skills and strategies.
- Daily On-Level lessons provide more practice and more opportunities to respond.
- Independent activities provide practice for core skills and extension and enrichment options.
- Leveled reader provides additional reading and practice for core skills and vocabulary.

A Advanced

- Daily Advanced lessons provide instruction for accelerated learning.
- Leveled reader provides additional reading tied to lesson concepts.

Additional Differentiated Learning Options

Reading Street Response to Intervention Kit
- Focused intervention lessons on the five critical areas of reading: phonemic awareness, phonics, vocabulary, comprehension, and fluency

My Sidewalks on Reading Street
- Intensive intervention for struggling readers

STEP 2 Monitor Progress

Don't Wait Until Friday

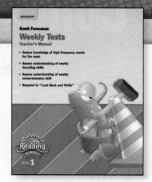
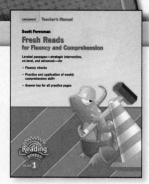

Use these tools during lesson teaching to **monitor student progress.**

- **Skill and Strategy** instruction during reading

- **Don't Wait Until Friday** boxes to check word reading, retelling, fluency, and oral vocabulary

- **Weekly Assessment** on Day 5 to check phonics and fluency

- **Reader's and Writer's Notebook** pages at point of use

- **Weekly Tests** to assess target skills for the week

- **Fresh Reads** for Comprehension and Fluency

Weekly Tests

Fresh Reads for Fluency and Comprehension

STEP 3 Assess and Regroup

Use these tools during lesson teaching assess and regroup.

- **Weekly Assessments** Record results of weekly assessments in retelling, phonics, and fluency to track student progress.

- **Unit Benchmark Test** Administer this test to check mastery of unit skills.

- **Regroup** We recommend the first regrouping to be at the end of Unit 1. Use weekly assessment information and Unit Benchmark Test performance to inform regrouping decisions. Then regroup at the end of each subsequent unit.

First Stop on Reading Street Assessment Chart

Group

Baseline Group Test → Regroup Units R and 1 → Regroup Unit 2 → Regroup Unit 3 → Regroup Unit 4 → **End of Year**

Unit R Weeks 1–6	Unit 1 Weeks 7–12	Unit 2 Weeks 13–18	Unit 3 Weeks 19–24	Unit 4 Weeks 25–30	Unit 5 Weeks 31–36

Outside assessments, such as DRA, TPRI, and DIBELS, may recommend regrouping at other times during the year.

STEP 4 Summative Assessment

Use these tools after lesson teaching to assess students.

- **Unit Benchmark Tests** Use to measure a student's mastery of each unit's skills.

- **End-of-Year Benchmark Test** Use to measure a student's mastery of program skills covered in all six units.

Unit and End-of-Year Benchmark Tests

Understanding By Design

Grant Wiggins, Ed.D.
Reading Street Author

"A big idea is a concept, theme, or issue that gives meaning and connection to discrete facts and skills…. In an education for understanding, a vital challenge is to highlight the big ideas, show how they prioritize the learning, and help students understand their value for making sense of all the 'stuff' of content."

Changes

THE BIG
?

What is changing in our world?

A Place to Play REALISTIC FICTION

❓ How do places change?

Paired Selection
My Neighborhood, Then and Now AUTOBIOGRAPHY

Ruby in Her Own Time ANIMAL FANTASY

❓ What do we learn as we grow and change?

Paired Selection
The Ugly Duckling FAIRY TALE

The Class Pet EXPOSITORY TEXT

❓ What can we learn about animals as they grow and change?

Paired Selection
Belling the Cat FABLE

Frog and Toad Together

ANIMAL FANTASY

❓ What changes happen in a garden?

Paired Selection
Growing Plants HOW-TO ARTICLE

I'm a Caterpillar LITERARY NONFICTION

❓ What changes can be seen in nature?

Paired Selection
My Computer 21ST CENTURY SKILLS

Where Are My Animal Friends? DRAMA

❓ What do animals do when the seasons change?

Paired Selection
"This Tooth," "Tommy," and "Where Do Fish Go in Winter?" POETRY

Concept Launch • **xxi**

UNIT 3

Small Group Time
Flexible Pacing Plans

Small Group Time

Sometimes you have holidays, programs, assemblies, or other interruptions to the school week. This plan can help you make Small Group Time decisions if you have less time during the week.

5 Day Plan

DAY 1	• Phonemic Awareness • Phonics • Reading Practice
DAY 2	• Phonemic Awareness • Phonics • Reading Practice
DAY 3	• Phonics • Leveled Reader
DAY 4	• High-Frequency Words • Reading Practice
DAY 5	• Phonics • Comprehension

4 Day Plan

DAY 1	• Phonemic Awareness • Phonics • Reading Practice
DAY 2	• High-Frequency Words • Leveled Reader
DAY 3	• Phonics • Leveled Reader
DAY 4	• High-Frequency Words • Reading Practice

3 Day Plan

DAY 1	• Phonemic Awareness • Phonics • Reading Practice
DAY 2	• Phonics • Leveled Reader
DAY 3	• High-Frequency Words • Reading Practice

5 Day Plan

DAY 1	• Frontload Concept • Preteach Skills • Conventions and Writing
DAY 2	• Review Concept and Skills • Frontload and Read Main Selection • Conventions and Writing
DAY 3	• Review Concept and Skills • Reread Main Selection • Conventions and Writing
DAY 4	• Review Concept and Skills • Read ELL or ELD Reader • Conventions and Writing
DAY 5	• Review Concept and Skills • Reread ELL or ELD Reader • Conventions and Writing

4 Day Plan

DAY 1	• Frontload Concept • Preteach Skills • Conventions and Writing
DAY 2	• Review Concept and Skills • Frontload and Read Main Selection • Conventions and Writing
DAY 3	• Review Concept and Skills • Reread Main Selection • Conventions and Writing
DAY 4	• Review Concept and Skills • Read ELL or ELD Reader • Conventions and Writing

3 Day Plan

DAY 1	• Frontload Concept • Preteach Skills • Conventions and Writing
DAY 2	• Review Concept and Skills • Frontload and Read Main Selection • Conventions and Writing
DAY 3	• Review Concept and Skills • Read ELL or ELD Reader • Conventions and Writing

A Place to Play

Common Core Standards
Weekly Planning Guide

Selection: A Place to Play
Genre: Realistic Fiction

Alignment of the Common Core Standards with This Week's Skills and Strategies

This Week's Common Core Standards for English Language Arts	Instructional Summary
Reading Standards for Literature	
Literature 1. Ask and answer questions about key details in a text.	The lesson focuses on the **sequence** of events in a story. Through the Listening Comprehension selection "We're Moving" and the main selection *A Place to Play,* the lesson helps children identify what happens first, next, and last in a story. The lesson's **summarize** strategy has children identify the most important parts of a story to help them understand and remember what they read.
Literature 3. Describe characters, settings, and major events in a story, using key details.	
Literature 4. Identify words and phrases in stories or poems that suggest feelings or appeal to the senses.	
Foundational Skills Standards	
Foundational Skills 3.g. Recognize and read grade-appropriate irregularly spelled words.	The lesson includes instruction in recognizing and spelling **irregularly spelled** high-frequency **words** used in *A Place to Play,* including such words as *always* and *nothing.* The fluency activities offer opportunities for children to reread for **accuracy** and **appropriate rate.**
Foundational Skills 4.b. Read on-level text orally with accuracy, appropriate rate, and expression on successive readings.	
Writing Standards	
Writing 3. Write narratives in which they recount two or more appropriately sequenced events, include some details regarding what happened, use temporal words to signal event order, and provide some sense of closure.	In the week's writing lesson, children use the writing process to write a **realistic narrative** with a focus on developing the beginning, middle, and end of a story. The use of **digital tools** is an integral part of the 21st Century Writing Project for Unit 3. In the project, children produce and publish a cooperatively written photo essay.
Writing 6. With guidance and support from adults, use a variety of digital tools to produce and publish writing, including in collaboration with peers.	
Speaking and Listening Standards	
Speaking/Listening 4. Describe people, places, things, and events with relevant details, expressing ideas and feelings clearly.	The listening and speaking activities in this lesson focus on **describing** an experience in sequence. Also, speakers are encouraged to prepare a poster they will present as they **share** their research and inquiry findings.
Speaking/Listening 5. Add drawings or other visual displays to descriptions when appropriate to clarify ideas, thoughts, and feelings.	
Language Standards	
Language 1.e. Use verbs to convey a sense of past, present, and future (e.g., *Yesterday I walked home; Today I walk home; Tomorrow I will walk home*).	The lesson helps children identify action **verbs.** It explicitly teaches the **spelling** of words with the vowel sounds of *y* and high-frequency words. **Spelling** and **decoding** instruction provide skills children can use to spell untaught words. Children are encouraged to identify familiar letter-sounds as part of their word-attack skills.
Language 2.d. Use conventional spelling for words with common spelling patterns and for frequently occurring irregular words.	
Language 2.e. Spell untaught words phonetically, drawing on phonemic awareness and spelling conventions.	

Additional Support for a Common Core Standard This Week

Use the following instruction to supplement the teaching of one of this week's Common Core Standards.

Common Core Standard: Language 1.e.
Write the following sentences on the board.
Present Tense: Today, I play soccer. Jorge plays soccer too.
Past Tense: Yesterday, I played soccer. Anna played soccer too.
Future Tense: Tomorrow, we will play soccer again.

• Tell children that they change the form of a verb to show whether something is happening now, has happened in the past, or will happen in the future.
• Review each tense, identifying the forms of the verb used. Then delete the verbs from the sentences.
• Ask children to provide the correct tense of the verb to complete each sentence.

ISBN-13: 978-0-328-64369-6 ISBN-10: 0-328-64369-1

Grade 1 • Unit 3 • Week 1
A Place to Play

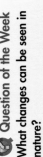

Unit 3
THE BIG Question
What is changing in our world?

Common Core Standards and Concept Development

- Introduce and explore this unit's weekly concepts through rich, structured conversations
- Develop complex content knowledge and vocabulary
- Expand on a single concept with engaging literature and nonfiction
- Build better readers in all content areas
- Align instruction to Common Core Anchor Standards

You Are Here: Week 1

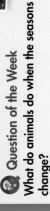
connect to **SOCIAL STUDIES**

A Place to Play
Question of the Week
How do places change?

As children answer this unit's Big Question and this week's Question of the Week, they will address:

Reading 1. Read closely to determine what the text says explicitly and to make logical inferences from it; cite specific textual evidence when writing or speaking to support conclusions drawn from the text.

Concept Talk Guide children as they discuss questions such as:
- What are some ways your neighborhood has changed?

As children answer this week's Concept Talk question, they will address:

Speaking/Listening 1. Prepare for and participate effectively in a range of conversations and collaborations with diverse partners, building on others' ideas and expressing their own clearly and persuasively. **(Also Speaking/Listening 4.)**

Writing Think about a place to play that you think is interesting. Now write a made-up story about children playing at that place.

As children write about this week's prompt, they will address:

Writing 3. Write narratives to develop real or imagined experiences or events using effective technique, well-chosen details, and well-structured event sequences.

Listening and Speaking On page 42, children learn to use time-order transition words when they tell a story. By doing so, they address:

Speaking/Listening 4. Present information, findings, and supporting evidence such that listeners can follow the line of reasoning and the organization, development, and style are appropriate to task, purpose, and audience.

Week 2

connect to **SOCIAL STUDIES**

Ruby in Her Own Time
Question of the Week
What do we learn as we grow and change?

Concept Talk Guide children as they discuss questions such as:
- What can you do now that you could not do when you were younger?

Writing Look at the pictures in *Ruby in Her Own Time*. Think about what Ruby does. Write sentences that tell two things Ruby does that you like.

Week 3

connect to **SCIENCE**

The Class Pet
Question of the Week
What can we learn about animals as they grow and change?

Concept Talk Guide children as they discuss questions such as:
- Think about different animals. How are the babies different from the adults?

Writing Write a summary of *The Class Pet*. Tell the most important events and ideas.

Week 4

connect to **SCIENCE**

Frog and Toad Together
Question of the Week
What changes happen in a garden?

Concept Talk Guide children as they discuss questions such as:
- What do seeds look like when you first plant them? Then what happens?

Writing Think of actions Toad tried to help his garden grow. Write a list telling what Toad did that really helped the garden grow. In another list, tell his actions that did not help.

Week 5

connect to **SCIENCE**

I'm a Caterpillar
Question of the Week
What changes can be seen in nature?

Concept Talk Guide children as they discuss questions such as:
- How do different kinds of animals change as they grow?

Writing Think of changes in nature. Plants and animals grow. Seasons change. Draw two pictures to show one way a plant or animal changes. Write captions about your pictures.

Week 6

connect to **SCIENCE**

Where Are My Animal Friends?
Question of the Week
What do animals do when the seasons change?

Concept Talk Guide children as they discuss questions such as:
- Why do you think squirrels gather and hide nuts in the fall?

Writing Think about Raccoon and Squirrel in *Where Are My Animal Friends?* What would they say if they could call Goose on a phone? Write a play scene showing what they would say.

This Week's ELL Overview

ELL Handbook

- Maximize Literacy and Cognitive Engagement
- Research Into Practice
- Full Weekly Support for Every Selection

  ### A Place to Play
  - Multi-Lingual Summaries in Five Languages
  - Selection-Specific Vocabulary Word Cards
  - Frontloading/Reteaching for Comprehension Skill Lessons
  - ELD and ELL Reader Study Guides

- Transfer Activities
- Professional Development

Daily Leveled ELL Notes

ELL notes appear throughout this week's instruction and ELL Support is on the DI pages of your Teacher's Edition. The following is a sample of an ELL note from this week.

English Language Learners

Beginning Children can draw story events, label them, and share with a partner, possibly one who speaks the same home language.

Intermediate Have children draw pictures or write phrases to express story event ideas. Have them describe the story plan to other children.

Advanced Have children draw pictures or write short sentences in their story charts. As they share the plan with partners, children can clarify and add ideas.

Advanced High Have children write short sentences in their story charts. Then organize children into small groups. As they share their plans, children can offer suggestions to make the plans better.

ELL by Strand

The ELL lessons on this week's Support for English Language Learners pages are organized by strand. They offer additional scaffolding for the core curriculum. Leveled support notes on these pages address the different proficiency levels in your class. See pages DI•12–DI•21.

ELL Guy
Dr. Jim Cummins

The Three Pillars of ELL Instruction

ELL Strands	Activate Prior Knowledge	Access Content	Extend Language
Vocabulary p. DI•16	Preteach	Teach/Model	Practice
Reading Comprehension p. DI•17	Preteach	Reteach/Practice	Leveled Practice Activities
Phonics, Spelling, and Word Analysis pp. DI•13–DI•14	Preteach	Listen and Write	Leveled Practice Activities
Listening Comprehension p. DI•15	Prepare for the Read Aloud	First Listening	Second Listening
Conventions and Writing pp. DI•20–DI•21	Preteach/Introduce Terms	Practice/Model	Leveled Practice Activities/ Leveled Writing Activities
Concept Development p. DI•12	Activate Prior Knowledge	Develop Concepts	Review Concepts and Connect to Writing

This Week's Practice Stations Overview

Six Weekly Practice Stations with Leveled Activities can be found at the beginning of each week of instruction. For this week's Practice Stations, see pp. 12h–12i.

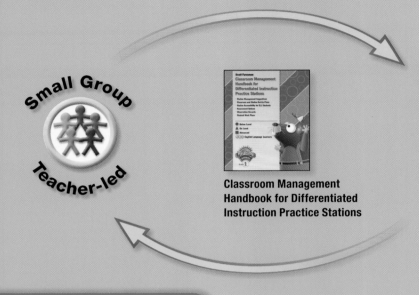

Classroom Management Handbook for Differentiated Instruction Practice Stations

Practice Stations

Daily Leveled Center Activities

○ Below   ◻ Advanced

△ On-Level   **E L L**

Practice Stations Flip Charts

						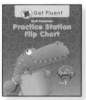
	Listen Up	**Word Work**	**Words to Know**	**Let's Write**	**Read for Meaning**	**Get Fluent**
Objectives	• Identify words with the sound /ē/.	• Sort and write words that have the long *e* sound. • Sort and write words that have the syllable pattern VC/CV.	• Identify high-frequency words *also, family, new, other, some, their.* • Write high-frequency words.	• Write complete sentences. • Use nouns in writing.	• Compare and contrast information in a selection and background knowledge.	• Read aloud with accuracy at an appropriate rate.
Materials	• *Listen Up* Flip Chart Activity 13 • six or seven Picture Cards, including *green, queen*	• *Word Work* Flip Chart Activity 13 • teacher-made Word Cards • pencils • T-charts	• *Words to Know* Flip Chart Activity 13 • High-Frequency Word Cards for Unit 2, Week 6 • paper • pencils	• *Let's Write* Flip Chart Activity 13 • paper • pencils	• *Read for Meaning* Flip Chart Activity 13 • Leveled Readers • paper • pencils	• *Get Fluent* Flip Chart Activity 13 • Leveled Readers

This Week on Reading Street!

Question of the Week
How do places change?

Daily Plan

Don't Wait Until Friday

Whole Group
- ◉ Vowel sounds of *y*
- ◉ Syllable Pattern CV
- ◉ Sequence
- • Fluency
- • Vocabulary

MONITOR PROGRESS		Success Predictor		
Day 1 Check Word Reading	Day 2 Check Word Reading	Day 3 Check High-Frequency Words/Retelling	Day 4 Check Fluency	Day 5 Check Oral Vocabulary

Small Group

Teacher-Led

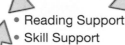

- • Reading Support
- • Skill Support
- • Fluency Practice

Practice Stations

Independent Activities

Customize Literacy More support for a Balanced Literacy approach, see CL•1–CL•47.

Customize Writing More support for a customized writing approach, see CW•1–CW•10.

Whole Group
- • Writing: Realistic Story
- • Conventions: Action Verbs

Assessment
- • Weekly Tests
- • Day 5 Assessment
- • Fresh Reads

You Are Here! Unit 3 Week 1

This Week's Reading Selections

Main Selection
Genre: **Realistic Fiction**

Paired Selection

Decodable Practice Readers

Leveled Readers

ELL and ELD Readers

Resources on Reading Street!

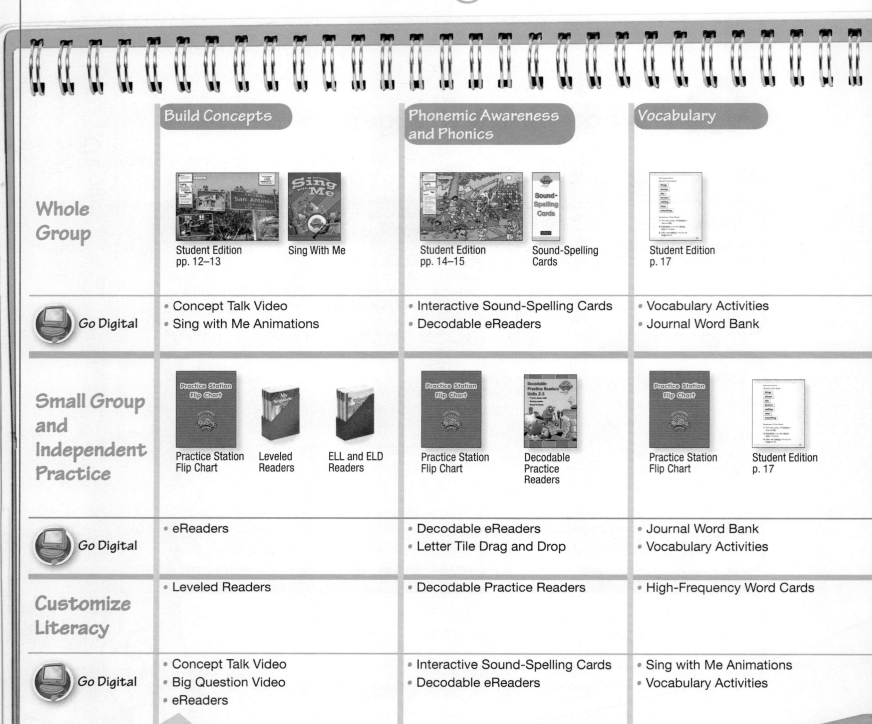

	Build Concepts	Phonemic Awareness and Phonics	Vocabulary
Whole Group	Student Edition pp. 12–13 / Sing With Me	Student Edition pp. 14–15 / Sound-Spelling Cards	Student Edition p. 17
Go Digital	• Concept Talk Video • Sing with Me Animations	• Interactive Sound-Spelling Cards • Decodable eReaders	• Vocabulary Activities • Journal Word Bank
Small Group and Independent Practice	Practice Station Flip Chart / Leveled Readers / ELL and ELD Readers	Practice Station Flip Chart / Decodable Practice Readers	Practice Station Flip Chart / Student Edition p. 17
Go Digital	• eReaders	• Decodable eReaders • Letter Tile Drag and Drop	• Journal Word Bank • Vocabulary Activities
Customize Literacy	• Leveled Readers	• Decodable Practice Readers	• High-Frequency Word Cards
Go Digital	• Concept Talk Video • Big Question Video • eReaders	• Interactive Sound-Spelling Cards • Decodable eReaders	• Sing with Me Animations • Vocabulary Activities

Question of the Week
How do places change?

Comprehension	Fluency	Conventions and Writing
 Student Edition pp. 20–35	Decodable Practice Readers	 Student Edition pp. 36–37
• Envision It! Animations • eSelections	• eSelections • eReaders	• Grammar Jammer
Practice Station Flip Chart Leveled Readers ELL and ELD Readers	Practice Station Flip Chart Decodable Practice Readers	Practice Station Flip Chart Reader's and Writer's Notebook
• eReaders • Story Sort	• Decodable eReaders	• Grammar Jammer
• Envision It! Skills and Strategies Handbooks • Leveled Readers	• Leveled Readers	• Reader's and Writer's Notebook
• Envision It! Animations • eReaders	• eReaders	• Grammar Jammer

You Are Here! Unit 3 Week 1

My 5-Day Planner for Reading Street!

Don't Wait Until Friday
SUCCESS PREDICTOR

	Check Word Reading **Day 1** pages 12j–17f	Check Word Reading **Day 2** pages 18a–33g

Get Ready to Read	**Concept Talk,** 12j–13
	Oral Vocabulary, 13a–13b
	  growth, population, public
	Phonemic Awareness, 14–15
	  Segment and Blend Phonemes
	Phonics, 15a–16a
	  ⊚ Vowel Sounds of *y*
	READ Decodable Practice Reader 13A,16b–16c
	Spelling, 16d Pretest
		Concept Talk, 18a–18b
		Oral Vocabulary, 18b
		  shuffle, teeter
		Phonemic Awareness, 18c
		  Segment and Blend Phonemes
		Phonics, 18d–19a
		  ⊚ Syllable Pattern CV
		READ Decodable Practice Reader 13B,19b–19c
		Review **Phonics,** 19d
		  Long *e,* Long *i,* and Vowel Sounds of *y*
		Spelling, 19e Practice

Read and Comprehend	**High-Frequency Words,** 17
	Introduce *always, become, day, everything, nothing, stays, things*
	Listening Comprehension, 17a–17b
	  ⊚ Sequence
		High-Frequency Words, 19
		Build Fluency *always, become, day, everything, nothing, stays, things*
		Story Words, 20a
		  Introduce *art, boy, grew, now, tower, sunset*
		Vocabulary, 20a Antonyms
		Build Background, 20b
		READ Main Selection–First Read, 20c–33a
		  A Place to Play
		Literary Text, 33b Realistic Fiction

Language Arts	**Conventions,** 17c Action Verbs
	Writing, 17d–17e
	  Realistic Story
	Research and Inquiry, 17f
	  Identify and Focus Topic
		Conventions, 33c Action Verbs
		Writing, 33d–33e Realistic Story
		  Writing Trait: Organization
		Handwriting, 33f
		  Letter *Y* and *y*: Letter Spacing
		Research and Inquiry, 33f
		  Research Skill: Interview

You Are Here!
Unit 3 Week 1

Question of the Week
How do places change?

Check High-Frequency Words Check Retelling **Day 3** pages 34a–37c	Check Fluency **Day 4** pages 38a–41e	Check Oral Vocabulary **Day 5** pages 42a–43k
Concept Talk, 34a–34b **Oral Vocabulary**, 34b *crooked* **Phonological Awareness**, 34c Rhyming Words **Phonics**, 34d–34e ◉ Vowel Sounds of *y* ◉ Syllable Pattern CV **Spelling**, 34f Dictation	**Concept Talk**, 38a–38b **Oral Vocabulary**, 38b *makeshift, spindly* **Phonemic Awareness**, 38c Add Initial Phonemes Review **Phonics**, 38d Long *e*, Spelled *e, ee;* Syllables VC/CV READ **Decodable Practice Reader 13C**, 38e–38f Review **Fluent Word Reading**, 38g **Spelling**, 38h Partner Review	**Concept Wrap Up**, 42a Review **Oral Vocabulary**, 42b **Phonemic Awareness**, 42c Add Initial Phonemes Review **Phonics**, 42c ◉ Vowel Sounds of *y* ◉ Syllable Pattern CV **Spelling**, 42d Test
Review **High-Frequency Words**, 34g *always, become, day, everything, nothing, stays, things* Review **Story Words**, 34g *art, boy, grew, now, tower, sunset* READ **Main Selection–Second Read**, 20–33, 34h–35a **Fluency**, 35b Accuracy and Appropriate Rate	**Social Studies in Reading**, 38i READ **Paired Selection**, 38–41 "My Neighborhood, Now and Then" **Fluency**, 41a Accuracy and Appropriate Rate	**Listening and Speaking**, 42–43 Tell About an Experience **Vocabulary**, 43a Antonyms **Fluency**, 43a Accuracy and Rate Review **Comprehension**, 43b ◉ Sequence Review **Vocabulary**, 43b High-Frequency Words and Story Words **Literary Text**, 43c Characters **Assessment**, 43d–43f Monitor Progress
Conventions, 36 Action Verbs **Writing**, 36–37a Realistic Story Writer's Craft: Sequence **Listening and Speaking**, 37b Relate an Experience in Sequence **Research and Inquiry**, 37c Gather and Record Information	**Conventions**, 41b Action Verbs **Writing**, 41c–41d Realistic Story Revising Strategy **Research and Inquiry**, 41e Review and Revise Topic	Review **Conventions**, 43g Action Verbs **Writing** 43h–43i Realistic Story Writer's Craft: Verbs **Research and Inquiry**, 43j Communicate **Wrap Up Your Week**, 43k How do places change?

Week 1

Grouping Options for Differentiated Instruction
Turn the page for the small group time lesson plan.

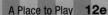

Planning Small Group Time on Reading Street!

SMALL GROUP TIME RESOURCES

Look for this Small Group Time box each day to help meet the individual needs of all your children. Differentiated Instruction lessons appear on the DI pages at the end of each week.

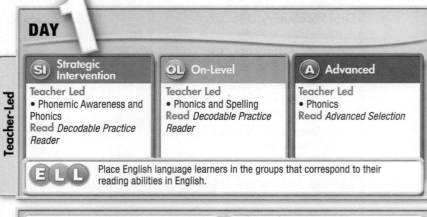

DAY 1

Teacher-Led

SI Strategic Intervention
Teacher Led
• Phonemic Awareness and Phonics
Read *Decodable Practice Reader*

OL On-Level
Teacher Led
• Phonics and Spelling
Read *Decodable Practice Reader*

A Advanced
Teacher Led
• Phonics
Read *Advanced Selection*

ELL Place English language learners in the groups that correspond to their reading abilities in English.

Practice Stations
• Listen Up
• Word Work

Independent Activities
• *Reader's and Writer's Notebook*
• Concept Talk Video

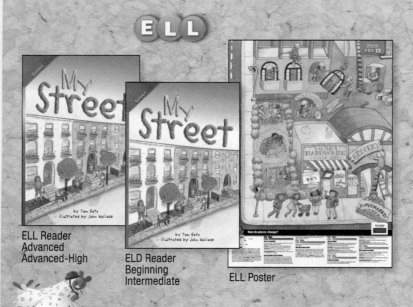

ELL

ELL Reader
Advanced
Advanced-High

ELD Reader
Beginning
Intermediate

ELL Poster

Day 1

SI Strategic Intervention		**Phonemic Awareness and Phonics**, DI•1 Read **Decodable Practice Reader 13A**, DI•1
OL On-Level		**Phonics and Spelling**, DI•6 Read **Decodable Practice Reader**, DI•6
A Advanced		**Phonics**, DI•9 Read **Advanced Selection**, DI•9
ELL English Language Learners		DI•12–DI•21 **Frontload Concept** **Preteach Skills** **Writing**

You Are Here!
Unit 3
Week 1

Reading Street Response to Intervention Kit

Reading Street Leveled Practice Stations Kit

SI Strategic Intervention   **OL** On-Level   **A** Advanced

Below-Level Reader

Decodable Practice Readers

On-Level Reader

Advanced Reader

Carlos Gets a Puppy

Advanced Selection

Concept Literacy Reader

Small Group Weekly Plan

Day 2	Day 3	Day 4	Day 5
Phonemic Awareness and Phonics, DI•2 Read **Decodable Practice Reader 13B**, DI•2	**Phonemic Awareness and Phonics**, DI•3 Read **Concept Literacy Leveled Reader**, DI•3	**High-Frequency Words**, DI•4 Read **Decodable Practice Reader 13C**, DI•4	**Phonics Review**, DI•5 Read **Below-Level Leveled Reader**, DI•5
Phonics and High-Frequency Words, DI•6 Read **Decodable Practice Reader 13B**, DI•6	Read **On-Level Leveled Reader**, DI•7	**Conventions**, DI•8 Reread **Main Selection**, DI•8	**Phonics Review**, DI•8 Reread **On-Level Leveled Reader**, DI•8
Phonics and Comprehension, DI•9 Read **Main Selection**, DI•9	Read **Advanced Leveled Reader**, DI•10	**Comprehension**, DI•11 Read **Paired Selection**, DI•11 Reread **Leveled Reader**, DI•11	**Fluency and Comprehension**, DI•11 Reread **Advanced Selection**, DI•11
DI•12–DI•21 **Review Concept** **Practice Skills** **Frontload Main Selection** **Writing**	DI•12–DI•21 **Review Concept** **Practice Skills** **Reread Main Selection** **Writing**	DI•12–DI•21 **Review Concept** **Practice Skills** **Read ELL or ELD Reader** **Writing**	DI•12–DI•21 **Review Concept** **Review Skills** **Writing**

Week 1

Practice Stations for Everyone on Reading Street!

Listen Up!
Match sounds and pictures.

Objectives
• Identify words with the sound /ē/.

Materials
• *Listen Up!* Flip Chart Activity 13
• Six or seven Picture Cards, including *green, queen*

Differentiated Activities

⬤ Find Picture Cards that have the same middle sound as *feet*. Now think of words that rhyme with *we*. What ending sound do you hear?

▲ Find Picture Cards that have the same middle sound as *feet*. Say the words, and then say words that rhyme with them. Now think of words that rhyme with *we*. What ending sound do you hear?

⬛ Find Picture Cards that have the same middle sound as *feet*. Say the words, and then say words that rhyme with them. Now think of words that rhyme with *we*. Take turns with a partner thinking of as many words as you can that have the long *e* sound.

Technology
• Interactive Sound-Spelling Cards

Word Work
Long e: e, ee; Syllables VC/CV

Objectives
• Sort and write words that have the long *e* sound.
• Sort and write words that have the syllable pattern VC/CV.

Materials
• *Word Work* Flip Chart Activity 13
• teacher-made word cards
• pencils
• T-charts

Differentiated Activities

⬤ On a T-chart, label one column "*ee or e.*" Label one column "VC/CV." Read the words on the word cards. Write the words in the columns in which they belong.

▲ On a T-chart, label one column "*ee or e.*" Label one column "VC/CV." Read the words on the word cards. Write the words in the columns in which they belong. Underline the letter or letters that make the long *e* sound. Draw a line to separate syllables.

⬛ On a T-chart, label one column "*ee or e.*" Label one column "VC/CV." Read the words on the word cards. Write the words in the columns in which they belong. Write sentences using some of the words you used.

Technology
• Interactive Sound-Spelling Cards

Words To Know
Practice high-frequency words.

Objectives
• Identify high-frequency words *also, family, new, other, some, their.*
• Write high-frequency words.

Materials
• *Words to Know* Flip Chart Activity 13
• High-Frequency Word Cards for Unit 2, Week 6
• paper
• pencils

Differentiated Activities

⬤ Using one of the Word Cards, say a sentence using that word. Have your partner point to the correct word card. Write each word you use on your paper.

▲ Using one of the Word Cards, say a sentence using that word. Have your partner point to the correct word card. Write each word you use on your paper.

⬛ Using one of the Word Cards, say a sentence using that word. Have your partner point to the correct word card. Write sentences using the words as you figure them out.

Technology
• Online Tested Vocabulary Activities

You Are Here!
Unit 3
Week 1

Use this week's materials from the
Reading Street Leveled Practice Stations
Kit to organize this week's stations.

Key

 Below-Level Activities

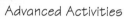 On-Level Activities

Advanced Activities

Practice Station
Flip Chart

Let's Write!
Write sentences using nouns.

Objectives
- Write complete sentences.
- Use nouns in writing.

Materials
- *Let's Write!* Flip Chart Activity 13
- paper
- pencils

Differentiated Activities

🔵 Think about an insect that lives in a community. Write a description of that insect community. Be sure each sentence begins with a capital letter and ends with a period. Underline the nouns.

🔺 Think about an insect that lives in a community. Write a description of that insect community. Be sure each sentence begins with a capital letter and ends with a period. Underline the nouns.

🟥 Think about an insect that lives in a community. Write a description of that insect community. Be sure each sentence begins with a capital letter and ends with a period. Underline the nouns.

Read For Meaning
Compare and contrast information.

Objectives
- Compare and contrast information in a selection and background knowledge.

Materials
- Read for Meaning Flip Chart Activity 13
- Leveled Readers
- paper
- pencils

Differentiated Activities

- To **compare** means to find what is alike. To **contrast** means to find what is different.

🔵 Read *Learn About Worker Bees.* Now use your background knowledge. Compare and contrast what a worker bee does in its family and what you do in your family. Share your ideas with a partner.

🔺 Read *Honey.* Now use your background knowledge. Compare and contrast what people do with honey and what people do with sugar. Write sentences that explain the comparisons and contrasts.

🟥 Read *Bees and Beekeepers.* Compare and contrast bees that live in hives they make and bees that live in a beekeeper's hive. Look for other comparisons and contrasts as you read. Write sentences about what you find.

Technology
- Leveled eReaders

Get Fluent
Practice fluent reading.

Objectives
- Read aloud with accuracy at an appropriate rate.

Materials
- *Get Fluent* Flip Chart Activity 13
- Leveled Readers

Differentiated Activities

🔵 Work with a partner. Take turns reading pages from *Learn About Worker Bees.* Think about what you're reading about. Be sure to read at an appropriate rate. Read as accurately as you can. Give your partner feedback.

🔺 Work with a partner. Take turns reading pages from *Honey.* Think about what you're reading about. Be sure to read at an appropriate rate. Read as accurately as you can. Give your partner feedback.

🟥 Work with a partner. Take turns reading pages from *Bees and Beekeepers.* Think about what you're reading about. Be sure to read at an appropriate rate. Read as accurately as you can. Give your partner feedback.

Technology
- Reading Street Readers CD-ROM

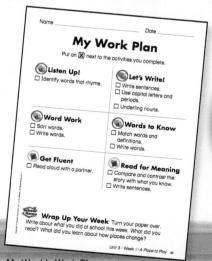

Week 1

Objectives
- Introduce concepts: places growing and changing.
- Share information and ideas about the concept.

Today at a Glance

Oral Vocabulary
growth, population, public

Phonemic Awareness
Segment and Blend Phonemes

Phonics and Spelling
◉ Vowel Sounds of *y*

Fluency
Oral Rereading

High-Frequency Words
always, become, day, everything, nothing, stays, things

Comprehension
◉ Sequence

Conventions
Action Verbs

Writing
Realistic Stories: Introduce

Research and Inquiry
Identify and Focus Topic

Concept Talk

Question of the Week
How do places change?

Introduce the concept

To build concepts and to focus children's attention, tell them that this week they will talk, sing, read, and write about how places change. Write the Question of the Week and track the print as you read it.

> **ROUTINE** **Activate Prior Knowledge** **Team Talk**
>
> 1. **Think** Have children think for a minute about how places change.
> 2. **Pair** Have pairs of children discuss the question.
> 3. **Share** Have children share their ideas with the group. Remind them to ask questions to clarify information. Guide discussion and encourage elaboration with prompts such as: What are some ways your neighborhood has changed?

Routines Flip Chart

Anchored Talk

Develop oral language

Have children turn to pages 12–13 in their Student Edition. Read the title and look at the photos. Use these questions to guide discussion and create the "How do places change?" concept map (shown on next page).

- The sign says "San Antonio, POP. 1,144,646." *POP.* is short for *population,* which means "the number of people who live somewhere." What might cause a change in population? (Possible response: People move there.) Let's add *People move to new places* to our map.

- What does the picture of the library have to do with growing and changing? (Possible response: As more children come to a school, they would need more books in the library.) Let's add *Some places are made better* to our map.

- What is shown in the picture above the library? (Possible response: It shows a new house being built.) Let's add *New homes are built* to our map.

Objectives
• Listen closely to speakers and ask questions to help you better understand the topic. • Share information and ideas about the topic. Speak at the correct pace.

Oral Vocabulary

Let's Talk About

Read Together

Growing and Changing
● Share information about growing and changing.
● Share ideas about how places can change.

READING STREET ONLINE CONCEPT TALK VIDEO
www.ReadingStreet.com

You've learned **1 4 2** Amazing Words so far this year!

ENTERING San Antonio CITY LIMIT POP. 1144646

12   13

Student Edition pp. 12–13

Amazing Words

You've learned **1 4 2** words so far.
You'll learn **0 0 8** words this week!

growth	teeter
population	crooked
public	makeshift
shuffle	spindly

Writing on Demand

Develop Writing Fluency
Ask children to write about what they know about how places change. Have them write for two to three minutes. Children should write as much as they can. Tell them to try to do their best writing. You may want to discuss what children wrote during writing conferences.

Connect to reading   Explain that this week, children will read about how neighbors work together to make places better. Let's add *Neighbors work together* to our map.

How do places change?

| People move to new places. | New homes are built. | Neighbors work together. | Some places are made better. |

ELL

English Language Learners
Listening Comprehension
English learners will benefit from additional visual support to understand the key terms in the concept map. Use the pictures on pp. 12–13 to scaffold understanding. For example, when talking about new homes being built, point to the picture of the new house.

ELL Support Additional ELL support and modified instruction are provided in the *ELL Handbook* and in the *ELL Support Lessons* on pp. DI•12–DI•21.

ELL **Preteach Concepts** Use the Day 1 instruction on ELL Poster 13 to assess and build background knowledge, develop concepts, and build oral vocabulary.

ELL Poster 13

A Place to Play   **12–13**

Objectives
- Build oral vocabulary.
- Discuss the concept to develop oral language.
- Share information and ideas about the concept.

Oral Vocabulary
Amazing Words

Introduce Amazing Words

Display p. 13 of the Sing with Me Big Book. Tell children they are going to sing about a town that is growing and changing. Ask children to listen for the Amazing Words *growth, population,* and *public* as you sing. Sing the song again and have children join you.

 Sing with Me Big Book Audio

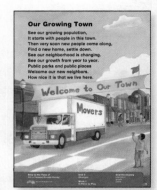

Sing with Me Big Book p. 13

Teach Amazing Words

Amazing Words Oral Vocabulary Routine

1. **Introduce the Word** Relate the word *growth* to the song. The song says we see the *growth* of the town from year to year. Supply a child-friendly definition: *Growth* means getting bigger. Have children say the word.

2. **Demonstrate** Provide examples to show meaning: When children have grown a lot in a short time, we say they have had a *growth* spurt. You can measure your *growth* in height with a ruler or a *growth* chart on the wall. Most plants have their *growth* season in the spring or summer.

3. **Apply** Have children demonstrate their understanding: Give examples of *growth* you have seen. It could be about you, a family member or friend, a community, an animal, or a plant.

See p. OV•1 to teach *population* and *public.*

Routines Flip Chart

Check understanding of Amazing Words

Have children look at the picture on p. 13. It looks like someone is moving to town. What would happen to the *population* if more people moved to town? Use *population* in your answer. (Possible response: The *population* would get bigger.)

What changes might happen in the town if the *population* gets bigger? Use *growth* in your answer. (Possible response: If there is a *growth* in *population,* new homes might be built.)

Name a *public* place near where you live. How might it need to change? (Possible response: The library is a *public* place. It might need to get bigger because it doesn't have enough space.)

Apply Amazing Words

Have children demonstrate their understanding of the Amazing Words by completing these sentences orally.

Eric's fast **growth** made his clothes _____.

As people move into a town, the **population** _____.

A _____ is a **public** place.

Corrective feedback

If... children have difficulty using the Amazing Words, then... remind them of the definitions and provide opportunities for children to use the words in sentences.

Preteach Academic Vocabulary

Write the following on the board:

- **sequence**
- **realistic fiction**
- **action verb**

Have children share what they know about this week's Academic Vocabulary. Use children's responses to assess their prior knowledge. Preteach the Academic Vocabulary by providing a child-friendly description, explanation, or example that clarifies the meaning of each term. Then ask children to restate the meaning of the Academic Vocabulary in their own words.

Amazing Words

growth	teeter
population	crooked
public	makeshift
shuffle	spindly

ELL

English Language Learners

Pronunciation Speakers of many languages have difficulty hearing and pronouncing the sound /th/. If children have difficulty pronouncing the /th/ in *growth,* say the word slowly, emphasizing the position of the tongue between the teeth, and have children repeat.

Cognates The words *population* and *public* may have cognates in children's home languages. Invite Spanish speakers to identify cognates *población* and *público.* Point out how this prior knowledge can help children with learning new words.

Objectives

- Segment and blend words with vowel sounds of *y*.
- ⊙ Associate the vowel sounds /ē/ or /ī/ with the spelling *y*.

Skills Trace

⊙ **Vowel Sounds of y**

Introduce U3W1D1

Practice U3W1D3; U3W1D4

Reteach/Review U3W1D5; U3W2D4

Assess/Test Weekly Test U3W1

Benchmark Test U3

KEY:

U=Unit   W=Week   D=Day

Student Edition pp. 14–15

Phonemic Awareness
Segment and Blend Phonemes

Introduce

Read together the first two bulleted points on pages 14–15 of the Student Editions. What is the weather like in the picture? (sunny) The last sound I hear in *sunny* is /ē/. Have children look at the picture to identify other items or actions that contain the long *e* sound. (bunny, twenty, sleepy) In the picture I can also see some birds. Where are the birds? (in the sky) The last sound I hear in *sky* is /ī/. Again, have children look at the picture but this time, have them identify words or actions that contain the long *i* sound. (tired, eye, try)

Model

Listen to the sounds in the word *sky*: /s/ /k/ /ī/. There are three sounds in *sky*. Let's blend those sounds to make a word: /s/ /k/ /ī/, *sky*. Continue modeling with *baby*.

Guide practice

Guide children as they segment and blend these words from the picture: *bunny, sleepy, fly,* and *sky*.

Corrective feedback

If... children make an error,

then... model by segmenting the word, and have them repeat the segmenting and blending of the word.

14–15   Changes • Unit 3 • Week 1

Phonics—Teach/Model
Vowel Sounds of *y*

Sound-Spelling Card 77

ROUTINE **Blending Strategy**

1 Connect Write the words *hide, me,* and *seed.* Ask children what they know about the vowel sounds in these words. (The vowel sounds are long; they say their names.) Explain that today they will learn how to spell and read words with vowel sounds of *y.*

2 Use Sound-Spelling Cards Display Card 77. Point to *y.* The long e sound, /ē/, can be spelled *y.* Have children say /ē/ several times as you point to *y.* Display Card 81. Point to *y.* The long i sound, /ī/, can be spelled *y.* Have children say /ī/ several times as you point to *y.*

3 Model Write *cry.* In this word, the letter *y* stands for the sound /ī/. Segment and blend *cry*; then have children blend with you: /k/ /r/ /ī/, *cry.* Follow this procedure to model *bunny.*

4 Guide Practice Continue the process in step 3. This time have children blend with you. Remind children that *y* can spell long *e* or long *i.*

Sound-Spelling Card 81

muddy	fry	puppy	shy	nanny	my
handy	try	fuzzy	sky	dandy	dry

5 Review What do you know about reading these words? (The letter *y* at the end of a word can spell the sounds /ē/ or /ī/. When *y* ends a word with two syllables, it usually spells the sound /ē/.)

Routines Flip Chart

Phonics—Build Fluency
Vowel Sounds of *y*

Model

Envision It!

Have children turn to page 16 in their Student Edition. Look at the pictures on this page. I see a picture of a *bunny* and a picture of a *sky*. The words *bunny* and *sky* both end with a vowel sound of *y*. When I say *bunny*, I hear /ē/ at the end. In *bunny*, long e is spelled *y*. When I say *sky*, I hear /ī/ at the end. In *sky*, long *i* is spelled *ý*.

Guide practice

For each word in "Words I Can Blend," ask for the sound of each letter or group of letters. Make sure that children identify the correct sound for *y*. Then have children blend the whole word.

Corrective feedback

If... children have difficulty blending a word,
then... model blending the word, and then ask children to blend it with you.

Student Edition p. 16

Objectives
• Decode words by using letter-sound patterns to understand the different sounds vowels make.

Envision It! | **Sounds to Know**

bunny

-y

sky

-y

READING STREET ONLINE
SOUND-SPELLING CARDS
www.ReadingStreet.com

Phonics
Vowel Sounds of *y*

Words I Can Blend

b	u	d	d	y
f	u	z	z	y
f	l	y
r	u	s	t	y
wh	y

Sentences I Can Read

1. His buddy shuts a rusty gate.
2. These fuzzy chicks can't fly.
3. Why did Jen run home?

16

Blend and Read

Decode words in isolation

After children can successfully segment and blend the words, point to words in random order and ask children to read them naturally.

Decode words in context

Have children read each of the sentences. Have them identify words in the sentences that have the vowel sounds *y*.

(Team Talk) Pair children and have them take turns reading each of the sentences aloud.

On their own

Use *Reader's and Writer's Notebook* p. 313.

Reader's and Writer's
Notebook p. 313

Differentiated Instruction

(A) **Advanced**

Extend Blending Provide children who can segment and blend all the words correctly with more challenging words such as: *magnify, lullaby, usually,* and *secretary.*

Spelling Patterns

/ē/ Spelled *y* The sound /ē/ may be spelled *y* at the end of a syllable or a single-syllable word.

/ī/ Spelled *y* The sound /ī/ may be spelled *y* at the end of a word of two or more syllables.

Don't Wait Until Friday

MONITOR PROGRESS — **Check Word Reading**
↺ **Vowel Sounds of *y***

Write the following words and have the class read them. Notice which words children miss during the group reading. Call on individuals to read some of the words.

by	dry	sky	cry	shy
buddy	happy	ugly	daddy	funny
yell	yummy	bumpy	yet	sly

Spiral Review
Row 3 contrasts the vowel sounds of y with the consonant sound of y.

If... children cannot blend words with the vowel sounds of *y* at this point,

then... use the Small-Group Time Strategic Intervention lesson, pp. DI•1, to reteach vowel sounds of *y*. Continue to monitor children's progress using other instructional opportunities during the week. See the Skills Trace on p. 14–15.

Day 1	**Day 2**	**Day 3**	**Day 4**	**Day 5**
Check Word Reading	Check Word Reading	Check High Frequency Words/Retelling	Check Fluency	Check Oral Vocabulary

Success Predictor

Objectives

- Apply knowledge of sound-spellings to decode unknown words when reading.
- Decode and read words in context and isolation.
- Practice fluency with oral rereading.

Decodable Practice Reader 13A
Vowel Sounds of *y*

Decode words in isolation

Have children turn to page 145. Have children decode each word.

Review High-frequency words

Review the previously taught words *what, wants, to, a, the, you,* and *are.* Have children read each word as you point to it on the Word Wall.

Decodable Practice Reader 13A

Preview Decodable Reader

Have children read the title and preview the story. Tell them they will decode words that end in *y* and have a long *e* or long *i* sound.

Decode words in context

Pair children for reading and listen as they decode. One child begins. Children read the entire story, switching readers after each page. Partners reread the story. This time the other child begins.

Decodable Practice Reader 13A

Corrective feedback

If... children have difficulty decoding a word, **then...** refer them to the Sound-Spelling Cards to identify the sounds in the word. Then prompt them to blend the word.

- What is the new word?
- Is the new word a word you know?
- Does it make sense in the story?

Check decoding and comprehension

Have children retell the story to include characters, setting, and events. Then have children find words that end in *y* in the story. For each word, have children tell whether the *y* spells the long *e* or long *i* sound. Children should supply *Billy, fly, my, silly, funny, Dotty, cry, why, try, sunny, sky, by, Freddy,* and *happy.*

Reread for Fluency

Have children reread Decodable Practice Reader 13A to develop automaticity decoding words with vowel sounds of *y.*

 **Oral Rereading**

1. **Read** Have children read the entire book orally.

2. **Reread** To achieve optimal fluency, children should reread the text three or four times.

3. **Corrective Feedback** Listen as children read. Provide corrective feedback regarding their fluency and decoding.

Routines Flip Chart

Professional Development

Fluency Fluency building begins in first grade. Poor readers especially need a fluency model to emulate. Pairing fluent and non-fluent readers together for practice gives struggling readers a chance to hear fluent reading in a one-on-one situation.

ELL

English Language Learners

Vowel sounds of *y* Beginning/Intermediate
Write several words with vowel sounds of *y* from the Decodable Practice Reader on the board, such as *fly, happy, my, cry,* and *sky.* Underline the *y* ending in each word. Say each word aloud with children. Then say the words again. Have children stand if they hear a long *i* sound, and sit if the word has a long *e* sound.

Advanced/Advanced High
Create a two-column chart with the headings "long *i*" and "long *e.*" Have pairs of children categorize words with vowel sounds of *y* on the first few pages of the Decodable Practice Reader by writing the words under the correct heading.

Advanced/Advanced High
After reading the story, have children use the pictures in the reader to make up their own sentences about Billy, using the long *e* and long *i* words that end in *y.*

Objectives
- Spell words with vowel sounds of *y*.
- Read high-frequency words.

Spelling Pretest
Vowel Sounds of *y*

Dictate spelling words

Dictate the spelling words and read the sentences. Have children write the words. If needed, segment the words for children, clarify the pronunciations, and give meanings of words. Have children check their pretests and correct misspelled words.

1. by*	I walk **by** the park on my way to school.
2. try	It is fun to **try** new foods.
3. sunny	It is a **sunny** day.
4. handy	Do you have a pencil **handy?**
5. fly	Would you like to **fly** a plane?
6. cry	A sad movie can make people **cry.**
7. lucky*	Ann felt **lucky** when she got a new bike.
8. silly	The **silly** clown made us laugh.
9. puppy	Jack is teaching his **puppy** a trick.
10. my	**My** dad and I like to read together.

* Words marked with asterisks come from the selection *A Place to Play*.

Let's Practice It!
TR DVD•126

On their own

Use Let's Practice It! p. 126 on the *Teacher Resource DVD-ROM.*

Small Group Time

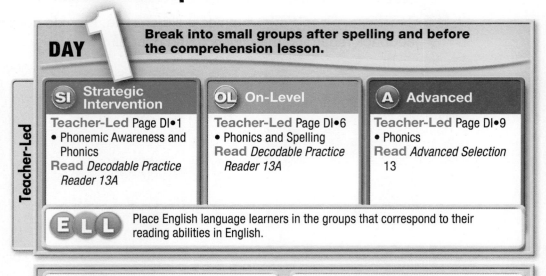

DAY 1

Break into small groups after spelling and before the comprehension lesson.

Teacher-Led

SI Strategic Intervention	**OL On-Level**	**A Advanced**
Teacher-Led Page DI•1 • Phonemic Awareness and Phonics **Read** *Decodable Practice Reader 13A*	**Teacher-Led** Page DI•6 • Phonics and Spelling **Read** *Decodable Practice Reader 13A*	**Teacher-Led** Page DI•9 • Phonics **Read** *Advanced Selection 13*

ELL Place English language learners in the groups that correspond to their reading abilities in English.

Practice Stations	**Independent Activities**
• Listen Up • Word Work	• Read independently/Reading Log on *Reader's and Writer's Notebook* p. RR 4 • Concept Talk Video

High-Frequency Words

ROUTINE **Nondecodable Words**

Introduce

① **Say and Spell** Look at p. 17. Some words we have to learn by remembering the letters rather than saying the sounds. We will say and spell the words to help learn them. **Point to the first word.** This word is *things.* The letters in *things* are t-h-i-n-g-s, *things.* Have children say and spell each word, first with you, and then without you.

② **Identify Familiar Letter-Sounds** Point to the first two letters in *things.* These two letters stand for one sound. What are these letters and what is their sound? (th, /th/)

③ **Demonstrate Meaning** Tell me a sentence using the word *things.* Repeat this routine with the other Words I Can Read.

Routines Flip Chart

Read words in isolation

Have children read the words on p. 17 aloud. Add the words to the Word Wall.

Read words in context

Have children read the sentences aloud. Have them identify this week's High-Frequency Words in the sentences.

On their own

Use *Reader's and Writer's Notebook* p. 314.

Reader's and Writer's Notebook, p. 314

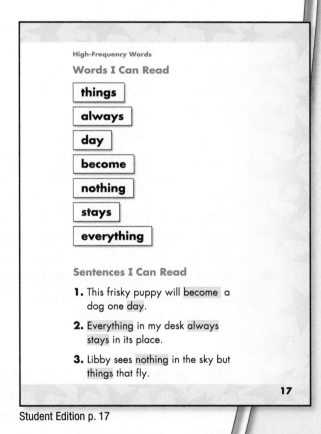

High-Frequency Words

Words I Can Read

things
always
day
become
nothing
stays
everything

Sentences I Can Read

1. This frisky puppy will become a dog one day.

2. Everything in my desk always stays in its place.

3. Libby sees nothing in the sky but things that fly.

17

Student Edition p. 17

Differentiated Instruction

 Advanced

Extend Spelling Challenge children who spell words correctly to spell more difficult words such as: *greedy, pry, shaggy, sleepy, reply,* and *fluffy*.

Phonics/Spelling Generalization

Each spelling word ends in *y,* which spells the long *i* or long *e* sound.

ELL

English Language Learners

Vowel *y* Emphasize that unlike in Spanish, where the vowel *y* only makes the long *e* sound, *y* can make either the long *e* or the long *i* sound in English.

Frontload Read Aloud Use the modified Read Aloud in the *ELL Support* pages to prepare children to listen to "We're Moving" on p. 17b.

Listening Comprehension
Sequence

Introduce

Envision It!

Events in a story happen in a certain order called **sequence**. Good readers pay attention to the sequence in which things happen because it helps them understand the story. Display the words *first, next,* and *last.* Authors may use clue words like these to help readers figure out the sequence.

Have children turn to p. EI•7 in their Student Editions. These pictures show an example of sequence. Discuss these questions using the pictures:

• What happened to the tree first? (It grew flowers.)
• What happened to the tree next? (It grew apples.)
• What happened to the tree last? (The boy picked an apple.)

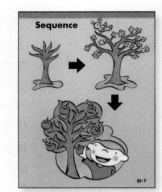
Student Edition EI•7

Model

Today we will read a story about people who are moving. Read "We're Moving." Use Graphic Organizer 21 to model sequence.

 Think Aloud When I read, I look for clue words to help me pay attention to the sequence. Hanna and her mom have lots to do before they move. The clue word *first* helps me know when they started packing boxes. I will add this to the sequence chart. Add *started packing boxes* to the top oval. Continue modeling *next* and *last* events.

We're Moving
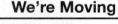
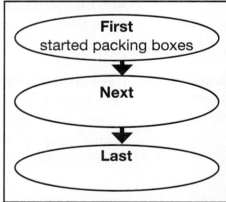

Graphic Organizer Flip Chart 21

Guide practice

After reading the story, have children choose one event from the sequence chart and draw it. Then have children share their drawings with the class, using a sequence word to describe their pictures.

On their own

Use *Reader's and Writer's Notebook* p. 315.

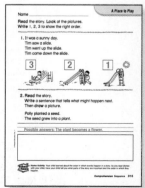
Reader's and Writer's Notebook, p. 315

We're Moving

"I don't want to move, Mama," said Hanna sadly, as she looked out her window at the familiar backyard of her apartment building.

"You know, sweetie," said Hanna's mom, pulling her onto her lap, "we're not moving far. Our new home is just down the street, so you won't be leaving your friends."

Hanna thought of how her neighborhood was changing. New homes and parks were being built. Her mom said this was because of the growth in population of their area. But Hanna missed the open field in which she and her friends used to play. Now it was a construction site.

Hanna and her mom had a lot to do before they moved. First they had to pack up all their belongings in boxes. Then they had to load their furniture into a huge van. Their friends helped them carry everything out to the van.

After the van was filled, they swept the floors, cleaned the cupboards, and washed the windows. Then they piled into the car with their plants and Hanna's special doll, Ruthie, and waved good-bye to their old apartment.

As the van pulled up to the new apartment, Hanna looked out the window. To her amazement, she saw a beautiful new park! There were swings and slides, and flowers and trees. "I wonder if our new park is open to the public yet!" said Hanna, her eyes bright with excitement.

"I bet it is, Hanna," her mom said as they pulled up in front of their new home. "And look! There's a bunch of kids already playing there!"

Hanna jumped out of the car and ran over to the new park. She was excited to meet her new friends!

Academic Vocabulary

sequence the order of events

Objectives
- Identify and use action verbs.
- Develop an understanding of sequence in a realistic story.
- Understand and recognize the features of a realistic story.

Conventions
Action Verbs

Action Verbs
Grammar Transparency 13
TR DVD

Model

Explain that an **action verb** is a word in a sentence that shows action. *Walk* and *sing* are action verbs.

Display Grammar Transparency 13. Read the definition aloud. Model identifying the action verb in each example. Then read the directions and model number 1.

- Verbs tell what someone or something does. *Ann plants a seed.* The word *plants* is the action verb. It tells what Ann does.

- I will circle the verb *plants.* This word tells the action. It is a verb.

Guide practice

Continue with items 2–6, having children identify the verb that tells the action in each sentence.

Connect to oral language

Have the class complete these sentence frames orally using action verbs.

1. Bill _____ home from school every day.

2. My mom _____ the best macaroni and cheese.

3. We _____ a new movie every weekend.

On their own

(Team Talk) Pair children and have them talk about things they like to do. Then have them identify the verbs that describe the action of what they enjoy doing.

MINI-LESSON

5 Day Planner
Guide to Mini-Lessons

DAY 1	Read Like a Writer
DAY 2	Sequence
DAY 3	Sequence in a Story
DAY 4	Revising Strategy: Adding Words
DAY 5	Proofread for Verbs and Transition Words

Writing—Realistic Story
Introduce

MINI-LESSON

Read a Like a Writer

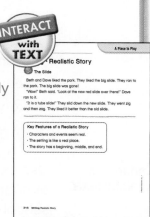

Reader's and Writer's Notebook p. 316

■ **Introduce** This week you will write a realistic story. A realistic story is made up, but it is like real life. You can imagine this kind of story really happening.

Prompt	Write a made-up story about children in a new place to play.
Trait	Organization
Mode	Narrative

■ **Examine Model Text** Let's listen to a realistic story. Track the print as you read aloud "The Slide" on *Reader's and Writer's Notebook* p. 316. Have children follow along.

■ **Key Features** Who are the two characters in this story? (Beth and Dave) Help children find and circle the names. Ask if Beth and Dave act like real children. (yes) Help children underline short phrases in the story that tell about the characters acting like real children, such as *They ran* and *They slid.* Then ask what the **setting** is—where the story takes place. (the park) Point out the word *park.* Ask if any parks or playgrounds in real life have slides. (yes)

This story has characters who are like real people. The writer told events that are like things that can really happen. The place is like a real park.

The story has a beginning as Beth and Dave run to the park. In the middle, they see that the old slide is gone and there is a new slide. At the end, they slide down the new slide. Do they like it? (yes)

Write Guy
Jeff Anderson

Use Mentor Text

Help children remember a realistic story they have read, such as the Unit 2 story *The Farmer in the Hat.* Children need to see, hear, and remember the kind of writing they are learning to do. As teachers, we can direct their attention to how writers make characters realistic and how they make up story events that really could happen.

Academic Vocabulary

action verb a word that shows action

setting where and when a story takes place

Daily Fix-It

1. i am lucki.
   I am lucky.
2. Alwas try your best
   Always try your best.

Discuss the Daily Fix-It corrections with children. Review sentence capitalization and punctuation, the *y* spelling of long *e* and long *i,* and the spelling of *always.*

English Language Learners
Options for Conventions Support To provide children with practice on action verbs, use the modified conventions lessons in the *ELL Handbook.*

Writing—Realistic Story
Introduce, continued

Review key features

Review key features of a realistic story with children. You may want to post these key features in the classroom to allow children to refer to them as they work on their stories.

Key Features of Realistic Story

- characters and events seem real
- setting is like a real place
- story has a beginning, middle, and end

Connect to familiar texts

Use examples from *The Farmer in the Hat* (Unit 2) or another realistic story familiar to children. In *The Farmer in the Hat,* the characters are children in school. There are realistic events at the beginning (children talk about who will be the farmer in a play), the middle (children make masks), and the end (they make animal sounds and a cat comes in). The setting, a school, is a realistic place for children.

Look ahead

Tell children that tomorrow they will plan their own realistic stories.

ROUTINE Quick Write for Fluency [Team Talk]

 Talk Read these questions aloud, and have children respond with action verbs.

What can children do at a park?

What can children do in the classroom?

 Write Have children write short sentences to answer the questions. Make sure their sentences include a subject and a verb.

 Share Partners can read their answers to one another.

Routines Flip Chart

Research and Inquiry
Identify and Focus Topic

Teach

Display and review the concept map about this week's question: *How do places change?* What ideas about change would you like to learn more about? Ask children to share their interests. Help them identify that change often occurs in their own neighborhoods.

Model

Think Aloud One way to learn about something new would be to conduct an interview. During an interview, one person asks questions about a subject, and the other person provides the answers. For example, if I wanted to learn more about your neighborhood, I might ask questions about what makes your neighborhood special. Then you would give me your answers.

Guide practice

Give children time to think about interview questions that, when answered, would help them learn more about changes in their neighborhood. Record children's questions in a chart.

Wrap Up Your Day

✔ **Phonics: Vowel Sounds of y** Write *happy* and *my.* Ask children what sound the *y* in *happy* has. (long *e*) Ask children what sound the *y* in *my* has. (long *i*)

✔ **Spelling: Vowel Sounds of y** Have children name the letter that spells each sound in *silly* and write the word. Continue with *try* and *puppy.*

✔ **Build Concepts** Ask children to recall what happened in the Read Aloud, "We're Moving." How do you think moving to a new home was an exciting change for Hanna? (Possible response: Hanna would have a brand new home and new friends, and she would be closer to the place where she loves to play.)

✔ **Homework** Send home this week's Family Times Newsletter from Let's Practice It! pp. 121–122 on the *Teacher Resource DVD-ROM.*

Let's Practice It!
TR DVD•121–122

Topic: Neighborhood Change	
Question	**Answer**
Are there any new stores in your neighborhood?	

Preview DAY 2

Tell children that tomorrow they will read about a brother and sister who discover new things at the neighborhood community center.

Objectives
- Discuss the concept to develop oral vocabulary.
- Build oral vocabulary.

Today at a Glance

Oral Vocabulary
shuffle, teeter

Phonemic Awareness
Segment and Blend Phonemes

Phonics and Spelling
◉ Vowel Sounds of *y*
◉ Syllable Pattern CV

Fluency
Paired Reading

High-Frequency Words

Story Words
art, boy, grew, now, sunset, tower

Comprehension
◉ Sequence
◉ Summarize

Vocabulary
Antonyms

Conventions
Action Verbs

Writing
Realistic Story

Handwriting
Letter *Y* and *y*/Letter Spacing

Research and Inquiry
Research Skill: Interview

Concept Talk

 Question of the Week

How do places change?

Build concepts

To reinforce concepts and to focus children's attention, have children sing "Our Growing Town" from the *Sing with Me* Big Book. Why is the town in the song changing? (New people are moving there.)

🔘 Sing with Me Big Book Audio

Introduce Amazing Words

Display the Big Book, *Mr. George Baker*. Read the title and identify the author. Explain that in the story, the author uses the words *shuffle* and *teeter* in place of the word *walk*. Have children listen as you read the story to find out who *teeters* and *shuffles*.

Use the Oral Vocabulary routine on the next page to teach *teeter* and *shuffle*.

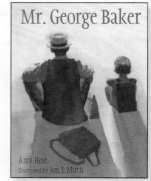

Big Book

ELL **Reinforce Vocabulary** Use the Day 2 instruction on ELL Poster 13 to reinforce the meaning of high-frequency words.

Oral Vocabulary
Amazing Words

Teach Amazing Words

Amazing Words

growth	teeter
population	crooked
public	makeshift
shuffle	spindly

Amazing Words — Oral Vocabulary Routine

1 **Introduce the Word** Relate the word *teeter* to the book. George's wife *teeters* out the screen door to give George a sack. Supply a child-friendly definition. *Teeters* means "wobbles a bit" or "moves unsteadily." Have children say the word.

2 **Demonstrate** Provide examples to show meaning. A baby might *teeter* as she learns to walk. After I get off a roller coaster, I *teeter* before I am able to walk the right way.

3 **Apply** Have children demonstrate their understanding. Tell about a time when you *teetered* or saw someone else *teeter*.

See p. OV•1 to teach *shuffle*.

Routines Flip Chart

Anchored Talk

Add to the concept map

Discuss how places change and how people can help places change.

- What does "Our Growing Town" say about how places change? (New people come to the town to find new homes.) Let's add *New people come* to our map. New people coming to a town means a *growth* in *population*. *Growth* and *population* were two of our Amazing Words from yesterday.

- In yesterday's Read Aloud, "We're Moving," what changes took place in Hanna's neighborhood because of the growth in population? (New apartments and a new park were built.) Let's add *apartments* and *new park* to the concept map.

Differentiated Instruction

SI Strategic Intervention

Sentence Production If children do not pronounce the sound /r/ at the end of the word *teeter*, say the sentence containing the word, stressing the sound /r/. Have children repeat it.

English Language Learners
Physical Response Teach the words *shuffle* and *teeter* by acting them out and having children join you. To reinforce understanding, look for opportunities to recycle the language in the day's activities. For example, have children shuffle as they line up and teeter while in line.

Objectives

- Segment and blend words with syllable pattern CV.
- ◉ Blend and read words with syllable pattern CV.
- ◉ Associate the sound /ē/ with *e*, /ī/ with *i*, and /ō/ with *o*.

Skills Trace

◉ **Syllable Pattern CV**
Introduce U3W1D2
Practice U3W1D3; U3W1D4
Reteach/Review U3W1D5; U3W2D4
Assess/Test Weekly Test U3W1
Benchmark Test U3

KEY:
U=Unit   W=Week   D=Day

Phonemic Awareness
Segment and Blend Phonemes

Model isolating sounds

Have children look at the picture on pages 14–15 in their Student Editions. I see two people greeting each other. We greet others by saying *hi*. The last sound I hear in *hi* is /ī/. I see a boy yawning. *He* is tired. The last sound in *he* is /ē/. I see a person who has started a race. He has just said *go*. The last sound in *go* is /ō/.

Student Edition pp. 14–15

Model segmenting and blending

Listen to the sounds in the word *go*: /g/ /ō/. There are two sounds in *go*. Let's blend those sounds to make a word: /g/ /ō/, *go*. Continue modeling with *hi* and *he*.

Guide practice

Guide children as they segment and blend these words from the picture: *she, hi, go, he,* and *we*.

Corrective feedback

If... children make an error,
then... model by segmenting the word, and have them repeat the segmenting and blending of the word.

Have children segment and blend the following words.

On their own

/h/ /ē/ **he**	/w/ /ē/ **we**	/s/ /ō/ **so**
/m/ /ō/ **Mo**	/h/ /ī/ **hi**	/m/ /ē/ **me**
/p/ /r/ /ō/ **pro**	/v/ /ī/ **Vi**	/b/ /ē/ **be**

Phonics—Teach/Model
↻ Syllable Pattern CV

Sound-Spelling Card 82

o

Sound-Spelling Card 75

_e

Sound-Spelling Card 78

_i

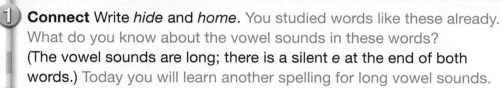

ROUTINE **Blending Strategy**

1 Connect Write *hide* and *home*. You studied words like these already. What do you know about the vowel sounds in these words? (The vowel sounds are long; there is a silent *e* at the end of both words.) Today you will learn another spelling for long vowel sounds.

2 Use Sound-Spelling Cards Display Card 82. The sound you hear at the end of *no* is /ō/. The sound /ō/ can be spelled *o*. Have children say /ō/ several times as you point to *o*. Follow the same procedure with Cards 75 and 78 and the sounds of long *e* and long *i*.

3 Model Write *go*. The *o* in this word says its name. When a word or syllable ends with one vowel, the vowel sound is usually long. This is how I blend this word. Segment and blend *go*. Follow this procedure to model blending *she* and *hi*.

4 Guide Practice Continue the process in step 3. This time have children blend with you.

we	so	he	hi	go	she
pro	me	hello	Jo	be	yoyo

5 Review What do you know about reading these words? (When a word or syllable ends with one vowel, the vowel is usually long.)

Routines Flip Chart

Vocabulary Support
You may wish to explain the meaning of this word.
pro in favor of something

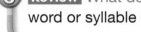

English Language Learners
Visual Support Model isolating sounds while using the pictures on pp. 14–15 of the Student Edition as visual support. For example: /s//k//ī/, *sky*. Who can point to birds in the sky? Now let's say the sounds of *sky* together: /s//k//ī/.

Phonics—Build Fluency
⟳ Syllable Pattern CV

Model

Envision It!

Have children turn to page 18 in their Student Editions. Look at the pictures on this page. The word in the first picture is *no*. When I say *no*, I hear /ō/. In *no*, long *o* is spelled *o*. The word in the next picture is *hi*. When I say *hi*, I hear /ī/ at the end. In *hi*, long *i* is spelled *i*. In the last picture, the word is *we*. When I say *we*, I hear /ē/ at the end. In *we*, long *e* is spelled *e*.

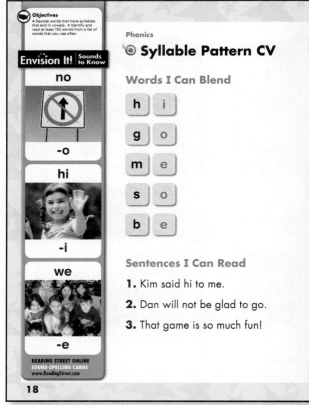

Student Edition p. 18

Guide practice

For each word in "Words I Can Blend," ask for the sound of each letter. Make sure that children identify the correct sound for the final vowel. Then have children blend the whole word.

Corrective feedback

If... children have difficulty blending a word,

then... model blending the word, and ask children to blend it with you.

Blend and Read

Decode words in isolation

After children can successfully segment and blend the words, ask them to read the words naturally.

Decode words in context

Have children read each of the sentences. Have them identify words in the sentences that have the syllable pattern CV.

[Team Talk] Pair children and have them take turns reading each of the sentences aloud.

On their own

Use *Reader's and Writer's Notebook* p. 317.

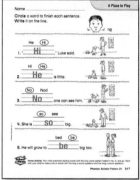

Reader's and Writer's Notebook p. 317

Differentiated Instruction

SI Strategic Intervention

Letter Tiles If children have difficulty reading words with contrasting long-vowel patterns, have them use letter tiles to help them sound out the words and differentiate between the patterns.

Spelling Patterns

Long e Spelled e The long e sound may be spelled with the letter e at the end of a word or syllable.

Long i Spelled i The long i sound may be spelled with the letter i at the end of a word or syllable.

Long o Spelled o The long o sound may be spelled with the letter o at the end of a word or syllable.

MONITOR PROGRESS   Check Word Reading   ↻ Syllable Pattern CV

Write the following words and have the class read them. Notice which children miss words during the group reading. Call on those individuals to read some of the words.

no	me	hi	she	go	**Spiral Review**
we	dive	so	my	these ←	Row 2 contrasts long-vowel patterns.
pet	he	robe	got	pro ←	Row 3 contrasts short- and long-vowel patterns.

If... children cannot blend words with syllable pattern CV,

then... use the Small Group Time Strategic Intervention lesson, p. DI•2, to reteach syllable pattern CV. Continue to monitor children's progress using other instructional opportunities during the week. See the Skills Trace on p. 18c.

Day 1	Day 2	Day 3	Day 4	Day 5
Check Word Reading	Check Word Reading	Check High-Frequency Words/Retelling	Check Fluency	Check Oral Vocabulary

Objectives

- Apply knowledge of sound-spellings to decode unknown words when reading.
- Decode and read words in context and in isolation.
- Practice fluency with oral rereading.

Decodable Practice Reader 13B
Syllable Pattern CV

Decode words in isolation

Have children turn to page 153. Have children decode each word.

Review High-frequency words

Review the previously taught words *said, want, I, now, saw, down, was, come, to, the,* and *a*. Have children read each word as you point to it on the Word Wall.

Preview

Have children read the title and preview the story. Tell them they will read words that end in syllable pattern CV.

Decode words in context

Pair children for reading, and listen as they decode. One child begins. Children read the entire story, switching readers after each page.

Decodable Practice Reader 13B

Decodable Practice Reader 13B

Corrective feedback

If... children have difficulty decoding a word, **then...** refer them to the Sound-Spelling Cards to identify the sounds in the word. Then prompt them to blend the word.

- What is the new word?
- Is the new word a word you know?
- Does it make sense in the story?

Check decoding and comprehension

Have children retell the story to include characters, setting, and events. Then have children find words that end in syllable pattern CV in the story. Children should supply *no, go, be, Mo, Vi, he, hi, she,* and *we.*

Reread for Fluency

Have children reread Decodable Practice Reader 13B to develop automaticity decoding words with syllable pattern CV.

 ROUTINE **Paired Reading**

1 **Reread** To achieve optimal fluency, have partners reread the text three or four times.

2 **Corrective Feedback** Listen as children read. Provide corrective feedback regarding their fluency and decoding.

Routines Flip Chart

Differentiated Instruction

 Strategic Intervention
Retelling If children have difficulty retelling the story, ask them questions regarding the events in the story.

E L L

English Language Learners
Syllable Pattern CV
Beginning After reading, point out the words that end with the syllable pattern CV on each page. Have children read them aloud. Then have children identify the story characters, Mo and Vi, in the illustration on p. 157.

Intermediate After reading, have children find pairs of rhyming words with the syllable pattern CV and say them aloud. For example: *no* and *go*; *she* and *be.*

Advanced/Advanced High After reading, have children find words that end with the syllable pattern CV. Have them make up questions using the words. For example: *Will Mo and Vi go to the picnic?* Allow other children to answer the questions.

Objectives
- Apply knowledge of letter-sound correspondences and syllable patterns to decode words in context and in isolation.
- Spell words with vowel sounds of *y*.

Phonics Review
Long *e*, Long *i*, and Vowel Sounds of *y*

Review Sound-spellings

Review the long-vowel spelling patterns *i_e, ee,* and the vowel sounds of *y* using Sound-Spelling Cards 80, 63, 77 and 81.

Decode words in isolation

Display these words. Have the class blend the words. Then point to the words in random order and ask children to read them quickly.

shy	hide	feet
muddy	tree	drive
teeth	carry	dry

Corrective feedback

Model blending decodable words and then ask children to blend them with you.

Decode words in context

Display these sentences. Have the class read the sentences.

Team Talk Have pairs take turns reading the sentences naturally.

> **Why** will **Mike** look at the **sky?**
>
> **My puppy** is **sweet** and **funny.**
>
> **Sandy likes** to **ride** in a **jeep.**

Spelling
Vowel Sounds of *y*

Guide practice

Tell children that you will segment the sounds in each spelling word. They should repeat the sounds in each word as they write the word. Check the spelling of each word before saying the next word.

1. /m/ /ī/ **my**
2. /b/ /ī/ **by**
3. /t/ /r/ /ī/ **try**
4. /s/ /u/ /n/ /ē/ **sunny**
5. /h/ /a/ /n/ /d/ /ē/ **handy**

6. /f/ /l/ /ī/ **fly**
7. /k/ /r/ /ī/ **cry**
8. /l/ /u/ /k/ /ē/ **lucky**
9. /p/ /u/ /p/ /ē/ **puppy**
10. /s/ /i/ /l/ /ē/ **silly**

On their own

Use *Reader's and Writer's Notebook* p. 318.

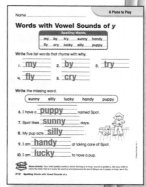

Reader's and Writer's Notebook p. 318

Small Group Time

DAY 2

Break into small groups after spelling and before the comprehension lesson.

Teacher-Led

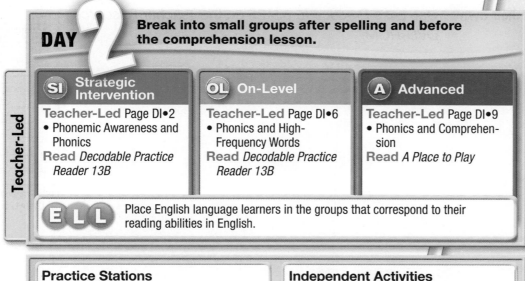

SI **Strategic Intervention**	OL **On-Level**	A **Advanced**
Teacher-Led Page DI•2	**Teacher-Led** Page DI•6	**Teacher-Led** Page DI•9
• Phonemic Awareness and Phonics	• Phonics and High-Frequency Words	• Phonics and Comprehension
Read *Decodable Practice Reader 13B*	**Read** *Decodable Practice Reader 13B*	**Read** *A Place to Play*

ELL Place English language learners in the groups that correspond to their reading abilities in English.

Practice Stations
• Listen Up
• Word Work

Independent Activities
• Read independently/Reading Log on Reader's and Writer's Notebook p. RR 4
• Audio Text of Main Selection

 **ELL**

English Language Learners

Long Vowels Spanish speakers may spell long *e* words with the letter *i*, and long *i* words with the letters *ai*.

DAY 2 Read and Comprehend 40–45 min.

Objectives

- Learn story words: *grew, art, boy, tower, now, sunset.*
- Review high-frequency words.
- Identify antonyms.

High-Frequency Words
Build Fluency

Read words in isolation

Remind children that there are some words we learn by remembering the letters, rather than by saying the sounds. Then have them read each of the highlighted high-frequency words aloud.

Read words in context

Chorally read the "I Can Read!" passage along with children. Then have them read the passage aloud to themselves. When they are finished, ask children to reread the high-frequency words.

Team Talk Have children choose two high-frequency words and give them time to create a sentence in which both words are used properly. Then have them share their sentence with a partner.

On their own

Use *Let's Practice It!* p. 125 on the *Teacher Resource DVD-ROM.*

I Can Read!

My pal Timmy and I always go to fun places. One day we met on Sandy Lane.

Timmy said, "Hi! Look! This used to be nothing but a muddy lot. Then men came to work. It has become a club for kids. We can do fun things, like skate, swim, and hike. Everything is free!"

"I am happy," I said. "I hope it stays!"

You've learned!
- Vowel Sounds of *y*
- Syllable Pattern CV

High-Frequency Words
things always day nothing
stays become everything

19

Student Edition p. 19

Let's Practice It!
TR DVD•125

Story Words
A Place to Play

Introduce story words

Use Vocabulary Transparency 13 to introduce this week's story words. Read each sentence as you track the print. Frame each underlined word and explain its meaning.

Vocabulary Transparency 13
TR DVD

boy	a male child
art	painting, drawing, or sculpture
tower	a tall building or part of a building
grew	got bigger
now	at this time
sunset	last time of the day when the sun is seen

Have children read each sentence with you.

Vocabulary
Antonyms

Model antonyms

Explain that *antonyms* are words that have opposite meanings. Draw a T-chart or display Graphic Organizer 4. List these words in the left column: *always, up, boy me,* and *sunset*. Explain that each word in the left column has an antonym.

always	never
up	down
boy	girl
me	you
sunset	sunrise

Graphic Organizer
Flip Chart 4

Think Aloud I see the word *always*. The opposite of *always* is *never*. So *always* and *never* are antonyms. I'll write *never* in the right column so I can see the antonyms together.

Guide practice

Have a volunteer give the antonym for *up* and write it in the right column (down). Repeat the procedure for the remaining words.

On their own

Have children choose a pair of antonyms and draw and label a picture that shows the meaning of each word.

Differentiated Instruction

SI Strategic Intervention

Pronunciation If children pronounce the /th/ in *nothing* and *everything* as /t/, then say each word, clearly pronouncing the /th/, and have children repeat it. If children do not pronounce the sound /ėr/ at the end of the word *never*, then say the word, clearly pronouncing the final /ėr/ sound and have children repeat it.

Academic Vocabulary

antonyms words that have opposite meanings

ELL

English Language Learners
Understand General Meaning Ask children to listen as you read aloud p. 19 in the Student Edition. After reading, have them restate the general ideas in the passage using the familiar language of the high-frequency words. Have children use strategies for understanding unfamiliar information: listening for important details and taking notes.

Multilingual Vocabulary Lists Children can apply knowledge of their home language to acquire new English vocabulary by using the Multilingual Vocabulary List (*ELL Handbook* pp. 465–476).

Objectives

- Build background on the steps for building a house.
- Preview and predict.
- Use key structure and elements of realistic fiction to improve understanding of text.
- Set a purpose for reading text.

Build Background
A Place to Play

Background-Building Audio

Have children listen to the CD. Tell them to listen for what the construction worker says are the steps in building a house.

 Background Building Audio

Discuss building a house

Team Talk Have children turn to a partner and use these questions for discussion:

- What is the first step in building a house?
- What is the second step in building a house?
- What is the third step in building a house?

Organize information in a chart

Draw a chart or display Graphic Organizer 31. Have children recall the three steps in building a house. Record their responses.

Step 1	Make a plan.
Step 2	Build the foundation and frame the house.
Step 3	Finish the inside and the outside of the house.

Graphic Organizer Flip Chart 31

Connect to selection

We learned about three steps in building a house. The last step is finishing the inside and outside. In the story we are about to read, *A Place to Play*, a community center is being built. We'll learn about some things that are done to finish the center.

Student Edition pp. 20–21

Double Day Read!

Main Selection—First Read
A Place to Play

Practice the skill

Sequence Remind children that events in a story happen in a certain order, or sequence. Display the words *first, next,* and *last*. These clue words can help them understand a story's sequence.

Introduce the strategy

Summarize Explain that when readers want to understand or remember what they read, they think about the most important parts. Have children turn to page EI•19 in their Student Edition.

Envision It!

Student Edition EI•19

Think Aloud Look at what is happening in this picture. What do you think this picture is mainly about? (a falling table) As I read *A Place to Play*, I will pay attention to what the story is about and the most important things that happen.

Introduce genre

Let's Read Together **Realistic fiction** is a made-up story that could happen in real life. As they read, ask children to look for events that indicate this could happen in real life.

Preview and predict

Have children identify the title of the story, the author, and the illustrator. Read aloud the names of the author and illustrator and have children describe the role of each. Help children activate prior knowledge by asking them to look through the selection and use the illustrations to predict events that might happen in the story.

Set a purpose

Good readers read for a purpose. Setting a purpose helps us to think and understand more as we read. Guide children to set a purpose for reading the story.

Tell children that today they will read *A Place to Play* for the first time. Use the Day 2 Guide Comprehension notes to help children develop their comprehension of the story.

Double Day Read!

First Read

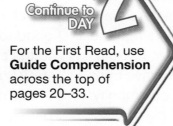
Continue to DAY 2

For the First Read, use **Guide Comprehension** across the top of pages 20–33.

INTERACT with TEXT

Strategy Response Log

Background Knowledge
Before reading, have children use p. RR25 of their *Reader's and Writer's Notebook* to draw a picture of their favorite place to play. Have them write a sentence explaining why this is their favorite place.

Academic Vocabulary

summarize to recall the important ideas in a text

realistic fiction a made-up story that could happen in real life

ELL

English Language Learners

Build Background Before children listen to the CD, build background and elicit prior knowledge. On the CD, you will hear about a construction worker. He is going to build a house. What do you think he might do *first, second,* and *third*?

Frontload Main Selection Ask children what they already know about a community center using the picture on pp. 20–21. Then do a picture walk of the selection so children can talk about and see activities that take place at a community center.

DAY 2

Guide Comprehension
Skills and Strategies

Connect to Concept
Growing and Changing Look at the pictures on pages 20 and 21. How is this place changing? (The outside of this building is changing because they are planting trees.)

Amazing Words
Sample Text Have children continue discussing the concept using the Amazing Words *growth, population, public, shuffle,* and *teeter* as they read.

Student Edition pp. 20–21

DAY 3

Extend Thinking
Think Critically

Higher-Order Thinking Skills
Analysis I see in the picture that there are trees and plants right next to the community center. Explain why it is a good idea to have trees and plants next to the community center.

If... children cannot explain why it is good to have trees and plants next to the community center,
then... ask children how trees and plants might make the building look better.

Strategies

⊙ **Summarize** Remind children that good readers look for important ideas as they read. Have them summarize what has happened in the story so far.

If... children have difficulty summarizing the text, **then...** model a summary statement. *The children have gone with Nai Nai to see what their parents have been doing.*

"This will <u>be</u> a fun <u>day</u>," <u>Benny</u> said to <u>Molly</u>. "Nai Nai can take <u>us</u> to see where Mom and Dad are working."

22

"I <u>spy</u> Dad and Mom!" said <u>Benny</u>. "What are you doing?"

"We are planting <u>things</u>. This <u>sunny</u> spot <u>is</u> good for growing plants," said Dad.

23

Student Edition pp. 22–23

Review **Author's Purpose**

Analysis On pages 22–23, what does the author want you to know about the community center? (The author wants us to know that Benny and Molly's parents are planting things at the community center because the center is not finished yet.)

Higher-Order Thinking Skills

Synthesis Describe the appearance of the outside of the community center. How would you make it look?

Skills and Strategies, continued

DAY 2

Skills
 **Sequence** What do Benny and Molly do after they find their mom and dad? (They go inside the community center.)

Vocabulary
Story Words Have children locate the story word *grew* on page 25. What does Ms. Torres mean when she says she grew up in the neighborhood? (She has lived there since she was a child.)

"It is muddy in that spot!" said Benny.

"Let us go inside," said Nai Nai.

"Here is a place for meetings," said Mom. "Look, Benny! There is Ms. Torres!"

"Hi, Benny!" said Ms. Torres. "I grew up in this neighborhood, so I want to help."

24

25

Student Edition pp. 24–25

Think Critically, continued

DAY 3

Higher-Order Thinking Skills
Evaluation Explain why growing up in the neighborhood would make Ms. Torres want to help.

If... children have trouble explaining why Ms. Torres would help, **then...** relate Ms. Torres's feelings about her neighborhood to children's feelings about the neighborhood they live in.

Word Reading

Decoding Have children check their reading of new words using these guidelines:

- Did I blend the sounds to read the word?
- Did I put the new word in the sentence to make sure it made sense?
- Did I look for word parts to help me understand the word?

Vocabulary

Antonyms I know that the words *playing* and *working* on page 27 are opposites. Words that are opposites are called antonyms. What word on page 27 is the antonym, or opposite, of *ground*? (sky) On page 26, what is the antonym for *far away*? (next to)

"This is a place for art," said Mom. Look at the wall with nothing on it. Now look at the wall next to it."

"That wall looks like my neighborhood!" said Benny. "I see people working and playing under a blue sky."

26

27

Student Edition pp. 26–27

Higher-Order Thinking Skills

Analysis What buildings did the artist paint in her picture on page 27? (an ice cream shop, a flower shop, and a library) Why do you think she chose to show these buildings in the painting? (They might be buildings from her neighborhood.)

Skills and Stragegies, continued

DAY 2

Skills

👁 **Sequence** What is the first thing that happens on pages 28–29? What happens next? (First, Benny talks to Mr. Gray. Then the family goes to the place where people will watch plays.)

Word Reading

High-Frequency Words Point out the words *stays, always,* and *become*. Have children practice reading these words.

"Do you like it?" asked Mr. Gray. Benny said, "Yes, I hope it stays there always!"

28

"This will become a place to watch plays," said Dad.

"Look, there is Mr. Jackson," said Mom. "He lives by us too."

29

Student Edition pp. 28–29

Think Critically, continued

DAY 3

Higher-Order Thinking Skills

Evaluation How can having a stage be a help to the community center?

If... children have difficulty explaining the benefits of a stage, **then...** ask when it would be useful for an adult to be able to speak out.

Connect to Social Studies

Community Centers The community center in Benny and Molly's neighborhood can be used for many activities and by many different people.

Team Talk Have children discuss with a partner why they think community centers are important.

Strategies

Summarize Have children summarize what has happened in *A Place to Play* in their own words.

Strategy Self-Check

Have children find a sentence in *A Place to Play* that summarizes the most important idea in the story. ("People from the neighborhood came together to work on everything in this place," Mom said.)

"People from the neighborhood came together to work on everything in this place," Mom said.

Benny saw a boy who seemed a little shy. "Do you like to play ball?" Benny asked.

"Go check out this next one," said Dad.

30

31

Student Edition pp. 30–31

Higher-Order Thinking Skills

Analysis Mom said that people from the neighborhood came together to work on the community center. How could the children have helped?

If... children have difficulty naming something the children could have helped with,
then... have children name something that they have helped with before at home.

Skills and Strategies, continued

Skills

DAY 2

◎ Sequence What is the last thing that the family sees before they go home? (They see the sunset.) Have children tell what happens in the beginning, in the middle, and at the end of the story.

If... children have trouble retelling the beginning, middle, and end of the story, **then...** have them look back at the pictures to refresh their memories.

Continue to DAY **2**
Comprehension Check p. 33a

"I will slide down!" Benny said. Mom and Molly went up in the tower.

"They are lucky," said Nai Nai. "I wish I had a place like this when I was a kid."

32

"See the sunset?" Mom asked.

Dad said, "It is time to go home."

"I like this place," said Benny. "It is a good place for all of us!"

33

Student Edition pp. 32–33

Think Critically, continued

DAY 3

Higher-Order Thinking Skills
Evaluation Why does Benny think that the community center is a good place for all of them?

If... children have difficulty explaining why the community center is a good place for all of them, **then...** ask volunteers to name a person in Benny's family and an activity that person could do at the community center.

Comprehension Check

Have children discuss each question with a partner.
Ask several pairs to share their responses.

☑ **Realistic fiction** Do you think this story could happen in real life? (Possible response: Yes, I think that people could work together to help build a community center in their neighborhood.)

☑ **Confirm predictions** How did you use pictures or story clues to predict what would happen next in the story? (Possible response: I used the picture of the people working outside to predict they would make the place nicer.)

☑ **Cause and effect** What will all the neighbors be able to do because of the changes at the community center? (Possible response: Neighbors will be able to watch plays on the new stage.)

☑ **Draw conclusions** How do you think Benny feels at the end of the story? Why? (Possible response: I think he is happy because he says that he likes the community center.)

☑ **Connect text to self** Benny meets a boy at the center who seems a little shy. Think about a time when you felt shy. How would you have felt if someone asked you to play? Why do you think Benny asks the shy boy if he likes to play ball? (Possible response: Benny wants to make the shy boy feel comfortable at the community center. So, he asks him to play with him.)

English Language Learners
Support Discussion Ask yes-or-no questions to start children's responses. For example: Could this story happen in real life? (Yes.) Extend language opportunities for children by asking follow-up questions, such as: Why? What things could happen?

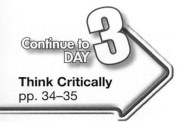

Think Critically
pp. 34–35

Objectives
- Identify and retell a story's beginning, middle, and end.
- Identify and use action verbs.

Literary Text
Realistic Fiction

Identify beginning, middle, and end

Use the book *Mr. George Baker* to have children retell the story's beginning, middle, and end.

- The book *Mr. George Baker* has a beginning, middle, and end. What happens at the beginning of the story? (Harry joins George on his porch.)
- What happens in the middle of the story? (They wait on the porch, and Mrs. Baker brings George a sack lunch.)
- What happens at the end of the story? (They get on the bus and go to school, where they are both learning to read.)

Guide practice

Explain that the class will now list the beginning, middle, and end of the story *A Place to Play* on Graphic Organizer 22. Ask children to tell what you should write in each space.

On their own

Divide children into small groups and assign each group a previously read story from the Student Edition. Have them identify the story's beginning, middle, and end. Have them share their information with the class.

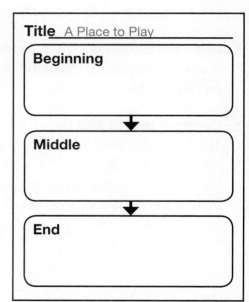

Graphic Organizer Flip Chart 22

Conventions
Action Verbs

Model action verbs

Write *The dog eats* on the board. Point to each word as you read it. Ask children to identify what the action is. (eats) Ask children to identify who is doing the action. (the dog) A verb tells what someone or something does. Many verbs show action. What do we call those verbs? (action verbs)

Guide Practice

Write the following sentences on the board. Have children read the sentences and identify the action verb in each sentence.

1. I spy Dad and Mom!   (spy)
2. Mom and Molly go into the tower.   (go)
3. He lives by us too.   (lives)
4. I like this place.   (like)

Connect to oral language

Have the class complete these sentence frames orally using action verbs.

1. Every day I _____ a song.
2. The bells _____ loudly in the morning.
3. The king _____ his horse.

On their own

Use *Reader's and Writer's Notebook* p. 319.

Reader's and Writer's Notebook p. 319

DAY 2 Language Arts

Objectives

- Generate realistic story ideas.
- Recognize features of a realistic story.
- Use sequence in writing a plan for a story.

Writing—Realistic Story
Writing Trait: Organization

Introduce the prompt

Review with children the key features of a realistic story. Point out that *A Place to Play* is a realistic story. Assure them that they can make up a brief story with characters that seem real and a setting like a real place. Explain that today children will plan their own story with events that really could happen. It will be a story with a beginning, middle, and end. Read aloud the writing prompt.

Writing Prompt

Write a made-up story about children at a new place to play.

Help children generate story ideas

Sharing the Writing

Think Aloud To plan a new story, think of places to play. Let's make a chart of places where children play and way they can play at each place. Display a T-chart. I'll start with the word *playground*.

Guide children in identifying places to play and ways to play in each place. Possible ideas are shown. Record the responses, and keep the chart so that children can refer to it as they plan and draft their stories.

Places to Play	Ways to Play
playground	ride on swings or slide, play in sandbox, play kickball
park	hide and seek, play with ball or kite
yard	run, play with toys or pet
indoor playground	climb on bars, jump in a ball pit

Have each child choose a setting for a new story. Circulate to guide them. Have them make up names for children who will be their characters.

MINI-LESSON

Sequence

■ **Introduce** Use *Reader's and Writer's Notebook* p. 320 to model story planning. To plan a story, I can use a chart. I don't need a title yet, but I have an idea for characters. I'll write about a girl and a boy. I'll call them *Sally* and *Eddy.* I'll write the names in the Characters box. In the Setting box, I'll write *playground.* Now I will plan what happens in the beginning, middle, and end of my story.

■ **Model** At the beginning, Sally and Eddy will walk to a new sandbox. I'll write that in the Beginning box. When I write the story, I also will tell that they carry a pail and a shovel. In the middle of the story, I plan that the characters will make a castle of sand. I'll write that in the Middle box. At the end, Sally and Eddy can say that they are queen and king of the playground. Now I'll write that idea in the End of Story box. Now plan for your story. **Circulate to guide and assist children.**

INTERACT with TEXT

Reader's and Writer's Notebook p. 320

ROUTINE

Quick Write for Fluency

Team Talk

1. **Talk** Have children take two minutes to tell their story events to a partner.

2. **Write** Each child briefly writes about the events at the beginning, middle, and end of the planned story.

3. **Share** Each child reads the story ideas to the partner.

Routines Flip Chart

Write Guy
Jeff Anderson

Sharing the Writing

Sharing writing tasks helps children learn to use language to express their ideas. Shared writing with a group or class pulls them into the literate community. Scaffold children's generation of ideas for realistic story settings and characters.

Differentiated Instruction

SI **Strategic Intervention**

Planning Setting If children find it difficult to think of a setting, have them look at the T-chart and decide which place they like best. Help them copy a word such as *yard* or *park.* Then have them think of ways that children play in that kind of place.

ELL

English Language Learners
Support Prewriting

Beginning Children can draw story events, label them, and share with a partner, possibly one who speaks the same home language.

Intermediate Have children draw pictures or write phrases to express story event ideas. Have them describe the story plan to other children.

Advanced/Advanced High Have children draw pictures or write short sentences in their story charts. As they share the plan with partners, children can clarify and add ideas.

Objectives

- Write letters legibly and with proper spacing.
- Understand and analyze the features of an interview.
- Understand how to use an interview to locate information.
- Apply knowledge of an interview to inquiry project.

Handwriting
Letter *Y* and *y*/Letter Spacing

Model letter formation

Display upper- and lower-case letters: *Yy*. Use the stroke instructions pictured below to model proper letter formation.

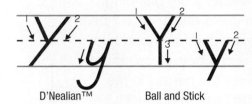

D'Nealian™   Ball and Stick

Model letter spacing

Explain that when we write a word, all the letters in that word should be evenly spaced. Write the word *happy* using correct spacing. When I write the letters in a word, I need to pay attention to the spaces between each letter. Write *happy* again, with the letters too close to each other. The letters should not be so close together that they touch each other. Write *happy* a third time, with the letters too far from each other. They should not be so far apart that it's hard to tell they spell out a word. By correctly spacing letters in words, I make it easier for others to understand what I write. Ask children which of the three writing examples is easiest to read and have them explain why.

Guide practice

Write the following sentence, using letter spacing that is too crowded. *Molly is happy.*

Team Talk Have children work in pairs to discuss what is wrong with the sentence and how it needs to be fixed. Have them share with the class.

On their own

Use the *Reader's and Writer's Notebook* p. 321.

Reader's and Writer's
Notebook p. 321

Research and Inquiry
Research Skill: Interview

Academic Vocabulary

source a person, place, or thing that provides information

Teach

Tell children that a **source** is a person, place, or thing that provides information. Review sources of information they have learned about and have them identify a source that tells where things are located. (a map) Explain that in an interview, your source is a person.

Model

Think Aloud — Display Research Transparency 13. This is an example of an interview. Let's see how an interview is organized. **Point out the title, author, questions, and answers.** Looking at the title, I can tell that this interview is about Building a Home. I see the name of the person is written before each question. The person who asks the questions is the author. I see the name of the person is written before each answer. The person who gives answers to the questions is the source. Read the first question and answer. Who is the author and who is the source?

Research Transparency 13
TR DVD

Guide practice

Continue reading each question and answer. Have children tell what they learn from each answer.

Wrap Up Your Day

✔ **Phonics: Syllable Pattern CV** Write the words *she, he, hi,* and *go.* Ask children to identify the long vowel sounds in these words and determine how they are spelled.

✔ **High-Frequency Words** Write the following sentence: *We will stop moving things to the new building at the end of the day.* Ask children to read the sentence. Then point to the high-frequency words *things* and *day,* and have children read them.

✔ **Build Concepts** Monitor children's use of oral vocabulary as they respond. Recall the Big Book, *Mr. George Baker.* Ask: What public place does Mr. George Baker go to? (the school) How is Mr. George Baker growing and changing? (He's learning to read.)

Preview DAY 3

Tell children that tomorrow they will reread *A Place to Play.*

Objectives
- Build oral vocabulary.
- Identify details in text.
- Share information and ideas about the concept.

Today at a Glance

Oral Vocabulary
crooked

Phonological Awareness
Rhyming Words

Phonics and Spelling
- Vowel Sounds of *y*
- Syllable Pattern CV

High-Frequency Words
always, become, day, everything, nothing, stays, things

Story Words
art, boy, grew, now, sunset, tower

Comprehension
Review Author's Purpose

Fluency
Accuracy and Appropriate Rate

Conventions
Action Verbs

Writing
Realistic Story

Writer's Craft: Draft

Listening and Speaking
Relate an Experience in Sequence

Research and Inquiry
Gather and Record Information

Concept Talk

Question of the Week

How do places change?

Build concepts

To reinforce concepts and to focus children's attention, have children sing "Our Growing Town" from the *Sing with Me* Big Book. Why do people sometimes need to find new places to live? (families grow; new jobs)

 Sing with Me Big Book Audio

Monitor listening comprehension

Display the Big Book *Mr. George Baker.* As children listen to the story, have them think about the friendship between Harry and Mr. George Baker. Then read the book aloud.

- What do Harry and Mr. Baker share? (Mr. Baker shares candy with Harry; they share a seat on the bus; they share an interest in learning to read.)
- How do we know that Mr. Baker is Harry's friend? (Mr. Baker sits with Harry on the bus every day.)

Big Book

ELL **Expand Vocabulary** Use the Day 3 instruction on ELL Poster 13 to help children expand vocabulary.

ELL Poster 13

Oral Vocabulary
Amazing Words

Amazing Words

growth	teeter
population	crooked
public	makeshift
shuffle	spindly

Teach Amazing Words

 **Oral Vocabulary Routine**

1 Introduce the Word Relate the word *crooked* to the book. Mr. George Baker's fingers were crookedy. That means they looked *crooked.* Supply a child-friendly definition: When something is *crooked,* it is bent, curved, or twisted. Have children say the word.

2 Demonstrate Provide examples to show meaning. The line I drew looks *crooked,* so I'll try hard to draw a straighter line. My grandpa's big toe is *crooked,* but it doesn't hurt him.

3 Apply Have children demonstrate their understanding. When you draw a line, how can you keep it from being *crooked?* What are some other things that often are *crooked?*

Routines Flip Chart

Anchored Talk

Add to the concept map

Use these questions to discuss how places change and how people can help places change as you add to the concept map.

• In *A Place to Play,* many neighbors are working together to make the community center. Let's add *community center* to the concept map.

• What kinds of things are being done to make the community center better? Let's add those things to the map.

English Language Learners
Vocabulary Help children understand that the story word *crookedy* is not a real word; it is a different way to emphasize that something, such as Mr. Baker's fingers, look *crooked.* Explain that *crookedy* and *crooked* both mean "twisted, bent, or curved."

Objectives
• Identify words that rhyme.
◉ Read words with vowel sounds of *y* and syllable pattern CV.

Phonological Awareness
Rhyming Words

Model producing rhyming words

Read together the last two bulleted points on pages 14–15 of the Student Edition. Today we are going to use this picture to help us produce rhyming words. Remember that **rhyming words** are words that end with the same sound. The directions tell us to find three words that rhyme with *by.* When I look at the picture, I see the *sky,* and I see two workers *high* on the roof. *Sky* and *high* rhyme with *by.*

Student Edition pp. 14–15

Guide practice

Guide children to use the picture to produce words that rhyme with *funny.* (sunny, bunny)

On their own

Have children produce words that rhyme with the following words.

sunny	we	cry
pro	so	see

Team Talk Allow children the opportunity to create pairs of rhyming words with a partner.

Phonics
Build Words

Model word building

Now we are going to build words with long *i* spelled *y*. Write *try* and blend it. Watch me change *t* in *try* to *c*. Model blending the new word, *cry*.

Guide practice

Have children spell *cry* with letter tiles. Monitor children's work as they build words.

- Change the *c* in *cry* to *f*.
  Say the new word together.

  f r y

- Change the *r* in *fry* to *l*.
  Say the new word together.

  f l y

- Change the *f* in *fly* to *s*.
  Say the new word together.

  s l y

- Change the *l* in *sly* to *k*.
  Say the new word together.

  s k y

Corrective feedback

For corrective feedback, model the correct spelling and have children correct their tiles.

Fluent Word Reading

Model

Write *smoky*. I know the sounds for *s*, *m*, *o*, *k*, and *y*. I blend them and read the word *smoky*.

Guide practice

Write the words below. Say the sounds in your head for each spelling you see. When I point to the word, we'll read it together. Allow one second per sound-previewing time for the first reading.

| try | me | fly | go | hi | sunny |

On their own

Have children read the list above three or four times, until they can read one word per second.

DAY 3 Get Ready to Read

Objectives
- ◎ Associate the vowel sounds of long *e* and long *i* with the spelling *y*.
- Blend and read words with the vowel sounds of y and words with syllable pattern CV.
- Decode words in context and in isolation.
- Spell words with vowel sounds of *y*.
- Spell high-frequency words.

🔁 Blend and Read

Decode words in isolation

Have children turn to pages 323–324 in the *Reader's and Writer's Notebook* and find the first list of words. Each word in this list ends with either a vowel sound of *y* or the syllable pattern CV. Let's blend and read these words. Be sure that children identify the correct final sound in each word.

Next, have children read the high-frequency words.

Reader's and Writer's Notebook pp. 323–324

Decode words in context

Chorally read the story along with children. Have children identify words in the story that have the vowel sounds of *y* or the syllable pattern CV.

Team Talk Pair children and have them take turns reading the story aloud to each other. Monitor children as they read to check for proper pronunciation and appropriate pacing.

On their own

To further develop automaticity, have children take the story home to reread.

Spelling
Vowel Sounds of *y*

Spell high-frequency words

Write *things* and *always* and point them out on the Word Wall. Have children say and spell the words with you and then without you.

Dictation

Have children write these sentences. Say each sentence. Then repeat it slowly, one word at a time.

> 1. **That silly puppy takes my things.**
> 2. **I always cry when I'm sad.**
> 3. **Jo will try to fly this kite.**

Proofread and correct

Write each sentence, spelling words one at a time. Have children circle and rewrite any misspelled words.

On their own

Use *Reader's and Writer's Notebook* p. 325.

Spelling Words

Vowel Sounds of *y*

1. my	6. fly
2. by	7. cry
3. try	8. lucky
4. sunny	9. silly
5. handy	10. puppy

High-Frequency Words

11. things	12. always

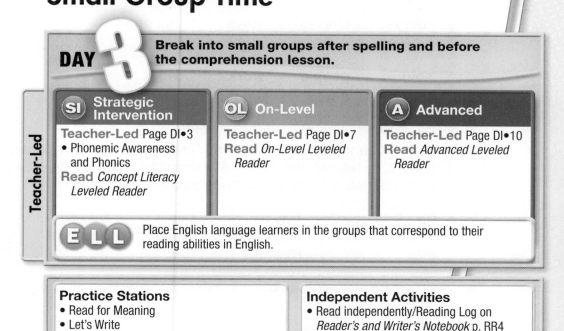

Reader's and Writer's Notebook, p. 325

Small Group Time

DAY 3

Break into small groups after spelling and before the comprehension lesson.

Teacher-Led

(SI) Strategic Intervention	(OL) On-Level	(A) Advanced
Teacher-Led Page DI•3 • Phonemic Awareness and Phonics **Read** *Concept Literacy Leveled Reader*	**Teacher-Led** Page DI•7 **Read** *On-Level Leveled Reader*	**Teacher-Led** Page DI•10 **Read** *Advanced Leveled Reader*

ELL Place English language learners in the groups that correspond to their reading abilities in English.

Practice Stations
• Read for Meaning
• Let's Write

Independent Activities
• Read independently/Reading Log on *Reader's and Writer's Notebook* p. RR4
• AudioText of Main Selection

ELL

English Language Learners

Spelling Dictation Children will benefit from hearing each dictated sentence read three times. First, have children listen to understand the sentence. The second time, they should write what they hear. The third time, they can check their work.

Objectives
- Read high-frequency words.
- Establish purpose for reading text.
- Review key features of realistic fiction.

Check High-Frequency Words
❗ **SUCCESS PREDICTOR**

High-Frequency and Story Words

Read words in isolation

Display and review this week's high-frequency words and story words. Have children read the words aloud.

Read words in context

Display the following sentence frames. Have children complete the sentences using high-frequency and story words. Have children read each completed sentence with you.

1. She can see *everything* when she is up in that _____. (tower)
2. This past fall, *nothing* _____ on my tall peach tree. (grew)
3. *Now* we make *things* with small sticks at my _____ camp. (art)
4. We can *always* take a bus home on that _____. (day)
5. When the _____ is at camp, his pet *stays* at home. (boy)
6. A blue, sunny sky may *become* deep red at _____. (sunset)

Don't Wait Until Friday

MONITOR PROGRESS ↻ **Check High-Frequency Words**

Point to these words on the Word Wall and have the class read them. Listen for children who miss words during the reading. Call on those children to read some of the words individually.

things	always	stays	become	**Spiral Review** Rows 3 and 4 review previously taught high-frequency words.
everything	nothing	day		
said	people	work	what	←
there	down	where		←

If... children cannot read these words,

then... use the Small Group Time Strategic Intervention lesson, p. DI•4, to reteach the words. Monitor children's fluency with these words during reading and provide additional practice.

Day 1	Day 2	Day 3	Day 4	Day 5
Check Word Reading	Check Word Reading	**Check High-Frequency Words/Retelling**	Check Fluency	Check Oral Vocabulary

Success Predictor

Main Selection—Second Read
A Place to Play

Review Author's Purpose

Recall this week's main selection, *A Place to Play*. Tell children that today they will read the story again. Remind children that the reason or reasons that an author writes is the **author's purpose**. Identifying the author's purpose can help us better understand what the author is saying and why certain information is included in the text. What are some reasons why authors write?

Review Genre: realistic fiction

Let's Read Together Remind children that realistic fiction is a made-up story that could happen in real life. Have children recall facts from *A Place to Play* that indicate that this story could happen in real life. (It has realistic characters and setting.)

Set a purpose

Remind children that good readers read for a purpose. Guide children to set a new purpose for reading *A Place to Play* today, perhaps to consider why different events occurred in the story.

Extend thinking

Tell children they will now read *A Place to Play* for the second time. Use the Day 3 Extend Thinking notes to encourage children to use higher order thinking skills to go beyond the details of the story.

 Continue to **DAY 3**
For the Second Read, use **Extend Thinking** across the bottom of pages 20–33.

Second Read

Story Words

boy a male child
art painting, drawing, or sculpture
tower a tall building or part of a building
grew got bigger
sunset last time of the day when the sun is seen
now at this time

Academic Vocabulary

author's purpose the reason or reasons why an author writes

ELL

English Language Learners
Words in Context Provide support by supplying a word bank for children during the sentence frames review activity on p. 34g.

Success Predictor

Objectives
- Retell a narrative.
- ◎ Identify sequence in a narrative text.
- Ask questions.
- Write clear, coherent sentences.

Check Retelling
SUCCESS PREDICTOR

Think Critically

1. Why might a community center be a good place to play? Text to World

2. Why do you think the author wrote this story? Author's Purpose

3. What do Benny and Molly see after they go inside? Sequence

4. What do you think is the most important idea in the story? Summarize

5. **Look Back and Write** Look back at page 23. Why is a sunny spot good for growing plants? Write about it.
TEST PRACTICE Extended Response

Meet the Illustrator

Maryann Cocca-Leffler

Maryann Cocca-Leffler is an illustrator who also writes many of her own stories. She has gotten a lot of the inspiration for her stories from her two daughters. But she admits that she still thinks like a kid, and that helps when she writes children's books.

Here are other books by Maryann Cocca-Leffler.

Use the Reading Log in the *Reader's and Writer's Notebook* to record your independent reading.

34   35

Student Edition pp. 34–35

Retelling

 Have children work in pairs, retelling the story to one another. Remind children that their partners should include the characters, setting, and events from the beginning, middle, and end of the story. Children should use the retelling strip in the Student Edition as they retell. Monitor children's retelling.

Scoring rubric

> **Top-Score Response** A top-score response makes connections beyond the text, elaborates on the author's purpose, and describes in detail the characters, setting, and plot.

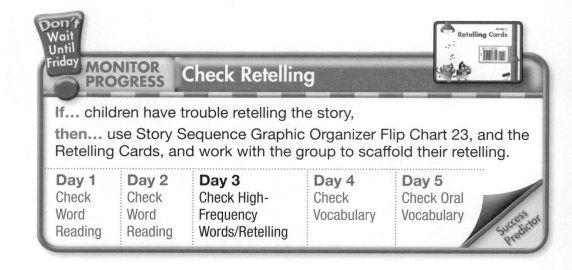

Don't Wait Until Friday

MONITOR PROGRESS Check Retelling

Retelling Cards

If... children have trouble retelling the story,

then... use Story Sequence Graphic Organizer Flip Chart 23, and the Retelling Cards, and work with the group to scaffold their retelling.

Day 1	Day 2	Day 3	Day 4	Day 5
Check Word Reading	Check Word Reading	Check High-Frequency Words/Retelling	Check Vocabulary	Check Oral Vocabulary

Success Predictor

Think Critically

Text to World

1. Possible response: A community center is a good place to play because it is close to where people live, and there are things for everyone to do.

Author's Purpose

2. Possible response: The author wants us to learn that things can change and be made better.

Sequence

3. They see Ms. Torres helping in a meeting room.

Summarize

4. Neighbors can work together to change something.

 Writing on Demand

5. **Look Back and Write** For writing fluency, assign a five-minute time limit. As children finish, encourage them to reread their response and proofread for errors.

Scoring rubric

> **Top-Score Response** A top-score response uses details from the text and the picture to tell why a sunny spot is good for growing plants. For example:
>
> Mom and Dad plant in the sunny spot to help things grow. It also makes the building look nice.

Meet the illustrator

Read aloud page 35 as children follow along. Ask children what an illustrator does.

Read Independently

After children enter their independent reading into their Reading Logs, have them paraphrase a portion of the text they have just read. Tell children that when we paraphrase, we express the meaning of what we have read using our own words.

Differentiated Instruction

 A **Advanced**

Look Back and Write Ask children who show proficiency with the writing prompt to explain why they believe Benny and Molly will continue to play at the community center.

INTERACT with TEXT

Strategy Response Log

Monitor and Clarify Have children revisit p. RR25 in their *Reader's and Writer's Notebook* where they drew a picture of their favorite place to play. After reading the story, have them add to their picture to show how they would change it if they could.

Plan to Assess Retelling

- ☑ This week: Assess Strategic Intervention children.
- ☐ Week 2: Advanced
- ☐ Week 3: Strategic Intervention
- ☐ Week 4: On-Level
- ☐ Week 5: Strategic Intervention
- ☐ Week 6: Assess any children you have not yet checked during this unit.

Retelling

Success Predictor

Model Fluency
Accuracy and Appropriate Rate

Model fluent reading

Have children turn to Student Edition pages 22–23. Follow along as I read these pages. I will try to read with no mistakes. I want to read just the way I speak.

Guide practice

Have children read the pages with you. Then have them reread the pages chorally without you until they read with no hesitation and no mistakes. Continue in the same way with pages 24–25.

Corrective feedback

If... children have difficulty reading with accuracy and appropriate rate, then... prompt:

• Which word is a problem? Let's read it together.
• Read the sentence again to be sure you understand it.
• Tell me the sentence. Now read it as if you are speaking it to me.

Reread for Fluency

ROUTINE Choral Reading

1. **Select a Passage** For *A Place to Play,* use pp. 26–27.
2. **Model** First, have children track the print as you read.
3. **Guide Practice** Then have children read along with you.
4. **Corrective Feedback** Have the class read aloud without you. Monitor progress and provide feedback. For optimal fluency, children should reread three to four times.

Routines Flip Chart

Check comprehension

Why do you think the characters in the story are helping to change their neighborhood? (They want to make their neighborhood a nicer and better place.)

Conventions
Action Verbs

Review
Action Verbs

Remind children that action verbs tell what someone or something does: *Rain falls. Billy hides.*

Guide practice

Write this sentence on the board and have children read it aloud.

Molly runs home.

What other verbs could we use in place of *runs* to make the sentence more interesting?

Team Talk Have children say the sentence using their action verbs.

Connect to oral language

Have children complete these sentence frames orally using action verbs.

1. The boats _____ on the pond.
2. Max _____ across the grass.
3. Jess _____ up the tree.

On their own

Use *Reader's and Writer's Notebook* p. 326.

Reader's and Writer's
Notebook, p. 326

Options for Oral Rereading

Use *A Place to Play* or one of this week's Decodable Practice Readers.

Professional Development

Fluency Fluency building begins in first grade, where the focus is primarily on accuracy and speed. Some fluency practice should occur with on-grade text in a whole-class situation. A teacher modeling fluent reading has a positive effect with minimal class disruption.

Daily Fix-It

5. Mi pupy is white.
   My puppy is white.
6. try not to cri.
   Try not to cry.

Discuss the Daily Fix-It corrections with children. Review sentence capitalization and punctuation, and the *y* spelling of long *e* and long *i*.

Objectives
- Write a draft of a realistic story.
- Use sequence in writing.

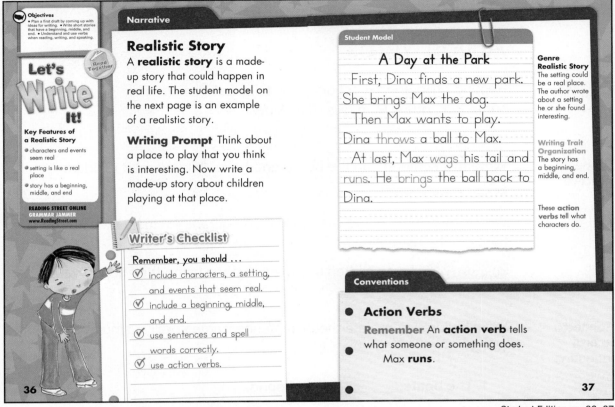

Student Edition pp. 36–37

Let's Write It!

Teach

Use pages 36–37 in the Student Edition. Read aloud the Key Features of a Realistic Story and the definition of a realistic story. Help children better understand the Writing Prompt by reading it aloud and discussing the Writer's Checklist with children.

Review the student model

Then read "A Day at the Park" on page 37 to children. Point out the realistic characters and events in the story. Ask children to identify the setting. (a new park) Use the words *First, Then,* and *At last* in the brief story to help children recognize the beginning, middle, and end. Read aloud and briefly discuss the side notes about Genre, the Writing Trait, and Action Verbs to help children understand how an author writes a realistic story.

Scoring rubric

Top-Score Response Help children understand that a top-score response has a beginning, middle, and end, uses strong action verbs, and uses transition words such as *first, next,* and *last.* For a complete rubric see Writing Rubric 13 from the Teacher Resource DVD-ROM.

Connect to conventions

Read to children the Conventions note about Action Verbs. Point out action verbs in the model story (such as *finds, throws,* and *wags*).

Writing—Realistic Story
Writer's Craft: Sequence

Developing Sequence Children may include more than one story event in the beginning, middle, or end of the story.

MINI-LESSON

Sequence in a Story

■ **Introduce** Use your story chart from yesterday and Writing Transparency 13A to model story events in sequence. When I wrote my story, I used my chart. Yesterday in the chart, I wrote that Sally and Eddy would walk to a new sandbox. In the middle of the story, the children will make a sand castle. It makes sense that they go to the sandbox first and then play there. At the end, Sally and Eddy will say they are the queen and king of the playground. After making the castle, they talk about being queen and king. One event comes after another. Read aloud the draft on the transparency to show how story events happen in the same sequence.

■ Explain how children can use story events they planned yesterday to draft the story: beginning, middle, and end. Today's goal is to write the story but not to rewrite each word perfectly. They can edit later to correct the words.

Fun at the Sandbox

One day Sally and Eddy walked to the new sandbox. They had a pail and a shovel.

The children made a castle out of sand. It was fun

They looked at the sand castel. Sally smiled. She said she was the queen of the playground. Eddy said he was the king.

Unit 3 A Place to Play   Writing Model **13A**

Writing Transparency 13A
TR DVD

 Write Guy
Jeff Anderson

Sharing the Writing

As children write stories, encourage them to use words that tell what happens. As they draft, they will use their knowledge of sound spellings to write. It helps them to use new nouns, verbs, and other words rather than limit themselves to the simplest words they know how to spell. For example, they might write a character's name such as *Emly* (for *Emily*) or a setting such as *yrd* (for *yard*). Help children focus on their story ideas, and assist their skill development. As you write words, model using sound-spellings to write correctly.

Guide story writing

Now it is time to write your story. Tell what your characters do at a new place to play. Have children use their story charts. Help them finish the ideas. Then guide children as they draft the stories.

ROUTINE **Quick Write for Fluency** **Team Talk**

1. **Talk** Have partners take one minute to talk about what children can do with a toy such as a ball, doll, or truck.

2. **Write** Each child writes a sentence about a child with a toy.

3. **Share** Partners point out action verbs in the others' sentences.

Routines Flip Chart

Listening and Speaking
Relate an Experience in Sequence

Teach sequence

Tell children that people often retell experiences that happened to them.

- Good speakers speak clearly.

- They use **sequence words,** such as *first, next,* and *last,* so the story makes sense.

- They choose strong action verbs and descriptive words that help listeners picture the experience.

Model

Use the passage below to model relating an experience in sequence.

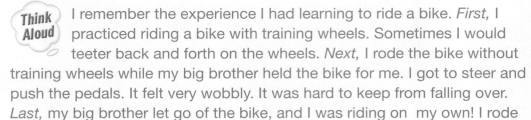 I remember the experience I had learning to ride a bike. *First,* I practiced riding a bike with training wheels. Sometimes I would teeter back and forth on the wheels. *Next,* I rode the bike without training wheels while my big brother held the bike for me. I got to steer and push the pedals. It felt very wobbly. It was hard to keep from falling over. *Last,* my big brother let go of the bike, and I was riding on my own! I rode the bike smoothly and didn't fall down.

Guide practice

Briefly discuss other things that children have learned to do. Make a list of ideas on the board. For one of the ideas, ask children the following questions:

1. What did you do first?

2. What did you do next?

3. What were you able to do last?

On their own

Have pairs of children take turns listening to and speaking about one of the other things they have learned to do. Remind children to listen politely and to speak clearly and at an appropriate pace. Encourage speakers to use the sequence words *first, next,* and *last.* Also be sure that children speak in complete sentences with correct subject-verb agreement.

Research and Inquiry
Gather and Record Information

Teach

Tell children that today they will conduct an interview in the class. Their goal is to find out more about changes in the neighborhoods where they live. Review and model the steps of conducting an interview.

Model

Display the list of questions that the class created on Day 1. *Before the interview, we know we have to prepare a list of questions. We already have our list. I'm interested in learning more about new stores in our neighborhoods. So, I'll ask: Are there any new stores in your neighborhood?* Ask a child to answer the question. Record the answer next to the question.

Guide practice

Have pairs ask or answer one of the inquiry questions. Explain that tomorrow they will review their topic and make sure all of their questions have been answered.

Topic: Neighborhood Change	
Questions	**Answers**
Are there any new stores in your neighborhood?	Yes, a new grocery store opened near our school.

On their own

Use *Reader's and Writer's Notebook* p. 322.

Differentiated Instruction

SI Strategic Intervention

Answering Interview Questions Some children may find it difficult giving interview answers beyond yes and no. Direct those children to then explain their yes or no answer.

Academic Vocabulary

sequence words clue words such as *first, next, then,* and *last* that signal the order of events in a story

Reader's and Writer's Notebook, p. 322

Wrap Up Your Day

✓ **Sequence** What clue words can help us tell the sequence of events?

✓ **Summarize** Have children recall why it is helpful to summarize important story ideas while reading.

Preview DAY 4

Tell children that tomorrow they will hear about a family who makes changes to a place in the country.

Objectives

• Discuss the concept to develop oral language.
• Build oral vocabulary.
• Identify details in text.

Today at a Glance

Oral Vocabulary
makeshift, spindly

Phonemic Awareness
Add Initial Phonemes

Phonics and Spelling
Review Long *e* Spelled *e, ee*
Review Syllables VC/CV

High-Frequency Words
Review

Comprehension
◉ Summarize

Fluency
Accuracy and Appropriate Rate

Conventions
Action Verbs

Writing
Realistic Story: Revise

Research and Inquiry
Interview: Review and Revise Topic

Concept Talk

Question of the Week
How do places change?

Build concepts

To reinforce concepts and to focus children's attention, have children sing "Our Growing Town" from the *Sing with Me* Big Book. What makes a park a public place? (Everyone can use it.) What other public places are in our neighborhoods?

 Sing with Me Big Book Audio

Review Genre: realistic fiction

Have children tell the key features of realistic fiction: it tells about made-up people and events, but the characters and events seem real. The setting of a realistic story seems real. Explain that today you will read about what other people do to build something in "Out in the Country," by Judy Pedersen.

"Out in the Country"

Monitor listening comprehension

Recall the work that Benny and Molly saw people doing to finish the community center. Have children listen to "Out in the Country" to find out what was built and who built it. Read the selection.

ELL **Produce Oral Language** Use the Day 4 instruction on ELL Poster 13 to extend and enrich language.

ELL Poster 13

Go Digital!   Sing with Me Animations   Concept Talk Video

Whole Group

Oral Vocabulary
Amazing Words

Teach Amazing Words

 Amazing Words   Oral Vocabulary Routine

1 **Introduce the Word** Relate the word *makeshift* to the story. The author says she lived in a *makeshift* cabin for a while. Supply a child-friendly definition. Something that is *makeshift* is a substitute for what you don't have when you need it. Have children say the word.

2 **Demonstrate** Provide examples to show meaning. I used the top of a book as a *makeshift* table. We used blankets as a *makeshift* shelter from the rain.

3 **Apply** Have children demonstrate their understanding. What could you use as a *makeshift* ball?

See p. OV•1 to teach *spindly*.

Routines Flip Chart

Anchored Talk

Add to the concept map

Discuss how people help places change.

- What was built in "Out in the Country"? (a country house) Where can we add this to our concept map?

- We read and sang about places changing. Why do some people move to different places? (Possible response: They want to live in the city or the country.) Where can we add this to our concept map?

Amazing Words

growth	teeter
population	crooked
public	makeshift
shuffle	spindly

Differentiated Instruction

A **Advanced**
Amazing Words Ask children who demonstrate an understanding of the word *makeshift* to locate several items in the classroom and explain various ways in which they could be used for other purposes.

 ELL

English Language Learners
Frontload Listening Use ELL Poster 13 to review things found in a city, such as apartments, stores, parks, and trees. Before reading, ask children: What are some things that can be found in the country? Record their answers on the board.

Phonemic Awareness
Add Initial Phonemes

Model

This week we read about a boy and a girl who find all kinds of new places. Listen as I say the sounds in *all*. Slowly model the sounds in *all*, /ȯ/ /l/. Now I will add /f/ to the word *all*, /f/ /ȯl/ We're going to make new words by adding a sound to the beginning of a word.

Guide practice

I will say a word, and you will add /f/ to the beginning of the word to make a new word. Say each word below; then guide children in adding /f/ to the beginning of each word to make a new word.

Corrective feedback

If children make an error, model the correct response. Return to the word later in the practice.

it (fit)	**lip** (flip)	**old** (fold)
ill (fill)	**lake** (flake)	**in** (fin)

On their own

Have children add /m/ to the beginning of the following words.

ice (mice)	**ash** (mash)	**ill** (mill)
end (mend)	**all** (mall)	**an** (man)

Phonics Review
Long e Spelled e, ee; Syllables VC/CV

Review Sound-spellings

To review last week's first phonics skill, write *she* and *sheet*. You studied words like these last week. What do you know about the sound you hear when a word ends with one vowel? (The vowel sound is usually long.) What letters spell the sound /ē/ in *sheet*? (The letters *ee* spell the sound long *e*.)

Corrective feedback

If children are unable to answer the questions about long *e*, refer them to Sound-Spelling Cards 63 and 75.

Review Syllabication

To review last week's second phonics skill, write *basket*. You can read this word because you know that if a word has two consonants in the middle, you can divide the word between the consonants and then blend the syllables together. What are the two syllables in this word? *(bas, ket)* What's the word? *(basket)*

Guide practice

Draw a T-chart. When I say a word, hold up one hand if the word has one syllable or two hands if it has two syllables: *hen, pencil, problem, sweep, cheese, insect, be, traffic, teeth, mitten*. Write each word in the appropriate column. Then have children decode the words. Have them identify words with long *e*. *(sweep, cheese, be, teeth)*

One Syllable	Two Syllables
hen	pencil
sweep	problem
cheese	insect
be	traffic
teeth	mitten

On their own

Use Let's Practice It! pp. 123–124 on the *Teacher Resource DVD-ROM*.

Let's Practice It! TR DVD•123

Let's Practice It! TR DVD•124

English Language Learners
Pronounce /f/ If children have difficulty pronouncing /f/, demonstrate how to produce the sound by biting the bottom lip gently with the upper teeth as you say /f/. Have children practice saying each word with initial /f/ several times.

Objectives
- Apply knowledge of sound-spellings to decode unknown words when reading.
- Decode words in context and in isolation.
- Practice fluency with oral rereading.

Decodable Practice Reader 13C
Syllable Pattern CV; Vowel Sounds of y

Decode words in isolation

Have children turn to page 161. Have children decode each word.

Review High-frequency words

Review the previously taught words *they, day, I, to, of, you, a,* and *wants*. Have children read each word as you point to it on the Word Wall.

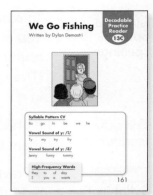

Decodable Practice Reader 13C

Preview

Have children read the title and preview the story. Tell them they will read words with the syllable pattern CV and words with vowel sounds of *y*.

Decode words in context

Pair children for reading and listen carefully as they decode. One child begins. Children read the entire story, switching readers after each page. Partners reread the story. This time the other child begins.

Jenny, Ty, and Bo will go fishing. They came to my home.

162

"Hi, Gwen," yelled Bo. "We will try to catch lots of fish."

163

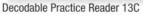
Decodable Practice Reader 13C

"Will you be fishing all day?" I asked.

164

Jenny asked, "Gwen, will you fish with us?"

165

We got poles, and Ty packed his bag.

166

Bo made a funny face as he fished. "I got a fish!"

167

Ty rubs his tummy. He wants a fish fry.

168

Corrective feedback

If... children have difficulty decoding a word, **then...** refer them to the Sound-Spelling Cards to identify the sounds in the word. Then prompt them to blend the word.

- What is the new word?
- Is the new word a word you know?
- Does it make sense in the story?

Check decoding and comprehension

Have children retell the story to include characters, setting, and events. Then have children find words that end in syllable pattern CV or include vowel sounds of *y* in the story. Children should supply *Bo, go, hi, be, we, he, Jenny, Ty, my, try, funny, tummy,* and *fry.*

Reread for Fluency

Have children reread Decodable Practice Reader 13C to develop automaticity decoding words with syllable pattern CV and vowel sounds of *y.*

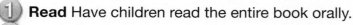

ROUTINE **Oral Rereading**

1. **Read** Have children read the entire book orally.
2. **Reread** To achieve optimal fluency, children should reread the text three or four times.
3. **Corrective Feedback** Listen as children read. Provide corrective feedback regarding their fluency and decoding.

Routines Flip Chart

English Language Learners
Decodable Reader

Beginning Before children read, lead them through *We Go Fishing.* Preview the story using the illustrations. Point out the words with vowel sounds of *y* and words with syllable pattern CV. Have children say the words aloud.

Intermediate After reading, have children find words with vowel sounds of *y* and syllable pattern CV and say them aloud. Then have children use each word in a sentence. For example: *I will go to the lake.*

Advanced/Advanced High After reading, have children find words with vowel sounds of *y* and syllable pattern CV and say them aloud. Then have them make up two sentences about the story character, Bo, using the following words: *Bo, go, he, try, my,* and *funny.*

Objectives
- Read words fluently in context and in isolation.
- Spell words with vowel sounds of *y*.
- Spell high-frequency words.

Fluent Word Reading
Spiral Review

Read words in isolation

Display these words. Tell children that they can blend some words on this list, and others are Word Wall words.

Have children read the list three or four times until they can read at the rate of two to three seconds per word.

peeping	met	good	Pete	these
kitten	there	Reed	paper	some
Ned	meet	family	be	down
other	new	me	also	picnic

Word Reading

Corrective feedback

If... children have difficulty reading whole words,
then... have them use sound-by-sound blending for decodable words, or have them say and spell high-frequency words.

If... children cannot read fluently at a rate of two to three seconds per word,
then... have pairs practice the list until they can read it fluently.

Read words in context

Display these sentences. Call on individuals to read a sentence. Then randomly point to review words and have children read them. To help you monitor word reading, high-frequency words are underlined and decodable words are italicized.

There are *these* other *chicks peeping* also.

My family *met* some new *people* at the *picnic*.

Pete will meet me down *by* the *paper bin*.

Ned and Reed will be good *and help* the *kitten*.

Sentence Reading

Corrective feedback

If... children are unable to read an underlined high-frequency word,
then... read the word for them and spell it, having them echo you.

If... children have difficulty reading an italicized decodable word,
then... guide them in using sound-by-sound blending.

Spelling
Vowel Sounds of *y*

Partner Review

Supply pairs of children with index cards on which the spelling words have been written. Have one child read a word while the other writes it. Then have children switch roles. Have them use the cards to check their spelling and correct any misspelled words.

On their own

Use *Reader's and Writer's Notebook* p. 327.

Reader's and Writer's Notebook, p. 327

Spiral Review

These activities review

- previously taught high-frequency words *also, down, family, good, new, other, paper, some, there.*

- long *e (e, ee, e_e)*; closed syllable CVC; short *e* spelled *e*.

Small Group Time

DAY 4

Break into small groups after spelling and before the comprehension lesson.

Teacher-Led

SI Strategic Intervention

Teacher-Led Page DI•4
- High-Frequency Words

Read *Decodable Practice Reader 13C*

OL On-Level

Teacher-Led Page DI•8
- Conventions

Reread *A Place to Play*

A Advanced

Teacher-Led Page DI•11
- Comprehension

Read "My Neighborhood, Then and Now"

Reread *Leveled Reader*

ELL Place English language learners in the groups that correspond to their reading abilities in English.

Practice Stations
- Words to Know
- Get Fluent

Independent Activities
- Read independently/Reading Log on *Reader's and Writer's Notebook* p. RR4
- AudioText of Paired Selection

ELL

English Language Learners

Fluent Word Reading Have children listen to a more fluent reader say the words. Then have them repeat the words.

Objectives

◎ Summarize important ideas.
- Recognize structure and elements of autobiography.
- Relate prior knowledge to new text.
- Set purpose for reading.

Social Studies in Reading

Preview and predict

Read the title and the first sentence of the selection. Have children look through the selection and predict what they might learn. (Possible response: We might learn about someone's neighborhood.) Ask them what clue helped them make that prediction. (Possible responses: the title of the selection or the photographs)

Let's Think About Genre

Autobiography Tell children that they will read an **autobiography.** Review the key features of an autobiography: it is a true story about a person's life written by that person. Explain that this selection is an autobiography because Emily is writing about her own life.

Activate prior knowledge

Ask children to recall what they have already learned about neighborhoods. (Sometimes people in a neighborhood work together to build something that everyone can use.)

Set a purpose

Let's Read Together As children read, have them pay attention to clues that would indicate that the selection is an autobiography.

Let's Think About... Autobiography

As you read "My Neighborhood, Then and Now" together, use Let's Think About in the Student Edition to focus on features of an autobiography.

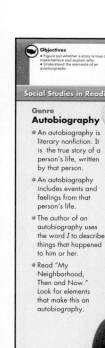

Objectives
● Figure out whether a story is true or make-believe and explain why.
● Understand the elements of an autobiography.

Social Studies in Reading

Genre
Autobiography

● An autobiography is literary nonfiction. It is the true story of a person's life, written by that person.

● An autobiography includes events and feelings from that person's life.

● The author of an autobiography uses the word *I* to describe things that happened to him or her.

● Read "My Neighborhood, Then and Now." Look for elements that make this an autobiography.

My Neighborhood, Then and Now

My name is Emily. I am ten.

This is my neighborhood.

It has changed since I was little.

When I was four, my family planted a tree.

The tree is taller now.

Let's **Think** About

How do you know this is an autobiography?
Autobiography

38   39

Student Edition pp. 38–39

Academic Vocabulary

autobiography the story of a real person's life written by that person

compare tell how things are the same

contrast tell how things are different

Social Studies Vocabulary

neighborhood area where you live

Guide Comprehension

Guide practice

⟳ Summarize

Think Aloud Good readers look for important ideas as they read so that they can summarize a story or selection. When I finished reading *A Place to Play*, I recalled that many neighbors worked together to make a place for all to enjoy. I will pay attention to the important ideas as I read "My Neighborhood, Then and Now."

Compare and contrast

Think Aloud I think about the title of this autobiography — "My Neighborhood, Then and Now." I wonder how the neighborhood is different now. I read that a tree planted by Emily's family has grown tall.

Let's **Think** About... Autobiography

Possible response: This is an autobiography because Emily is writing about her own life. This is a true story, not a fantasy. One clue is that she uses the word *I*. The photographs are also a clue that this is a true story.

Objectives

- Summarize an autobiography.
- Read aloud fluently with accuracy and at an appropriate rate.

Check Fluency WCPM

SUCCESS PREDICTOR

Student Edition pp. 40–41

Guide Comprehension, continued

Sequence What is the next change that Emily writes about? (The neighborhood has a big, new library.)

Summarize Summarize what you read in Emily's autobiography. Remember that to summarize, you think about the most important information that you read. (Although Emily has always liked her neighborhood, she likes the changes in it too.)

Reading Across Texts Have children find words and sentences in the texts of *A Place to Play* and "My Neighborhood, Then and Now" to show how Benny and Emily feel about their neighborhoods.

Writing Across Texts Children might list the new community center for Benny's neighborhood and the tall tree and the new library for Emily's neighborhood.

Fluency
Accuracy and Appropriate Rate

Guide practice

- Have children turn to pages 24–25 in *A Place to Play*.
- Have children follow along as you read the pages accurately and at an appropriate rate.
- Have the class read the pages with you and then reread the pages as a group without you until they read with no hesitation and no mistakes. To provide additional fluency practice, pair non-fluent readers with fluent readers.

ROUTINE **Paired Reading**

(1) **Select a Passage** For A Place to Play, use pp. 28–29.

(2) **Model** First, have children track the print as you read.

(3) **Guide Practice** Then have children read along with you.

(4) **On Their Own** For optimal fluency, have partners reread three or four times.

Routines Flip Chart

MONITOR PROGRESS **Check Fluency WCPM**

As children reread, monitor their progress toward their individual fluency goals. Current Goal: 20–30 words correct per minute. End-of-Year Goal: 60 words correct per minute.

If... children cannot read fluently at a rate of 20–30 words correct per minute,
then... have children practice with text at their independent level.

Day 1	Day 2	Day 3	Day 4	Day 5
Check Word Reading	Check Word Reading	Check High-Frequency Words/Retelling	Check Fluency	Check Oral Vocabulary

Success Predictor

Differentiated Instruction

 Advanced

WCPM If children already read at 60 words correct per minute, allow them to read independently.

Fluency Assessment Plan

Do a formal fluency assessment with 8 to 10 children every week. Assess 4 to 5 children on Day 4 and 4 to 5 children on Day 5. Use the reproducible fluency passage, Teacher's Edition, page 43f.

Options for Oral Rereading

Use *A Place to Play* or one of this week's Decodable Practice Readers.

Fluency WCPM

Success Predictor

Objectives
- Identify and use action verbs.
- Revise a draft by adding words to clarify meaning.
- Use time-order transition words.

Conventions
Action Verbs

Test practice

Use *Reader's and Writer's Notebook* p. 328 to help children understand how to identify verbs in test items. Recall that verbs tell what someone or something does: *run, say,* or *takes.* Model identifying a verb in a sentence by writing this sentence on the board, reading it aloud, and underlining the verb.

> **Mom likes the garden.**

Then read the *Reader's and Writer's Notebook* p. 328 directions. Guide children as they mark the answer for number 1.

Reader's and Writer's Notebook, p. 328

On their own

Use *Reader's and Writer's Notebook* p. 328.

Connect to oral language

After children mark the answers to numbers 1–6, review the correct choices aloud, and have children read each sentence, emphasizing the verb.

Writing—Realistic Story
Revising Strategy

MINI-LESSON

Revising Strategy: Adding Words

■ Yesterday we wrote realistic stories about children at a new place to play. Today we will revise. We can help people who read the stories. We can make the stories clearer or more interesting. We can use words that tell what happens first, next, and at the end.

■ Display the Revising Tips. Explain that this is a time for making the story clear for anyone who will read it. Tomorrow children will proofread to correct any errors such as misspellings, missing capital letters, or misplaced sentence periods.

Revising Tips

☐ Make sure your story tells who the characters are.
☐ Add words to make the sequence of events clear.

■ Use Writing Transparency 13B to **model adding time-order transition words.** In my realistic story "Fun at the Sandbox," Sally and Eddy walk to a sandbox. In the middle of the story, the children make a sand castle. I can add the word Then: "Then the children made a sand castle." **Add** *Then* to the sentence on the transparency.

Tell children that they can add words to their story as they revise.

Writing Transparency 13B
TR DVD

Peer conferencing

Peer Revision Pair up children and tell half to read the partner's story. Allow one to two minutes. Then have the readers use one or two minutes to tell what happens at the beginning, middle, and end. Repeat with second partners reading and telling about the other story. Have each writer listen for any part of the story that the reader has not understood. Circulate to assist children planning to revise their stories. As appropriate, suggest adding words including time-order transition words such as *first, next,* and *after that.*

Differentiated Instruction

SI Strategic Intervention

Test Formats A child may prepare to underline or mark verbs in sentences. Make sure children understand that, on *Reader's and Writer's Notebook* p. 328, they should mark the circle for each sentence in which the verb is already underlined rather than sentences in which other words are underlined.

Academic Vocabulary

time-order transition words words that show readers the order of events or steps: *first, next, then, later, now, tomorrow, last, finally* (and others)

Daily Fix-It

7. The puppie ran by the door
   The <u>puppy</u> ran by the door<u>.</u>

8. i am allways late.
   <u>I</u> am <u>always</u> late.

Discuss the Daily Fix-It corrections with children. Review the *y* spelling of long *e*, the end-of-sentence period, the capitalization of *I,* and the spelling of *always*.

English Language Learners
Capitalization of Names Be sure children understand that words such as mom and dad are capitalized when they are substituted for the person's name.

Objectives
- Revise a draft for story sequence or clarity.
- Review answers to inquiry questions.

Writing
Realistic Story, continued

Guide practice

Have children revise their stories. For those not sure how to revise, have children refer to the Revising Tips or the Key Features of Realistic Stories.

Corrective feedback

Circulate to monitor and conference with children as they write. Remind them that they will have time to proofread and edit tomorrow. Today they can make changes in story events or make sentences clearer. Help them understand the benefits of adding or changing words. Encourage them to make the beginning, middle, and end interesting.

ROUTINE   Quick Write for Fluency   Team Talk

1) **Talk** Read these sentences aloud, and have children tell which action should be first and which second.

   Then we sang that song.

   We learned a new song.

2) **Write** Have children write two short sentences about two things that happen one after another.

3) **Share** Partners can read the sentences to one another and orally add the word *first* to one sentence.

Routines Flip Chart

Research and Inquiry
Review and Revise Topic

Teach

Tell children that the next step in the inquiry project is to review our topic to see if we have the information we set out to find. Or, did our answers lead to a different topic?

Model

We wanted to find out more about how our neighborhoods have changed. Display the list of inquiry questions and the answers recorded during the interview. First I asked, "Are there any new stores in your neighborhood?" The answer is, "Yes, a new grocery store opened near our school." This answer gives me a good example of change in our neighborhoods. So, we have answered our original topic, and it does not need to change.

Guide practice

Read the remaining inquiry questions and answers. After each answer is read, have children turn to a partner to discuss whether or not the answer gives information about change in our neighborhoods. Note any new questions the children have and revise the original topic if necessary. Finally, tell children that tomorrow they will organize all the information in order to share it with others.

Wrap Up Your Day

✔ **Phonics Review** List words that end with vowel sounds of *y* and syllable pattern CV. Have children read each word and identify the vowel sound at the end of each word.

✔ **Fluency** Write *Happy people try to work together to make a place to play.* Have children read the sentence three or four times until they can do so fluently.

Preview DAY 5

Remind children that they heard about a family that built a house in the country. Tomorrow they will hear about the family again.

Objectives

- Review the concept: places growing and changing.
- Build oral vocabulary.
- Identify details in text.

Today at a Glance

Oral Vocabulary
Review

Phonics
- Review Vowel Sounds of *y*
- Review Syllable Pattern CV

Comprehension
- Sequence

Story Words
Review

High-Frequency Words
Review

Conventions
Action Verbs

Writing
Realistic Story

Research and Inquiry
Communicate

Check Oral Vocabulary
SUCCESS PREDICTOR

Concept Wrap Up

Question of the Week
How do places change?

Review Concept

This week we have read and listened to stories about how places grow and change. Today you will listen to find out what changes took place as the country house was built. **Read the story.**

- How did the country change when the family built their house? (Possible responses: Rocks were moved to make the foundation; trees were cut down to make planks of wood to frame the house.)

Review Amazing Words

Orally review the meanings of this week's Amazing Words. Then display this week's concept map. Have children use Amazing Words such as *growth, population,* and *public,* as well as the concept map, to answer the question "How do places change?"

"Out in the Country"

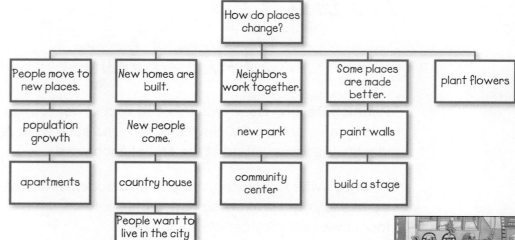

How do places change?

People move to new places.	New homes are built.	Neighbors work together.	Some places are made better.	plant flowers
population growth	New people come.	new park	paint walls	
apartments	country house	community center	build a stage	
	People want to live in the city or country.			

ELL **Check Concepts and Language** Use the Day 5 instruction on ELL Poster 13 to monitor children's understanding of the lesson concept.

Oral Vocabulary
Amazing Ideas

Connect to the Big Question

[Team Talk] Pair children and have them discuss how the Question of the Week connects to this unit's Big Question, "What is changing in our world?" Tell children to use the concept map and what they've learned from this week's Anchored Talks and reading selections to form an Amazing Idea—a realization or "big idea" about **change**. Then ask each pair to share their Amazing Idea with the class.

Amazing Ideas might include these key concepts:

• A town grows and changes when new people move there.

• People can work together to change a place and make it better.

It's Friday

MONITOR PROGRESS | Check Oral Vocabulary

Call on individuals to use this week's Amazing Words to talk about how places change. Prompt discussion with the questions below. Monitor children's ability to use the Amazing Words and note which words children are unable to use.

• **What changes happen when there is a *growth* in the *population*?**

• **Would people who *shuffle* or *teeter* want an elevator in a new building?**

• **What can community workers do to *spindly* weeds in a *public* park?**

• **How could you use a *crooked* branch as a *makeshift* flagpole?**

If... children have difficulty using the Amazing Words,

then... reteach the unknown words using the Oral Vocabulary Routines, pp. 13a, 18b, 34b, 38b.

Day 1	Day 2	Day 3	Day 4	**Day 5**
Check Word Reading	Check Word Reading	Check High-Frequency Words/Retelling	Check Fluency	**Check Oral Vocabulary**

Success Predictor

Amazing Words

growth	teeter
population	crooked
public	makeshift
shuffle	spindly

E L L

English Language Learners

Amazing Words Use pantomime or gesture to give children clues as you review the Amazing Words.

Oral Vocabulary

Success Predictor

Objectives
- Add initial sound to create a new word.
- ◎ Review words with vowel sounds of *y*.
- ◎ Review words with syllable pattern CV.

Assess
- Spell words with vowel sounds of *y*.
- Spell high-frequency words.

Phonemic Awareness
Add Initial Phonemes

Review
Initial consonants and digraphs

Have children add a beginning sound to each word below to make a new word. If children make an error, model the correct response. Return to the word later in the practice.

/l/and **land**	/b/end **bend**	/r/ice **rice**
/g/ate **gate**	/ch/ill **chill**	/k/lock **clock**
/b/old **bold**	/p/age **page**	/s/tack **stack**

Phonics
↻ Vowel Sounds of *y*; Syllable Pattern CV

Review
Target phonics skills

Write the following sentences on the board. Have children read each one, first quietly to themselves and then aloud as you track the print.

1. Danny gave me fifty cents.
2. Why did Di try to go?
3. This jelly is so messy!
4. No, my fussy kitty will not eat cat food.

Team Talk Have children discuss with a partner which words have vowel sounds of *y* and which words have syllable pattern CV. Then call on individuals to share with the class.

Spelling Test
Vowel Sounds of y

Dictate spelling words

Say each word, read the sentence, repeat the word, and allow time for children to write the word.

1. **puppy**	My **puppy** can do funny tricks.
2. **lucky**	Jo keeps a **lucky** stone in her desk.
3. **handy**	A notebook is **handy** for writing notes.
4. **my**	**My** jacket is nice and warm.
5. **sunny**	The weather was hot and **sunny**.
6. **try**	**Try** to work together.
7. **cry**	What makes you **cry**?
8. **by**	Andy likes to run **by** the lake.
9. **fly**	See the kites **fly** up in the sky.
10. **silly**	Dad tells **silly** jokes.

High-Frequency Words

11. **things**	Put these **things** on the top shelf.
12. **always**	Beth **always** reads before going to bed.

Differentiated Instruction

SI Strategic Intervention
Check Spelling Have children choose the correct spelling of each word from three random spellings.

A Advanced
Extend Spelling Have children who have demonstrated proficiency in spelling individual words spell each word in a self-made sentence.

Small Group Time

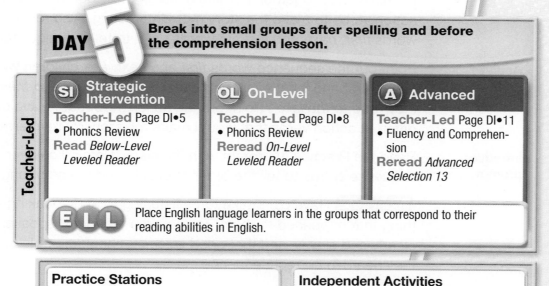

DAY 5

Break into small groups after spelling and before the comprehension lesson.

SI Strategic Intervention
Teacher-Led Page DI•5
• Phonics Review
Read *Below-Level Leveled Reader*

OL On-Level
Teacher-Led Page DI•8
• Phonics Review
Reread *On-Level Leveled Reader*

A Advanced
Teacher-Led Page DI•11
• Fluency and Comprehension
Reread *Advanced Selection 13*

ELL Place English language learners in the groups that correspond to their reading abilities in English.

Practice Stations
• Read for Meaning
• Words to Know

Independent Activities
• Read independently/Reading Log on *Reader's and Writer's Notebook* p. RR4
• Concept Talk Video

Objectives
- Relate an experience in sequence.
- Speak clearly at an appropriate rate.
- Listen attentively.
- Identify antonyms.
- Read aloud fluently with accuracy and at an appropriate rate.

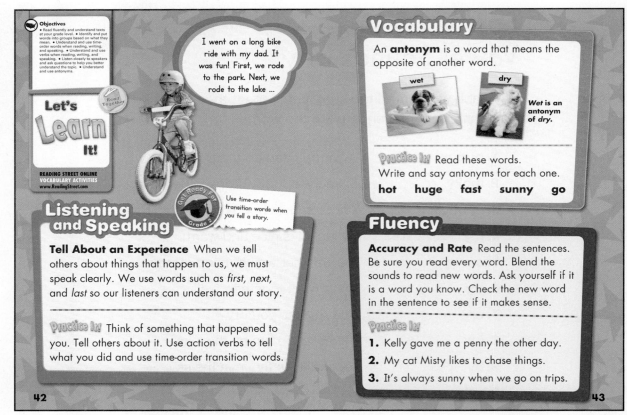

Student Edition pp. 42–43

Listening and Speaking
Tell About an Experience

Teach
Have children turn to page 42 of the Student Edition. Read and discuss the girl's story together. Remind children that good speakers use strong action verbs to make the story more interesting. Also remind them that the words *first*, *next*, and *last* are words used to tell the sequence.

Analyze model
Point out the sequence words *first* and *next*. Ask children what event happened first and what event was next. (*First, they rode to the park. Next, they rode to the lake.*) Point out the action verb *rode*. Have children name different action verbs that would make the story more interesting.

Introduce prompt
Read the Practice It! prompt with the class. Remind children to use sequence words to tell the order of events and to use strong action verbs.

Team Talk Have pairs take turns listening to and speaking about something that happened to them. Tell children that good speakers speak clearly and slowly, and that good listeners should be able to retell the story they heard in correct sequence.

Vocabulary
Antonyms

Teach

Read and discuss the Vocabulary lesson on page 43 of the Student Edition. Use the model to explain how antonyms are words that are opposites of each other.

Model

Point to the photos. What is different about the dog in the two photos? (In the first photo, the dog is wet. In the second photo, the dog is dry.) *Wet* is the opposite of *dry*. So, *wet* is an antonym of *dry*.

Guide practice

Read the instructions for the Vocabulary Practice It! activity. Read the first word and then have children repeat after you.

I need to find an antonym for the word *hot*. The opposite of *hot* is *cold*. So, I will say and write the word *cold*.

On their own

Have children continue saying and writing antonyms for the remaining words in the list.

Corrective feedback

Circulate around the room and listen as children say the antonyms. Provide assistance as needed.

Fluency
Accuracy and Rate

Teach

Read and discuss the Fluency instructions.

Read words in context

Give children a moment to look at the sentences. Then have them read each sentence three or four times until they can read each sentence with accuracy and at an appropriate rate.

Differentiated Instruction

 Strategic Intervention
Visual Skills Some children might find it helpful to see additional visual representations of the vocabulary skill, antonyms.

Tell About an Experience

In addition to using time-order transition words when telling about an experience, children at Grade 2 should also be able to be expressive, use complete sentences, avoid pauses and repetitive words, and use an appropriate voice level.

English Language Learners
Use Sentence Frames Provide this sentence frame to help children structure their understanding of antonyms: The opposite of _____ is _____.

Objectives
- ◎ Identify sequence in a story.
- • Review high-frequency and story words.
- • Identify and describe characters.

Comprehension

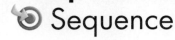 Sequence

Review
Sequence

Remember that events in a story happen in a certain order: first, next, and last. What is this order of events called? (sequence)

To check understanding of sequence, read aloud the following story and have children answer the questions that follow.

> Jake had a great day at his new school! First, he was asked to become the teacher's helper. Then, he spelled everything correctly on his spelling test. After lunch, things got better when he became friends with Sally. Finally, after school his mom took him for ice cream! Nothing could go wrong.

1. What is the first thing that happened to Jake? (First, he became the teacher's helper.)

2. What is something that happened in the middle? (Next, he spelled everything correctly. He became friends with Sally.)

3. What was the last thing that happened to Jake? (Last, Jake's mom took him for ice cream.)

Vocabulary
High-Frequency and Story Words

Review
High-frequency words

Review this week's high-frequency words: *always, day, become, everything, stays, things,* and *nothing.* Provide an example of a riddle for one of the words for the class to solve, such as: I am the opposite of never. I have six letters. (always)

Team Talk Have children orally give riddles for the remaining six words to a partner to solve.

Review
Story words

Write the words *grew, art, boy, tower, now,* and *sunset.* Read them aloud together. Then have children tell what each word means.

Corrective feedback

If... children cannot tell what the story words mean,
then... review the definitions on page 20a.

Literary Text
Character

Review Genre

Review with children that realistic fiction is not a real story, but it seems real. Realistic fiction stories happen in places that seem real. The characters in realistic fiction act and talk like real people.

Teach

Benny is a main character, or one of the most important characters, in *A Place to Play*. In the story, Benny asks another boy if he likes to play ball. This lets me know that Benny is friendly and curious. Let's see what else we can discover about Benny by how he acts and what he says.

Model

Think Aloud I know the story says that Benny thinks it will be a fun day, and I know real children want their days to be fun too. Benny spies his mom and dad and asks them questions about what they are doing. I know that real children ask their parents a lot of questions! Benny acts and talks like a real child!

Guide practice

Ask the following questions to guide children in describing a character in realistic fiction and determining reasons for the character's actions.

- Why would Benny think the day will be fun? (Possible response: He will learn and see new things.)

- In the story Benny says a spot is muddy. How do you think he knows what mud is? (Possible response: Benny has probably been outside after it has rained and has seen mud before.)

On their own

Benny says he hopes the picture of the neighborhood at the community center "stays there always." Why do you think he feels that way? (Accept any answers that children offer if they can give reasons for their answers.)

Differentiated Instruction

SI Strategic Intervention

Thinking Like a Character If children have difficulty answering questions about a character, ask the questions putting them in the character's position. For example: Why would you want to have fun? How do you know what mud is?

Academic Vocabulary

main character one of the most important characters in a story

Assess
- ◉ Words with Vowel Sounds of *y*
- ◉ Words with Syllable Pattern CV
- • High-Frequency Words
- • Fluency: WCPM
- ◉ Sequence

Fluency Goals
Set individual fluency goals for children to enable them to reach the end-of-year goal.
- • Current Goal: 20-30 WCPM
- • End-of-Year Goal: 60 WCPM

Assessment
Monitor Progress

For a written assessment of vowel sounds of *y*, syllable pattern CV, high-frequency words, and sequence, use Weekly Test 13, pages 109–114.

Assess words in context

Sentence reading Use the following reproducible page to assess children's ability to read words in context. Call on children to read two sentences aloud. Start over with sentence one if necessary.

> **MONITOR PROGRESS** **Sentence Reading**
>
> **If...** children have trouble reading vowel sounds of *y* or syllable pattern CV,
>
> **then...** use the Reteach Lessons on p. 209–210 of *First Stop*.
>
> **If...** children cannot read all the high-frequency words,
>
> **then...** mark the missed words on a high-frequency word list and have the child practice reading the words with a fluent reader.

Assess

Fluency Take a one-minute sample of children's oral reading. Have children read the fluency passage on page 43f.

Comprehension Have the child read the entire passage. If the child has difficulty with the passage, you may read it aloud. Then have the child retell the passage by stating the events in sequence.

> **MONITOR PROGRESS** **Fluency and Comprehension**
>
> **If...** a child does not achieve the fluency goal on the timed reading,
>
> **then...** copy the passage and send it home with the child for additional fluency practice, or have the child practice with a fluent reader.
>
> **If...** a child cannot retell the events in sequence,
>
> **then...** use the Reteach Lesson on p. 252 of *First Stop*.

Monitor accuracy

Record scores Have children monitor their accuracy by recording their scores using the Sentence Reading Chart and by recording the number of words read correctly per minute on their Fluency Progress Chart in *First Stop*.

Name _____

Read the Sentences

1. She tells jokes that are always so funny.

2. Nothing is muddy this week.

3. We will try to stack things on that shelf.

4. A puppy will be fine if it stays sweet.

5. Lee becomes happy at lunch time.

6. I made everything in my shop.

7. A bunny will hop on that day.

MONITOR PROGRESS
- Fluency
- Vowel sounds of *y*
- Words with syllable pattern CV
- High-frequency words

Name _____

Read the Story

A Happy Trip

    Do you like to take trips? Jo likes to go on   11
trips. She gets her things together. Then she   19
packs her three bags. When she has left, she   28
likes to stop and look at the big green hills.   38
When Jo has looked at all the hills she drives   48
to her last stop. She wants to get gifts for her   59
pals. She has a lot of fun! She stays for five   70
days. Then, it is time to go home. She drives   80
past a lot of bikes, buses, and trucks. She   89
sees sheep on the grass. The last thing she   98
does is go inside her home so she can take   108
a nap!   110

MONITOR PROGRESS
- Check Fluency
- Sequence

Objectives
- Identify verbs.
- Understand and use verbs in writing.

Conventions
Action Verbs

Review

Remind children that verbs are action words. Have them give several examples of verbs.

Guide to practice

Write the following sentences. Have children write a verb that makes sense in each blank.

> 1. I _____ with the ball.
>
> 2. My dog _____ with me.
>
> 3. My mom _____ me home.

Connect to oral language

Display and read the following sentence frame. Have children work in pairs to name as many action verbs as they can that could be used to complete the sentence. Then have children share their responses with the class.

> **My friend and I _____.**

On their own

Use Let's Practice It! p. 127 on the *Teacher Resource DVD-ROM.*

Let's Practice It!
TR DVD•127

Daily Fix-It

9. mom loks at the trees.
<u>Mom looks</u> at the trees.

10. The bear driinks from the lak.
The bear <u>drinks</u> from the <u>lake</u>.

Discuss the Daily Fix-It corrections with children. Review sentence capitalization and punctuation and the correct spellings of *looks, drinks,* and *lake.*

Objectives
- Edit a draft for spelling, punctuation, and capitalization.
- Create final draft and present.

Writing—Realistic Story
Writer's Craft: Verbs

Review Revising Remind children that yesterday they revised their stories. They may have added words to make the events clearer. Today they will proofread their stories.

MINI-LESSON

Proofread for Verbs and Transition Words

■ **Teach** In our stories, if we spell the words correctly, readers will know what words we mean. When we proofread, we check to make sure the words are correct. We can check to make sure the verbs are correct. We also can look at the words such as *first*, *then*, and *last* to make sure they are spelled correctly. I can use our word lists or a dictionary to check them.

■ **Model** Let us look at my story about the boy and girl who play in the sandbox. Display Writing Transparency 13C. Explain that you will look at the verbs and at time-order transition words such as *then*. Show how you would change any misspellings (such as *castel* for *castle*). Quickly show how to check a word's spelling in a classroom dictionary or word list. Model how you would change a letter at the beginning of a sentence if it were not capitalized or add a period if one were missing at the end of a sentence or if it were in the wrong place.

Writing Transparency 13C
TR DVD

Proofread Display the Proofreading Tips. Have children proofread their stories to correct any misspellings, missing capital letters, or errors with periods. Circulate to assist children with verbs, transition words, or other words.

Proofreading Tips

✔ Are my verbs spelled correctly? Check a dictionary.

✔ Are words such as *first, then,* and *last* spelled correctly?

✔ Do my sentences begin with a capital letter?

✔ Did I use periods correctly?

Present Have children make a final draft of their stories, with their revisions and proofreading corrections. Help as appropriate.

Choose an option for children to present their stories.

They might take turns reading them aloud to partners.	They might draw a picture of one character or event, to accompany the story in a wall display.

When they have finished, help them complete a Self-Evaluation form.

ROUTINE **Quick Write for Fluency** **Team Talk**

1. **Talk** Have partners take one minute to find a strong action verb (such as *run*, *jump*, *catch*, or *stop*) in each of their stories.
2. **Write** Each child writes a new short sentence using one of the verbs.
3. **Share** Partners trade sentences and read them aloud.

Routines Flip Chart

Teacher Note

Self-Evaluation Make copies of the Self-Evaluation form from the Teacher Resource DVD-ROM, and hand them out to children.

English Language Learners
Support Editing For children to whom the sounds and spelling of English still are not very familiar, look for spelling improvement little by little from week to week rather than rapid development. Help children make progress a word at a time and learn word meanings.

Research and Inquiry
Communicate

Teach

Tell children that today they will organize the information from the interview, create a poster that displays the information, and share the information with others.

Model

Think Aloud Display the list of inquiry questions and the answers recorded during the interview. I will review the interview answers and circle the changes that I would like to tell others about. For instance, I was interested in the question "Are there any new stores in your neighborhood?" The answer is "Yes, a new grocery store opened near our school." I'll circle the words *new grocery store*. On my poster, I will make sure to show that a *new grocery store* is one of the changes to our neighborhoods.

Guide practice

Review the answers from the interview with children, and have them prompt you to circle the changes to their neighborhoods.

On their own

Have children choose the changes they would like to share and create a poster that illustrates these changes. Have children share their posters in small groups. Remind them how to be good speakers and listeners:

• Good speakers talk at a pace that everyone can understand. So, be careful not to talk too fast or too slow.

• Good listeners wait until the speaker has finished speaking before raising their hands to ask a question.

Topic: Neighborhoods Change

Questions	Answers	Evidence to Change Topic
Are there any new stores in your neighborhood?	Yes, a new grocery store opened near our school.	No change. The answer gives us information about the topic.

Wrap Up Your Week!

 Question of the Week

How do places change?

Think Aloud This week we explored how places grow and change. In the story *A Place to Play*, we read about how neighbors worked together to make a new community center. In the story "My Neighborhood, Then and Now," we read about how Emily's neighborhood changed over time. **Have children recall their Amazing Ideas about growth and change. Then have children use these ideas to help them demonstrate their understanding of the Question of the Week.**

English Language Learners

Poster Preview Prepare children for next week by using Week 20, ELL Poster 14. Read the Poster Talk-Through to introduce the concept and vocabulary. Ask children to identify and describe objects and actions in the art.

Selection Summary
Send home the summary of *Ruby in Her Own Time* in English and the child's home language if available. Children can read the summary with family members.

Preview NEXT WEEK

Tell children that next week they will read about things people and animals learn as they grow and change.

DAY 5 Assessment Checkpoints for the Week

Weekly Assessment

Use pp. 109–114 of *Weekly Tests* to check:

✔ 🎯 **Phonics** Vowel Sounds of *y*

✔ 🎯 **Phonics** Syllable Pattern *CV*

✔ 🎯 **Comprehension Skill** Sequence

✔ **High-Frequency Words**

always	nothing
become	stays
day	things
everything	

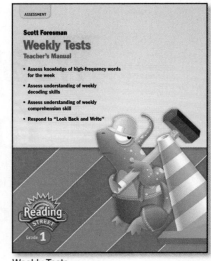

Weekly Tests

Advanced

On-Level

Strategic Intervention

Differentiated Assessment

Use pp. 109–114 of *Fresh Reads for Fluency and Comprehension* to check:

✔ 🎯 **Comprehension Skill** Sequence

✔ Review **Comprehension Skill** Author's Purpose

✔ **Fluency** Words Correct Per Minute

Fresh Reads for Fluency and Comprehension

Managing Assessment

Use *Assessment Handbook* for:

✔ **Weekly Assessment Blackline Masters for Monitoring Progress**

✔ **Observation Checklists**

✔ **Record-Keeping Forms**

✔ **Portfolio Assessments**

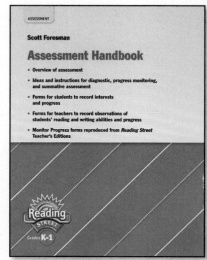

Assessment Handbook

Carlos Gets a Puppy

On Carlos's seventh birthday, he asked for a puppy. "Maybe we should get an adult dog," suggested his mother. "An adult dog is already trained so it won't be so messy and won't be such a big responsibility." But Carlos wanted a puppy.

A week later, when Carlos got home from school, he found his mother in the kitchen holding a tiny little animal. "What's that?" he asked.

"It's a puppy," said his mother. Carlos looked carefully at the tiny animal, which looked more like a mouse or a squirrel.

"It's only three weeks old," said his mother. "The animal shelter was full, so I said I'd help take care of it. I was hoping you'd help me." Carlos helped his mother feed the tiny puppy.

When they were done feeding the puppy, Carlos asked, "Can I play with it now?"

"No," said his mother. "A puppy this little needs to eat and sleep."

Carlos was disappointed. He had wanted a puppy to play with, but it was too small to play.

In time, and with lots of rest, the puppy grew bigger and stronger. Carlos and his mother took the puppy to the vet, who said that the little dog was healthy. "What's its name?" he asked.

"We call him Tiny," said Carlos, "but if he keeps growing, he may need a new name!"

Advanced Selection 13   Vocabulary: adult, healthy

Small Group Time

5 Day Plan

DAY 1	• Phonemic Awareness/ Phonics • Decodable Reader
DAY 2	• Phonemic Awareness/ Phonics • Decodable Reader
DAY 3	• Phonemic Awareness/ Phonics • Leveled Reader
DAY 4	• High-Frequency Words • Decodable Reader
DAY 5	• Phonics Review • Leveled Reader

3 or 4 Day Plan

DAY 1	• Phonemic Awareness/ Phonics • Decodable Reader
DAY 2	• Phonemic Awareness/ Phonics • Decodable Reader
DAY 3	• Phonemic Awareness/ Phonics • Leveled Reader
DAY 4	• High-Frequency Words • Decodable Reader

3 Day Plan: Eliminate the shaded box.

SI *Strategic Intervention*

DAY 1

Phonemic Awareness•Phonics

■ **Segment and Blend Phonemes** Reteach pp. 14–15 of the Teacher's Edition. Model segmenting and blending these words. Then have children practice segmenting and blending on their own.

sly /s/ /l/ /ī/   **funny** /f/ /u/ /n/ /ē/   **pry** /p/ /r/ /ī/

■ ◉ **Vowel Sounds of y** Reteach p. 15a of the Teacher's Edition. Then have children spell *my* using letter tiles. Monitor their work.

• Change the *m* in *my* to *fr*. What is the new word?

• Change the *r* in *fry* to *l*. What is the new word?

• Change the *fl* in *fly* to *wh*. What is the new word?

Decodable Practice Reader 13A

■ **Review** Review words with the vowel sounds of *y* and the high-frequency words *wants, to, a, the, what, you,* and *are.* Then have children blend and read these words from the story: *silly, Billy, trying, bump, Dotty, buzzing.*

> **If...** children have difficulty with any of these words, **then...** reteach the word by modeling. Have children practice the words, with feedback from you, until they can read them independently.

Have children reread the text orally. To achieve optimal fluency, children should reread the text three or four times.

Decodable Practice Reader 13A

Objectives
• Blend spoken phonemes to form one- and two-syllable words, including consonant blends.
• Combine sounds from letters to create recognizable words.

 SI *Strategic Intervention* **DAY 2**

Phonemic Awareness•Phonics

■ **Segment and Blend Phonemes** Reteach p. 18c of the Teacher's Edition. Model segmenting and blending these words. Then have children practice segmenting and blending on their own.

flow /f/ /l/ /ō/   **be** /b/ /ē/   **solo** /s/ /ō/ /l/ /ō/

■ **Syllable Pattern CV** Reteach p. 18d of the Teacher's Edition. Then have children spell *be* using letter tiles. Monitor their work.

• Change the *b* in *be* to *sh*. What is the new word?

• Drop the *s* in *she*. What is the new word?

• Add *llo* to the word *he*. What is the new word?

Decodable Practice Reader 13B

■ **Review** Review words with syllable pattern CV and the high-frequency words *said, want, come, to, the,* and *a.* Then have children blend and read these words from the story: *picnic, race, safe, pass.*

> **If…** children have difficulty with any of these words.
> **then…** reteach the word by modeling. Have children practice the words, with feedback from you, until they can read them independently.

Have children reread the text orally. To achieve optimal fluency, children should reread the text three or four times.

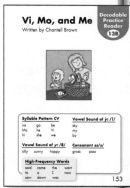

Decodable Practice Reader 13B

More Reading

Use Leveled Readers or other text at children's instructional level to develop fluency.

SI *Strategic Intervention*

Phonemic Awareness•Phonics

- **Rhyming Words** Model rhyming words. Say each sound in the word *cat*: /k/ /a/ /t/. Have children say the sounds with you and then say the sounds by themselves. Now listen as I say another word with the same ending sounds as *cat*. Model the sounds of the word *pat*. Have children say the sounds with you and then say the sounds by themselves. Point out that *cat* and *pat* are rhyming words.

- ◉ **Vowel Sounds of *y* and Syllable Pattern CV** Reteach p. 34e of the Teacher's Edition. Have children blend and read these additional words to help them practice the target phonics skills.

we	bunny	try	no	she	smelly

For a complete literacy instructional plan and additional practice with this week's target skills and strategies, see the **Leveled Reader Teaching Guide.**

Concept Literacy Leveled Reader

- **Preview and Predict** Read the title and the author's name. Have children look at the cover and ask them to describe what they see. Help children activate their prior knowledge by asking them to look through the story and to use the photos to predict things that might take place.

- **Set a Purpose** Remind children that setting a purpose for reading can help them better understand what they read. Guide children to pay attention to how things in a garden change over time.

- **Read** Provide corrective feedback as children read the story orally. During reading, ask them if they were able to confirm any of the predictions they made prior to the story.

If... children have difficulty reading the story individually,

then... read a sentence aloud as children point to each word. Then have the group reread the sentences as they continue pointing. Continue reading in this way until children read individually.

- **Retell** Have children take turns retelling the story. Help them identify how the garden changed over time by asking, What was the garden like at the beginning of the story? As time passed, how did the garden change?

Concept Literacy

Objectives
- Orally generate a series of original rhyming words using a variety of phonograms.
- Decode words in context and isolation by applying common letter-sound correspondences, including: single letters (vowels).

  DAY 4

More Reading
Use Leveled Readers or other text at children's instructional level.

High-Frequency Words

■ **Review** Write *things, always, day, become, nothing, stays, everything* on the board. Model saying each word. Then have children read each word, spell each word as you point to each letter, and have them say each word again. Allow time for children to practice reading these high-frequency words using the word cards.

Decodable Practice Reader 13C

■ **Review** Use the word lists to review the vowel sounds of *y* and the syllable pattern CV. Be sure that children understand that words with the vowel sounds of *y* make the long *i* and long *e* sounds, and the words with syllable pattern CV end with long vowel sounds. Then have children blend and read the two different groups of words.

Decodable Practice Reader 13C

If... children have difficulty reading the story individually, **then...** read a sentence aloud as children point to each word. Then have the group reread the sentences as they continue pointing. Continue reading in this way until children read individually.

Check comprehension by having children retell the story including the characters, plot, and setting. Have children locate words in the story that have the vowel sounds of *y* and the syllable pattern CV. List the words children identify. Then have children sort the words in a chart with columns labeled *Long i, Long e,* and *Long o*.

Long i	Long e	Long o
Ty	Jenny	Bo
my	funny	go
try	tummy	
fry	he	
hi	we	
	be	

Small Group Time

More Reading

Use Leveled Readers or other text at children's instructional level.

SI *Strategic Intervention*

DAY 5

Phonics Review

■ **Vowel Sounds of *y* and Syllable Pattern CV** Write these sentences on the board. Have children read them aloud as you track the print. Then call on individuals to blend and read the underlined words.

<u>Patty</u> will <u>try</u> to <u>fly</u> a kite.

Can <u>he</u> pet my <u>fluffy</u> <u>bunny</u>?

<u>Go</u> to a <u>sunny</u> place and <u>dry</u> it.

<u>No</u>, I am not <u>sleepy</u> yet.

For a complete literacy instructional plan and additional practice with this week's target skills and strategies, see the **Leveled Reader Teaching Guide.**

Below-Level Leveled Reader

Preview and Predict Read the title, the author's name, and the illustrator's name. Have children look at the cover and ask them to describe what they see. Help children activate their prior knowledge by asking them to look through the story and to use the illustrations to predict things that might take place.

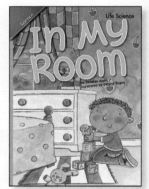

Below-Level Reader

■ **Set a Purpose** Remind children that setting a purpose for reading can help them better understand what they read. Guide children to pay attention to the order of events, or sequence, in which the story takes place.

■ **Read** Provide corrective feedback as children read the story orally. During reading, ask them if they were able to confirm any of the predictions they made prior to the story.

> **If...** children have difficulty reading the story individually,
> **then...** read each sentence aloud as children point to each word. Then have the group reread the sentences as they continue pointing.

■ ◉ **Summarize** Have children identify what they think is the most important part of the story. Then prompt them to explain why it is important.

Objectives
- Decode words in context and in isolation by applying common letter-sound correspondences, including: single letters (vowels).
- Retell a story's beginning, middle, and end with attention to the sequence of events.

Go Digital! eReaders

Differentiated Instruction

OL On-Level — DAY 1

Phonics•Spelling

- ◉ **Vowel Sounds of y** Write the following words on the board and have children practice reading words with vowel sounds of y.

  penny   pry   lucky   spy

  Then have children identify whether the word ends with the long e or the long i sound of y.

- **Long e and Long i Spelled y** Remind children that each spelling word ends in y, which spells the long e or long i sound. Clarify the pronunciation and meaning of each word. For example, say: A *puppy* is a young dog. Have children identify the same letters and sounds in rhyming words such as *by, try, fly, cry,* and *my.*

Objectives
- Decode words in context and isolation by applying common letter-sound correspondences, including: single letters (vowels).

OL On-Level — DAY 2

Phonics•High-Frequency Words

- ◉ **Syllable Pattern CV** Write the following words on the board and have children practice reading words with the syllable pattern CV. Then have children identify whether the word ends with the long e, long i, or long o sound.

  she   hello   hi   be

- **High-Frequency Words** Hold up this week's High-Frequency Word Cards *(things, always, day, become, nothing, stays, everything)* and review proper pronunciation. Continue holding the cards and have children chorally read each word. To help children demonstrate their understanding of the words, provide them with oral sentence frames such as: The sun shines during the _____. (day)

High-Frequency Word Cards for Grade 1

Objectives
- Use common syllabication patterns to decode words, including: open syllable.
- Read at least 100 high-frequency words from a commonly used list.

Pacing Small Group Instruction

20–30 min.

5 Day Plan

DAY 1	• Phonics • Spelling • Decodable Reader
DAY 2	• Phonics • High-Frequency Words • Decodable Reader
DAY 3	• Leveled Reader
DAY 4	• Conventions • Main Selection
DAY 5	• Phonics Review • Leveled Reader

3 or 4 Day Plan

DAY 1	• Phonics • Spelling • Decodable Reader
DAY 2	• Phonics • High-Frequency Words • Decodable Reader
DAY 3	• Leveled Reader
DAY 4	• Conventions • Main Selection

3 Day Plan: Eliminate the shaded box.

Decodable Practice Readers Units 2-3
- Practice phonics skills
- Blending practice
- Reread for fluency

Decodable Practice Readers

A Place to Play **DI•6**

Small Group Time

DAY **3**

For a complete literacy instructional plan and additional practice with this week's target skills and strategies, see the **Leveled Reader Teaching Guide.**

On-Level Leveled Reader

On-Level

■ **Preview and Predict** Read the title, the author's name, and the illustrator's name. Have children look at the cover and ask them to describe in detail what they see. Help children preview the story by asking them to look through the story and to use the pictures to predict things that might take place.

■ ◉ **Sequence** Before reading, remind children that setting a purpose for reading can help them better understand what they read. Guide children to pay attention to the sequence, or order, of events in the story.

■ **Read** During reading, monitor children's comprehension by providing higher-order thinking questions. Ask:

• What do you think life was like for the children before the park was built?

• How will seeds end up making the park prettier?

To help children gain a better understanding of the text, build upon their responses with a group discussion.

■ ◉ **Summarize** With a partner, have children take turns summarizing the story by identifying the most important ideas. Ask:

• Why do you think it was important for the people to help build the park?

• How did the place where the park was built change?

■ **Text to Self** Help children make personal connections to the story. Ask:

• Have you or someone you know helped change something in your neighborhood? What did you change?

Objectives
• Describe characters in a story and the reasons for their actions.
• Make inferences about text.

On-Level DAY **4**

Conventions

■ **Action Verbs** Remind children that words that tell what someone or something does are called verbs.

• *Run* is an action verb because it tells what a person or animal can do.

Pantomime the word *run*, write the word *run*, and use it in an oral sentence. The girls *run* to school each day.

• *Shine* is an action verb because it tells what a person, animal, or thing can do. Write the word *shine* and use it in an oral sentence. The stars *shine* bright at night.

Continue modeling in the same way with other action verbs such as *work* and *play*. Ask children to create a list of other action verbs. Reread the list as a group and have children pantomime the action verbs. Then have them use the action verbs in oral sentences.

Objectives

• Identify words that name actions (verbs).

More Reading

Use Leveled Readers or other text at children's instructional level to develop fluency.

On-Level DAY **5**

Phonics Review

■ **Vowel Sounds of *y* and Syllable Pattern CV** Have children practice blending and reading words that contain this week's target phonics skills. Write the following words on the board, and say and sound out each word with the children.

happy	reply	she	cargo	fuzzy
we	yummy	why	so	sunny

Then have children sort the words that end with the same long vowel sound into different groups.

Objectives

• Decode words in context and in isolation by applying common letter-sound correspondences, including: single letters (vowels).

Small Group Time

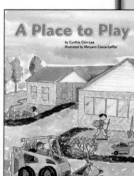

Pacing Small Group Instruction

20–30 mins.

5 Day Plan

DAY 1	• Phonics • Advanced Selection
DAY 2	• Phonics • Comprehension • Main Selection
DAY 3	• Leveled Reader
DAY 4	• Comprehension • Paired Selection
DAY 5	• Fluency • Comprehension • Advanced Selection

A Advanced

Phonics•Advanced Selection

■ 🔊 **Vowel Sounds of y** Have children practice with longer words containing *y* with the long *i* and long *e* sounds.

heavy	reply	beauty	bumpy	cycle
lullaby	magnify	secretary	usually	family

Have children write the words on cards and sort them by the sounds of *y*. Then have them use the words in sentences.

Advanced Selection 13

■ **Advanced Selection 13** Before reading, have children identify these story words: *adult* and *healthy*. Provide oral sentences with the words in context to help children determine their meaning. After reading, have children recall the two most important ideas of the story.

Objectives
• Decode words in context and in isolation by applying common letter-sound correspondences, including: single letters (vowels).

---

3 or 4 Day Plan

DAY 1	• Phonics • Advanced Selection
DAY 2	• Phonics • Comprehension • Main Selection
DAY 3	• Leveled Reader
DAY 4	• Comprehension • Paired Selection

3 Day Plan: Eliminate the shaded box.

A Advanced

Phonics•Comprehension

■ 🔊 **Syllable Pattern CV** Have children practice with longer words containing the syllable pattern CV.

potato	human	maybe	agent	zebra
secret	giant	bicycle	spider	program

Have children write the words and divide the syllables. Show children how breaking a word into syllables can help them read it.

A Place to Play

■ **Comprehension** Have children silently read this week's main selection, *A Place to Play.* Have them retell the story, identifying characters, setting, and the sequence of events. Discuss what makes *A Place to Play* realistic fiction. Point out that although the characters are not real, they act and speak like real people.

Objectives
• Use common syllabication patterns to decode words, including: open syllable.

 Advanced

DAY 3

For a complete literacy instructional plan and additional practice with this week's target skills and strategies, see the **Leveled Reader Teaching Guide.**

Advanced Leveled Reader

Advanced Reader

- **Activate Prior Knowledge** Read the title, the author's name, and the illustrator's name. Have children look at the cover and describe in detail what they see. Remind them that something that is *public* is for all people. Then activate children's prior knowledge by asking them to identify *public* places in their community and to describe how these places are used.

- **Sequence** Before reading, remind children that setting a purpose for reading can help them better understand what they read. Guide children to pay attention to the sequence, or order, in which the new library was built.

- **Read** During reading, monitor children's comprehension by providing higher-order thinking questions. Ask:

  • How will a bigger library help the growing town?

  • What other changes to public places might a growing town need?

  Build on children's answers to help them gain a better understanding of the text.

- **Summarize** With a partner, have children take turns summarizing the story by identifying the most important ideas. Ask:

  • What are the steps that were used to build the new library?

  • What changes took place as a result of the new library?

- **Text to Text** Help children make connections to the story. Ask:

  • What other books or stories have you read where people changed something in order to make it better? Explain the changes that were made.

More Reading
Use Leveled Readers or other text at children's instructional level.

Objectives
• Retell a story's beginning, middle, and end with attention to the sequence of events.
• Make inferences about text.

Small Group Time

More Reading

Use Leveled Readers or other text at children's instructional level.

A Advanced   DAY **4**

Comprehension

■ **Comprehension** Have children silently read this week's paired selection, "My Neighborhood, Then and Now." Have them retell the story, identifying the characters, setting, and sequence of events. Then have them summarize what they think were the most important ideas from the story.

Talk about what makes "My Neighborhood, Then and Now" an autobiography. Ensure that children understand that an autobiography is a true story about a person's life written by that person.

My Neighborhood, Then and Now

■ **Text to Text** Have children identify other autobiographies they may have read and explain how they were similar to "My Neighborhood, Then and Now."

Objectives
• Retell a story's beginning, middle, and end with attention to the sequence of events.

A Advanced   DAY **5**

Fluency•Comprehension

■ **Fluency** Using the first few sentences of Advanced Selection 13, model reading with accuracy and at an appropriate pace. Then have children read the selection to a partner as you listen to their reading. Provide corrective feedback as needed.

■ **Comprehension** After they have finished reading the selection, have children retell what happened by stating the story events in sequence. Then, on the back of the selection page, have them write three sentences that describe a pet they would like to have.

Advanced Selection 13

Objectives
• Read aloud grade-level appropriate text with fluency and comprehension.
• Retell a story's beginning, middle, and end with attention to the sequence of events.

English Language Learners

The ELL lessons are organized by strands. Use them to scaffold the weekly lesson curriculum or during small-group time.

Concept Development

How do places change?

■ **Activate Prior Knowledge** Write the Question of the Week and read it aloud. Underline the word *change* and have children say it with you. *Change* means that something is different. Show a picture of a construction site. This place will change. Right now, there is no building here. People are building a house. That will be a big change! Have children talk about how other places change. A park can change in the spring when new things grow. A school can change when builders add rooms for new students.

■ **Connect to New Concept** Have children turn to pages 12–13 in the Student Edition. Read the title and have children track the print as you read it. Point to the pictures one at a time and use them to guide a discussion about how places change. For example, point to the house under construction. What is this? (new house) People are building a new house. A city changes when new people come. New houses are made.

■ **Develop Concepts** Display ELL Poster 13 and have children identify neighborhood places they know. (apartment, park, grocery store, street) What changes do you see? Have children point to places that are changing on the Poster. (new building, new store sign) Use the leveled prompts below to assess understanding and build oral language. Point to pictures on the poster as you guide discussion.

Leveled Support

Beginning Ask yes/no questions, such as, Does the grocery store stay the same? Are the new signs in English and Spanish?

Intermediate Ask children questions that can be answered with simple sentences. What is changing in the poster? How does the grocery store change? What are the workers building?

Advanced/Advanced-High Have children answer the Question of the Week by giving specific examples from the poster and their own experiences.

■ **Review Concepts and Connect to Writing** Review children's understanding of the concept at the end of the week. Ask them to write in response to these questions: What changes do you see in our city? What English words did you learn this week? Write and display key ideas from the discussion.

Objectives
• Internalize new basic and academic language by using and reusing it in meaningful ways in speaking and writing activities that build concept and language attainment.

Content Objective
• Use prior experiences.

Language Objectives
• Share information orally.
• Use basic vocabulary for describing cities.

Daily Planner	
DAY 1	• **Frontload Concepts** • **Preteach** Comprehension Skill, Vocabulary, Phonemic Awareness/Phonics, Conventions/Writing
DAY 2	• **Review** Concepts, Vocabulary, Comprehension Skill • **Frontload Main Selection** • **Practice** Phonemic Awareness/Phonics, Conventions/Writing
DAY 3	• **Review** Concepts, Comprehension Skill, Vocabulary, Conventions/Writing • **Reread Main Selection** • **Practice** Phonemic Awareness/Phonics
DAY 4	• **Review Concepts** • **Read ELL/ELD Readers** • **Practice** Phonemic Awareness/Phonics, Conventions/Writing
DAY 5	• **Review** Concepts, Vocabulary, Comprehension Skill, Phonemic Awareness/Phonics, Conventions/Writing • **Reread ELL/ELD Readers**

*See the ELL Handbook for ELL Workshops with targeted instruction.

Concept Talk Video

Use this week's Concept Talk Video to help children build background knowledge about change. See the Concept Talk Video Routine (*ELL Handbook*, page 500) for suggestions on using the video.

Support for English Language Learners

Language Objectives

- Segment and blend phonemes.

- Decode words by segmenting and blending phonemes.

ELL Teaching Routine

For more practice with the vowel sounds of *y,* use the Sound-by-Sound Blending Routine (*ELL Handbook,* page 493).

ELL English Language Learners

Phonemic Awareness: Blend and Segment Phonemes

■ **Preteach** the Sounds /ī/ and /ē/

- Have children open to pp. 14–15. What are the birds doing? (flying) Say the word *fly* slowly. I am going to say the sounds in *fly*. Listen for the last sound: /f/ /l/ /ī/. The last sound I hear is /ī/. Say /ī/ with me. Say these words as you point to corresponding pictures: *cry, baby, high, knee, sky.* Have children repeat the word and wave hi if they hear the /ī/ sound.

- What animal is this? (puppy) Listen to the last sound in *puppy*. Slowly segment and blend the sounds: /p/ /u/ /p/ /ē/, *puppy*. What is the last sound in *puppy*? (/ē/) Yes, say the last sound in *puppy* with me: /ē/.

- Have children point out other items with the sound of /ī/ or /ē/.

■ **Practice** Listen again as I say all the sounds in *sky*. Stretch the sounds as you say them /fff/ /lll/ /ī ī ī/, *fly*. Now you try. Write the words on the board. Have children use the strategy of segmenting and blending the phonemes to decode the words suggested by the images on pp. 14–15.

/b/ /ā/ /b/ /ē/, baby	/k/ /r/ /ī/, cry	/h/ /a/ /p/ /ē/, happy
/b/ /u/ /n/ /ē/, bunny	/sh/ /ī/, shy	/t/ /r/ /ī/, try

Phonics: Vowel Sounds of *y*

■ **Preteach** Display Sound-Spelling Card 77. This is a bunny. What sound do you hear at the end of *bunny*? (/ī/) Say it with me: /ī/. Point to *y*. The long e sound /ē/ is spelled *y* in *bunny*. Display Sound-Spelling Card 81. This is the sky. What sound do you hear at the end of *sky*? (/ē/) Say it with me: /ē/. Point to *y*. The long i sound /ī/ is spelled *y* in *sky*.

■ **Listen and Write** Distribute Write and Wipe Boards.

- Write the word *shy* on the board. Copy this word. As you write *y*, say the sound to yourself: /ī/. Now say the sound aloud. (/ī/) Underline *y* in *shy*. The letter *y* spells /ī/ in *shy*.

- Repeat the instruction for *y* spelled /ē/ using the word *baby*. The letter *y* spells /ē/ in *baby*.

Objectives
- Recognize elements of the English sound system in newly acquired vocabulary such as long and short vowels, silent letters, and consonant clusters
- Learn relationships between sounds and letters of the English language and decode (sound out) words using a combination of skills such as recognizing sound-letter relationships and identifying cognates, affixes, roots and base words.

 English Language Learners

■ **Reteach and Practice** Write the following words on the board and have children read them aloud with you: *cry, my, handy, sky, funny, Billy.* Segment and blend each word with children. Point out the final vowel sounds. Leave the words on the board, but erase the letter *y* and replace it with a blank. Have children fill in the missing *y*.

 Leveled Support

Beginning Have children read the word aloud. Monitor for accurate pronunciation. Ask them if *y* sounds like /ī/ or /ē/.

Intermediate Have children read the word aloud. Monitor for accurate pronunciation. Ask them to tell the vowel sound spelled by *y*.

Advanced/Advanced-High Have children read the word aloud and name another rhyming word with the same vowel sound.

Phonics: CV Words

■ **Preteach** Have children turn to Envision It! on page 18 of the Student Edition.

- The word for the first picture is *no.* Shake your head to indicate the meaning. What sound do you hear at the end of *no*? (/ō/) Say it with me: /ō/. Point to *o*. The long *o* sound /ō/ is spelled *o* in *no.*

- The word in the next picture is *hi.* Wave. What sound do you hear at the end of *hi*? (/ī/) Point to *i*. The long *i* sound /ī/ is spelled *i* in *hi.*

- The word for the last picture is *we. We are in school.* What sound do you hear at the end of *we*? (/ē/) The long *e* sound /ē/ is spelled *e* in *we.*

■ **Practice** Distribute Letter Tiles *i, e, o, s, g, h,* and *m* to pairs.

- Blend the sounds in *so* and have pairs spell *so* with their tiles: /s/ /ō/, *so.*

- Replace the *s.* Spell *go.*

- Replace both letters. Spell /h/ /ī/, *hi.*

- Replace *i.* Spell /h/ /ē/, *he.*

- Replace *h.* Spell /m/ /ē/, *me.*

Language Objectives
- Associate the vowel sounds /e/ or /i/ with the spelling *y.*
- Use linguistic support.
- Read words with open syllable pattern CV.

Catch Up
The letters *a, e, i, o, u* and sometimes *y* are vowels. Every word in English has at least one of these letters.

 ## Transfer Skills
Sound-Spelling In Spanish, the letter i is always pronounced as long *e*, as in *día.* The long *e* sound is spelled *ai* or *ay* in Spanish.

Long e In Spanish, the letter *y* is pronounced like the long *e* in English, so the long *e* sound of *y* in words such as *funny* and *happy* may be familiar to beginning Spanish readers.

Practice Page
ELL Handbook page 297 provides additional practice for this week's skill.

Support for English Language Learners

Content Objective
- Monitor and adjust oral comprehension.

Language Objectives
- Discuss oral passages.
- Use a graphic organizer to take notes.

ELL Teacher Tip
You might have children use the story map to retell the story in their own words. They can retell the story to partners.

ELL *English Language Learners*

Listening Comprehension

A New Home

Hanna was sad. She did not want to move. She was going to miss her yard and her friends. "We are not moving far," Hanna's mom said. "We are moving down the street. You can still play with your friends."

There were many things for Hanna and her mom to do. First, they packed their things. Then, a big van came to move furniture. Then they cleaned. They cleaned the floors. They washed the windows. Their friends helped.

Finally Hanna and her mom were ready to go. They put their plants and Hanna's doll in the car. They waved goodbye. Soon they came to their new neighborhood. Hanna looked out the window. "A park!" she said. There were swings and slides. There were flowers and trees. "Look Hanna! Kids are playing in the park," her mom said. Hanna jumped out of the car. She was excited to meet her new friends.

Prepare for the Read Aloud The modified Read Aloud above prepares children for listening to the oral reading "We're Moving" on page 17b.

- **First Listening: Listen to Understand** Write the title of the Read Aloud on the board. Did you ever move? Do you know someone who moved? I am going to read a story about someone who is moving to a new place. How do you think she feels? Listen to find out who is moving and how she feels. After reading, ask children to recall the names of the characters and the events. Who is moving? (Hanna) How did she feel about it? (She felt sad.) What happens when she moves? (She feels happy because she sees a park.)

- **Second Listening: Listen to Check Understanding** Using Story Map A (*ELL Handbook*, page 506), work with children to recall the characters and the events in the story. Ask questions to prompt answers as you fill in the graphic organizer.

Objectives
- Demonstrate listening comprehension of increasingly complex spoken English by following directions, retelling or summarizing spoken messages, responding to questions and requests, collaborating with peers, and taking notes commensurate with content and grade-level needs.

High-Frequency Words

■ **Preteach** Distribute copies of this week's Word Cards (*ELL Handbook,* p. 137). Have children point to or hold up the corresponding card when you say a word in a sentence or make a gesture. When appropriate, use opposites to reinforce meaning.

- *Day* is the time of light between sunrise and sunset. The sun shines during the *day*. (night)

- Point to items such as books and pencils and say *things.*

- Hold out empty hands and say *nothing. (something/everything)*

- *The word everything* is made up of *every* and *thing.* Point to a set of things that are blue. *Everything* here is blue. (nothing)

- *Always* tells about all the time. I *always* ride the bus to school. (never)

- Puppies *become* dogs. Kittens *become* cats.

- *Stays* is the word *stay* with *s* at the end. Walk a few steps. I move about. Stand in one place. I *stay* in one spot.

■ **Practice** Briefly repeat each clue as children hold up the corresponding Word Cards.

■ **Speaking with High-Frequency Words**

- **Teach/Model** Review correct pronunciation of the high-frequency words with children.

- **Practice** Play a game of Beanbag Word Toss. Tape the Word Cards to the floor and give each child a chance to throw the beanbag at a word. Then tell children to say the word and use it in a sentence.

Beginning If children mispronounce the word, ask them to say it aloud with you.

Intermediate Help each child use the word in a sentence.

Advanced/Advanced-High Ask children to use the word in a complete sentence.

Language Objectives
- Use accessible language to learn new and essential language.
- Use high-frequency English words.
- Understand the general meaning of spoken language.
- Write using newly-acquired basic vocabulary.

Mini-Lesson: Listening
Turn to the Student Edition, p. 19, and read the passage aloud as children listen. Ask them questions to be sure that they have understood the general message of the spoken passage: What used to be on Sandy Lane? What is there now? How do people feel about the changes? Discuss strategies for getting the central message in a piece of writing, such as listening for important details, taking notes, and so on.

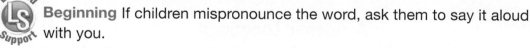
Objectives
- Use strategic learning techniques such as concept mapping, drawing, memorizing, comparing, contrasting, and reviewing to acquire basic and grade-level vocabulary.
- Internalize new basic and academic language by using it and reusing it in meaningful ways in speaking and writing activities that build language attainment.
- Understand the general meaning, main points, and important details of spoken language ranging from situations in which topics, language, and contexts are familiar to unfamiliar.

Support for English Language Learners

Content Objectives

- Identify sequence.
- Identify the sequence of events to aid comprehension.

Language Objectives

- Discuss evidence of sequential order.
- Demonstrate comprehension by retelling events in sequential order.
- Write events in sequential order.
- Recognize directionality.

Beginning Learners

Directionality As you read a text aloud, put your finger on the starting point in the text on the page. Show that you read from left to right and from top to bottom by moving your finger along lines of text. Have children use their fingers to show the correct movement as you read the text aloud again. Demonstrate directionality with p. EI•7 in the Student Edition as you point to pictures in sequence.

E L L English Language Learners

Guide Comprehension
Sequence

■ **Preteach** Model by pantomiming as you define *sequence*. Sequence is the order that things happen. If I bat in a baseball game, first I get a bat. Next I get ready for the pitch. Last, I swing the bat.

■ **Practice** Have children turn to Envision It! on page EI•7 in the Student Edition. Discuss the pictures. Have them point to what happens first, next, and last as you narrate the events in order. Then have children retell the events in order themselves. They can use sequence words such as *first, then,* and *last*.

■ **Reteach/Practice** Distribute copies of the Picture It! (*ELL Handbook,* p. 138) Read the text aloud twice. Prepare for the second reading by asking children to think about what happens first, next, and last. After reading, have children help you put sentence strips with the events in the correct order. Guide children in completing the practice exercises at their language proficiency level. (**Answers** *First*: Lili puts on her jacket. *Next:* She tells her mom that her jacket is too small. *Last:* She tries on a new jacket that fits.)

Beginning/Intermediate Use physical response to practice comprehension of directions. Start with simple commands, such as Draw a (circle, square, letter). Then add more commands, such as Color it (blue, red, green). As children become more proficient, add more complicated commands such as First, take out a pencil. Next, draw a circle. Then color it blue.

Advanced/Advanced-High Children can practice giving each other commands using *first, next,* and *last*. Pair them with Beginning/Intermediate level children and have them give oral commands with *first, next,* and *last* as appropriate.

MINI-LESSON

Academic Language

Directions tell you what to do. Listen as I tell you directions: *First, stand up. Next, turn around. Last, sit down again. Now listen to the directions again. Then follow the directions when I clap.* Give directions for simple classroom tasks, such as lining up with girls on one side and boys on the other. Take their suggestions as you craft directions for another simple task, such as watering the class plant. Finally, children can practice giving directions to you and to each other.

Objectives
- Understand the general meaning, main points, and important details of spoken language ranging from situations in which topics, language, and contexts are familiar to unfamiliar.

ELL *English Language Learners*

Reading Comprehension
A Place to Play

Student Edition pp. 20–21

■ **Frontloading**

- **Background Knowledge** Read the title aloud and discuss it. Where do you like to play? Are there places in your neighborhood for children to play? Support children who may not have places to play.

- **Preview** Guide children on a picture walk through the story, asking them to identify people, places, and actions. Reteach these words using visuals in the Student Edition: *community center* (p. 26), *neighborhood* (p. 28), *plays*—as in "drama" (p. 30), and *tower* (p. 33).

- **Predict** Where do you think the children in the story will play?

Sheltered Reading Ask questions such as the following to guide children's comprehension:

- p. 24: Point to Dad. Who is this? (Dad) What is Dad doing? (digging and planting)

- p. 26: Point to the tools on Ms. Torres's belt. What kind of work do you think Ms. Torres does? (She is a carpenter; she builds things.) Lead children to pantomime what Ms. Torres does on the job.

- pp. 26–27: Point to the wall with the art on it. Is this a window or a wall? Yes, it's a wall. It is art. Point to the tool that shows you this is art on the wall. (paintbrush) Have children identify places and things in the picture they know.

- p. 32: What do Benny and Molly play? Point to pictures of them playing. Tell what they do. (Benny plays basketball; Molly slides.)

■ **Fluency: Accuracy and Rate** Remind children that reading accurately means recognizing words and saying them correctly. Read page 22 aloud, modeling proper rate and accuracy. Tell children that the rate, or speed, at which you read should not be too fast or too slow. Have pairs read page 23 aloud to each other as their partners listen and offer feedback. Have children monitor for understanding of spoken language by retelling each section their partners read.

After Reading Help children summarize the text with the Retelling Cards. Ask questions that prompt children to summarize the important parts of the text.

Content Objectives
- Monitor and adjust comprehension.
- Use teacher support to develop background knowledge.
- Make and adjust predictions.

Language Objectives
- Read grade-level text with expression.
- Distinguish intonation patterns of English.
- Summarize text using visual support.
- Monitor understanding of spoken language.

Audio Support
Children can prepare for reading *A Place to Play* by using the eSelection or the Audio-Text CD.

English Summary
Read the English summary of *A Place to Play* (*ELL Handbook,* page 139). Children can ask questions about ideas or unfamiliar words. Send copies home for children to read with family members.

Objectives
- Distinguish sounds and intonation patterns of English with increasing ease.
- Use visual and contextual support and support from peers and teachers to read grade-appropriate content area text, enhance and confirm understanding, and develop vocabulary, grasp of language structures, and background knowledge needed to comprehend increasingly challenging language.

Support for English Language Learners

For additional leveled instruction, see the **ELL/ELD Reader Teaching Guide.**

ELL Reader ELD Reader

Comprehension: *My Street*

- **Before Reading** Distribute copies of the ELL and ELD Readers, *My Street*, to children at their reading level.

  - **Preview** Read the title aloud with children: This is a story about a street and how it changes. Activate prior knowledge. The story in our book was about changes in a place to play. This story is about changes too. What changes can happen on a street? Has anything ever changed on your street?

  - **Set a Purpose for Reading** Let's read to find out what changes on this street.

- **During Reading** Follow this Reading Routine for both reading groups.

  1. Read the entire Reader aloud slowly as children follow along and finger point.

  2. Reread the Reader one sentence at a time, having children echo read after you.

- **After Reading** Use the exercises on the inside back cover of *My Street* and invite children to share drawings and writing. In a whole-group discussion, ask children to list all of the ways a street can change. Encourage children to identify changes that take place at the beginning, middle, and end of the story. Children can point to examples in the book of the changes on the street.

ELD Reader Beginning/Intermediate

- **pp. 2–5** Point to the tree. How does a tree change? Can you share all the ways that the tree changes in this story?

- **pp. 6–7** What is new on the street? Point to it. (There is a new playground.)

Writing Draw a picture of the tree in one part of the book. Label your picture. Ask children to work in pairs and share their picture with the whole class. Have them compare the differences in their pictures and tell how the tree changes.

ELL Reader Advanced/Advanced-High

- **p. 2** What are some things on Tom's Street? (a apartment building, small trees, kids)

- **pp. 3–4** What are some new things on Tom's street? (The Barr family lives on the street with their dog; the trees have blossoms; the building next to Tom's building is now white; there are many flowers; there is a new boy named Dan on the street.)

Study Guide Distribute copies of the ELL Reader Study Guide (*ELL Handbook*, page 142). Scaffold comprehension by having children point to the trees in the Reader as the seasons change. Review their responses together. (**Answers** See *ELL Handbook*, pp. 245–248.)

Objectives

- Demonstrate English comprehension and expand reading skills by employing inferential skills such as predicting, making connections between ideas, drawing inferences and conclusions from text and graphic sources, and finding supporting text evidence commensurate with content area needs.

Go Digital! **eReaders**

Conventions
Action Verbs

■ **Preteach** Point to the image on page 25 of the Student Edition. *Molly stomps in the mud. The word* stomps *tells something that Molly does.* Pantomime stomping and encourage children to join you. *Stomps is an action verb. Any word that tells something we can do is an action verb.*

■ **Practice** Action verbs are a language structure in classroom materials. Use the Student Edition to have children identify verbs and how those verbs are used in sentences. Focus on pp. 23, 27, and 31.

Beginning Point to an action picture in the Student Edition and say a simple sentence, such as *Benny slides.* Have children identify the action verb.

Intermediate Point to an action picture. Ask children to say a verb that names the action. Write their responses on the board.

Advanced/Advanced-High Have children create simple sentences to tell about the action in a picture. Then ask them to identify the action verb.

■ **Reteach**

• Write "The boy plays outside" on the board. *The first part of the sentence tells who the sentence is about. Who is this sentence about?* (the boy) *The next part tells what the boy does. What does he do?* (plays outside) *What is the action verb?* (plays) Underline *plays.*

• Write simple verbs on index cards, such as *run, jump, sing, fly,* and so on. Ask a child to choose a card. Then work with children to create simple sentences with the verbs. Emphasize the order in the sentence. The *who* comes before the action verb.

■ **Practice** Use the summary of "A Place to Play" (*ELL Handbook,* page 139) to practice identifying and using action verbs.

Beginning Choose simple sentences from the summary to read aloud. Ask children to raise their hand or give a "thumbs up" when they hear action verbs. Have them repeat the action verbs.

Intermediate Write a few sentences from the summary on paper to make sentence strips, one sentence per strip. Have children work in pairs and underline or cut the verbs from the sentences.

Advanced/Advanced-High Repeat the intermediate activity. Then ask children to choose a verb to use in a sentence of their own. Have children check to make sure that they use the correct tense of the action verbs.

Objectives
• Speak using a variety of grammatical structures, sentence lengths, sentence types, and connecting words with increasing accuracy and ease as more English is acquired.

Content Objectives
• Identify and use action verbs.
• Correctly use action verbs in sentences.

Language Objectives
• Speak using action verbs in sentences.
• Write phrases and sentences with action verbs.
• Comprehend the language structure of action verbs in classroom materials.

Grammar Jammer
For more practice with verbs, use the Grammar Jammer for this target skill. See the Grammar Jammer Routine (*ELL Handbook,* page 501) for suggestions on using this learning tool.

Social Language
Have children name outdoor games they enjoy, such as baseball, basketball, hide and seek, or tag. Brainstorm action verbs for the games, such as *run, hop, walk, jump,* and *throw*. Record children's ideas. Children can pantomime the action verbs for their classmates to guess.

Support for English Language Learners

Content Objectives

- Identify words that indicate parts of a story.
- Identify the characteristics of a realistic story.

Language Objectives

- Write story sentences using sequence words.
- Share feedback for editing and revising.
- Narrate with increasing specificity and detail.

Mini-Lesson: Speaking

Tell children that not only can you write stories, you can also narrate, or tell, them. Turn to the Student Edition, p. 36, and read the prompt. Discuss a place where children could play. Then have children tell a story about the place. Prompt them to include details and specific ideas. Where is this place? Is this place new? What can you do in this place?

ELL English Language Learners

Write Story Sentences

- **Introduce Terms** Write *realistic story* on the board and explain each word as you point to it. A story is made up. It comes from your mind. Circle the word *real* inside *realistic*. See the word *real*? *Real* means that it's not make-believe. A realistic story is about things that could really happen. In a realistic story, a dog could not fly. In a realistic story, a dog could bark and wag its tail.

- **Describe Story Parts** Explain that a good story has a beginning, middle, and end. Write this sentence on the board: *James planted a seed.* Have children suggest things James would need to do to plant a seed. Record their answers on the board. Model supplying the first action: *James dug a hole in the dirt.*

- **Model** Draw three large boxes connected with arrows on the board. Label them *First, Next,* and *Last.* Engage children in naming three things that James would do when he planted a seed. Write sentences for each action in the boxes.

First ——→ Next ——→ Last

- **Write** Have children copy this story starter: *Carly went to the playground.* Have them draw three large boxes under the sentence and label them *First, Next,* and *Last.* Have partners work together to think of a game that Carly could play with her friends on the playground. What would happen first, next, and last in the game?

Beginning Supply the graphic organizer. Write the words *First, Next,* and *Last* in your boxes. Think of a game Carly could play. Draw three things that happen in the game. Have children tell about their pictures. Supply the action words and have children copy them in the appropriate boxes.

Intermediate Guide children's writing. What action words will you use? What words can you use to tell more about the playground? Help children with their spelling.

Advanced/Advanced-High Have children use the boxes for prewriting. Then have them write their sentences in paragraph form.

Objectives

- Write using newly acquired basic vocabulary and content-based grade-level vocabulary.
- Narrate, describe, and explain with increasing specificity and detail as more English is acquired.

Common Core Standards
Weekly Planning Guide

Selection: Ruby in Her Own Time
Genre: Animal Fantasy

Alignment of the Common Core Standards with This Week's Skills and Strategies

This Week's Common Core Standards for English Language Arts	Instructional Summary
Reading Standards for Literature	
Literature 4. Identify words and phrases in stories or poems that suggest feelings or appeal to the senses.	The lesson guides children as they **compare and contrast** the looks, behaviors, and experiences of the growing ducklings in the main selection *Ruby in Her Own Time*. After introducing **inferring** as a reading strategy, the lesson asks questions that help children make inferences about the story by using story illustrations and details as well as what they already know.
Literature 7. Use illustrations and details in a story to describe its characters, setting, or events.	
Literature 9. Compare and contrast the adventures and experiences of characters in stories.	
Foundational Skills Standards	
Foundational Skills 2.c. Isolate and pronounce initial, medial vowel, and final sounds (phonemes) in spoken single-syllable words.	In the phonics activities for this lesson, children **segment, blend,** and read words with the consonant patterns *ng* and *nk*. Children identify and read **verbs that end with -s** in conventions activities. In the story, children read words with endings *-ing, -ed,* and *-er*. In fluency activities, the lesson includes opportunities to use **appropriate phrasing** to help children reread with expression.
Foundational Skills 3.f. Read words with inflectional endings.	
Foundational Skills 4.b. Read on-level text orally, with accuracy, appropriate rate, and expression on successive readings.	
Writing Standards	
Writing 1. Write opinion pieces in which they introduce the topic or name the book they are writing about, state an opinion, supply a reason for the opinion, and provide some sense of closure.	This week children write comments about a story character. They learn that **story comments** express opinions by telling what the writer thinks or feels. In the Research and Inquiry section, children select a topic, identify facts about it, and choose one to share with the class.
Writing 2. Write informative/explanatory texts in which they name a topic, supply some facts about the topic, and provide some sense of closure.	
Speaking and Listening Standards	
Speaking/Listening 1.b. Build on others' talk in conversations by responding to the comments of others through multiple exchanges.	In this week's listening and speaking activities, children participate in a **conversation** about respect and tell about a favorite toy, using the correct form of a present tense verb in their **sentences.**
Speaking/Listening 6. Produce complete sentences when appropriate to task and situation. (See grade 1 Language standards 1 and 3 on page 26 for specific expectations.)	
Language Standards	
Language 1.c. Use singular and plural nouns with matching verbs in basic sentences (e.g., *He hops; We hop*).	In the Conventions section, the lesson focuses on the forms of **present tense verbs.** The lesson explicitly teaches the **spelling** of words with the consonant patterns of *ng* and *nk* and high-frequency words. In the Vocabulary section, children identify synonyms or words that are **related by meanings.**
Language 2.d. Use conventional spelling for words with common spelling patterns and for frequently occurring irregular words.	
Language 5. With guidance and support from adults, demonstrate understanding of word relationships and nuances in word meanings.	

Additional Support for a Common Core Standard This Week

Use the following instruction to supplement the teaching of one of this week's Common Core Standards.

Common Core Standard: Foundational Skills 3.f.
Write the following words in a column on the board: *walk, walks, walked, walking*.

- Underline the base word in each word and tell children that the word *walk* is the main part of each word.
- Circle the endings and tell children that these endings change the verb.
- Use each word in a sentence: *I walk every day. Michael walks home from school. We walked to the park yesterday. Are we walking to the park?*
- Ask children to add *-s, -ed,* and *-ing* to these words and to use the words they make in a sentence: *call* and *play.*

ISBN-13: 978-0-328-64369-6   ISBN-10: 0-328-64369-1

Week 6

Where Are My Animal Friends?

Question of the Week

What do animals do when the seasons change?

Concept Talk Guide children as they discuss questions such as:

- Why do you think squirrels gather and hide nuts in the fall?

Writing Think about Raccoon and Squirrel in *Where Are My Animal Friends?* What would they say if they could call Goose on a phone? Write a play scene showing what they would say.

connect to **SCIENCE**

Week 5

I'm a Caterpillar

Question of the Week

What changes can be seen in nature?

Concept Talk Guide children as they discuss questions such as:

- How do different kinds of animals change as they grow?

Writing Think of changes in nature. Plants and animals grow. Seasons change. Draw two pictures to show one way a plant or animal changes. Write captions about your pictures.

connect to **SCIENCE**

Week 4

Frog and Toad Together

Question of the Week

What changes happen in a garden?

Concept Talk Guide children as they discuss questions such as:

- What do seeds look like when you first plant them? Then what happens?

Writing Think of actions Toad tried to help his garden grow. Write a list telling what Toad did that really helped the garden grow. In another list, tell his actions that did not help.

connect to **SCIENCE**

Unit 3

THE BIG QUESTION 2

What is changing in our world?

Common Core Standards and Concept Development

- Introduce and explore this unit's weekly concepts through rich, structured conversations
- Develop complex content knowledge and vocabulary
- Expand on a single concept with engaging literature and nonfiction
- Build better readers in all content areas
- Align instruction to Common Core Anchor Standards

COMMON CORE Grade 2

Week 3

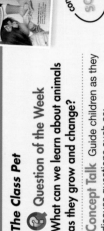

The Class Pet

Question of the Week

What can we learn about animals as they grow and change?

Concept Talk Guide children as they discuss questions such as:

- Think about different animals. How are the babies different from the adults?

Writing Write a summary of *The Class Pet*. Tell the most important events and ideas.

connect to **SCIENCE**

Week 1

A Place to Play

Question of the Week

How do places change?

Concept Talk Guide children as they discuss questions such as:

- What are some ways your neighborhood has changed?

Writing Think about a place to play that you think is interesting. Now write a made-up story about children playing at that place.

connect to **SOCIAL STUDIES**

You Are Here: Week 2

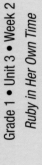

Ruby in Her Own Time

Question of the Week

What do we learn as we grow and change?

As children answer this unit's Big Question and this week's Question of the Week, they will address:

Reading 7. Integrate and evaluate content presented in diverse media and formats, including visually and quantitatively, as well as in words. **(Also Reading 9.)**

Concept Talk Guide children as they discuss questions such as:

- What can you do now that you could not do when you were younger?

As children answer this week's Concept Talk question, they will address:

Speaking/Listening 1. Prepare for and participate effectively in a range of conversations and collaborations with diverse partners, building on others' ideas and expressing their own clearly and persuasively.

Writing Look at the pictures in *Ruby in Her Own Time.* Think about what Ruby does. Write sentences that tell two things Ruby does that you like.

As children write about this week's prompt, they will address:

Writing 2. Write informative/explanatory texts to examine and convey complex ideas and information clearly and accurately through the effective selection, organization, and analysis of content.

Listening and Speaking On page 82, children learn to be polite to their listeners. By doing so, they address:

Speaking/Listening 6. Adapt speech to a variety of contexts and communicative tasks, demonstrating command of formal English when indicated or appropriate.

connect to **SOCIAL STUDIES**

COMMON CORE Grade 2

This Week's ELL Overview

ELL Handbook

- Maximize Literacy and Cognitive Engagement
- Research Into Practice
- Full Weekly Support for Every Selection

Ruby in Her Own Time

- Multi-Lingual Summaries in Five Languages
- Selection-Specific Vocabulary Word Cards
- Frontloading/Reteaching for Comprehension Skill Lessons
- ELD and ELL Reader Study Guides

- Transfer Activities
- Professional Development

Daily Leveled ELL Notes

ELL notes appear throughout this week's instruction and ELL Support is on the DI pages of your Teacher's Edition. The following is a sample of an ELL note from this week.

English Language Learners

Beginning Children can share orally with a partner how Ruby's actions make them feel.

Intermediate Have children write phrases to describe Ruby's actions. Have them describe to partners how they feel and why.

Advanced Have children write short descriptions in their charts. Have children share their ideas with partners.

Advanced High Organize children into pairs. Have them create a list of descriptive words from the story and use the words to discuss the characters and setting.

ELL by Strand

The ELL lessons on this week's Support for English Language Learners pages are organized by strand. They offer additional scaffolding for the core curriculum. Leveled support notes on these pages address the different proficiency levels in your class. See pages DI•33–DI•42.

ELL Guy
Dr. Jim Cummins

The Three Pillars of ELL Instruction

ELL Strands	Activate Prior Knowledge	Access Content	Extend Language
Vocabulary p. DI•37	Preteach	Teach/Model	Practice
Reading Comprehension p. DI•38	Preteach	Reteach/Practice	Leveled Practice Activities
Phonics, Spelling, and Word Analysis pp. DI•34–DI•35	Preteach	Listen and Write	Leveled Practice Activities
Listening Comprehension p. DI•36	Prepare for the Read Aloud	First Listening	Second Listening
Conventions and Writing pp. DI•41–DI•42	Preteach/Introduce Terms	Practice/Model	Leveled Practice Activities/ Leveled Writing Activities
Concept Development p. DI•33	Activate Prior Knowledge	Develop Concepts	Review Concepts and Connect to Writing

This Week's Practice Stations Overview

Six Weekly Practice Stations with Leveled Activities can be found at the beginning of each week of instruction. For this week's Practice Stations, see pp. 44h–44i.

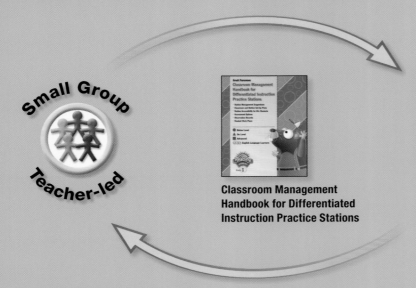

Practice Stations

Daily Leveled Center Activities

○ Below   ☐ Advanced
△ On-Level   Ⓔ Ⓛ Ⓛ

Classroom Management Handbook for Differentiated Instruction Practice Stations

Practice Stations Flip Charts

 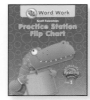    

	Listen Up	Word Work	Words to Know	Let's Write	Read for Meaning	Get Fluent
Objectives	• Identify words with the vowel sound of y. • Identify one-syllable words with /ī/, /ē/, /ō/.	• Write words that contain y: long e, long i. • Write words that contain open syllables long e, long i, long o.	• Identify high-frequency words *things, always, day, become, nothing, stays, everything.* • Write high-frequency words. • Determine antonyms.	• Identify and use action verbs in sentences.	• Identify the sequence of a story. • Identify the beginning, middle, and end of a story.	• Read aloud with accuracy at an appropriate rate.
Materials	• *Listen Up* Flip Chart Activity 14	• *Word Work* Flip Chart Activity 14 • pencils • teacher-made Word Cards • 3-column charts	• *Words to Know* Flip Chart Activity 14 • High-Frequency Word Cards for Unit 3, Week 1 • T-charts • pencils • Unit 3 Student Book	• *Let's Write* Flip Chart Activity 14 • paper • pencils	• *Read for Meaning* Flip Chart Activity 14 • Leveled Readers • paper • pencils • crayons	• *Get Fluent* Flip Chart Activity 14 • Leveled Readers

This Week on Reading Street!

Changes

 Question of the Week

What do we learn as we grow and change?

Daily Plan

Don't Wait Until Friday

Whole Group

- ◉ Consonant Patterns *ng, nk*
- ◉ Compound Words
- ◉ Compare and Contrast
- • Fluency
- • Vocabulary

MONITOR PROGRESS	Success Predictor			
Day 1 Check Word Reading	Day 2 Check Word Reading	Day 3 Check High-Frequency Words/Retelling	Day 4 Check Fluency	Day 5 Check Oral Vocabulary

Small Group

Teacher-Led

- • Reading Support
- • Skill Support
- • Fluency Practice

Practice Stations

Independent Activities

Customize Literacy More support for a Balanced Literacy approach, see CL•1–CL•47.

Customize Writing More support for a customized writing approach, see CW•1–CW•10.

Whole Group

- • Writing: Comments About a Story
- • Conventions: Verbs That Add *-s*

Assessment

- • Weekly Tests
- • Day 5 Assessment
- • Fresh Reads

You Are Here! Unit 3 Week 2

This Week's Reading Selections

Main Selection
Genre: **Animal Fantasy**

Paired Selection

Decodable Practice Readers

Leveled Readers

ELL and ELD Readers

Resources on Reading Street!

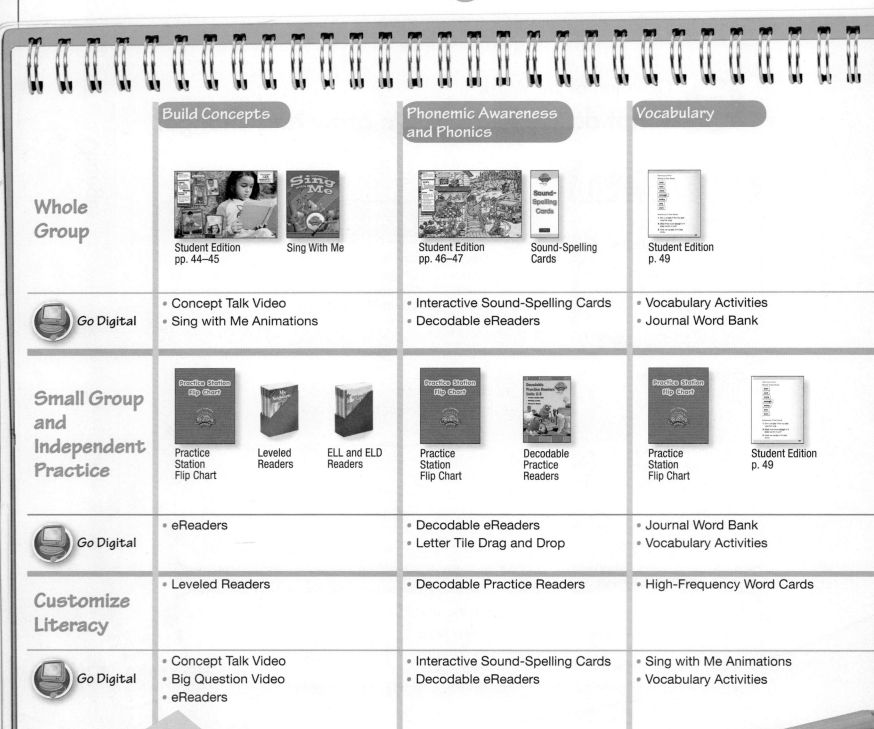

	Build Concepts	Phonemic Awareness and Phonics	Vocabulary
Whole Group	Student Edition pp. 44–45 · Sing With Me	Student Edition pp. 46–47 · Sound-Spelling Cards	Student Edition p. 49
Go Digital	• Concept Talk Video • Sing with Me Animations	• Interactive Sound-Spelling Cards • Decodable eReaders	• Vocabulary Activities • Journal Word Bank
Small Group and Independent Practice	Practice Station Flip Chart · Leveled Readers · ELL and ELD Readers	Practice Station Flip Chart · Decodable Practice Readers	Practice Station Flip Chart · Student Edition p. 49
Go Digital	• eReaders	• Decodable eReaders • Letter Tile Drag and Drop	• Journal Word Bank • Vocabulary Activities
Customize Literacy	• Leveled Readers	• Decodable Practice Readers	• High-Frequency Word Cards
Go Digital	• Concept Talk Video • Big Question Video • eReaders	• Interactive Sound-Spelling Cards • Decodable eReaders	• Sing with Me Animations • Vocabulary Activities

Question of the Week

What do we learn as we grow and change?

Comprehension	Fluency	Conventions and Writing
 Student Edition pp. 52–73	 Decodable Practice Readers	 Student Edition pp. 76–77
• Envision It! Animations • eSelections	• eSelections • eReaders	• Grammar Jammer
 Practice Station Flip Chart Leveled Readers ELL and ELD Readers	 Practice Station Flip Chart Decodable Practice Readers	 Practice Station Flip Chart Reader's and Writer's Notebook
• eReaders • Story Sort	• Decodable eReaders	• Grammar Jammer
• Envision It! Skills and Strategies Handbooks • Leveled Readers	• Leveled Readers	• Reader's and Writer's Notebook
• Envision It! Animations • eReaders	• eReaders	• Grammar Jammer

Week 2

You Are Here!
Unit 3
Week 2

My 5-Day Planner for Reading Street!

Don't Wait Until Friday SUCCESS PREDICTOR

Check Word Reading

Day 1 pages 44j–49f

Check Word Reading

Day 2 pages 50a–73g

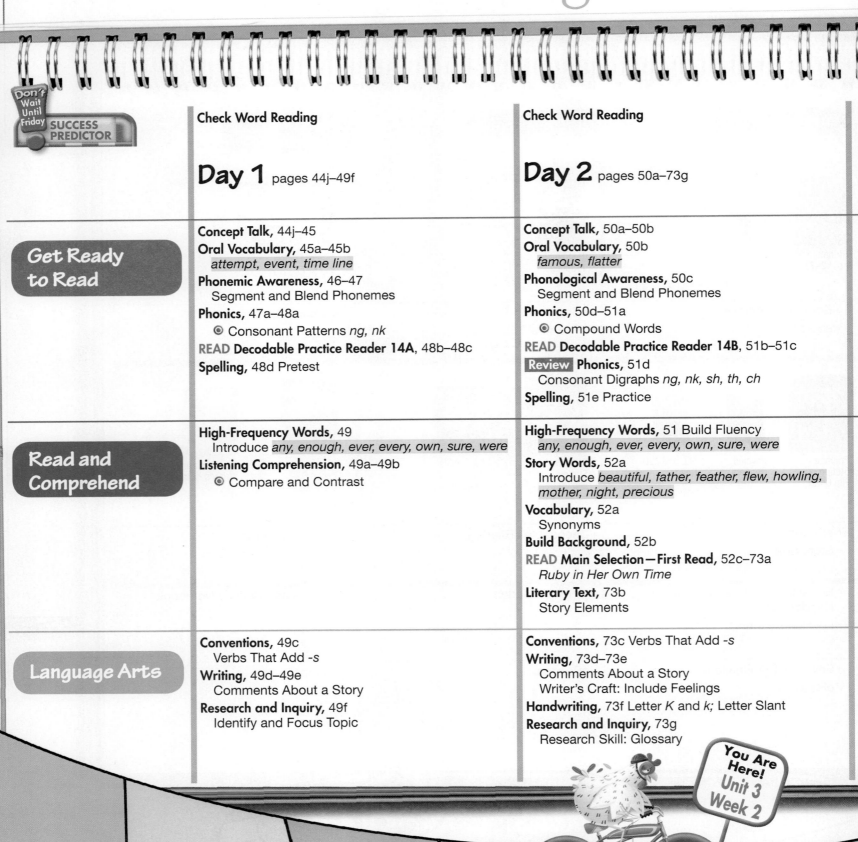

Get Ready to Read	**Concept Talk,** 44j–45 **Oral Vocabulary,** 45a–45b *attempt, event, time line* **Phonemic Awareness,** 46–47 Segment and Blend Phonemes **Phonics,** 47a–48a ◉ Consonant Patterns *ng, nk* READ **Decodable Practice Reader 14A,** 48b–48c **Spelling,** 48d Pretest	**Concept Talk,** 50a–50b **Oral Vocabulary,** 50b *famous, flatter* **Phonological Awareness,** 50c Segment and Blend Phonemes **Phonics,** 50d–51a ◉ Compound Words READ **Decodable Practice Reader 14B,** 51b–51c Review **Phonics,** 51d Consonant Digraphs *ng, nk, sh, th, ch* **Spelling,** 51e Practice
Read and Comprehend	**High-Frequency Words,** 49 Introduce *any, enough, ever, every, own, sure, were* **Listening Comprehension,** 49a–49b ◉ Compare and Contrast	**High-Frequency Words,** 51 Build Fluency *any, enough, ever, every, own, sure, were* **Story Words,** 52a Introduce *beautiful, father, feather, flew, howling, mother, night, precious* **Vocabulary,** 52a Synonyms **Build Background,** 52b READ **Main Selection—First Read,** 52c–73a *Ruby in Her Own Time* **Literary Text,** 73b Story Elements
Language Arts	**Conventions,** 49c Verbs That Add *-s* **Writing,** 49d–49e Comments About a Story **Research and Inquiry,** 49f Identify and Focus Topic	**Conventions,** 73c Verbs That Add *-s* **Writing,** 73d–73e Comments About a Story Writer's Craft: Include Feelings **Handwriting,** 73f Letter *K* and *k;* Letter Slant **Research and Inquiry,** 73g Research Skill: Glossary

You Are Here! Unit 3 Week 2

Question of the Week
What do we learn as we grow and change?

Check High-Frequency Words Check Retelling	Check Fluency	Check Oral Vocabulary
Day 3 pages 74a–77c	**Day 4** pages 78a–81e	**Day 5** pages 82a–83k

Concept Talk, 74a–74b
Oral Vocabulary, 74b
  correct
Phonemic Awareness, 74c
  Add Phonemes
Phonics, 74d–74e
  ◉ Consonant Patterns -*ng*, -*nk*
  ◉ Compound Words
Spelling, 74f Dictation
	Concept Talk, 78a–78b
	Oral Vocabulary, 78b
	  lovely, common
	Phonological Awareness, 78c
	`Review` **Phonics,** 78d
	  Vowel Sounds of *y*;
	  Syllable Pattern CV
	**READ Decodable Practice Reader
	14C,** 78e–78f
	`Review` **Fluent Word Reading,** 78g
	Spelling, 78h Partner Review
		Concept Wrap Up, 82a
		`Review` **Oral Vocabulary,** 82b
		Phonemic Awareness, 82c
		  Add Final Phonemes
		`Review` **Phonics,** 82c
		  ◉ Consonant Patterns -*ng*, -*nk*
		  ◉ Compound Words
		Spelling, 82d Test

`Review` **High-Frequency Words,** 74g
*any, enough, ever, every, own,
sure, were*
`Review` **Story Words,** 74g
*beautiful, father, feather, flew,
howling, mother, night, precious*
READ Main Selection–Second Read,
52–73, 74h–75a
Fluency, 75b
  Appropriate Phrasing
	Social Studies in Reading, 78i
	READ Paired Selection, 78–81
	  "The Ugly Duckling"
	Fluency, 81a
	  Appropriate Phrasing
		Listening and Speaking, 82–83
		  Share Information and Ideas
		Vocabulary, 83a Synonyms
		Fluency, 83a Appropriate Phrasing
		`Review` **Comprehension,** 83b
		  ◉ Compare and Contrast
		`Review` **Vocabulary,** 83b
		  High-Frequency and Story Words
		Genre, 83c Fairy Tale
		Assessment, 83d–83f
		  Monitor Progress

Conventions, 76a–77a
  Verbs That Add -*s*
Writing, 76–77a
  Comments About a Story
  Writing Trait: Voice
Listening and Speaking, 77b
  Respect
Research and Inquiry, 77c
  Gather and Record Information
	Conventions, 81b
	  Verbs That Add -*s*
	Writing, 81c–81d
	  Comments About a Story
	  Revising Strategy
	Research and Inquiry, 81e
	  Review and Revise Topic
		`Review` **Conventions,** 83g Verbs That
		Add -*s*
		Writing, 83h–83i
		  Writer's Craft: Verbs That Add -*s*
		Research and Inquiry, 83j
		  Communicate
		Wrap Up Your Week, 83k
		  ❓ What do we learn as we grow
		  and change?

Week 2

Grouping Options for Differentiated Instruction
Turn the page for the small group time lesson plan.

Planning Small Group Time on Reading Street!

SMALL GROUP TIME RESOURCES

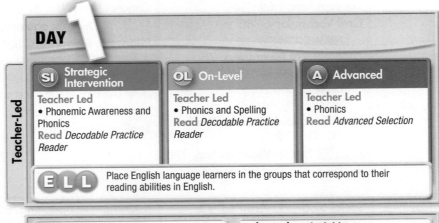

Look for this Small Group Time box each day to help meet the individual needs of all your children. Differentiated Instruction lessons appear on the DI pages at the end of each week.

DAY 1

Teacher-Led

SI Strategic Intervention

Teacher Led
• Phonemic Awareness and Phonics
Read *Decodable Practice Reader*

OL On-Level

Teacher Led
• Phonics and Spelling
Read *Decodable Practice Reader*

A Advanced

Teacher Led
• Phonics
Read *Advanced Selection*

ELL Place English language learners in the groups that correspond to their reading abilities in English.

Practice Stations
• Listen Up
• Word Work

Independent Activities
• *Reader's and Writer's Notebook*
• Concept Talk Video

ELL

ELL Reader
Advanced
Advanced-High

ELD Reader
Beginning
Intermediate

ELL Poster

Day 1

 **SI Strategic Intervention**	**Phonemic Awareness and Phonics**, DI•22 **Read Decodable Practice Reader 14A**, DI•22
OL On-Level	**Phonics and Spelling**, DI•27 **Read Decodable Practice Reader 14A**, DI•27
A Advanced	**Phonics**, DI•30 **Read Advanced Selection**, DI•30
 **ELL English Language Learners**	DI•33–DI•42 **Frontload Concept Preteach Skills Writing**

You Are Here!
Unit 3
Week 2

Reading Street Response to Intervention Kit

Reading Street Leveled Practice Stations Kit

SI Strategic Intervention

Below-Level Reader

Hank's Song
by Dale Cooper
illustrated by CD Hullinger

Decodable Practice Readers

Decodable Practice Readers Units 2-3
• Practice phonics skills
• Blending practice
• Reread for fluency

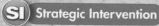
Concept Literacy Reader

I Can Read
By Josh Murphy

OL On-Level

On-Level Reader

Mac Can Do It!
by Dale Cooper
illustrated by Linda Howard Bittner

A Advanced

Advanced Reader

Paul's Bed
by Ruth Renolo
illustrated by Al Lorenz

Advanced Selection

Hank Rides a Bike

Small Group Weekly Plan

Day 2	Day 3	Day 4	Day 5
Phonemic Awareness and Phonics, DI•23 **Read Decodable Practice Reader 14B,** DI•23	**Phonemic Awareness and Phonics,** DI•24 **Read Concept Literacy Leveled Reader,** DI•24	**High-Frequency Words,** DI•25 **Read Decodable Practice Reader 14C,** DI•25	**Phonics Review,** DI•26 **Read Below-Level Leveled Reader,** DI•26
Phonics and High-Frequency Words, DI•27 **Read Decodable Practice Reader 14B,** DI•27	**Read On-Level Leveled Reader,** DI•28	**Conventions,** DI•29 **Reread Main Selection,** DI•29	**Phonics Review,** DI•29 **Reread On-Level Leveled Reader,** DI•29
Phonics and Comprehension, DI•30 **Read Main Selection,** DI•30	**Read Advanced Leveled Reader,** DI•31	**Comprehension,** DI•32 **Read Paired Selection,** DI•32 **Reread Leveled Reader,** DI•32	**Fluency and Comprehension,** DI•32 **Reread Advanced Selection,** DI•32
DI•33–DI•42 **Review Concept** **Practice Skills** **Frontload Main Selection** **Writing**	DI•33–DI•42 **Review Concept** **Practice Skills** **Reread Main Selection** **Writing**	DI•33–DI•42 **Review Concept** **Practice Skills** **Read ELL or ELD Reader** **Writing**	DI•33–DI•42 **Review Concept** **Review Skills** **Writing**

Week 2

Practice Stations for Everyone on Reading Street!

Listen Up!
Generate words with long vowels.

Objectives
• Identify words with the vowel sounds of *y*.
• Identify one-syllable words with /ī/, /ē/, /ō/.

Materials
• *Listen Up!* Flip Chart Activity 14

Differentiated Activities

⬤ Think of words that have the same ending sounds as *funny* and *sky*. Say them. Now think of one-syllable words that have the same ending sounds as *he, hi,* and *no*. Say them. Talk to a partner about the ending sounds you hear.

▲ Think of words that have the same ending sounds as *funny* and *sky*. Say them. Now think of one-syllable words that have the same ending sounds as *he, hi,* and *no*. Say them. Talk to a partner about the ending sounds you hear.

■ Think of words that have the same ending sounds as *funny* and *sky*. Say them. Now think of one-syllable words that have the same ending sounds as *he, hi,* and *no*. Say them. Take turns saying rhyming words with a partner.

Technology
• Interactive Sound-Spelling Cards

Word Work
Vowel sounds of *y*; open syllable pattern

Objectives
• Write words that contain *y*: long *e*, long *i*.
• Write words that contain open syllables long *e*, long *i*, long *o*.

Materials
• *Word Work* Flip Chart Activity 14
• pencils
• teacher-made word cards
• 3-column charts

Differentiated Activities

⬤ Label the columns "Ends with Long *e*," "Ends with Long *i*," and "Ends with Long *o*." Quietly read the words on the cards. Listen to the ending sound of each word as you read it. Write the word in the right column.

▲ Label the columns "Ends with Long *e*," "Ends with Long *i*," and "Ends with Long *o*." Quietly read the words on the cards. Listen to the ending sound of each word as you read it. Write the word in the right column. Underline the letter that makes the long vowel sound.

■ Label the columns "Ends with Long *e*," "Ends with Long *i*," and "Ends with Long *o*." Quietly read the words on the cards. Listen to the ending sound of each word as you read it. Write the word in the right column. Think of more words and add them to the chart.

Technology
• Interactive Sound-Spelling Cards

Words to Know
Practice high-frequency words.

Objectives
• Identify and read high-frequency words *things, always, day, become, nothing, stays, everything*.
• Determine antonyms.

Materials
• *Words to Know* Flip Chart Activity 14
• High-Frequency Word Cards for Unit 3, Week 1
• T-charts
• pencils

Differentiated Activities

⬤ Use the Word Cards. Read the words to a partner. Have your partner think of antonyms for the words *always, day, nothing,* and *stays*.

▲ On a T-chart, label the left column "Words to Know." Label the right column "Antonyms." Write the Words to Know in the left column, and then write antonyms for the words in the right column. (Some of the words may not have antonyms.)

■ On a T-chart, label the left column "Words to Know." Label the right column "Antonyms." Write the Words to Know in the left column, and then write antonyms for the words in the right column. (Some of the words may not have antonyms.) Add more words and their antonyms to your chart.

Technology
• Online Tested Vocabulary Activities

You Are Here!
Unit 3
Week 2

Key

● Below-Level Activities

▲ On-Level Activities

■ Advanced Activities

Practice Station Flip Chart

Let's Write!
Use verbs in writing.

Objectives
• Identify and use action verbs in sentences.

Materials
• *Let's Write!* Flip Chart Activity 14
• Student Edition pp. 46–47
• paper
• pencils

Differentiated Activities

Display the ELL Poster so that it is visible to all children.

● Look at your Student Edition, pp. 46–47. Think about action verbs that tell what is happening in the picture. Write a sentence about what one of the animals is doing. Underline the action verb you use.

▲ Look at your Student Edition, pp. 46–47. Think about action verbs that tell what is happening in the picture. Write sentences that tell what some of the animals are doing. Underline each action verb you use.

■ Look at your Student Edition, pp. 46–47. Think about action verbs that tell what is happening in the picture. Write a paragraph about what one of the animals is doing. Underline the action verbs you use.

Read For Meaning
Identify sequence.

Objectives
• Identify the sequence of a story.
• Identify the beginning, middle, and end of a story.

Materials
• *Read for Meaning* Flip Chart Activity 14
• Leveled Readers
• paper
• pencils
• crayons

Differentiated Activities

● Read *In My Room.* Use sequence to retell the beginning, middle, and end of the story to a partner. Draw three pictures of the boy's room—one from the beginning, one from the middle, and one from the end.

▲ Read *Let's Build a Park!* Use sequence to retell the beginning, middle, and end of the story to a partner. Draw three pictures of the events that take place—one from the beginning, one from the middle, and one from the end. Write a sentence describing each picture.

■ Read *A New Library.* Use sequence to retell the beginning, middle, and end of the story to a partner. Draw three pictures of the library—one from the beginning, one from the middle, and one from the end. Write a sentence describing each picture.

Technology
• Leveled eReaders

Get Fluent
Practice fluency.

Objectives
• Read aloud with accuracy at an appropriate rate.

Materials
• *Get Fluent* Flip Chart Activity 14
• Leveled Readers

Differentiated Activities

● Work with a partner. Take turns reading pages from *In My Room.* Think about what you're reading about. Be sure to read at an appropriate rate. Read as accurately as you can. Give your partner feedback.

▲ Work with a partner. Take turns reading pages from *Let's Build a Park!* Think about what you're reading about. Be sure to read at an appropriate rate. Read as accurately as you can. Give your partner feedback.

■ Work with a partner. Take turns reading pages from *A New Library.* Think about what you're reading about. Be sure to read at an appropriate rate. Read as accurately as you can. Give your partner feedback.

Technology
• Reading Street Readers CD-ROM

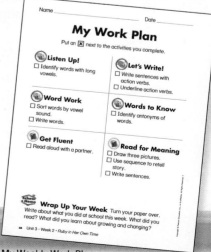

My Weekly Work Plan

week 2

Objectives
- Introduce concepts: what people learn as they grow and change.
- Share information and ideas about the concept.

Today at a Glance

Oral Vocabulary
attempt, event, time line

Phonemic Awareness
Segment and Blend Phonemes

Phonics and Spelling
⊚ Consonant Patterns *ng, nk*

Fluency
Oral Rereading

High-Frequency Words
any, enough, ever, every, own, sure, were

Comprehension
⊚ Compare and Contrast

Conventions
Verbs That Add *-s*

Writing
Comments About a Story: Introduce

Research and Inquiry
Identify and Focus Topic

Concept Talk

Question of the Week

What do we learn as we grow and change?

Introduce the concept

To build concepts and to focus children's attention, tell them that this week they will talk, sing, read, and write about how people learn as they grow and change. Write the Question of the Week and track the print as you read it.

> **ROUTINE** **Activate Prior Knowledge** **Team Talk**
>
> **Think** Have children think for a minute about what they have learned as they have grown and changed.
>
> **Pair** Have pairs of children discuss the question.
>
> **Share** Have children share information and their ideas with the group. Remind them to ask questions to clarify information. Guide discussion and encourage elaboration with prompts such as: What can you do now that you could not do when you were younger?

Routines Flip Chart

Anchored Talk

Develop oral language

Have children turn to pages 44–45 in their Student Edition. Read the title and look at the photos. Use these questions to guide discussion and create the "What do we learn as we grow and change?" concept map shown on the next page.

- One way we learn is by attempting new skills. *Attempt* means "try." What new skill is the baby in blue shorts attempting to do? (**Possible response: He is attempting to walk.**) Let's add *We learn new skills* to our map.

- Children learn different skills as they grow older. What order would you put the pictures in to show which skill children learn first, next, and so on? (**Possible response: crawl, walk, draw, ties shoes, read**) Let's add these skills to our map.

Oral Vocabulary

Let's Talk About

Read Together

Growing and Changing

● Share information about growing and changing.

● Share ideas about what we learn as we grow and change.

READING STREET ONLINE
CONCEPT TALK VIDEO
www.ReadingStreet.com

Objectives
● Listen closely to speakers and ask questions to help you better understand the topic. ● Share information and ideas about the topic. Speak at the correct pace.

You've learned **150** Amazing Words so far this year!

44   45

Student Edition pp. 44–45

Connect to reading

Explain that this week, children will read about how a duck grows and changes, and what her family comes to understand about her.

Let's add We understand ourselves and others better to our map.

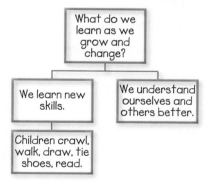

What do we learn as we grow and change?

We learn new skills.

We understand ourselves and others better.

Children crawl, walk, draw, tie shoes, read.

ELL **Preteach Concepts** Use the Day 1 instruction on ELL Poster 14 to assess and build background knowledge, develop concepts, and build oral vocabulary.

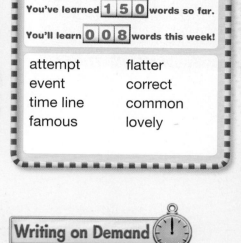

Amazing Words

You've learned **1 5 0** words so far.

You'll learn **0 0 8** words this week!

attempt	flatter
event	correct
time line	common
famous	lovely

Writing on Demand

Develop Writing Fluency

Ask children to write about what they know about how we grow and change. Have them write for two or three minutes. Children should write as much as they can. Tell them to try to do their best writing. You may want to discuss what children wrote during writing conferences.

ELL

English Language Learners

Activate Prior Knowledge Ask children to recall some important skills they have learned. Children can identify these skills in their home language and then in English, or demonstrate them using pantomime.

Language Production Have children point to each photo and complete this sentence frame: The child learns to _____.

ELL Support Additional ELL support and modified instruction are provided in the *ELL Handbook* and in the ELL Support Lessons on pp. DI•33–DI•42.

ELL Poster 14

Ruby in Her Own Time   **44–45**

Objectives
- Build oral vocabulary.
- Discuss the concept to develop oral language.
- Share information and ideas about the concept.

Oral Vocabulary
Amazing Words

Introduce Amazing Words

Display page 14 of the *Sing with Me* Big Book. Tell children they are going to sing about how people learn in different ways and at different times. Ask children to listen for the Amazing Words *attempt*, *event*, and *time line* as you sing. Sing the song again and have children join you.

 Sing with Me Big Book Audio

Sing with Me Big Book p. 14

Teach Amazing Words

Amazing Words Oral Vocabulary Routine

1 Introduce the Word Relate the word *event* to the song. The song says that learning a new thing is an important event. Supply a child-friendly definition: An *event* is something that happens. Have children say the word.

2 Demonstrate Provide examples to show meaning: Losing a tooth is an exciting *event*. The talent show was the main *event* at the school fair. The newspaper reports on interesting local and world *events*.

3 Apply Have children demonstrate their understanding: Tell about an important *event* in your life this year.

See p. OV•2 to teach *attempt* and *time line*.

Routines Flip Chart

Check understanding of Amazing Words

Have children look at the picture on page 14. Two of the children are *attempting* to learn to ride a two-wheeler. What new skill will you *attempt* to learn someday? Use *attempt* in your answer. (Possible response: I will attempt to learn to swim.)

The first time you ride a two-wheeler is an exciting *event*. What are some other exciting *events* for children? Use the word *event* in your answer. (Possible response: A birthday is an exciting event.)

How might you use a *time line* to show what a child learns to do as he or she grows? (Possible response: I could put the most important events on the time line, to show how the child changed as he or she got older.)

Apply Amazing Words

Have children demonstrate their understanding of the Amazing Words by completing these sentences orally.

The team wanted to **attempt** to _____.

_____ is an important **event** at the Olympics.

I have a **time line** for learning how to _____.

Corrective feedback

If... children have difficulty using the Amazing Words, **then...** remind them of the definitions and provide opportunities for children to use the words in sentences.

Preteach Academic Vocabulary

Write the following on the board:

- compare and contrast
- animal fantasy
- verbs that add *-s*

Have children share what they know about this week's Academic Vocabulary. Use children's responses to assess their prior knowledge. Preteach the Academic Vocabulary by providing a child-friendly description, explanation, or example that clarifies the meaning of each term. Then ask children to restate the meaning of the Academic Vocabulary in their own words.

Amazing Words

attempt	flatter
event	correct
time line	common
famous	lovely

English Language Learners

Extend Language Help children recognize that an *event* is something that happens. People use the word *event* to identify important things that happen. To understand the word *attempt*, children can think of the word *try*. Ask them to identify events in life when children attempt something new (such as going to school for the first time or learning to ride a bike).

Sentence Production Use gestures and pantomime to help children complete the sentences.

Objectives

- Segment and blend words with the consonant sounds /ng/ and /ngk/.
- ◎ Associate the consonant sounds /ng/ and /ngk/ with the spellings *ng* and *nk*.

Skills Trace

◎ **Consonant Patterns *ng, nk***
Introduce U3W2D1
Practice U3W2D3; U3W2D4
Reteach/Review U3W2D5; U3W3D4
Assess/Test Weekly Test U3W2
Benchmark Test Unit 3

KEY:
U=Unit   W=Week   D=Day

Student Edition pp. 46–47

Phonemic Awareness
Segment and Blend Phonemes

Introduce   Read together the third bulleted point on page 46 of the Student Edition. What is the alligator in the center of the picture wearing on her hand? (a ring) The last sound I hear in *ring* is /ng/. Have children look at the picture to identify other items or actions that end with /ng/. (Possible responses: swing, sling, wing, sing) In this picture, I also see a piggy *bank*. The last sound in *bank* is /ngk/. Again, have children look at the picture but this time, have them identify words or actions that end with /ngk/. (Possible responses: sink, chipmunk, tank)

Model   Listen to the sounds in the word *ring*: /r/ /i/ /ng/. There are three sounds in *ring*. Let's blend those sounds to make a word: /r/ /i/ /ng/, *ring*. Continue modeling with *bank*.

Guide practice   Guide children as they segment and blend these words from the picture: *sing, young, bring, wing, drink, pink, wink, tank,* and *honk*.

Corrective feedback   If... children make an error, model by segmenting the word,
then... have them repeat the segmenting and blending of the word.

Phonics—Teach/Model
 ## Consonant Patterns *ng, nk*

Sound-Spelling
Card 44

Sound-Spelling
Card 45

ROUTINE **Blending Strategy**

1. **Connect** Write the word *mixing*. Have children say the word. Remind them that they already know that the ending *–ing* stands for the sounds /i//ng/. Explain that today they will learn how to spell and read words that end with the letters *ng* or *nk*.

2. **Use Sound-Spelling Cards** Display Card 44. Point to *ng*. The letters *ng* stand for the sound /ng/. Have children say /ng/ several times as you point to *ng*. Display Card 45. Point to *nk*. The letters *nk* stand for the sound /ngk/. Have children say /ngk/ several times as you point to *nk*.

3. **Model** Write *sing*. In this word, the letters *ng* stand for the sound /ng/. Segment and blend *sing*; then have children blend with you: /s/ /i/ /ng/. Follow this procedure to model *junk*.

4. **Guide Practice** Continue the process in step 3. This time have children blend with you. Remind children that *ng* spells the sound /ng/ and *nk* spells the sound /ngk/.

king	lung	sank	ring	drank	swing
tank	bunk	wink	sang	bring	blank

5. **Review** What do you know about reading these words? (The letters *ng* spell the sound /ng/; the letters *nk* spell the sound /ngk/.)

Routines Flip Chart

Differentiated Instruction

SI Strategic Intervention

Blend *nk* Words If children have a tendency to weaken or drop the /n/ in the final blend *nk*, pronounce and then have children repeat words such as *skunk, thank,* and *pink.*

Vocabulary Support

You may wish to explain the meaning of these words.

lung the part of your body that holds the air you breathe

bunk a narrow bed, often stacked one above another

English Language Learners

Pronounce /ng/ Speakers of Cantonese, Khmer, and Korean will be familiar with /ng/. Other English learners may need to practice pronouncing words such as *rang, king,* and *sung.*

Pronounce /ngk/ In Spanish, words often end in vowels, and they don't end with two consonants. As a result, speakers of Spanish may delete or substitute final consonant sounds. Be sure to give them plenty of practice pronouncing words with final *nk*, such as *sink, junk,* and *drank.*

Phonics—Build Fluency
🎯 Consonant Patterns *ng, nk*

Model

Envision It!

Have children turn to page 48 in their Student Edition. Look at the pictures on this page. I see a picture of a *swing* and a picture of a *skunk*. When I say *swing*, I hear the sound /ng/ at the end. The /ng/ sound is spelled *ng*. When I say *skunk*, I hear the sound /ngk/ at the end. The /ngk/ sound is spelled *nk*.

Guide practice

For each word in "Words I Can Blend", ask for the sound of each letter or group of letters. Make sure that children identify the correct sound for *ng* or *nk*. Then have children blend the whole word.

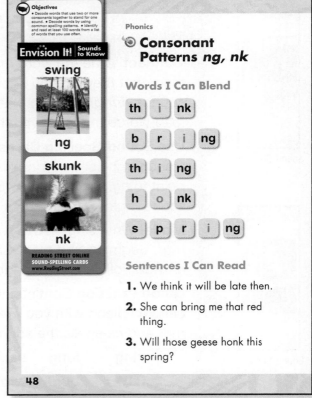

Student Edition p. 48

Corrective feedback

If... children have difficulty blending a word,

then... model blending the word, and then ask children to blend it with you.

Blend and Read

Decode words in isolation

After children can successfully segment and blend the words, point to words in random order and ask children to read them naturally.

Decode words in context

Have children read each of the sentences. Have them identify words in the sentences that have the consonant sound /ng/ or /ngk/.

Team Talk Pair children and have them take turns reading each of the sentences aloud.

On their own

Use *Reader's and Writer's Notebook* p. 329.

Reader's and Writer's Notebook p. 329

Don't Wait Until Friday

MONITOR PROGRESS | Check Word Reading Consonant Patterns *ng, nk*

Write the following words and have the class read them. Notice which words children miss during the group reading. Call on individuals to read some of the words.

king	hunk	rang	junk	wink	**Spiral Review** Row 2 reviews short vowels and initial consonant blends.
trunk	bring	drink	stung	swing	
thank	thing	think	chunk		Row 3 reviews short vowels and initial digraphs *ch* and *th*.

If... children cannot blend *ng* and *nk* words at this point,

then... use the Small-Group Time Strategic Intervention lesson, p. DI•22, to reteach /ng/ spelled *ng* and /ngk/ spelled *nk*. Continue to monitor children's progress using other instructional opportunities during the week. See the Skills Trace on pp. 46–47.

Day 1	Day 2	Day 3	Day 4	Day 5
Check Word Reading	Check Word Reading	Check High-Frequency Words/Retelling	Check Fluency	Check Oral Vocabulary

Success Predictor

Differentiated Instruction

A Advanced

Extend Blending Provide children who can segment and blend all the words correctly with more challenging words such as: *mustang* and *chipmunk*.

Spelling Patterns

ng The sound /ng/ is spelled *ng*.

nk The sound /ngk/ is spelled *nk*.

ELL

English Language Learners

Produce Final /ng/, /ngk/ For children who speak Greek, Italian, Spanish, and some other languages, producing final consonant sounds may be challenging. Demonstrate how to pronounce words with final /ng/ and /ngk/. Have children practice the words. Then have them practice blending onsets and rimes.

Word Reading

Success Predictor

Decodable Practice Reader 14A
Consonant Patterns *ng, nk*

Decode words in isolation

Have children turn to page 169. Have children decode each word.

Review High-frequency words

Review the previously taught words *a*, *could*, *I*, *from*, *into*, *now*, *the*, and *to*. Have children read each word as you point to it on the Word Wall.

Preview Decodable Reader

Have children decode the title and preview the story. Tell them they will read words with consonant patterns *ng* and *nk*.

Decode words in context

Pair children for reading and listen as they decode. One child begins. Children read the entire story, switching readers after each page. Partners reread the story. This time the other child begins.

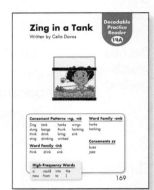

Decodable Practice Reader 14A

Zing is in a tank.
He honks with his wings.
Buzz, buzz.

170

I will not let Zing go!
He will be mad at us.
We could get stung.

171

Decodable Practice Reader 14A

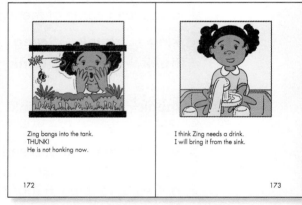

Zing bangs into the tank.
THUNK!
He is not honking now.

172

I think Zing needs a drink.
I will bring it from the sink.

173

I will let Zing go.
Will he try to sting me?

174

Zing is flying to the dish.
He is drinking.

175

Buzz, buzz.
Zing honks jazz with his wings.
He is a happy bee.
I think he winked at me.

176

Corrective feedback

If... children have difficulty decoding a word,
then... refer them to the Sound-Spelling Cards to identify the sounds in the word. Then prompt them to blend the word.

- What is the new word?
- Is the new word a word you know?
- Does it make sense in the story?

Check decoding and comprehension

Have children retell the story to include characters, setting, and events. Then have children find words with *ng* and *nk* in the story and tell if the word has the /ng/ or the /ngk/ sound. Explain that some story words with these letters will have an *–s*, *–ing*, or *–ed* ending. Children could supply *Zing, honks, wings, stung, bangs, honking, bring, sting, tank, thunk, think, drink, sink, drinking,* and *winked*.

Reread for Fluency

Have children reread Decodable Practice Reader 14A to develop automaticity decoding words with consonant patterns *ng* and *nk*.

 Oral Rereading

1 **Read** Have children read the entire book orally.

2 **Reread** To achieve optimal fluency, children should reread the text three or four times.

3 **Corrective Feedback** Listen as children read. Provide corrective feedback regarding their fluency and decoding.

Routines Flip Chart

Professional Development

Words with *ng* The sound /ng/ spelled *ng* is never heard at the beginning of a word. It always follows a vowel.

English Language Learners
Beginning Before children read, lead them on a picture walk through the story. Point out and pronounce the *ng* and *nk* words that are pictured. Then write a pictured word and have children pronounce it and find its picture.

Intermediate Before reading, help children pronounce *ng* and *nk* words in the story title, *Zing in a Tank*. Then have them use the words *Zing* and *Tank* to make a prediction about what the story will be about.

Advanced/Advanced High After reading, have children find *ng* and *nk* words and use them to tell what might happen next, now that Zing is out of the tank.

DAY 1 Get Ready to Read

Objectives
- Spell words with the sounds /ng/ and /ngk/.
- Read high-frequency words.

Spelling Pretest
Consonant Patterns *ng, nk*

Dictate spelling words

Dictate the spelling words and read the sentences. Have children write the words. If needed, segment the words for children, clarify the pronunciations, and give meanings of words. Have children check their pretests and correct misspelled words.

1. **bring**   I will **bring** a fruit salad to the picnic.

2. **trunk**   You can find bark on a tree **trunk**.

3. **pink**   Mix red and white paint to get **pink** paint.

4. **bank**   Save your money in a piggy **bank**.

5. **sang**   We **sang** a song about learning.

6. **wing***   The mother bird lifted her **wing**.

7. **rink**   Dad and I skate at the ice **rink**.

8. **blank**   Write on a clean, **blank** sheet of paper.

9. **rang**   The bell **rang** at the end of the school day.

10. **sunk**   The ship had **sunk** to the bottom of the ocean.

* Words marked with asterisks come from the selection *Ruby in Her Own Time*.

On their own

Use Let's Practice It! p. 134 on the *Teacher Resource DVD-ROM*.

Let's Practice It! TR DVD•134

Small Group Time

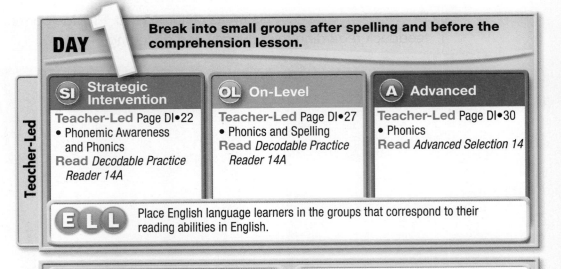

DAY 1   Break into small groups after spelling and before the comprehension lesson.

Teacher-Led	SI Strategic Intervention	OL On-Level	A Advanced
	Teacher-Led Page DI•22 • Phonemic Awareness and Phonics **Read** *Decodable Practice Reader 14A*	**Teacher-Led** Page DI•27 • Phonics and Spelling **Read** *Decodable Practice Reader 14A*	**Teacher-Led** Page DI•30 • Phonics **Read** *Advanced Selection 14*

ELL Place English language learners in the groups that correspond to their reading abilities in English.

Practice Stations	**Independent Activities**
• Listen Up • Word Work	• Read independently/Reading Log on *Reader's and Writer's Notebook* p. RR4 • Concept Talk Video

High-Frequency Words

Introduce

 ROUTINE **Nondecodable Words**

1 **Say and Spell** Look at p. 49. Some words we have to learn by remembering the letters rather than saying the sounds. We will say and spell the words to help learn them. **Point to the first word.** This word is *ever*. The letters in *ever* are e-v-e-r, *ever*. Have children say and spell each word, first with you, and then without you.

2 **Identify Familiar Letter-Sounds** Point to the first letter in *ever*. This letter makes the same sound you hear at the beginning of *elephant*. What is this letter and what is its sound? (e, /e/)

3 **Demonstrate Meaning** Tell me a sentence using the word *ever*. Repeat this routine with the other Words I Can Read.

Routines Flip Chart

Read words in isolation
Have children read the words on p. 49 aloud. Add the words to the Word Wall.

Read words in context
Have children read the sentences aloud. Have them identify this week's High-Frequency Words in the sentences.

On their own
Use *Reader's and Writer's Notebook* p. 330.

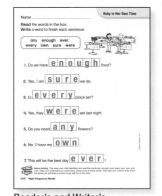

Reader's and Writer's Notebook, p. 330

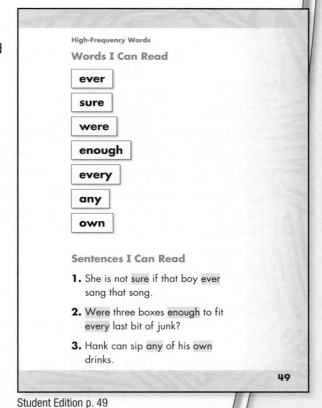

Student Edition p. 49

Differentiated Instruction

SI **Strategic Intervention**
Check Spelling Have children choose the correct spelling of each word from three random spellings.

A **Advanced**
Extend Spelling Have children learn to spell these more difficult words with *ng* and *nk* and write them in original sentences: *spring, strung, shrink, wrong, hanger, kingdom.*

Phonics/Spelling Generalization

Consonant Patterns *ng, nk* Each spelling word ends in either *ng* or *nk*, which have the /ng/ and /ngk/ sound, respectively.

ELL

English Language Learners
Survival Vocabulary Have children use the word *every* to talk about school. Children might say, *We read **every** morning.*

Objectives
◎ Compare and contrast within text.

Skills Trace

◎ **Compare and Contrast**

Introduce U2W6D1; U3W2D1; U5W3D1

Practice U2W6D2; U2W6D3; U2W6D4; U3W2D2; U3W2D3; U3W2D4; U5W3D2; U5W3D3; U5W3D4

Reteach/Review U2W6D5; U3W2D5; U3W3D2; U3W6D2; U4W4D2; U5W3D5; U5W4D2

Assess/Test Weekly Tests U2W6; U3W2; U5W3

Benchmark Tests U3

KEY:
U=Unit   W=Week   D=Day

Listening Comprehension
◎ Compare and Contrast

Introduce

When we **compare** things in a story, we look for ways in which they are alike. When we **contrast** things in a story, we look for ways in which they are different.

Compare and Contrast

Student Edition EI•3

Envision It!

Have children turn to p. EI•3 in their Student Edition. This picture shows a boy holding two things. Let's compare and contrast them. **Discuss these questions using the pictures:**

• What does the boy have in his hands? (two hats)

• How are the hats the same? (They both have some blue.)

• How are they different? (One has red on it; the other does not.)

Model

Today we will read a story about a little chick named Cheep. She is learning how to live on the farm. **Read "Something Else to Do." Use Graphic Organizer 28 to model how to compare and contrast.**

 Think Aloud When I read, I can compare and contrast the different animals on the farm. I'll label one circle *Ducks* and the other *Chickens*. What is the same about ducks and chickens? They are both birds. I'll put *birds* in the middle to show that both ducks and chickens are birds. I use evidence from the text to support my understanding. The text says *There some other birds were quacking happily.* What is different about ducks and chickens? Ducks can swim, but chickens cannot. I'll put *can swim* in the circle labeled *Ducks* and *cannot swim* in the circle labeled *Chickens*. What evidence from the text tells us this?

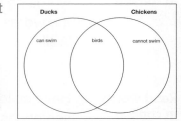

Graphic Organizer Flip Chart 28

Guide practice

Let's compare and contrast cats and chickens. **Label one circle *Cats* and the other *Chickens*. What is the same about cats and chickens? Look in the text for evidence. (They are both animals.)** Let's put *animals* in the middle. What is different about the cats and chickens? (Cats chase mice; chickens do not.) Let's put *chase mice* in the *Cats* circle, and *do not chase mice* in the *Chickens* circle.

On their own

Use *Reader's and Writer's Notebook*, p. 331.

Reader's and Writer's Notebook, p. 331

Read Aloud

Something Else to Do

Mother Hen was very proud when her eggs hatched. It was quite a happy event. She kissed each one of her darling little chicks and told them all about how to live on the farm.

"You can find the most tasty bugs in the dirt over there," she said. "And the straw in the back of the barn is the best place for naps."

The littlest chick, Cheep, didn't think this sounded like much fun.

"I don't want to eat bugs and sleep in the barn," she said. "I'll find something else to do!"

And so she hopped around the farm until she came to the pond. There some other birds were quacking happily as they flew through the air and splashed into the water.

"I can do that too!" Cheep cried and jumped into the water. She sank and sank until a duck fished her out.

"Little chicks shouldn't attempt to swim," the duck said kindly. "That's what ducks do!" She put Cheep gently down on the ground.

"Okay," Cheep said. "I'll find something else to do!"

And so she hopped around the farm until she came to a field. There some other animals purred happily as they ran over the grass and chased the field mice.

"I can do that too!" Cheep cried and ran into the field. She ran and ran after the mice until she realized that the cats were chasing her! Just as a cat was about to catch her, a mouse pulled her behind a rock to hide.

"Little chicks shouldn't attempt to chase mice," the mouse whispered kindly. "That's what cats do!" He pointed out the way back to the farmyard.

"Okay," Cheep said. "I'll find something else to do!"

And so she hopped back to the farm. There the chickens were pecking at the dirt for bugs.

"I can do that too!" Cheep cried, and she ate and ate.

"Hmm," she said once she was full. "I guess being a little chick isn't so bad after all." And she hopped off to the barn to take a nap.

Academic Language

animal fantasy a story in which animals talk and act like humans

DAY 1 Language Arts

20–25 min.

Objectives

- Use present tense verbs with correct subject-verb agreement.
- Use inflectional endings to spell present tense verbs correctly.
- Understand and recognize the features of comments about a story.

MINI-LESSON

5 Day Planner
Guide to Mini-Lessons

DAY **1**	Read Like a Writer
DAY **2**	Include Feelings
DAY **3**	Voice
DAY **4**	Revising Strategy: Adding a Sentence
DAY **5**	Proofread for Verbs That Add -s

Conventions
Verbs That Add -s

Model   Explain that a **verb** is the word in a sentence that shows the action. *Hops, climbs,* and *kicks* are verbs. A verb in the **present tense** means the action is happening now.

Display Grammar Transparency 14. Read the definition aloud. Model identifying the verb in each example. Then read the directions and model number 1.

- I see one baby. The baby is doing something now.
- One person is doing something now, so the verb should have *s* at the end. I will underline the verb *crawls.* The baby crawls across the floor.

Grammar Transparency 14
TR DVD

Guide practice   Continue with items 2–6, having children identify the present tense form of the verb in each sentence.

Connect to oral language   Have the class complete these sentence frames orally using the present tense forms of the verbs *run* and *jump.*

> He _____.
>
> She _____.
>
> The dog _____.

On their own   **Team Talk** Pair children and have them talk about things they like to do. Then have them identify the present tense form of the verbs they use.

Writing—Comments About a Story
Introduce

Write Guy
Jeff Anderson

Writers Write!

Young writers succeed in classrooms where they write. Simple, isn't it? Are you trying to meet some mandate or standard with such blinders on that you're forgetting daily writing? Children need to read every day and to write every day. Teachers do not need to read and assess everything that children write.

MINI-LESSON

Read Like a Writer

■ **Introduce** This week you will write comments about a story. Comments about a story talk about a certain part of a story and tell how you feel about the story.

Prompt	Look at the pictures in *Ruby in Her Own Time*. Think about what Ruby does. Write sentences to tell two things Ruby does that you like.
Trait	Voice
Mode	Expository

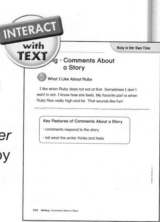

INTERACT with TEXT

Reader's and Writer's Notebook p. 332

■ **Examine Model Text** Let's listen to comments about a story. Track the print as you read aloud "What I Like About Ruby" on *Reader's and Writer's Notebook* p. 332. Have children follow along.

■ **Key Features** What are the two things this writer says about Ruby? (She doesn't eat at first. She flies really high and far.) Help children find and circle the ideas. Ask if the writer gives reasons for liking these things. (yes) Help children underline the reasons. (*I know how she feels. That sounds like fun!*)

These comments respond directly to the story. The writer picks two things Ruby does in the story to talk about.

The writer tells how she feels about Ruby. She uses words that share her feelings, such as *like, favorite,* and *fun*.

Academic Vocabulary

action verb a word that shows action

Daily Fix-It

1. i sang on the way to the rinc.
   <u>I</u> sang on the way to the <u>rink</u>.
2. Put the blanck book in the trunk
   Put the <u>blank</u> book in the trunk<u>.</u>

Discuss the Daily Fix-It corrections with children. Review sentence capitalization, the *k* spelling of the hard *k* sound, and sentence punctuation.

English Language Learners
Options for Conventions Support To provide children with practice on verbs that add *-s,* use the modified grammar lessons in the *ELL Handbook*.

DAY 1 Language Arts

Objectives

- Understand and recognize the features of comments about a story.
- Develop an understanding of voice and preference in comments about a story.
- Identify a topic connected to this week's concept.
- Narrow the focus of the topic by formulating inquiry questions related to the topic.
- Explore growing and changing.

Writing—Comments About a Story
Introduce, continued

Review key features Review key features of comments about a story with children. You may want to post these key features in the classroom to allow children to refer to them as they work on their comments.

> **Key Features of Comments About a Story**
>
> - comments respond to the story
> - tell what the writer thinks or feels

Connect to familiar texts Use examples from book reviews found in children's literary magazines. In book reviews, writers share comments about a story. They tell how they feel about a story. They use words that show how they feel.

Look ahead Tell children that tomorrow they will plan their own comments about a story.

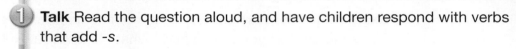

ROUTINE **Quick Write for Fluency** **Team Talk**

1. **Talk** Read the question aloud, and have children respond with verbs that add -s.

   What does Ruby do?

2. **Write** Have children write short sentences to answer the question. Make sure their sentences include a subject and a verb that adds -s.

3. **Share** Partners can read their answers to one another.

Routines Flip Chart

Research and Inquiry
Identify and Focus Topic

Teach

Display and review the concept map about this week's question: *What do we learn as we grow and change?* What are some things you have learned that you would like to tell people about? Ask children to share their ideas. Point out that they can learn facts and information as well as how to do things.

Model

Think Aloud I have learned lots of things as I have grown! When I was in high school, I learned how to surf. Surfing is certainly a topic I could tell someone about. I also have learned lots of facts about the ocean. Maybe I could tell one of those facts. For example, I learned that there are mountains in the ocean. That is an interesting fact I could tell another person.

Guide practice

Give children time to think of topics they have learned about as they have grown. Record children's suggestions in a list.

Wrap Up Your Day

✓ **Phonics: Consonant Patterns *ng, nk*** Write *sing* and ask children which letters in *sing* stand for the /ng/ sound. (*ng*) Write *think* and ask children which letters stand for the /ngk/ sound. (*nk*)

✓ **Spelling: Words with *ng, nk*** Have children name the spelling for each sound in *rang*. Write the spelling as children write the letters in the air. Continue with *bank, bring,* and *trunk.*

✓ **Build Concepts** Ask children to recall what happened in the Read Aloud "Something Else to Do." What do you think Cheep learned? (Possible response: She learned that just being a little chick is not so bad after all.)

✓ **Homework** Send home this week's Family Times Newsletter from Let's Practice It! pp. 129–130 on the *Teacher Resource DVD-ROM.*

Let's Practice It!
TR DVD•129–130

Preview DAY 2

Tell children that tomorrow they will read about a family of ducklings who learn how to do many new things as they grow up.

Objectives

- Discuss the concept to develop oral vocabulary.
- Build oral vocabulary.

Today at a Glance

Oral Vocabulary
famous, flatter

Phonological Awarenes
Segment and Blend Phonemes

Phonics and Spelling
◉ Consonant Patterns *ng, nk sh, th, ch*
◉ Compound Words

Fluency
Paired Reading

High-Frequency Words

Story Words
beautiful, father, feather, flew, mother, precious, night, howling

Comprehension
◉ Compare and Contrast
◉ Inferring

Vocabulary
Synonyms

Literary Text
Story Elements

Conventions
Verbs That Add *-s*

Writing
Comments About a Story

Handwriting
Letter *Kk*/Letter Slant

Research and Inquiry
Research Skill: Glossary

Concept Talk

 Question of the Week
What do we learn as we grow and change?

Build concepts

To reinforce concepts and to focus children's attention, have children sing "On Our Own Time Line" from the *Sing with Me* Big Book. What skills do the children in the song learn? (reading, writing, riding a bike)

🔘 Sing with Me Big Book Audio

Introduce Amazing Words

Display the Big Book, *Mr. George Baker*. Read the title and identify the author. Explain that in the story, the author uses the words *famous* and *flatter*. Have children listen as you read the story to find out who is *famous* and what it means to *flatter* someone.

Use the Oral Vocabulary routine on the next page to teach the words *famous* and *flatter*.

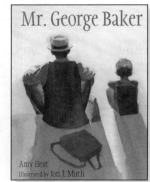

Mr. George Baker

Amy Hest
Illustrated by Jon J. Muth

Big Book

ELL **Reinforce Vocabulary** Use the Day 2 instruction on ELL Poster 14 to reinforce the meanings of high-frequency words.

ELL Poster 14

Oral Vocabulary
Amazing Words

Teach Amazing Words

 **Oral Vocabulary Routine**

① **Introduce the Word** Relate the word *famous* to the book. Mr. George Baker is a *famous* drummer. Supply a child-friendly definition. A *famous* person is someone who is well known. Have children say the word.

② **Demonstrate** Provide examples to show meaning. Everyone recognized the *famous* baseball player. The author is *famous* for her books about horses.

③ **Apply** Have children demonstrate their understanding. Name some people who are *famous*. Tell why they are *famous*.

See p. OV•2 to teach *flatter*.

Routines Flip Chart

Add to the concept map

Anchored Talk

Discuss what we learn as we grow and change and how others may learn differently than we learn.

- What does "On Our Own Time Line" tell us about how different people learn the same skill? (People learn in different ways.) Let's add *We learn in different ways* to our map.

- What does the song mean when it says that we each learn on our own time line? (People learn the same skill at different times.) Let's add *We learn at different times* to our map.

- In yesterday's Read Aloud "Something Else to Do," Cheep could not learn every skill she attempted. What could she not do? (swim, catch mice) Let's add *We aren't able to do some things* to our map.

 Amazing Words

attempt	flatter
event	correct
time line	common
famous	lovely

Differentiated Instruction

Ⓐ **Advanced**
Using Amazing Words
Encourage children who have demonstrated mastery of the Amazing Words to revisit *Mr. George Baker* and give examples of things they would say to flatter the different characters.

English Language Learners
Physical Response Teach the words *famous* and *flatter* by acting them out and having children join you. To reinforce understanding, look for opportunities to recycle language in the day's lessons. For example, in social studies lessons, have children recall famous people from history.

Phonological Awareness
Segment and Blend Phonemes

Model isolating sounds

Have children look at the picture on pages 46–47 in their Student Edition. I see *sunflowers* growing outside the window. *Sunflower* is a compound word that is made from the two shorter words, *sun* and *flower*. I hear three sounds in the word *sun*. The first sound I hear is /s/. The second sound is /u/. The last sound is /n/.

Student Edition pp. 46–47

Model segmenting and blending

Listen to the sounds in the word *flower*: /f/ /l/ /ou/ /ėr/. Let's blend those sounds to make a word: /f/ /l/ /ou/ /ėr/. Continue modeling with *dragon, fly,* and *dragonfly.*

Guide practice

Guide children as they segment and blend these words from the picture: *strawberries, watermelon, shoelace, blue, bluebird,* and *blueberry.*

Corrective feedback

If... children make an error,
then... model by segmenting the word, and have them repeat the segmenting and blending of the word.

On their own

Have children segment and blend the following compound words.

/b/ /e/ /d/ /t/ /ī/ /m/ **bedtime**	/s/ /a/ /n/ /d/ /b/ /o/ /ks/ **sandbox**
/p/ /a/ /n/ /k/ /ā/ /k/ **pancake**	/b/ /ā/ /s/ /b/ /ô/ /l/ **baseball**
/s/ /u/ /n/ /r/ /ī/ /z/ **sunrise**	/d/ /r/ /ī/ /v/ /w/ /ā/ **driveway**

After children segment and blend, have them say each part of the compound words. For example, for *bedtime* they would say *bed* and *time.*

Phonics—Teach/Model
↻ Compound Words

compound
word

Sound-Spelling
Card 108

Routines Flip Chart

ROUTINE **Word Parts Strategy**

① **Connect** Write the words *bed* and *time*, and have children say them. Remind children that they already know how to read words like these. Today you will learn to read long words that are made from two shorter words like *bed* and *time*.

② **Model** Write *bedtime*. *Bedtime* is a compound word. A compound word is made from two or more shorter words. The meaning of the compound word often comes from the meanings of the smaller words. *Bedtime* means "the time to go to bed."

Segment and blend *bedtime*. Explain that you read the two shorter words together as one longer compound word.

③ **Guide Practice** Have children identify the two shorter words in each of these compound words. Then have them read the compound words with you. Discuss the meaning of each word.

sidewalk	flagpole	bathtub	beehive
lipstick	sandbox	weekend	sunblock

④ **Review** What do you know about reading these words? (These compound words are made of two smaller words. We read the two words together to say the compound word.)

Differentiated Instruction

Ⓐ **Advanced**

Read Compound Words Have children divide the following compound words into their smaller words and use each in a sentence: *afternoon, scarecrow, thunderstorm, peppermint, understand, inchworm, tablecloth, sweatshirt, seashore,* and *sailboat.*

Vocabulary Support

You may wish to explain the meanings of some of the shorter words that appear in the compound words.

pole a long, slender, usually round piece of wood or metal

tub a large, open container that holds water

English Language Learners
Practice Compound Words
Display and read the following words, and have children repeat them: *sandbox, pancake, sunrise,* and *everything.* Have children find the short words in each one. Discuss the meaning of each compound word by looking at the shorter words. Point out that *pancake* means a flat cake that is cooked in a pan.

Objectives
- ◎ Blend and read compound words.
- • Decode words in context and in isolation.

Check Word Reading
SUCCESS PREDICTOR

Phonics—Build Fluency
Compound Words

Model

Envision It!

Have children turn to page 50 in their Student Edition. Look at the picture on this page. I see a picture of a football. *Football* is a compound word. A compound word is a longer word made from two or more shorter words. To read a compound word, I blend and read the two shorter words together: *foot, ball, football*. We can also use the words *foot* and *ball* to give us clues about the compound word *football*. In football, the foot is sometimes used to move the ball across the field. The words *foot* and *ball* make up the compound word *football*.

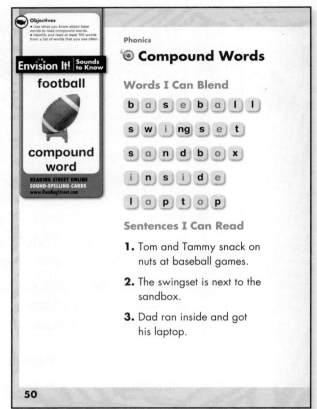

Student Edition p. 50

Guide practice

For each word in "Words I Can Blend," ask for the sound of each smaller word within the compound word. Make sure children pronounce each part of the compound word correctly. Then guide children in explaining how the two base words in each compound word give clues to the meaning of the compound word.

Corrective feedback

If... children have difficulty blending a word,
then... model blending the word, and ask children to blend it with you.

Blend and Read

Decode words in isolation

After children can successfully segment and blend the words, ask them to read the words naturally.

Decode words in context

Have children read each of the sentences. Have them identify compound words in the sentences.

Team Talk Pair children and have them take turns reading each of the sentences aloud.

On their own

Use *Reader's and Writer's Notebook* p. 333.

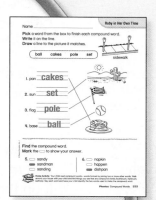

Reader's and Writer's
Notebook p. 333

Don't Wait Until Friday

MONITOR PROGRESS | Check Word Reading | Compound Words

Write the following words and have the class read them. Notice which children miss words during the group reading. Call on those individuals to read some of the words.

pigpen	quicksand	outside	treetops	gumball	**Spiral Review** Row 2 reviews high-frequency and selection words.
sunset	sunlight	into	inside	nowhere	
basketball	paperback	everything	jellyfish	understand	Row 3 reviews two-syllable words as part of compounds.

If... children cannot blend compound words,

then... use the Small Group Time Strategic Intervention lesson, p. DI•23, to reteach compound words. Continue to monitor children's progress using other instructional opportunities during the week. See the Skills Trace on p. 50c.

Day 1	Day 2	Day 3	Day 4	Day 5
Check Word Reading	Check Word Reading	Check High-Frequency Words/ Retelling	Check Fluency	Check Oral Vocabulary

Success Predictor

Differentiated Instruction

(A) Advanced

Listing Compound Words Give children a common word part, such as *sun*, and instruct them to come up with as many other word parts as they can that will form compound words. Guide them to write and pronounce each new compound word.

Spelling Patterns

Compound A compound is a word made up of two or more shorter words.

English Language Learners
Recognize Compound Words Children who speak languages in which words mostly consist of only one syllable, such as Cantonese, Hmong, and Vietnamese, may need extra practice reading, writing, and saying compound words.

Word Reading

Success Predictor

Objectives
- Apply knowledge of sound-spellings to decode unknown words when reading.
- Decode words in context and isolation.
- Practice fluency with oral rereading.

Decodable Practice Reader 14B
⟲ Compound Words

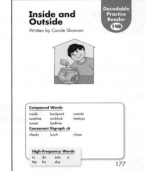

Decodable Practice Reader 14B

Decode words in isolation

Have children turn to page 177. Have children decode each word.

Review High-frequency words

Review the previously taught words *day, do, eats, for,* and *to.* Have children read each word as you point to it on the Word Wall.

Preview

Have children decode the title and preview the story. Tell them they will read compound words.

Decode words in context

Pair children for reading and listen as they decode. One child begins. Children read the entire story, switching readers after each page.

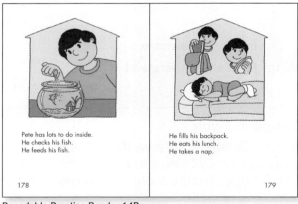

Pete has lots to do inside.
He checks his fish.
He feeds his fish.

178

He fills his backpack.
He eats his lunch.
He takes a nap.

179

Pete can go outside.
Pete has lots to do
in the nice sunshine.

180

Pete likes to jump.
He can jump rope.
He jumps and jumps.

181

Decodable Practice Reader 14B

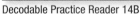
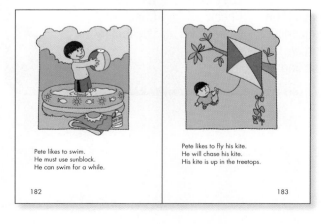

Pete likes to swim.
He must use sunblock.
He can swim for a while.

182

Pete likes to fly his kite.
He will chase his kite.
His kite is up in the treetops.

183

At sunset, Pete must go home.
It is bedtime.
Pete has had a big day!

184

Corrective feedback

If... children have difficulty decoding a word, **then...** refer them to the Sound-Spelling Cards to identify the sounds in the word. Then prompt them to blend the word.

- What is the new word?
- Is the new word a word you know?
- Does it make sense in the story?

Check decoding and comprehension

Have children retell the story to include characters, setting, and events. Then have children find compound words in the story. Children should supply *inside, backpack, outside, sunshine, sunblock, treetops, sunset,* and *bedtime*. Have children discuss how the two base words give clues to the meaning of the compound word they form.

Reread for Fluency

Have children reread Decodable Practice Reader 14B to develop automaticity decoding compound words.

> ## ROUTINE **Paired Reading**
>
> 1. **Reread** To achieve optimal fluency, have partners reread the text three or four times.
> 2. **Corrective Feedback** Listen as children read. Provide corrective feedback regarding their fluency and decoding.

Routines Flip Chart

Differentiated Instruction

 Strategic Intervention

Retelling If children have difficulty identifying the setting, ask them to find some words from the story that tell where things happened.

ELL

English Language Learners

Beginning Show children several compound words in *Inside and Outside*, and explain the meanings of the individual words that make up each compound. For example, say, "It is a pack for your back. It is a backpack."

Intermediate Have children read the sentences with compound words, and then repeat them, substituting the two individual words that make up each compound word—for example, "It is bedtime." / "It is time to go to bed."

Advanced/Advanced High Have children find compound words in *Inside and Outside* and then use each one in a sentence.

Objectives

- Apply knowledge of letter-sound correspondences and consonant digraphs to decode words in context and in isolation.
- Spell words with the consonant digraphs *ng* and *nk*.

Phonics Review

Consonant Patterns *ng, nk, sh, th, ch*

Review Sound-spellings

Review the following consonant patterns: the *ng* spelling for /ng/, the *nk* spelling for /ngk/, the *sh* spelling for /sh/, the *th* spelling for /th/ and /ŦH/, and the *ch* spelling for /ch/. Use Sound-Spelling Cards 34, 44, 45, 47, 50 and 51.

Decode words in isolation

Display these words. Have the class blend the words. Then point to the words in random order and ask children to decode them quickly.

wing	sink	stung	chunk
bath	fish	such	math
crash	thank	fresh	which

Corrective feedback

Model blending decodable words and then ask children to blend them with you.

Decode words in context

Display these sentences. Have the class read the sentences.

Team Talk Have pairs take turns reading the sentences naturally.

Sing a **song** with me.

The new **king** is **rich**.

Take this **junk** to the **trash** can.

Spelling
Consonant Patterns *ng, nk*

Guide practice

Tell children that you will segment the sounds in each spelling word. They should repeat the sounds in each word as they write the word. Check the spelling of each word before saying the next word.

1. /r/ /a/ /ng/ **rang**
2. /b/ /a/ /ngk/ **bank**
3. /t/ /r/ /u/ /ngk/ **trunk**
4. /b/ /r/ /i/ /ng/ **bring**
5. /s/ /u/ /ngk/ **sunk**

6. /b/ /l/ /a/ /ngk/ **blank**
7. /s/ /a/ /ng/ **sang**
8. /r/ /i/ /ngk/ **rink**
9. /p/ /i/ /ngk/ **pink**
10. /w/ /i/ /ng/ **wing**

On their own

Use *Reader's and Writer's Notebook* p. 334.

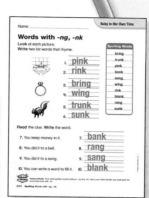

Reader's and Writer's Notebook p. 334

Small Group Time

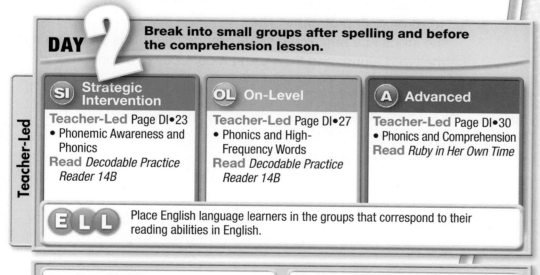

DAY 2 Break into small groups after spelling and before the comprehension lesson.

Teacher-Led

(SI) Strategic Intervention
Teacher-Led Page DI•23
• Phonemic Awareness and Phonics
Read *Decodable Practice Reader 14B*

(OL) On-Level
Teacher-Led Page DI•27
• Phonics and High-Frequency Words
Read *Decodable Practice Reader 14B*

(A) Advanced
Teacher-Led Page DI•30
• Phonics and Comprehension
Read *Ruby in Her Own Time*

ELL Place English language learners in the groups that correspond to their reading abilities in English.

Practice Stations
• Listen Up
• Word Work

Independent Activities
• Read independently/Reading Log on *Reader's and Writer's Notebook* p. RR4
• AudioText of Main Selection

Objectives
- Learn story words: *beautiful, father, feather, flew, mother, precious, night, howling.*
- Review high-frequency words.
- Identify synonyms.

High-Frequency Words
Build Fluency

Read words in isolation

Remind children that there are some words we learn by remembering the letters, rather than by saying the sounds. Then have them read each of the highlighted high-frequency words aloud.

Read words in context

Chorally read the "I Can Read!" passage along with the children. Then have them read the passage aloud to themselves. When they are finished, ask children to reread the high-frequency words.

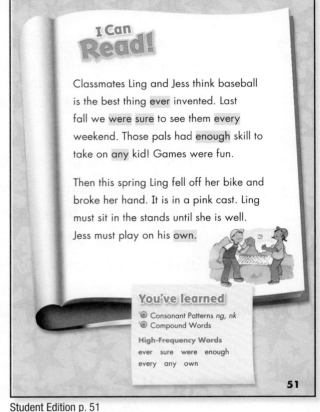

I Can Read!

Classmates Ling and Jess think baseball is the best thing ever invented. Last fall we were sure to see them every weekend. Those pals had enough skill to take on any kid! Games were fun.

Then this spring Ling fell off her bike and broke her hand. It is in a pink cast. Ling must sit in the stands until she is well. Jess must play on his own.

You've learned
- Consonant Patterns *ng, nk*
- Compound Words

High-Frequency Words
ever sure were enough
every any own

51

Student Edition p. 51

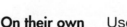 **Team Talk** Write each word on a strip of paper. Put the strips in a bag. Have small groups take turns choosing a strip, reading the word aloud, and then using it correctly in a sentence.

On their own

Use Let's Practice It! p. 133 on the *Teacher Resource DVD-ROM.*

Let's Practice It! TR DVD●133

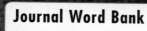
Story Words
Ruby in Her Own Time

Introduce story words

Use Vocabulary Transparency 14 to introduce this week's story words. Read each sentence as you track the print. Frame each underlined word and explain its meaning.

mother	a woman who has a child or children
precious	having great value
feather	one of the light, soft things that cover a bird's body
howling	making a loud, whining sound
father	a man who has a child or children
flew	took off and moved in the air
night	time of day between sunset and sunrise
beautiful	very pretty to see or hear

A Bird Family

1. A mother bird sits on her nest.
2. She keeps her precious eggs safe.
3. When the baby birds hatch, they have no feathers.
4. They will be howling for food.
5. Where is the father bird?
6. He flew off to get food.
7. The father bird will be back by night.
8. The baby birds will grow to be big beautiful birds.

Vocabulary Transparency 14 TR DVD

Have children read each sentence with you.

Vocabulary
Synonyms

Model synonyms

Explain that **synonyms** are words that have nearly the same meanings. Draw a two-column chart or display Graphic Organizer 4. List these words in the left column: *mother, father,* and *beautiful*. Explain that each of these words has a synonym.

Word	Synonym
mother father beautiful	mom

Graphic Organizer 4

Think Aloud I see the word *mother*. What other words have the same meaning? I call my mother *mom*. I'll write that *mom* is a synonym for *mother*.

Guide practice

Have a volunteer give the synonym for *father* and write it in the right column (dad). Repeat the procedure for *beautiful* (pretty).

On their own Have children choose a pair of synonyms, draw a picture that shows their shared meaning, and label the picture with both synonyms.

Ruby in Her Own Time **52a**

Differentiated Instruction

 Strategic Intervention

Similar Words If children have trouble differentiating between *feather* and *father*, have them make flash cards for each and practice pronouncing each word and saying each definition.

Academic Vocabulary

synonym a word that has the same or nearly the same meaning as another word

English Language Learners
Multilingual Vocabulary Lists
Children can apply knowledge of their home language to acquire new English vocabulary by using the *Multilingual Vocabulary List* (*ELL Handbook* pp. 465–476).

Objectives

- Build background about the life of a duck.
- Preview and predict.
- Use key structure and elements of animal fantasy to improve understanding of text.
- Set a purpose for reading text.

Build Background
Ruby in Her Own Time

Background Building Audio

Have children listen to the CD. Tell them to listen to find out how ducks grow and change over time.

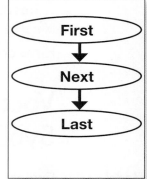 Background Building Audio

Discuss the life of a duck

 Have children turn to a partner and use these questions for discussion:

- How are adult ducks different from baby ducks? How are they the same?
- What happens when ducks are ready to hatch?
- Do you think learning to fly is easy for ducks? Explain.

Organize information in a chart

Draw a chart or display Graphic Organizer 21. Have children recall what they learned from the CD about how ducks grow and change. Record their responses.

First

Next

Last

Graphic Organizer Flip Chart 21

Connect to selection

We learned how ducks grow and change over time. First, ducks grow inside an egg. Then they hatch. Eventually they learn to fly. Ruby is a baby duck in the story we are about to read. As we read, we'll find out what Ruby learns as she grows up.

Student Edition pp. 52–53

Main Selection—First Read
Ruby in Her Own Time

Practice the skill

 Compare and Contrast Review comparing and contrasting. Comparing is telling how two things are alike. Contrasting is telling how they are different. Children can use words such as *both* or *too* to compare. They can use words such as *but* or *though* to contrast.

Introduce the strategy

Inferring Explain that good readers think about more than what is on the page. They think about what they already know. They use that knowledge to come up with new ideas about what they read. Have children turn to page EI•14 in their Student Edition.

 **Envision It!**

 Think Aloud Look at this picture. What do you see? (The bag is torn, and the eggs are broken.) What do you think happened? (The bottom of the bag ripped and the eggs fell out.) As I read *Ruby in Her Own Time*, I will use what I already know to come up with new ideas about what I am reading.

Student Edition EI•14

Introduce genre

Let's Read Together **Animal fantasy** is a made-up story with animals that do things real animals can't do. As they read *Ruby in Her Own Time*, children should look for things the ducks do that real ducks cannot.

Preview and predict

Have children read the title of the story. Read the names of the author and illustrator, and have children describe the role of each. Have children activate prior knowledge by looking through the story and predicting what it will be about.

Set a purpose

Good readers read for a purpose. Setting a purpose helps us to think and understand more as we read. Guide children to set a purpose for reading the story.

Tell children that today they will read *Ruby in Her Own Time* for the first time. Use the Day 2 Guide Comprehension notes to help children develop their comprehension of the story.

 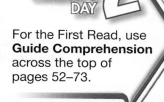 **Continue to DAY 2**

For the First Read, use **Guide Comprehension** across the top of pages 52–73.

First Read

 INTERACT with TEXT **Strategy Response Log**

Genre Have children use p. RR26 in their *Reader's and Writer's Notebook* to identify the characteristics of animal fantasy.

Academic Vocabulary

inferring combining background knowledge with information in the text to interpret and draw conclusions about what is not explicitly stated

ELL

English Language Learners

Build Background Before children listen to the CD, build background and elicit prior knowledge. On the CD, you will hear about how ducks change as they grow. What do you think ducks learn to do after they hatch from eggs?

Frontload Main Selection Ask children what they already know about ducks using the picture on pp. 52–53. Then do a picture walk of the selection so children can talk about and see the things ducks learn as they grow.

Objectives

◎ Make inferences about text.
◎ Compare and contrast elements in text.
• Determine word meaning and use newly acquired vocabulary.
• Discuss ideas related to, but not expressed in, the literature.

DAY 2

Guide Comprehension

Skills and Strategies

Connect to Concept

Growing and Changing Look at the pictures on pages 52 and 53. What is one way the duckling might change? (Possible response: The duckling will grow bigger as it gets older.)

Amazing Words Have children continue discussing the concept using the Amazing Words *attempt, event, time line, famous,* and *flatter* as they read.

Student Edition pp. 52–53

DAY 3

Extend Thinking

Think Critically

Higher-Order Thinking Skills

Synthesis *Ruby in Her Own Time* tells how a duckling learns to eat, swim, and fly. What are some other things animals can learn to do? (Possible response: Dogs can learn to sit, fetch, and roll over.)

If... children cannot name other activities animals can learn, **then...** encourage them to think about pets they know and the training or tricks their owners have taught them.

Strategies

Inferring Remind children that good readers make inferences as they read a story. They use what they already know and what the author tells them to come up with their own ideas about the story. Have children infer why Mother Duck sits on the nest all day and all night.

If... children have trouble inferring, **then...** review with them that birds hatch from eggs and lead them to understand that Mother Duck is keeping the eggs warm until they hatch.

Once upon a time upon a nest beside a lake, there lived two ducks—a mother duck and a father duck.

There were five eggs in the nest. Mother Duck sat upon the nest, all day and all night . . .

through howling wind and driving rain, looking after the eggs—all five of them.

Student Edition pp. 54–55

Higher-Order Thinking Skills

Analysis Mother Duck sits on the eggs in her nest even when it is windy and rainy. What does that tell you about her? (Possible response: She is a good mother. She keeps her eggs safe even when the weather is bad.)

Skills and Strategies, continued

Skills

DAY 2

🎯 **Compare and Contrast** Have children tell how Mother Duck and Father Duck are alike and different. (Possible response: Mother and Father Duck are both parents. Mother Duck is yellow with an orange beak, but Father Duck is brown and green with a yellow beak.)

If... children have trouble coming up with similarities and differences, **then...** encourage them to use the illustrations for clues.

Then, one bright <u>morning</u>, the eggs began to hatch.

One, two, three, four little beaks poked out into the <u>sunlight</u>.

One, two, three, four little <u>ducklings</u> shook their feathers in the breeze.

"We'll call them Rufus, Rory, Rosie, and Rebecca," said Father Duck. And Mother Duck agreed.

56

57

Student Edition pp. 56–57

Think Critically, continued

DAY 3

 Review **Sequence**
Evaluation Think about what happened first, next, and last as the eggs hatched. What do you think might happen after Father Duck names the ducklings? (Possible response: The ducklings will learn how to walk.)

Vocabulary

Story Words Have children locate the story word *precious* on page 59. What does Mother Duck mean when she says Ruby is precious? (She means that Ruby is very special and valuable to her.)

Strategies

Inferring Why does Mother Duck think Ruby is a good name for someone who is precious? (A ruby is a jewel that is very valuable, and *precious* means "very valuable.")

But the fifth egg did <u>nothing</u>.
"Will it ever hatch?" said Father Duck.

"It will," said Mother Duck, "in its own time."

And—
sure enough—
it did.

"She's very small," said Father Duck.
"What shall we call her?"

"We'll call her Ruby," said Mother Duck, "because she's small and precious."

58

59

Student Edition pp. 58–59

Higher-Order Thinking Skills

Synthesis Mother Duck and Father Duck name the last duckling Ruby because she is small and precious. What do you think would have been another good name for her?

If... children cannot think of other appropriate names for Ruby,
then... review what they know about Ruby (for example, she is small, precious, independent, and brave).

DAYS 2&3 Read and Comprehend

Skills and Strategies, continued

Skills

DAY 2

◉ **Compare and Contrast** How is Ruby different from her brothers and sisters? (Ruby's brothers and sisters will eat anything and everything, but Ruby eats nothing.)

If... children have trouble contrasting Ruby with her brothers and sisters, **then...** ask them to think about what Ruby and her siblings eat on pages 60–61.

Rufus, Rory, Rosie, and Rebecca ate whatever they were given. They ate anything and everything.

But Ruby ate nothing.

"Will she ever eat?" said Father Duck.

"She will," said Mother Duck, "in her own time."

60

61

Student Edition pp. 60–61

Think Critically, continued

DAY 3

Higher-Order Thinking Skills

Evaluation Why might parents worry about a child like Ruby more than they would worry about other children? (Possible response: She is very small, and she doesn't eat.)

If... children have trouble thinking of reasons parents might worry, **then...** encourage them to think about the different things parents are concerned with, such as their children's health.

Word Reading

Decoding Have children check their reading of new words using these questions:

- Did I blend the sounds to read the word?
- Did I put the new word in the sentence to make sure it made sense?
- Did I look for word parts to help me understand the word?

Student Edition pp. 62–63

Higher-Order Thinking Skills

Synthesis What might happen to a duck if it did not learn to swim? (Possible response: It would have trouble finding food.)

If... children cannot think of reasons ducks must learn to swim,
then... review what you have learned about ducks' lives, such as what kinds of foods they eat and where those foods are found.

Skills and Strategies, continued

DAY 2

Word Reading
High-Frequency Words Point out the words *ever, own, sure,* and *enough.* Have children practice reading these words.

Skills
Compare and Contrast From what you read on these pages, how are Ruby and her brothers and sisters alike? (Possible response: They all grow bigger.)

But Ruby swam nowhere.

"Will she ever swim?" said Father Duck.

"She will," said Mother Duck, "in her own time."

And—
sure enough—
she did.

64

Rufus, Rory, Rosie, and Rebecca grew bigger.

And Ruby grew bigger too. Her feathers grew out, and her wings grew broad and beautiful.

65

Student Edition pp. 64–65

Think Critically, continued

DAY 3

Higher-Order Thinking Skills
Evaluation On page 65, what does the author tell you about Ruby's wings? (They are broad and beautiful.) Why are Ruby's wings so important? (Ruby uses her wings to become the best flyer of all her brothers and sisters.)

Connect to Social Studies
Respecting Differences Explain that it is important to be patient when trying to teach someone a new skill.

Team Talk Have children discuss a time they have had to be patient when teaching a younger sibling or neighbor how to do something.

Skills

⟳ Compare and Contrast From what you read on these pages, what do Ruby and her brothers and sisters have in common? (Possible response: They all learn how to fly.)

Word Reading

Story Words Have children locate the story word *flew* on pages 66 and 67. What were the new places the ducks could go once they could fly? (Possible response: The ducks could go among the trees and above the water.)

And when Rufus, Rory, Rosie, and Rebecca began to fly . . .

Ruby flew too!

Rufus, Rory, Rosie, and Rebecca flew far and wide. They flew out across the water. They flew up among the trees.

66

67

Student Edition pp. 66–67

Higher-Order Thinking Skills

Synthesis Think about the things the ducks learn to do and the places they go. In what kind of environment do you think the ducks live? (Possible response: They probably live in a woodland environment.)

If... children have trouble thinking of different possible environments,
then... review several environments and their features, asking if the ducks would be able to swim and fly among the trees in each.

Skills and Strategies, continued

DAY 2

Vocabulary

Synonyms I know that the words *flew* and *soared* on pages 68 and 69 have nearly the same meaning. Words that have nearly the same meaning are called synonyms. What word on page 69 is a synonym for *lovely*? (beautiful)

Skills

Compare and Contrast From what you read on these pages, how is Ruby different from her brothers and sisters? (Ruby flies much farther and higher than her brothers and sisters do.)

But Ruby flew farther and wider. She flew out beyond the water.

She flew up above the trees.

68

She flew anywhere and everywhere. She stretched out her beautiful wings and soared high among the clouds.

69

Student Edition pp. 68–69

Think Critically, continued

DAY 3

Higher-Order Thinking Skills

Evaluation Once Ruby learns how to fly, she flies farther and higher than the other ducklings. Does this fit what you know about Ruby so far? (Possible response: Yes. Ruby has always done things a little differently than the other ducklings.)

If... children are unable to connect Ruby's flying to her other behavior, **then...** review the different instances of Ruby acting independently and doing things "in her own time" throughout the story.

Strategies

Inferring Why do you think Father Duck is so sure that Ruby will come back? (Ruby has always done everything in her own time.)

Word Reading

Decoding Have children check their reading of new words using these questions:

- Did I blend the sounds to read the word?
- Did I put the new word in the sentence to make sure it made sense?
- Did I look for word parts to help me understand the word?

Mother Duck and Father Duck watched Ruby flying off into the distance.

"Will she ever come back?" said Mother Duck.

"She will," said Father Duck, "in her own time."

70

71

Student Edition pp. 70–71

Higher-Order Thinking Skills

Analysis On pages 70–71, Ruby flies far away. What are some places she might be going? Where do you think her brothers and sisters fly? (Possible response: Ruby is probably going to visit other parts of the world. Her brothers and sisters will probably stay close to home.)

If... children have a hard time predicting where Ruby's brothers and sisters fly,
then... remind children that the ducks stayed close to home when they first learned to fly and were not as daring as Ruby.

Skills and Strategies, continued

DAY 2

Strategy Self-Check
🔄 **Inferring** Have children talk about how they solved any problems they encountered as they read. Then have them identify the clues they used to make inferences.

Word Reading
High-Frequency Words Point out the words *sure* and *enough*. Have children practice reading these words.

Continue with DAY 2

Comprehension Check p. 73a

And—
sure enough—
she did.

72

73

Student Edition pp. 72–73

Think Critically, continued

DAY 3

Higher-Order Thinking Skills
Analysis Look at the illustration of the ducks on pages 72 and 73. Who are these new ducks? Why do you think that? (Possible response: The ducklings are Ruby's children. She started her own family while she was away.)

If... children have trouble identifying the ducklings as Ruby's children, **then...** review the illustrations from the beginning of the story that show what baby ducks and parent ducks look like.

Comprehension Check

Have children discuss each question with a partner. Ask several pairs to share their responses.

✓ **Animal fantasy** How is this story different from a story about real ducks? (Possible response: In this story, the ducks talk. Real ducks can't talk.)

✓ **Draw conclusions** How do Mother and Father Duck feel when Ruby flies off into the distance? (Possible response: They're proud because she is grown up and can fly like the other ducks, but they are sad to see her leave.)

✓ **Plot** What was the main problem in this story? How was it solved? (Possible response: Ruby did not learn how to do some things as quickly as the other ducklings. By the end, she learned how to do everything in her own time, and she was an even better flyer than her brothers and sisters.)

✓ **Confirm predictions** How did you use pictures or story clues to predict what would happen next in the story? How did you confirm or change your predictions? (Possible response: I could tell that Ruby would be different from her brothers and sisters because the pictures show all of them doing one thing and her doing another. When I read the story, I found out my predictions were correct.)

✓ **Connect text to self** In the story, Ruby's family teaches her how to do lots of new things, such as swimming and flying. What are some things you have learned how to do? Who taught you how to do them? (Possible response: I learned how to tie my shoes. My older brother taught me how.)

ELL

English Language Learners
Support Discussion Supply sentence starters to aid children's responses. For example: I learned how to _____.

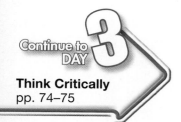
Continue to DAY **3**
Think Critically
pp. 74–75

Objectives
- Identify story elements in literary text.
- Identify and correctly use verbs that add -s when reading, speaking, and writing.

Literary Text
Story Elements

Identify story elements

Use the story *Ruby in Her Own Time* to have children identify story elements in literary text. Record information on Graphic Organizer 23.

- Who are the characters in *Ruby in Her Own Time?* (Mother Duck, Father Duck, and their children: Rufus, Rory, Rosie, Rebecca, and Ruby) Who is the main character? (Ruby) How do you know? (Possible response: Most of the story is about Ruby and how she does things in her own time.)

- Where does *Ruby in Her Own Time* take place? What is the setting? (The setting is a lake where ducks live.)

- What is a story's series of events called? (the plot) In one sentence, how would you summarize the basic plot of *Ruby in Her Own Time?* (A family of ducklings grows up near a lake.)

Title _____	
Characters	**Setting**

Events	
1. First	
2. Next	
3. Then	
4. Last	

Graphic Organizer Flip Chart 23

Guide practice

Explain that the class will now take a closer look at the story's plot. Continue to use Graphic Organizer 23. Let's start at the beginning of the story. What is the first thing that happens in *Ruby in Her Own Time?* (Mother Duck sits on the five eggs in her nest.) Repeat this process with the remaining events in the story. Have children study the finished story sequence chart. Review the definitions of all story elements.

On their own

Divide children into small groups and assign each group a previously read story from the Student Edition. Have them identify the story elements. Have them share their information with the class.

Conventions
Verbs That Add -*s*

Model verbs that add -*s*
On the board, write *Mr. George Baker sits*. Point to each word as you read it. Ask children to identify the verb in the sentence. (sits) What does Mr. George Baker do? (sits) When does he do it? (now) How many people are sitting? (one) We add *s* to the verb to show what one person does now. For this sentence to be correct, there must be the ending -*s* on the verb.

Guide Practice
Write the following sentence frame:

> **Mr. George Baker _____ .**

Display the Big Book *Mr. George Baker*, p. 5. Point to Mr. George Baker waving. What verb names what he is doing now? (*wave*). Write *wave* on the line and read the sentence aloud. Only one person is waving now, so what must I add to wave? (-*s*) Add the -*s* and read the corrected sentence aloud.

Repeat this routine with verbs suggested by illustrations on p. 18 (*tap, drum*), p. 20 (*walk*), and p. 23 (*read*).

Connect to oral language
Have the class use verbs with -*s* to complete these sentence frames orally.

> **1. Harry _____ on the step.**
>
> **2. Mrs. Baker _____ a lunch for Mr. Baker.**

On their own
Use *Reader's and Writer's Notebook* p. 335.

Reader's and Writer's Notebook p. 335

Differentiated Instruction

SI Strategic Intervention

Verbs in Sentences Have children write three short sentences for the subjects *he, she,* and *it* using verbs that end in -*s*. Children may use the names of people or things instead of these pronouns. Then have children point out the *s* at the end of each verb.

Daily Fix-It

3. The bird's wing Is pink
   The bird's wing is pink.

4. bring your skates to the rinck.
   Bring your skates to the rink.

Discuss the Daily Fix-It corrections with children. Review sentence capitalization and punctuation, and the *k* spelling of /k/.

ELL

English Language Learners
Practice Verbs with -*s* Provide simple sentences. *Dad sings. Mom hums.* Read the sentences, stressing the final *s* sound. Have children repeat. Have children identify each verb and use it in sentences of their own.

Objectives

- Generate comments about a story.
- Recognize features of comments about a story.
- Use words that show feelings in comments about a story.

Writing—Comments About a Story
Writer's Craft: Include Feelings

Introduce the prompt

Review with children the key features of comments about a story. Point out that *Ruby in Her Own Time* is a story with characters and events. Explain that when children write comments about a story, they might respond to any aspect of the story. Explain that today children will plan their own comments about a story. They will use words that show how they feel. Read aloud the writing prompt.

Writing Prompt

> Look at the pictures in *Ruby in Her Own Time*. Think about what Ruby does. Write sentences to tell two things Ruby does that you like.

Help children generate ideas

Sharing the Writing

 The prompt tells us we will write about what Ruby does. First, we need to look at the pictures and see what Ruby does. Let's make a list of the things Ruby does. Then you can choose the two things you like most to write about.

Guide children in identifying Ruby's actions. List the main actions for children and have them review the actions to choose two to write about.

What Ruby Does

- *She hatches late.*
- *She doesn't eat at first.*
- *She swims later than her brothers and sisters.*
- *She grows big.*
- *She flies farther than anyone.*
- *She comes home with a new family of her own.*

Have each child choose two things Ruby does to write about. Circulate to guide them. Have them choose two things they like and that they are able to express why they like them.

MINI-LESSON

Include Feelings

■ **Introduce** Use *Reader's and Writer's Notebook* p. 336 to model planning comments. I know when I write comments about a story I need to tell about the story. I also need to tell about how the story makes me feel. I can use a chart to help me plan my comments about the story.

Reader's and Writer's Notebook p. 336

■ **Model** I see that the first column of the chart says "I Like When Ruby…" This lets me know I have to write something that Ruby does that I like. I really like it when Ruby swims. I will write that in the first column. Now I can move to the next column. I need to think about how it makes me feel when Ruby swims. I am excited for Ruby. I will write *excited.* Now I need to tell why. It took me a long time to learn to swim. I was just like Ruby. When she swims, it reminds me of how I felt when I first swam. Now it is your turn to plan your comments about a story. Use the chart to list the things Ruby does, how they make you feel, and why they make you feel that way. **Circulate to guide and assist children.**

ROUTINE   Quick Write for Fluency   Team Talk

(1) **Talk** Have children take two minutes to tell the actions they chose to write about.

(2) **Write** Each child briefly writes how one of Ruby's actions makes him or her feel.

(3) **Share** Each child reads the comments to the partner.

Routines Flip Chart

Differentiated Instruction

SI Strategic Intervention

Naming Feelings If children find it difficult to name their feelings, give them a list of words that describe feelings and help them choose appropriate words to complete their charts: *happy, glad, excited, thrilled, surprised.*

E L L

English Language Learners
Support Prewriting

Beginning Children can share orally with a partner how Ruby's actions make them feel.

Intermediate Have children write phrases to describe Ruby's actions. Have them describe the way they feel and why to partners.

Advanced/Advanced-High Have children write short descriptions in their charts. Have children share their ideas with partners.

Handwriting
Letter *K* and *k*/Letter Slant

Model letter formation

Display upper- and lower-case letters: *Kk.* Use the stroke instructions pictured below to model proper letter formation.

D'Nealian™   Ball and Stick

Model letter slant

Explain that when we write a word, all of the letters in that word should be slanted correctly and consistently. Write the word *bang* with the letters all slanted correctly. When I write the letters in a word, I need to make sure that they all are going the correct way. Write the word *bang* again, this time with the letters going in different directions. This word is hard to read! If I write a word with the letters all slanted in the correct way, it is easier for others to understand what I write.

Guide practice

Write the following words. Make sure that two of them have consistent, correct letter slant, and two of them are written with letters in different directions.

wink	hang	bank	strong

Team Talk Have children work in pairs to discuss which words are slanted correctly and which ones are not. Have them determine how to fix the words and share their ideas with the class.

On their own

Use the *Reader's and Writer's Notebook* p. 337.

Reader's and Writer's Notebook
p. 337

Research and Inquiry
Research Skill: Glossary

Academic Vocabulary

glossary an alphabetical list of words and their definitions, usually found at the back of a book

Teach

Tell children that a **glossary** is an alphabetical list of words and their definitions. Have children turn to the glossary at the end of their Student Edition. Explain that a glossary is often helpful when you are reading facts about a topic. If you do not understand a word you have read, you may be able to look it up in the glossary.

Model

Think Aloud In *Ruby in Her Own Time*, the story says that the wind was *howling*. That sounds interesting, but I am not exactly sure what *howling* means. I will look for it in the glossary. Point out *howling* on page 221 of the glossary, and read the definition. The glossary explains what *howling* means. Now the sentence makes sense.

Guide practice

On the board, write: *A ruby is a precious jewel*. With children, find the word *precious* in the glossary. Then have children explain how the definition helps them understand the fact.

Wrap Up Your Day

✔ **Compound Words** Write the words *backpack, outside,* and *sunshine*. Have children identify the two words that make up each compound word.

✔ **High-Frequency Words** Point to these words on the Word Wall: *ever, sure, were, enough, every, any,* and *own*. Have children read each word and use it in a sentence.

✔ **Build Concepts** Monitor children's use of oral vocabulary as they respond. Recall *Mr. George Baker*. Ask: What does Mr. George Baker attempt to learn? (He attempts to learn how to read.) How do you know Mr. George Baker is on his own time line? (He is 100 years old, but he still wants to learn how to read.)

Preview DAY 3

Tell children that tomorrow they will reread *Ruby in Her Own Time*.

Objectives
- Build oral vocabulary.
- Identify details in text.
- Share information and ideas about the concept.

Today at a Glance

Oral Vocabulary
correct

Phonemic Awareness
Add Phonemes

Phonics and Spelling
- Consonant Patterns *-ng, -nk*
- Compound Words

High-Frequency Words
ever, sure, were, enough, every, any, own

Story Words
beautiful, father, feather, flew, mother, precious, night, howling

Comprehension
Sequence

Fluency
Appropriate Phrasing

Conventions
Verbs That Add *-s*

Writing
Comments About a Story
Writer's Craft:

Listening and Speaking
Share Information and Ideas

Research and Inquiry
Gather and Record Information

Concept Talk

 Question of the Week

What do we learn as we grow and change?

Build concepts

To reinforce concepts and to focus children's attention, have children sing "On Our Own Time Line" from the *Sing with Me* Big Book. What are some things that were hard or easy for you to learn? (Possible response: It was hard for me to learn to ride a bike. It was easy for me to learn to tie my shoe.)

Sing with Me Big Book Audio

Monitor listening comprehension

Display the Big Book *Mr. George Baker*. As children listen to the story, have them think about what Harry and Mr. George Baker attempt to learn. Then read the book aloud.

- What skill is hard for Harry and Mr. George Baker to learn? (how to read)

- How can you tell that Mr. Baker thinks reading is important? (Mr. Baker is much older than Harry, but he still goes to school every day.)

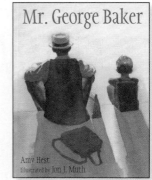

Big Book

ELL Expand Vocabulary Use the Day 3 instruction on ELL Poster 14 to expand children's use of English vocabulary to communicate about lesson concepts.

ELL Poster 14

Oral Vocabulary
Amazing Words

Teach Amazing Words

Amazing Words **Oral Vocabulary Routine**

1. **Introduce the Word** Relate the word *correct* to the book. Mr. George Baker never learned to read. He wants to correct that. Supply a child-friendly definition: When you *correct* something, you change it to make it right. Have children say the word.

2. **Demonstrate** Provide examples to show meaning. You can *correct* the answers you got wrong by giving the right answers. You can *correct* someone if they pronounce your name the wrong way.

3. **Apply** Have children demonstrate their understanding. How can you *correct* yourself if you are riding a bike and begin to tip over?

Routines Flip Chart

Anchored Talk

Add to the concept map

Use these questions to discuss what we learn about ourselves and others as we grow and change as you add to the concept map.

- In *Ruby in Her Own Time*, the ducklings learn as they grow and change. Let's add *ducklings* to our concept map.

- What new skills do the ducklings learn? (They learned to eat, swim, and fly.) Let's add those things to the map.

- Ruby learns to do new things in her own time. What does this tell you about how each of us learns new things? (We learn the same things at different times.)

English Language Learners

Words in Context Have children work with the word *correct*. Have them tell how they would correct this math statement: $2 + 2 = 5$.

Objectives

• Add initial sound to create a new word.
• Build words with *–ink*.
◎ Read words with *ng*, words with *nk*, and compound words.

Phonemic Awareness
Add Phonemes

Model adding phonemes

Read together the fourth bullet point on pages 46–47 of the Student Edition. Today we are going to use this picture to help us add new sounds to the beginning of words. The directions tell us to add the sound /s/ in front of the word *wing*. When I add /s/ to *wing*, I make a new word: *swing*. Now I will look for a picture of that new word, *swing*.

Student Edition pp. 46–47

Guide practice

Help children add an initial sound to each word below to make a new word. Then have them point to the matching picture in their Student Edition.

/b/ring **bring**   /d/rink **drink**   /p/ink **pink**

On their own

Have children add initial /s/ to the following words to make new words.

and (sand)   **lap** (slap)   **tack** (stack)

ash (sash)   **top** (stop)   **end** (send)

Team Talk Have partners think of other initial sounds they could add to *end* to make new words (*bend, lend, mend*). Ask children to share their words.

Phonics
Build Words

h	i	k	l	n	r	s	t	w	

Model word building

Now we are going to build words that end with the sound /ngk/. Write *pink* and blend it. Watch me change /p/ to /w/. Model blending the new word, *wink*.

Guide practice

Have children spell *wink* with letter tiles. Monitor children's work.

- Change the /w/ in *wink* to /s/. Say the new word together.
- Change the /s/ in *sink* to /l/. Say the new word together.
- Change the /l/ in *link* to /r/. Say the new word together.
- Change the /r/ in *rink* to /th/. Say the new word together.

Corrective feedback

For corrective feedback, model the correct spelling and have children correct their tiles.

Fluent Word Reading

Model

Write *king*. I know the sounds for *k*, *i*, and *ng*. I blend them and read the word *king*.

Guide practice

Write the words below. Say the sounds in your head for each spelling you see. When I point to the word, we'll read it together. Allow one second per sound previewing time for the first reading.

bang	skunk	sandbox	anthill
sung	tank	pancake	

On their own

Have children read the list above three or four times, until they can read one word per second.

Differentiated Instruction

 Advanced

Build *nk* Words If children are able to build the words in the class activity easily and independently, have them use letter tiles to build these more difficult words with *nk*: *drink, shrink, blank, spank, chipmunk*

ELL

English Language Learners

Produce Initial Blends Children whose first language is Spanish may need support with words with initial *s* blends, such as *swing* and *skunk*. Model the formal pronunciation and have children repeat the words.

Objectives

- ◎ Associate the consonant sounds /ng/ and /ngk/ with the spellings *ng* and *nk*.
- Blend and read words with the consonant patterns *ng* or *nk* and compound words.
- Decode words in context and isolation.
- Spell words with the consonant patterns *ng* and *nk*.

⟲ Blend and Read

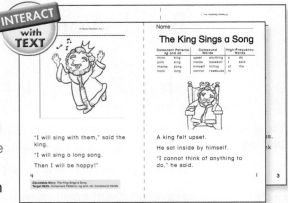

Reader's and Writer's Notebook pp. 339–340

Decode words in isolation

Have children turn to pages 339–340 in the *Reader's and Writer's Notebook* and find the first list of words. Each word in this list either has the consonants *ng* or *nk* or is a compound word. Let's blend and read these words. Be sure that children identify the correct final sound in words that end with *ng* or *nk*.

Next, have children read the high-frequency words.

Decode words in context

Chorally read the story along with children. Have children identify words in the story that are compound words or that have the consonant pattern *ng* or *nk*.

Team Talk Pair children and have them take turns reading the story aloud to each other. Monitor children as they read to check for proper pronunciation and appropriate pacing.

On their own

To further develop automaticity, have children take the story home to reread.

Spelling
Words with *ng, nk*

Spell high-frequency words

Write *every* and *sure* and point them out on the Word Wall. Have children say and spell the words with you and then without you.

Dictation

Say each sentence. Then repeat each slowly, one word at a time. Have children write the sentences.

1. **Hank rang every bell.**
2. **Put the pink dress in the trunk.**
3. **We sang at the ice rink.**

Proofread and correct

Write each sentence, spelling words one at a time. Have children circle and rewrite any misspelled words.

On their own

Use *Reader's and Writer's Notebook* p. 341.

Spelling Words

Consonant Patterns *ng, nk*

1. bring	6. wing
2. trunk	7. rink
3. pink	8. blank
4. bank	9. rang
5. sang	10. sunk

High-Frequency Words

11. every	12. sure

Reader's and Writer's Notebook p. 341

Small Group Time

DAY 3

Break into small groups after spelling and before the comprehension lesson.

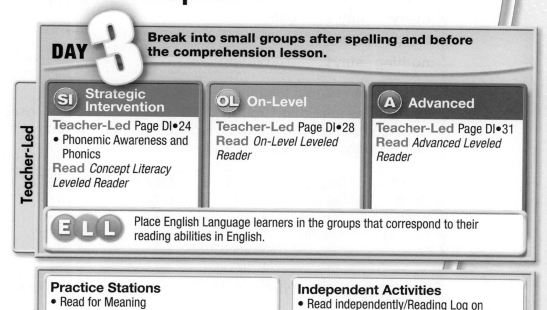

Teacher-Led

(SI) Strategic Intervention

Teacher-Led Page DI•24
• Phonemic Awareness and Phonics
Read *Concept Literacy Leveled Reader*

(OL) On-Level

Teacher-Led Page DI•28
Read *On-Level Leveled Reader*

(A) Advanced

Teacher-Led Page DI•31
Read *Advanced Leveled Reader*

ELL Place English Language learners in the groups that correspond to their reading abilities in English.

Practice Stations
• Read for Meaning
• Let's Write

Independent Activities
• Read independently/Reading Log on *Reader's and Writer's Notebook* p. RR4
• AudioText of Main Selection

ELL

English Language Learners

Letter Tiles Write these words on the board: *sang, ring, bunk,* and *sank.* Say the word *sang,* have children repeat it, and then erase it from the board. Have partners spell the word with letter tiles. Continue the exercise with the remaining words or other words that end in *ng* or *nk.*

Objectives
- Read high-frequency words.
- Establish purpose for reading text.
- Review key features of animal fantasies.

Check High-Frequency Words

SUCCESS PREDICTOR

High-Frequency and Story Words

Read words in isolation

Display and review this week's high-frequency words and story words. Have children read the words aloud.

Read words in context

Display the following sentence frames. Have children complete the sentences using high-frequency and story words. Have the children read each completed sentence with you.

1. I *own* a hat with a red _____. (feather)

2. Did you *ever* hear a dog _____? (howling)

3. The ____ bird finds *enough* food for her baby. (mother)

4. My cat sleeps on my bed *every* _____. (night)

5. The mother and ____ *were* with their son. (father)

6. I am *sure* the robin _____ into that tree. (flew)

Don't Wait Until Friday

MONITOR PROGRESS | **Check High-Frequency Words**

Point to these words on the Word Wall and have the class read them. Listen for children who miss words during the reading. Call on those children to read some of the words individually.

ever	sure	were	enough	
every	any	own		
thing	always	day	become	
nothing	stays	everything		

Spiral Review
Rows 3 and 4 review previously taught high-frequency words.

If... children cannot read these words,

Then... use the Small Group Time Strategic Intervention lesson, p. DI•25, to reteach the words. Monitor children's fluency with these words during reading and provide additional practice.

Day 1	Day 2	Day 3	Day 4	Day 5
Check Word Reading	Check Word Reading	Check High-Frequency Words/ Retelling	Check Fluency	Check Oral Vocabulary

Success Predictor

Main Selection—Second Read
Ruby in Her Own Time

Review
Sequence

Recall this week's main selection, *Ruby in Her Own Time*. Tell children that today they will read the story again. Remind children that the order of events in a story is its **sequence**. Paying attention to the sequence helps us understand what happens in a story. What is the first thing that happens in *Ruby in Her Own Time*? (Possible response: Mother Duck sits on her eggs.) What happens next? (Possible response: Four of the eggs hatch.)

Review
Genre: animal fantasy

Let's Read Together Remind children that animal fantasy is a made-up story with animals that do things real animals can't do. Have children recall things the ducks in *Ruby in Her Own Time* do that real ducks can't do. (Possible response: They can talk.)

Set a purpose

Remind children that good readers read for a purpose. Guide children to set a new purpose for reading *Ruby in Her Own Time* today, perhaps to consider why Ruby does things differently than her brothers and sisters do.

Extend thinking

Tell children they will now read *Ruby in Her Own Time* for the second time. Use the Day 3 Extend Thinking notes to encourage children to use higher order thinking skills to go beyond the details of the story.

Story Words

mother a woman who has a child or children

precious having great value

feather one of the light, soft things that cover a bird's body

howling making a loud, whining sound

father a man who has a child or children

flew took off and moved in the air

night the time between sunset and sunrise

beautiful very pretty to see or hear

Academic Vocabulary

sequence the order of events in a selection

English Language Learners
Story Elements Have children review the plot of *Ruby in Her Own Time* in preparation for their second reading. Encourage them to identify the story problem and what the main character does to try to solve it.

Continue to **DAY 3**

For the Second Read, use **Extend Thinking** across the bottom of pages 52–73.

Second Read

High-Frequency Words

Success Predictor

Objectives

- Retell a narrative.
- Make inferences in a narrative text.
- Compare and contrast.
- Write clear, coherent sentences.

Check Retelling
SUCCESS PREDICTOR

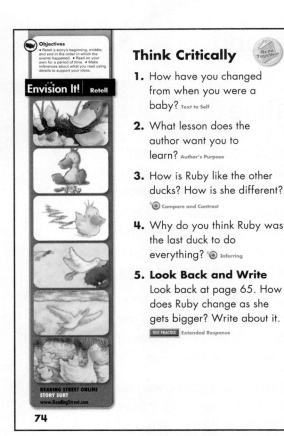

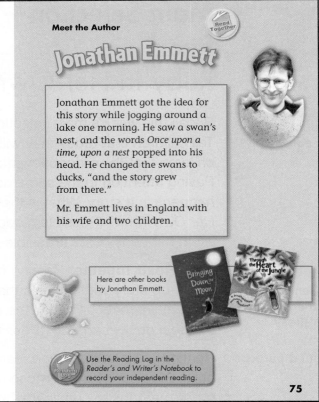

Student Edition pp. 74–75

Retelling

Envision It! Have children work in pairs, retelling the story to one another. Remind children that their partners should include the characters, setting, and events from the beginning, middle, and end of the story. Children should use the retelling strip in the Student Edition as they retell. Monitor children's retelling.

Scoring rubric

> **Top-Score Response** A top-score response makes connections beyond the text, elaborates on the author's purpose, and describes in detail the characters, setting, and plot.

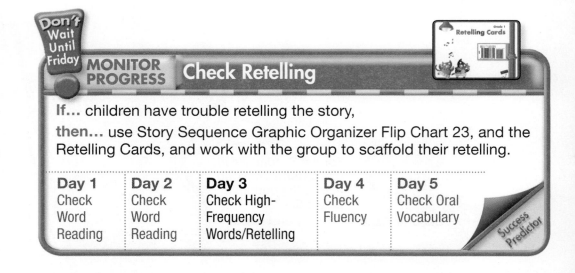

Don't Wait Until Friday

MONITOR PROGRESS   Check Retelling

If... children have trouble retelling the story,

then... use Story Sequence Graphic Organizer Flip Chart 23, and the Retelling Cards, and work with the group to scaffold their retelling.

Day 1	Day 2	Day 3	Day 4	Day 5
Check Word Reading	Check Word Reading	Check High-Frequency Words/Retelling	Check Fluency	Check Oral Vocabulary

Think Critically

Text to Self

Author's Purpose

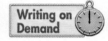**Compare and Contrast**

Inferring

Writing on Demand

1. Possible response: I have gotten taller.

2. Possible response: The author wants us to learn that we all grow and learn new things at different times.

3. Ruby grew bigger and learned to fly at the same time as her brothers and sisters. She hatched later and learned to do some things more slowly than her brothers and sisters.

4. She hatched later and was smaller than her brothers and sisters.

5. Look Back and Write For writing fluency, assign a five minute time limit. As children finish, encourage them to reread their response and proofread for errors.

> **Top-Score Response** A top-score response uses details from the text and the pictures to tell how Ruby changed as she got bigger. For example:
>
> Ruby's feathers got fluffy. Her wings became wide and beautiful. She began to fly.

Meet the author

Read aloud page 75 as children follow along, and track the print. Ask children what authors do.

Read independently

After children enter their independent reading into their Reading Logs, have them paraphrase a portion of the text they have just read. Tell children that when we paraphrase, we express the meaning of what we have just read using our own words.

Differentiated Instruction

A **Advanced**

Look Back and Write Ask children who show proficiency with the writing prompt to explain why they think Ruby returns home at the end of the story.

INTERACT with TEXT

Strategy Response Log

Inferring Have children revisit p. RR26 in their *Reader's and Writer's Notebook.* Have them draw pictures to show the knowledge they used to make an inference as they read.

Plan to Assess Retelling

- [ ] **Week 1:** Strategic Intervention
- [x] **This week: Assess Advanced children.**
- [ ] **Week 3:** Strategic Intervention
- [ ] **Week 4:** On-Level
- [ ] **Week 5:** Strategic Intervention
- [ ] **Week 6:** Assess any children you have not yet checked during this unit.

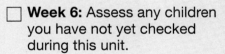Retelling

Success Predictor

Model Fluency
Appropriate Phrasing

Model fluent reading

Have children turn to Student Edition page 58. Point to the question mark. This is a question mark. It tells me that I should read this sentence as if I am asking a question.

Guide practice

Have children read the page with you. Then have them reread the page as a group until they read with appropriate phrasing, paying attention to punctuation. Make sure they correctly read the question (the second sentence). Continue in the same way with page 59.

Corrective feedback

If... children have difficulty reading with appropriate phrasing, **then...** prompt:

- Do you look at the end marks?
- How should your voice sound when you read a sentence that ends with a question mark?
- Read the sentence as if you are asking a friend a question.

Reread for Fluency

> **ROUTINE** Choral Reading
>
> 1. **Select a Passage** For *Ruby in Her Own Time,* use pp. 60–61.
> 2. **Model** First, have children track the print as you read.
> 3. **Guide Practice** Then have children read along with you.
> 4. **Corrective Feedback** Have the class read aloud without you. Monitor progress and provide feedback. For optimal fluency, children should reread three to four times.

Routines Flip Chart

Check comprehension

What do Ruby and her brothers and sisters have in common? How are they different? (Possible response: They all learn to do the same things, but Ruby does things in her own time, which is more slowly than her brothers and sisters.)

Conventions
Verbs That Add -s

Review verbs that add -s

Remind children that we add -s to the end of a verb to show what one person, animal, or thing does now: Mom *bakes*. The dog *barks*.

Guide practice

Write this sentence on the board and have children read it aloud.

Ruby swim every day.

What letter must we add to the end of *swim* to make the sentence correct? (-s) Add -s to *swim* and read the corrected sentence aloud.

Team Talk Have children say the same sentence correctly, using the verbs *eat*, *play*, and *nap*.

Connect to oral language

Have children complete these sentence frames orally with a verb that tells what one baby animal does now.

One puppy _____.

A kitten _____.

The chick _____.

On their own

Use *Reader's and Writer's Notebook* p. 342.

Reader's and Writer's Notebook p. 342

Options for Oral Rereading

Use *Ruby in Her Own Time* or one of this week's Decodable Practice Readers.

Professional Development

Fluency Fluency building begins in first grade where the focus is primarily on accuracy and speed. A teacher modeling fluent reading has a positive effect with minimal class disruption.

Daily Fix-It

5. I have a pinc piggy bank
   I have a pin<u>k</u> piggy bank<u>.</u>
6. are you shure you want to bring that?
   <u>A</u>re you <u>s</u>ure you want to bring that?

Discuss the Daily Fix-It corrections with children. Review sentence capitalization and punctuation, the *k* spelling of /k/, and the *s* spelling of /sh/.

ELL

English Language Learners

Verbs That Add –s Pronounce and then act out verbs that a first grader might do in the classroom: *paint, write,* and *read*. Have children select a word to act out. Then have them use the word again in this sentence frame: *A first grader* _____.

Objectives
- Write a draft of comments about a story.
- Use voice in writing.

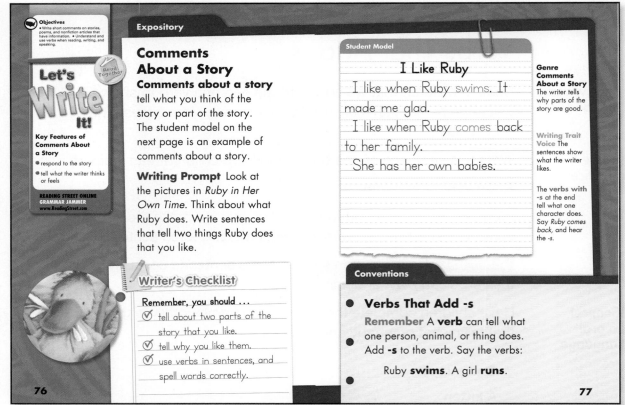

Student Edition pp. 76–77

Let's Write It!—Comments About a Story

Teach

Use pages 76–77 in the Student Edition. Read aloud the Key Features of Comments About a Story and the paragraph that begins with the words *Comments about a story*. Help children better understand the Writing Prompt by reading it aloud and discussing the Writer's Checklist with children.

Review the student model

Then read "I Like Ruby" on page 77 to children. Point out that the writer comments on two things Ruby does—she swims and comes back to her family. Read aloud and briefly discuss the side notes about Genre, the Writing Trait, and Verbs That Add -*s* to help children understand how an author writes comments about a story.

Scoring rubric

Top-Score Response Help children understand that a top-score response has comments about things Ruby does and includes the writer's feelings. For a complete rubric see Writing Rubric 14 from the Teacher Resource DVD-ROM.

Connect to conventions

Read to children the Conventions note about Verbs That Add -*s*. Point out these verbs in the model (*swims, comes*).

Writing—Comments About a Story
Writing Trait: Voice

MINI-LESSON

Voice

■ **Introduce** Use your chart from yesterday and Writing Transparency 14A to model writing comments about a story. Yesterday I recorded my ideas about Ruby. I wrote down how she made me feel. Today, I can use my chart to help me write comments about a story. I will say what Ruby does. Then I will tell how it makes me feel. I will pick words that show my voice. I will tell why I feel the way I do. **Read aloud the draft on the Transparency to show how to turn the chart into comments about a story.**

What Ruby Does Best

I like when Ruby first swim. She swims after everyone else. I was so excited for her. It is great when Ruby flies high in the air. It makes me fel happy. Ruby must be having fun way up there.

Unit 3 Ruby in Her Own Time   Writing Model **14A**

Writing Transparency 14A
TR DVD

■ Explain how children can use their charts from yesterday to draft the comments about a story. Today's goal is to write but not to rewrite each word perfectly. They can edit later to correct the words.

Guide writing Now it is time to write your comments about a story. Tell what Ruby does that you like and why. **Have children use their charts to write their comments. Guide children as needed.**

ROUTINE **Quick Write for Fluency** **Team Talk**

1. **Talk** Have partners take one minute to talk about why they like Ruby.
2. **Write** Each child writes a sentence about their preference.
3. **Share** Partners point out words that show feelings in others' sentences.

Routines Flip Chart

Differentiated Instruction

 Advanced

Voice Challenge children to use words that show exactly how they feel. If necessary, children can use a thesaurus to look up precise adjectives to describe their reactions.

Objectives

- Understand that it is OK to disagree.
- Acknowledge another point of view.
- Ask questions and make comments in an appropriate tone of voice.
- Express ideas through speaking and writing.
- Gather information for an inquiry project.

Listening and Speaking
Share Information About Respect

Introduce respect

Respect helps you work and play well with others. When you show respect, you show that you are thinking about how another person feels. What if Tommy wants to play soccer at recess, and Gina wants to play tag? How can they talk about it and show respect?

- Gina can sit quietly and listen while Tommy is speaking.
- Gina can raise her hand to get permission to speak.
- She can use a nice tone of voice when speaking.
- She can tell Tommy she understands why he wants to play soccer, even if she wants to play tag.

Have children brainstorm other ways they have learned to show respect. (Possible examples: not cutting in line, asking before taking, saying please and thank you)

Model

 What if Sarah wants to play with blocks during our free time, and Joey wants to draw? Let's put on a little play to show what happens when we don't show respect for each other. Who would like to help me act it out? Now let's imagine the same scene, only this time Sarah and Joey show respect for each other. How do you think Sarah and Joey feel after each play?

Guide practice

After the plays, divide the children into pairs or groups. Draw a T-chart on the board, and have each pair or group draw one on paper. Label the columns "Showing Respect" and "Not Showing Respect." Work with children to write words or phrases to fill each column. Then have children work in pairs or groups to add to their own charts. Walk around the room and take dictation as needed. Then have volunteers share their work with the class. As children speak, have them speak in complete sentences with correct subject-verb agreement.

On their own

Have children draw a picture of themselves showing respect to a friend. Encourage children to write a sentence about their picture, offering assistance as needed.

Research and Inquiry
Gather and Record Information

Teach

Tell children that today they will look through sources of information to find facts about a topic. They will write a sentence telling a fact about something they have learned as they have grown.

Model

 Think Aloud Display the list of topics the class created on Day 1. Before we can write a fact sentence, we have to pick a topic. It's best to choose a topic you already know something about. So, I'll ask: What topic do you know the most about? You can gather information about your topic from a source like a textbook. If you see a word you don't know, you can look it up in the glossary.

Guide practice

Have children choose a topic from the list. Then tell them to use reference works to locate information about the topic. Encourage children to find two or three facts about their topic and to record the information they have found. Explain that they will use this information to write a sentence about the topic.

On their own

Use *Reader's and Writer's Notebook* p. 338.

Wrap Up Your Day

✔ **Compare and Contrast** Have children think about Ruby from *Ruby in Her Own Time*. How are you like Ruby? How are you different?

✔ **Inferring** Remind children that, when they infer, they must consider what they already know as well as what is in the text they are reading.

Differentiated Instruction

SI Strategic Intervention

Taking Notes Some children may have trouble taking notes on a topic. Tell these children that they do not need to write down full sentences. They can just write down words or phrases and develop their ideas later in the week.

Reader's and Writer's Notebook p. 338

Preview DAY 4

Tell children that tomorrow they will read about a special crab.

Objectives
- Discuss the concept to develop oral language.
- Build oral vocabulary.
- Identify details in text.

Today at a Glance

Oral Vocabulary
common, lovely

Phonological Awareness
Blend and Segment Syllables

Phonics and Spelling
Review Vowel Sounds of *y*
Review Syllable Pattern CV

High-Frequency Words
Review

Comprehension
◉ Compare and Contrast

Fluency
Appropriate Phrasing

Conventions
Verbs That Add *-s*

Writing
Comments About a Story: Revise

Research and Inquiry
Review and Revise Topic

Concept Talk

Question of the Week
What do we learn as we grow and change?

Build concepts

To reinforce concepts and to focus children's attention, have children sing "On Our Own Time Line" from the *Sing with Me* Big Book. How should we treat people who can't do the same things that we can do? (Possible response: We should be kind to them and help them.)

🔘 Sing with Me Big Book Audio

Review Genre: animal fantasy

Have children tell the key features of animal fantasy: it is a made-up story with animals that do things real animals can't do. Explain that today you will read about a hermit crab who wants to be special in "Hermia's Shell."

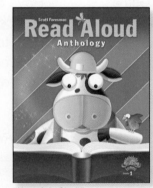

"Hermia's Shell"

Monitor listening comprehension

Recall that Ruby was different from her brothers and sisters because she was smaller and learned more slowly. Have children listen to "Hermia's Shell" to find out how Hermia is different from the other hermit crabs. Read the selection.

ELL **Produce Oral Language** Use the Day 4 instruction on ELL Poster 14 to extend and enrich language.

ELL Poster 14

Oral Vocabulary
Amazing Words

Teach Amazing Words

Amazing Words **Oral Vocabulary Routine**

① **Introduce the Word** Relate the word *lovely* to the story. Hermia's new shell had *lovely* ridges. Supply a child-friendly definition. Something that is *lovely* is very beautiful. Have children say the word.

② **Demonstrate** Provide examples to show meaning. The different colors on the flowers looked *lovely*. The sunset over the lake was *lovely*.

③ **Apply** Have children demonstrate their understanding. Name a word that means the opposite of *lovely*.

See p. OV•2 to teach *common*.

Routines Flip Chart

Anchored Talk

Add to the concept map

Discuss what we learn as we grow and change.

• We read about a hermit crab today in "Hermia's Shell." How does Hermia change over time? (She gets bigger and needs a new shell.)

• What does Hermia learn after her time alone living in her beautiful shell? (Her friends are more important than having a beautiful shell.) What can people learn from Hermia's experience? (Friends are more important than things.) Add *Friends are more important than things* to the concept map.

Amazing Words

attempt	flatter
event	correct
time line	common
famous	lovely

Differentiated Instruction

Ⓐ **Advanced**

Extend Amazing Words Ask questions such as the following. Encourage children to use the words in discussion and writing.

• What is something that you think could be *lovely*?

• What are some *common* foods served at your house?

ELL

English Language Learners

Demonstrate To illustrate the meaning of *lovely*, show children various pictures or paintings and have them explain why each one is *lovely*.

Objectives
- Segment and blend words with two syllables.
- Read words with vowel sounds of *y* and syllable pattern CV.

Phonological Awareness
Segment and Blend Syllables

Model
This week we read about a duck named Ruby. Listen as I say the two syllables in Ruby. **Slowly model the syllables:** /rü/ • /bē/. Now I will blend the two syllables together to say the name: /rü/ • /bē/, Ruby.

Guide practice
I will say two syllables. Repeat them after me. Then blend the syllables to make a word from the story. **Say each syllable pair below. Have children say and then blend the syllables to form a word.**

Corrective feedback
If children make an error, model the correct response. Return to the word later in the practice.

/duk/ • /ling/ (duckling)	/in/ • /tü/ (into)	/ə/ • /mong/ (among)
/ə/ • /pon/ (upon)	/flī/ • /ing/ (flying)	/muᴛʜ/ • /ər/ (mother)

On their own
Have children segment and blend the following two-syllable words.

/sun/ • /līt/ (sunlight)	/ver/ • /ē/ (very)	/môr/ • /ning/ (morning)
/nō/ • /hwer/ (nowhere)	/drīv/ • /ing/ (driving)	/ā/ • /bəl/ (able)

Phonics Review
Vowel Sounds of *y*; Syllable Pattern CV

Review
Sound-spellings

To review last week's first phonics skill, write *fly* and *fluffy*. You studied words like these last week. What do you know about the sound of *y* at the end of a one-syllable word? (The *y* stands for the sound /ī/.) What do you know about the sound of *y* at the end of a two-syllable word? (The *y* stands for the sound /ē/.)

Corrective feedback

If children are unable to answer your questions about the vowel sounds in the words you wrote, refer them to Sound-Spelling Cards 77 and 81.

Review
CV pattern

To review last week's second phonics skill, write *me*, *hi*, and *go*. You also studied words like these. What sounds do the letters *e*, *i*, and *o* stand for in these words? (The *e* stands for the sound /ē/, the *i* for the sound /ī/, and the *o* for the sound /ō/.)

Guide practice

Use Graphic Organizer 4. When I say a word, hold up one hand if the word has one syllable or two hands if it has two syllables: *my, smelly, cry, be, candy, sloppy, fussy, hi, no, silly*. Write each word in the appropriate column. Have children identify words with the sound /ē/ *(be, smelly, candy, sloppy, fussy, silly)* and the sound /i/ *(my, cry, hi)*.

One Syllable	Two Syllables
my	smelly
cry	candy
be	sloppy
hi	fussy
no	silly

On their own

Use Let's Practice It! pp. 131–132 on the *Teacher Resource DVD-ROM*.

Let's Practice It!
TR DVD•131

Let's Practice It!
TR DVD•132

ELL

English Language Learners

Produce Final /ī/ For Spanish speakers, the long *i* sound in words such as *fly* may need additional practice. Say the word slowly, stressing the final /ī/, and have children repeat the word to learn its formal pronunciation.

Objectives

- Apply knowledge of sound-spellings to decode unknown words when reading.
- Decode words in context and isolation.
- Practice fluency with oral rereading.

Decodable Reader 14C
Consonant Patterns *ng, nk*; Compound Words

Decodable Practice Reader 14C

Decode words in isolation

Have children turn to p. 185. Have children decode each word.

Review High-frequency words

Review the previously taught words *for, the, of, put, wanted, new, to,* and *a.* Have children read each word as you point to it on the Word Wall.

Preview

Have children read the title and preview the story. Tell them they will read words with consonant patterns *ng* and *nk* and compound words.

Decode words in context

Pair children for reading and listen carefully as they decode. One child begins. Children read the entire story, switching readers after each page. Partners reread the story. This time the other child begins.

Decodable Practice Reader 14C

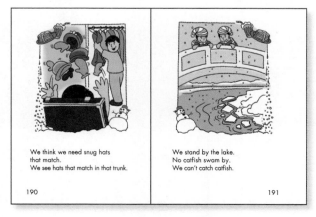

Corrective feedback

If... children have difficulty decoding a word,
then... refer them to the Sound-Spelling Cards to identify the sounds in the word or the base words in a compound word. Then prompt them to blend the word.

- What is the new word?
- Is the new word a word you know?
- Does it make sense in the story?

Check decoding and comprehension

Have children retell the story to include characters, setting, and events. Then have children find words with consonant patterns *ng* and *nk* and compound words in the story. Children could supply *rang, drank, things, long, think, trunk, hang, pancakes, milkshakes, outside, catfish,* and *inside*.

Reread for Fluency

Have children reread Decodable Practice Reader 14C to develop automaticity decoding words with consonant patterns *ng* and *nk* and compound words.

ROUTINE   Oral Rereading

 Read Have children read the entire book orally.

 Reread To achieve optimal fluency, children should reread the text three or four times.

 Corrective Feedback Listen as children read. Provide corrective feedback regarding their fluency and decoding.

Routines Flip Chart

English Language Learners

Beginning After they have read the story, have children look at the drawings that border each picture and identify the two compound words pictured in the top corner (pancakes, milkshake).

Intermediate Review the word *things* from the story. Then challenge children to think of another word they could add to *thing* to form a compound word. (Possible answers: *some, every, any*)

Advanced/Advanced High Have children construct a sentence telling what they think might happen next. Encourage them to use one word with consonant pattern *ng* or *nk* or one compound word.

Objectives

- Read words fluently in context and in isolation.
- Spell words with the consonant digraphs *ng* and *nk*.
- Spell high-frequency words.

Fluent Word Reading
Spiral Review

Read words in isolation

Display these words. Tell children that they can blend some words on this list and others are Word Wall words.

Have children read the list three or four times until they can read at the rate of two to three seconds per word.

always	day	food	everything	me
stays	my	by	grow	nothing
around	Jimmy	become	horse	go
happy	try	we	stall	sky

Word Reading

Corrective feedback

If... children have difficulty reading whole words,
then... have them use sound-by-sound blending for decodable words or have them say and spell high-frequency words.

If... children cannot read fluently at a rate of two to three seconds per word,
then... have pairs practice the list until they can read it fluently.

Read words in context

Display these sentences. Call on individuals to read a sentence. Then randomly point to review words and have children read them. To help you monitor word reading, high-frequency words are underlined and decodable words are italicized.

My happy <u>horse</u> *always has* <u>food</u> <u>around</u> *his stall.*

<u>Everything</u> *will* <u>grow</u> <u>day</u> *by* <u>day</u> *and* <u>become</u> *big.*

Jimmy <u>stays</u> *with me, and we try* <u>to</u> *make things.*

<u>Nothing</u> *can go up in* <u>the</u> *sky* <u>now</u>.

Sentence Reading

Corrective feedback

If... children are unable to read an underlined high-frequency word,
then... read the word for them and spell it, having them echo you.

If... children have difficulty reading an italicized decodable word,
then... guide them in using sound-by-sound blending.

Spelling
Words with *ng, nk*

Partner Review

Supply pairs of children with index cards on which the spelling words have been written. Have one child read a word while the other writes it. Then have children switch roles. Have them use the cards to check their spelling and correct any misspelled words.

On their own

Use *Reader's and Writer's Notebook* p. 343.

Reader's and Writer's Notebook p. 343

Small Group Time

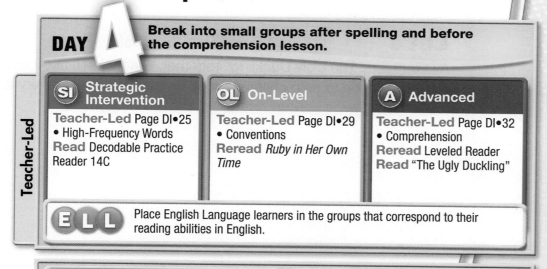

DAY 4 Break into small groups after spelling and before the comprehension lesson.

Teacher-Led

SI Strategic Intervention
Teacher-Led Page DI•25
• High-Frequency Words
Read Decodable Practice Reader 14C

OL On-Level
Teacher-Led Page DI•29
• Conventions
Reread *Ruby in Her Own Time*

A Advanced
Teacher-Led Page DI•32
• Comprehension
Reread Leveled Reader
Read "The Ugly Duckling"

ELL Place English Language learners in the groups that correspond to their reading abilities in English.

Practice Stations
• Words to Know
• Get Fluent

Independent Activities
• Read independently/Reading Log on *Reader's and Writer's Notebook* p. RR4
• AudioText of Paired Selection

Spiral Review

These activities review

• previously taught high-frequency words *always, around, become, day, everything, food, grow, horse, nothing, stays.*

• /ī/ and /ē/ spelled *y*, long vowels (CV), and initial consonant blends.

English Language Learners
Fluent Word Reading Have children listen to a more fluent reader say the words. Then have them repeat the words.

Objectives

- Recognize structure and elements of a fairy tale.
- Relate prior knowledge to new text.
- Set purpose for reading.

Read Together

Social Studies in Reading

Preview and predict

Read the title and the first sentence of the selection. Have children look through the selection and predict what they might learn. (Possible response: They might learn about the ugly duckling.) Ask them what clue helped them make that prediction. (Possible responses: the title of the selection or the pictures)

Let's Think About Genre

Fairy Tale Tell children that they will read a **fairy tale**. Review the key features of a fairy tale: it is a story with made-up characters that are sometimes animals; it often begins with the phrase "Once upon a time" and ends with the phrase "happily ever after." Explain that this selection is a fairy tale because it is a short story with animal characters, and it begins with "Once upon a time" and ends with "The swan lived happily ever after."

Activate prior knowledge

Ask children to recall what they have already learned about growing and changing. (Possible response: Sometimes we learn in our own way and sometimes other people help us learn.)

Set a purpose for reading

Let's Read Together Have children read to look for elements of a fairy tale.

Let's Think About... Fairy Tale

As you read "The Ugly Duckling" together, use Let's Think About in the Student Edition to help children focus on the features of a fairy tale.

Objectives
• Explain why some of the same phrases are used in different stories.

Social Studies in Reading

Genre
Fairy Tale

• A fairy tale is a story with made-up characters that are sometimes animals.

• A fairy tale often begins with the phrase "Once upon a time." This phrase means that the story happened long ago, and that it is probably a fantasy.

• A fairy tale often ends with the phrase "They lived happily ever after." This phrase means that no matter what problems the characters have during the story, things get better for them later.

• As you read "The Ugly Duckling," look for elements of a fairy tale.

The Ugly Duckling

Once upon a time, Mother Duck's seven eggs hatched. Six of the ducklings looked alike. One was different.

Let's **Think** About...

This story begins with the phrase "Once upon a time." What does that tell you?
Fairy Tale

78
79

Student Edition pp. 78–79

Academic Vocabulary

character a person or animal in a story

compare tell how things are the same

contrast tell how things are different

Social Studies Vocabulary

nest a place used by birds to lay their eggs and then raise their babies

Guide Comprehension
↺ Compare and Contrast

Guide practice

Think Aloud Good readers compare and contrast as they read to see how things in the story are alike and different. When I finished reading *Ruby in Her Own Time*, I recalled that Ruby was different from her brothers and sisters. She learned to do things in her own time. As I read "The Ugly Duckling," I will pay attention to how the characters are alike and different.

Let's 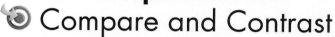 About... Fairy Tale

Possible response: The phrase "Once upon a time" tells me that this story is probably a fairy tale. The phrase means that the story happened a long time ago and that the story is probably a fantasy.

Objectives

- Connect text to personal experiences.
- Discuss the function of recurring phrases in a fairy tale.
- Read aloud fluently with accuracy and at an appropriate rate.

Check Fluency WCPM
SUCCESS PREDICTOR

Student Edition pp. 80–81

Guide Comprehension, continued

Compare and Contrast How is the "ugly duckling" different at the end of the story than at the beginning? (Possible response: At the beginning, it looked like an ugly duckling, but by the end, it is a beautiful swan.)

Connect text to self The ugly duckling is different from the other ducklings. It is special. What are some things that make you different and special? (Possible response: I love to draw. That makes me special.)

Let's Think About... Fairy Tale

Possible response: I know the story is a fairy tale because it is a made-up story with animal characters. The story starts with the phrase "Once upon a time." The story ends with "happily ever after." In this story, that means that the swan will have a good life.

Reading Across Texts Ruby's problem is that she learns to do things in her own time. The ugly duckling's problem is that it looks different from the other ducklings.

Writing Across Texts Children might note that Ruby's parents would love the ugly ducking and let it grow up in its own way.

Fluency
Appropriate Phrasing

Guide practice

- Have children turn to pp. 64–65 in *Ruby in Her Own Time*.
- Have children follow along as you read the pages with appropriate phrasing.
- Have the class read the pages with you and then reread the pages as a group without you until they read with appropriate phrasing. To provide additional fluency practice, pair nonfluent readers with fluent readers.

ROUTINE — Paired Reading

1. **Select a Passage** For *Ruby in Her Own Time*, use pp. 68–69.
2. **Model** First, have children track the print as you read.
3. **Guide Practice** Then have children read along with you.
4. **On Their Own** For optimal fluency, have partners reread three or four times.

Routines Flip Chart

 Don't Wait Until Friday

MONITOR PROGRESS — Check Fluency WCPM

As children reread, monitor their progress toward their individual fluency goals. Current Goal: 20–30 words correct per minute. End-of-Year Goal: 60 words correct per minute.

If... children cannot read fluently at a rate of 20–30 words correct per minute,

then... have children practice with text at their independent level.

Day 1	Day 2	Day 3	Day 4	Day 5
Check Word Reading	Check Word Reading	Check High-Frequency Words/ Retelling	Check Fluency	Check Oral Vocabulary

Success Predictor

Differentiated Instruction

 A **Advanced**

WCPM If children already read at 60 words correct per minute, allow them to read independently.

Fluency Assessment Plan

Do a formal fluency assessment with 8 to 10 children every week. Assess 4 to 5 children on Day 4 and 4 to 5 children on Day 5. Use the reproducible fluency passage, Teacher's Edition, page 83f.

Options for Oral Rereading

Use *Ruby in Her Own Time* or one of this week's Decodable Readers.

Fluency WCPM

Success Predictor

Objectives
- Use present tense verbs with correct subject-verb agreement.
- Spell present tense verbs with correct inflectional endings.
- Revise a draft.

Conventions
Verbs That Add -s

Test practice

Use *Reader's and Writer's Notebook* p. 344 to help children understand present tense verbs in test items. Recall that present tense verbs tell what someone or something does now: *sings, dances,* or *makes.* Model identifying a present tense verb in a sentence by writing this sentence on the board, reading it aloud, and underlining the present tense verb.

> Willy <u>skates</u> on the sidewalk.

Then read the *Reader's and Writer's Notebook* p. 344 directions. Guide children as they mark the answer for number 1.

On their own

Use *Reader's and Writer's Notebook* p. 344.

Connect to oral language

After children mark the answers to numbers 1–6, review the correct choices aloud, and have children read each sentence, emphasizing the present tense verbs.

Reader's and Writer's Notebook p. 344

Writing—Comments About a Story
Revising Strategy

MINI-LESSON

Revising Strategy: Adding a Sentence

■ Yesterday we wrote comments about a story. Today we will revise. We can look for missing information in our comments. We will decide if we left out any important ideas. Then we can add a sentence if we did.

Writing Transparency 14B
TR DVD

■ Display the Revising Tips. Explain that this is a time for making the comments clear for anyone who will read them. Tomorrow children will proofread to correct any errors such as misspellings, and incorrect use of verbs that add -s.

Revising Tips
☑ Make sure your comments are about the story.
☑ Add sentences if you left out important ideas.

■ Use Writing Transparency 14B to model adding a sentence. In my comments, I say I was excited for Ruby, but I don't tell why. I need to add a sentence to explain why I was excited. Add the sentence *It took me a long time to swim, too* to the transparency.
Tell children that they can add a sentence as they revise.

Peer conferencing

Peer Revision Have pairs exchange papers and mark each sentence with a 1, 2, or 3. Write the key on the board: 1 = What Ruby Does. 2 = How Writer Feels. 3 = Why Writer Feels. Once children are done reading and marking, they can return papers and make suggestions for additional sentences based on the numbering system. For example, if a paper has sentences numbered 1, 2, 1, 2, 3, then the writer might add a sentence telling why he or she feels as she does to the sentence labeled 2.

Differentiated Instruction

SI **Strategic Intervention**

Support Revising Remind children that during revising, they need to make sure that they have all the important ideas down. They should check that these ideas make sense. Guide children through identifying the key features of comments about a story. Children should make sure they tell two things Ruby does and share their reactions to those two things.

Daily Fix-It

7. Are you sur the phone rangg?
   Are you <u>sure</u> the phone <u>rang</u>?
8. Take this chek to the banc.
   Take this <u>check</u> to the <u>bank</u>.

Discuss the Daily Fix-It corrections with children. Review the spelling of *sure* and *rang* and of the hard *k* sound as *ck* and *k*.

English Language Learners

Verbs That Add -s Be sure children understand when to add -s to nouns and verbs. A noun that names one thing has no added -s. A verb that tells one thing's action has an -s.

Objectives
- Revise a draft for clarity.
- Review answers to inquiry questions.

Writing
Comments About a Story, continued

Guide practice

Have children revise their comments about a story. For those not sure how to revise, have children refer to the Revising Tips or the Key Features of Comments About a Story.

Corrective feedback

Circulate to monitor and conference with children as they write. Remind them that they will have time to proofread and edit tomorrow. Today they can identify any missing ideas and add a sentence to make the writing complete and the ideas clear.

ROUTINE Quick Write for Fluency · Team Talk

 Talk Have children share their new sentences with partners.

 Write Have children write a sentence that tells why they added that new sentence.

 Share Partners can read the explanations to one another.

Routines Flip Chart

Research and Inquiry
Review and Revise Topic

Teach

Tell children that the next step in the inquiry project is to review our topic to see if we have the information we set out to find. Or, did our answers lead to a different topic?

Model

 Think Aloud We wanted to come up with a fact about a topic we have learned about. First, we listed topics we already knew about. Then we picked the one we knew best. Last, we gathered some information about the topic. Now I will look at the information I gathered. I will see if I found any good facts I can write a sentence about. If I did not, I can always gather more information. If there are any words I do not understand, I may be able to look them up in the glossary.

Guide practice

Have children look at the information they gathered during Day 3. Instruct them to work with a partner to choose the most interesting fact about the topic. If necessary, they can conduct more research to collect more facts. Finally, tell children that tomorrow they will organize all the information in order to share it with others.

Wrap Up Your Day

✓ **Phonics** List several compound words and words ending *ng, nk*. Have children read each word and identify which are compound words.

✓ **Fluency** Write *Who is this duck? Will she be back?* Have the class reread the questions until they can do so with appropriate phrasing.

Preview DAY 5

Remind children that they heard about a swan that thought he was a duck. Tomorrow they will hear about the swan again.

Objectives

- Review the concept: what we learn as we grow and change.
- Build oral vocabulary.
- Identify details in text.

Today at a Glance

Oral Vocabulary
Review

Phonics
◉ Review Consonant Patterns *ng, nk*
◉ Review Compound Words

Comprehension
◉ Compare and Contrast

Story Words
Review

High-Frequency Words
Review

Conventions
Verbs That Add *–s*

Writing
Comments About a Story

Research and Inquiry
Communicate

Check Oral Vocabulary
SUCCESS PREDICTOR

Concept Wrap Up

Question of the Week
What do we learn as we grow and change?

"Hermia's Shell"

Review Concept

This week we have read and listened to stories about things we learn as we grow and change. Today you will listen to find out how Hermia learns about herself as she grows and changes. **Read the story.**

- What did Hermia learn as she grew and changed? (Possible responses: She learned that having a beautiful shell wasn't that important. She learned that her friends didn't like her bragging about her shell.)

Review Amazing Words

Orally review the meaning of this week's Amazing Words. Then display this week's concept map. Have children use Amazing Words such as *attempt, correct,* and *event,* as well as the concept map, to answer the question, "What do we learn as we grow and change?"

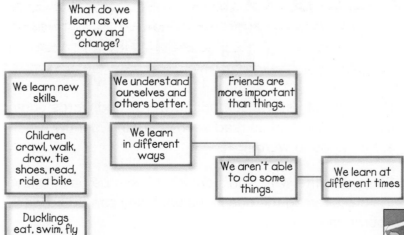

ELL Check Concepts and Language Use the Day 5 instruction on ELL Poster 14 to monitor children's understanding of the lesson concept.

ELL Poster 14

Oral Vocabulary
Amazing Ideas

Connect to the Big Question

Team Talk Pair children and have them discuss how the Question of the Week connects to this unit's Big Question, "What is changing in our world?" Tell children to use the concept map and what they've learned from this week's Anchored Talks and reading selections to form an Amazing Idea—a realization or "big idea" about **change**. Then ask each pair to share their Amazing Idea with the class.

Amazing Ideas might include these key concepts:

- Children change as they grow.
- As children grow and change, they learn new skills, such as walking, drawing, or riding a bike.

It's Friday

MONITOR PROGRESS **Check Oral Vocabulary**

Call on individuals to use this week's Amazing Words to talk about what we learn as we grow and change. Prompt discussion with the questions below. Monitor children's ability to use the Amazing Words and note which words children are unable to use.

- **What new skill will you *attempt* to learn?**
- **When might a person look *lovely*?**
- **What is one skill you learned on your own *time line*?**
- **What is one way a person can become *famous*?**
- **What was one exciting *event* in your life?**
- **How could you *flatter* your friends?**
- **What do you do to *correct* your mistakes?**
- **What is a *common* color for school buses?**

If... children have difficulty using the Amazing Words,

then... reteach the unknown words using the Oral Vocabulary Routines, pp. 45a, 50b, 74b, 78b.

Day 1	Day 2	Day 3	Day 4	Day 5
Check Word Reading	Check Word Reading	Check High-Frequency Words/Retelling	Check Fluency	Check Oral Vocabulary

Success Predictor

Amazing Words

attempt	flatter
event	correct
time line	lovely
famous	common

English Language Learners
Amazing Words Use pantomime or gesture to give children clues as you review the Amazing Words.

Objectives
◎ Review words with the consonant patterns *ng* and *nk*.
◎ Review compound words.
• Add final sound to create a new word.

Assess
• Spell words with the consonant patterns *ng* and *nk*.
• Spell high-frequency words.

Phonemic Awareness
Add Final Phonemes

Review
Final consonants and digraphs

Have children add a final sound to each word below to make a new word. If children make an error, model the correct response. Return to the word later in the practice.

an/t/ **ant**	bar/n/ **barn**	see/d/ **seed**
for/k/ **fork**	fir/m/ **firm**	how/l/ **howl**
ram/p/ **ramp**	too/th/ **tooth**	pea/ch/ **peach**

Phonics

↻ Consonant Patterns *ng, nk*; Compound Words

Review
Target phonics skills

Write the following sentences on the board. Have children read each one, first quietly to themselves and then aloud as you track the print.

1. **Hank put the junk outside on the driveway.**
2. **Do you think the king can sing?**
3. **Thank Frank for bringing the homemade food.**
4. **Mom put on pink lipstick.**

Team Talk Have children discuss with a partner which words have *ng*, which words have *nk*, and which words are compound words. Then call on individuals to share with the class.

Spelling Test
Words with *ng, nk*

Dictate spelling words

Say each word, read the sentence, repeat the word, and allow time for children to write the word.

1. **blank**	Fill the **blank** sheet of paper.
2. **sunk**	The stone had **sunk** in the lake.
3. **wing**	Look out at the **wing** of the plane.
4. **pink**	I have a **pink** backpack.
5. **bring**	**Bring** the cat inside.
6. **rink**	We'll go to the ice **rink** on the weekend.
7. **trunk**	Shut the lid of the **trunk.**
8. **rang**	The bells **rang**.
9. **bank**	Go to the **bank** with your check.
10. **sang**	We **sang** at the baseball game.

High-Frequency Words

11. **every**	**Every** man at the desk had a laptop.
12. **sure**	Are you **sure** you can sing?

Small Group Time

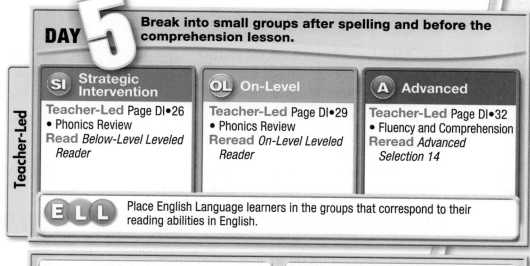

DAY 5

Break into small groups after spelling and before the comprehension lesson.

Teacher-Led

SI Strategic Intervention
Teacher-Led Page DI•26
• Phonics Review
Read *Below-Level Leveled Reader*

OL On-Level
Teacher-Led Page DI•29
• Phonics Review
Reread *On-Level Leveled Reader*

A Advanced
Teacher-Led Page DI•32
• Fluency and Comprehension
Reread *Advanced Selection 14*

ELL Place English Language learners in the groups that correspond to their reading abilities in English.

Practice Stations
• Words to Know
• Read for Meaning

Independent Activities
• Read independently/Reading Log on *Reader's and Writer's Notebook* p. RR4
• Concept Talk Video

Differentiated Instruction

SI Strategic Intervention
Segment Words Help children spell each word on the test by saying the individual sounds in each word, for example: /b/ /l/ /a/ /ngk/.

English Language Learners

Spelling Dictation Be sure to clearly pronounce beginning consonant blends in *blank*, *bring*, and *trunk*, as speakers of Asian languages, such as Chinese, Korean, and Vietnamese, may have difficulty hearing the sounds /l/ and /r/ in the blends.

Objectives

- Share information and ideas effectively.
- Speak clearly and at an appropriate pace.
- Use the conventions of language when speaking.
- Listen attentively.
- Identify synonyms.
- Read aloud fluently with appropriate phrasing.

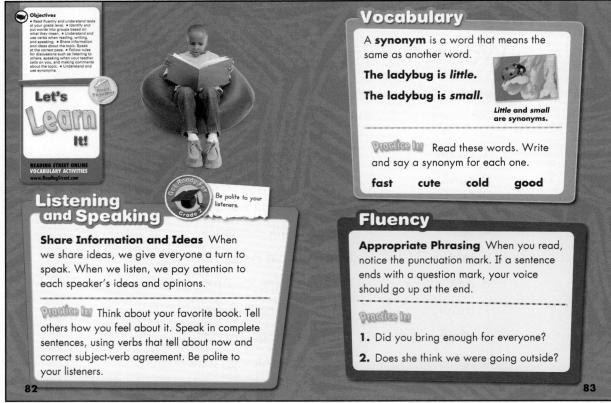

Let's Learn It!

READING STREET ONLINE
VOCABULARY ACTIVITIES
www.ReadingStreet.com

Vocabulary

A **synonym** is a word that means the same as another word.

The ladybug is *little*.

The ladybug is *small*.

Little and *small* are synonyms.

Practice It! Read these words. Write and say a synonym for each one.

fast   cute   cold   good

Listening and Speaking

Share Information and Ideas When we share ideas, we give everyone a turn to speak. When we listen, we pay attention to each speaker's ideas and opinions.

Practice It! Think about your favorite book. Tell others how you feel about it. Speak in complete sentences, using verbs that tell about now and correct subject-verb agreement. Be polite to your listeners.

Be polite to your listeners.

Fluency

Appropriate Phrasing When you read, notice the punctuation mark. If a sentence ends with a question mark, your voice should go up at the end.

Practice It!

1. Did you bring enough for everyone?
2. Does she think we were going outside?

82   83

Student Edition pp. 82–83

Listening and Speaking
Share Information and Ideas

Teach

Have children turn to pages 82–83 of the Student Edition. Remind children that good speakers wait to be called on before they speak. Good listeners pay attention to everyone's ideas.

Analyze model

Read the top part of the box with children. Model how to pay attention to a speaker. I look at the speaker and sit quietly. I do not think about what I want to say later. Have children add other ideas about listening attentively. (Possible response: Do not interrupt.)

Introduce prompt

Read the Practice It! prompt with the class. Remind children that good speakers use active verbs, including verbs that add -s.

Team Talk Have children take turns telling others about their favorite book. Tell children that good speakers speak clearly and slowly, and that good listeners look directly at the speaker.

Vocabulary
Synonyms

Teach

Read and discuss the Vocabulary lesson on page 83 of the Student Edition. Use the model to explain that a synonym is a word that has the same meaning as another word.

Model

Point to the illustration. What do we see in this picture? It's a *little* ladybug. What does *little* mean? (not large; small in size). We could also say, The ladybug is *small*. *Little* and *small* have the same meaning. They are synonyms.

Guide practice

Read the instructions for the Vocabulary Practice It! activity. Read the first word and then have children repeat after you.

What is a word that means the same thing as *fast*? *Quick* is a synonym for fast. They both mean "to move with speed."

On their own

Have children continue identifying synonyms for the other words in the list.

Corrective feedback

Circulate around the room and listen as children say the other words and their synonyms. Provide assistance as needed.

Fluency
Appropriate Phrasing

Teach

Read and discuss the Fluency instructions.

Read words in context

Give children a moment to look at the sentences. Then have them read each sentence three or four times until they can read each sentence with appropriate phrasing.

Differentiated Instruction

 Advanced

Self-Reflection Have children write a few sentences about how effectively they spoke about their favorite book. What did they do well? What could they do better next time?

Share Information and Ideas

To prepare themselves for skills needed at Grade 2, children should be able to effectively share information and ideas using appropriate phrasing.

ELL

English Language Learners
Language Production Have children point to each word and complete this sentence frame: Another word for _____ is _____.

Objectives

◎ Compare and contrast elements of a story.

• Read high-frequency and story words.

• Identify the features of a fairy tale.

Comprehension
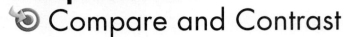
Compare and Contrast

Review
Compare and contrast

Remember that good readers tell how the things they read about are alike and different. What is telling how things are alike called? (**comparing**) What is telling how things are different called? (**contrasting**)

To check understanding of compare and contrast, read aloud the following story and have children answer the questions that follow.

> Today, Javier's family got a little bigger. Javier's father brought home two puppies, Meg and Jack! Both Meg and Jack are tiny cocker spaniels. Meg has golden fur, but Jack is black and white. Meg's ears are huge and floppy! Jack has big ears, too. Meg is a girl dog, but Jack is a boy dog. Most importantly, they both love to play with Javier!

1. What is one way Meg and Jack are alike? (**Possible response: They are both cocker spaniels.**)

2. What is one way Meg and Jack are different? (**Possible response: Meg is golden, but Jack is black and white.**)

Vocabulary
High-Frequency and Story Words

Review
High-frequency words

Review this week's high-frequency words: *any, enough, ever, every, own, sure,* and *were*. Model making up a sentence that tells something about this week's selection and includes a high-frequency word. For example: Father Duck wondered if Ruby would ever swim.

Team Talk Have children retell *Ruby in Her Own Time,* one sentence at a time. Encourage them to use at least one of the remaining six words in each sentence.

Review
Story words

Write the words *beautiful, father, feather, flew, mother, precious, night,* and *howling.* Read them aloud together. Then have children tell what each word means.

Corrective feedback

If... children cannot tell what the story words mean,

then... review the definitions on page 52a.

Genre
Fairy Tale

Review Genre

Review with children that a fairy tale is a timeless story that has been passed down by word of mouth. Fairy tales have magical characters and events, and they often include well-known phrases or sentences such as "once upon a time." The author wants readers to connect the events and characters in a fairy tale to their own experience.

Teach

In "The Ugly Duckling," Mother Duck has seven ducklings. Six of the ducklings look the same, but one duckling is different. They call the different one the "ugly duckling." Later, though, the "ugly duckling" grows up to be a beautiful swan and lives a happy life.

Model

 Think Aloud I can tell "The Ugly Duckling" is a fairy tale because it is a story that could be told at any time and in any place. It also includes the common phrase "once upon a time." This story reminds me of my friend's experience growing up. She had bright red hair, and everyone made fun of her because she was different. But when she got older, people thought her red hair was beautiful and special.

Guide practice

Ask the following questions to guide children in describing a fairy tale and connecting it to their own experience.

- What is magical about this story? (The duckling grows up and turns into a beautiful swan.)

- What is another example of a well-known phrase in this story? ("happily ever after")

- How does this fairy tale remind you of your own life? (Possible response: Sometimes people make comments because I wear glasses. They think I am different.)

On their own

The six ducklings make fun of the "ugly duckling" because it is different. Why do you think the ducklings make fun of their sibling? (Possible response: They make fun of the "ugly duckling" because they want to feel better about the way they look. Maybe they *really* think the "ugly" duckling is beautiful.)

Differentiated Instruction

A Advanced

Challenge children to write a different ending for "The Ugly Duckling." Have children share their new endings with the class.

Academic Vocabulary

fairy tale a folk story with magical characters and events

Assess

- ◉ Words with Consonant Patterns *ng, nk*
- ◉ Compound Words
- • High-Frequency Words
- • Fluency: WCPM
- ◉ Compare and Contrast

Fluency Goals

Set individual fluency goals for children to enable them to reach the end-of-year goal.

- • **Current Goal:** 20–30 WCPM
- • **End-of-Year Goal:** 60 WCPM

Assessment
Monitor Progress

For a written assessment of consonant patterns *ng* and *nk*, compound words, high-frequency words, and comparing and contrasting, use Weekly Test 14, pp. 115–120.

Assess words in context

Sentence reading Use the following reproducible page to assess children's ability to read words in context. Call on children to read two sentences aloud. Start over with sentence one if necessary.

> **MONITOR PROGRESS** **Sentence Reading**
>
> **If...** children have trouble reading the consonants,
> **then...** use the Reteach Lesson on p. 211 of *First Stop*.
>
> **If...** children cannot read all the high-frequency words,
> **then...** mark the missed words on a high-frequency word list and have the child practice reading the words with a fluent reader.
>
>

Assess

Fluency Take a one-minute sample of children's oral reading. Have children read the fluency passage on page 83f.

Comprehension Have the child read the entire passage. (If the child has difficulty with the passage, you may read it aloud.) Then have the child compare and contrast "Cupcake and Link."

> **MONITOR PROGRESS** **Fluency and Comprehension**
>
> **If...** a child does not achieve the fluency goal on the timed reading,
> **then...** copy the passage and send it home with the child for additional fluency practice, or have the child practice with a fluent reader.
>
> **If...** a child cannot compare and contrast,
> **then...** use the Reteach Lesson on p. 254 of *First Stop*.

Monitor accuracy

Record scores Have children monitor accuracy by recording their scores using the Sentence Reading Chart and by recording the number of words read correctly per minute on the Fluency Progress Chart in *First Stop*.

Name _____

Read the Sentences

1. Did you ever skate at an outside rink?

2. Frank made his treehouse big enough.

3. There were some pinecones by the swings.

4. Sandy put her own things in her backpack.

5. We will bring any homework we need.

6. My family sang every day last weekend.

7. Hank sure ate that pancake fast.

MONITOR PROGRESS
- Fluency
- Consonant patterns *ng, nk*
- Compound words
- High-frequency words

Name _____

Read the Story

Cupcake and Link

Last weekend, Frank gave his dog Cupcake   7
a bath. He filled the bathtub with water. Then Frank   17
picked up Cupcake. He put Cupcake into the bathtub.   26
Plunk! Cupcake sat inside the bathtub. Frank sang   34
a song. Everything was fine. Cupcake got her bath.   43

Frank also gave his cat Link a bath. The bathtub   53
was too big. So, Frank filled the sink with water. He put 65
Link in the sink. Link flung water all around. Then he   76
yanked himself from Frank's hands and jumped out.   84

Link sure did not like the bath. How could Frank   94
keep Link in the sink? He had to think of something.   105
Frank looked inside his backpack. He got a little   114
ball. When Link had the ball, he did not jump out   125
of the sink. So, Link got his bath, too.   134

MONITOR PROGRESS
• Fluency
• Compare and Contrast

Objectives
- Use present tense verbs with correct subject-verb agreement.
- Use inflectional endings to spell verbs correctly.

Conventions
Verbs That Add -s

Review

Remind children that present tense verbs are verbs that tell what someone or something is doing now. Have them give examples of present tense verbs.

Guide practice

Write the following sentences. Have children write a verb that makes sense in each blank.

> 1. Dad _____ at Willy.
>
> 2. Willy _____ Dad.
>
> 3. Ruby _____ away.

Connect to oral language

Display and read the following sentence frame. Have children work in pairs to name as many present tense verbs as they can that could be used to complete the sentence. Then have children share their responses with the class.

> **A first grader _____ at school.**

On their own

Use Let's Practice It! p. 135 on the *Teacher Resource DVD-ROM.*

Let's Practice It!
TR DVD•135

Daily Fix-It

9. I am <u>shure</u> the dog swims.
   I am sure the dog swims.

10. The cat <u>cin jumps</u>.
    The cat can jump.

Discuss the Daily Fix-It corrections with children. Review subject-verb agreement and the spelling of present tense verbs.

Objectives
- Edit a draft for spelling, punctuation, and capitalization.
- Create final draft and present.

Writing—Comments About a Story
Writer's Craft: Verbs That Add -s

Review
Revising

Remind children that yesterday they revised their comments about a story. They may have added sentences to make the ideas clearer. Today they will proofread their comments about a story.

MINI-LESSON

Proofread for Verbs That Add -s

■ **Teach** When we write, we need to spell words correctly and use the words we mean. If we do this, then our readers will understand us. We can share our ideas with each other. No one will be confused. I will read through my comments about a story. Each time I read, I will check for a different mistake.

Writing Transparency 14C
TR DVD

■ **Model** Let's look at my comments about a story. Display Writing Transparency 14C. Explain that you will look at the verbs to make sure you have added -s where it is needed. Stop after reading the first sentence. Explain that *swim* needs an -s because it tells what one animal (Ruby) does. Model adding the -s using the proofreading marks. Continue reading, checking for verbs, punctuation, and spelling. Model correcting the misspelling of *feel*. Tell children they will use the proofreading marks to make corrections to their own comments.

Proofread

Display the Proofreading Tips. Have children proofread their comments to correct any misspellings, missing -s endings on verbs, or errors with periods. Circulate to assist children with verbs or other words.

Proofreading Tips

✓ Do my verbs need an -s?

✓ Are my words spelled correctly? Check a dictionary.

✓ Do my sentences begin with a capital letter?

✓ Did I use periods correctly?

Present

Have children make a final draft of their comments about a story, with their revisions and proofreading corrections. Help as appropriate.

Choose an option for children to present their comments about a story.

They might draw pictures to illustrate their comments and post them on the bulletin board.	They might put their comments together in a classroom volume of comments about Ruby.

When they have finished, help them complete a Self-Evaluation form.

ROUTINE — Quick Write for Fluency — Team Talk

1. **Talk** Have partners take one minute to find a feeling word in their comments about a story.
2. **Write** Each child writes a new short sentence using one of the feeling words.
3. **Share** Partners trade sentences and read them aloud.

Routines Flip Chart

Teacher Note

Self-Evaluation Make copies of the Self-Evaluation form from the Teacher Resource DVD-ROM and hand them out to children.

ELL

English Language Learners
Support Editing For children whose first language does not distinguish between plural and singular verbs in the same manner, identifying errors in verbs that add -s may be particularly challenging. Before children begin editing, give them a list of two-word sentences about Ruby to say aloud. Then have them consult the list as they edit. Examples: *Ruby hatches. Ruby eats. Ruby swims. Ruby flies.*

Objectives
- Review concept: people learning as they grow and change.
- Organize information.
- Present results of an inquiry project.

Research and Inquiry
Communicate

Teach

Tell children that today they will write a sentence that tells a fact about their topic and share the information with others.

Model

Think Aloud Display the list of facts about the topic. I will review my facts and circle the one I think is the most interesting. That will be the fact I will write my sentence about. My topic was the ocean. The fact I think is the most interesting is "some ocean animals, like whales, use echolocation to find food." Before I write my sentence, I will make sure I know what all the words in my fact mean. I'm not sure what *echolocation* means. I checked a dictionary to find out. The dictionary says that echolocation is using sound echoes to locate objects. That definition helps me understand more about my topic.

Guide practice

Review children's topics and facts. Work with them to state each fact as a complete sentence.

On their own

Have children choose the fact they would like to share with the class and write it in one sentence on a sheet of paper. Have children break themselves into groups based on the similarity of their responses. Then instruct them to read aloud their sentences to one another. Remind them how to be good speakers and listeners:

- Good speakers pay close attention to end marks like question marks.
- Good listeners pay attention to the speaker and do not talk while someone else is speaking.

Wrap Up Your Week!

? Question of the Week

What do we learn as we grow and change?

Think Aloud This week we explored the topic of growing and changing. In the story *Ruby in Her Own Time,* we read about some of the things ducklings learn to do as they grow up. In the fairy tale "The Ugly Duckling," we read about how an ugly duckling changes into a beautiful swan as it grows. Have children recall their Amazing Ideas about growing and changing. Then have children use these ideas to help them demonstrate their understanding of the Question of the Week.

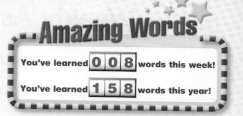

Amazing Words

You've learned **0 0 8** words this week!

You've learned **1 5 8** words this year!

ELL

English Language Learners

Poster Preview Prepare children for next week by using Week 3, ELL Poster 15. Read the Poster Talk-Through to introduce the concept and vocabulary. Ask children to identify and describe objects and actions in the art.

Selection Summary
Send home the summary of *The Class Pet* in English and the child's home language if available. Children can read the summary with family members.

Preview NEXT WEEK

Tell children that next week they will read about a group of students who get a new class pet.

Weekly Assessment

Use pp. 115–120 of *Weekly Tests* to check:

✔ 🔊 **Phonics** Consonant Patterns *ng, nk*

✔ 🔊 **Phonics** Compound Words

✔ 🔊 **Comprehension Skill** Compare and Contrast

✔ **High-Frequency Words**

any	own
enough	sure
ever	were
every	

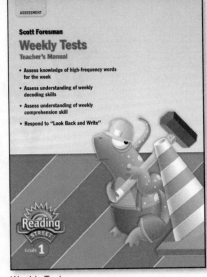

Weekly Tests

A Advanced

OL On-Level

SI Strategic Intervention

Differentiated Assessment

Use pp.115–120 of *Fresh Reads for Fluency and Comprehension* to check:

✔ 🔊 **Comprehension Skill** Compare and Contrast

✔ Review **Comprehension Skill** Sequence

✔ **Fluency** Words Correct Per Minute

Fresh Reads for Fluency Comprehension

Managing Assessment

Use *Assessment Handbook* for:

✔ **Weekly Assessment Blackline Masters for Monitoring Progress**

✔ **Observation Checklists**

✔ **Record-Keeping Forms**

✔ **Portfolio Assessment**

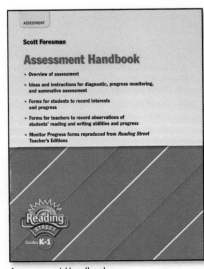

Assessment Handbook

Hank Rides a Bike

Hank hung his head.

"We'll try again next time," Dad said with a wink. It was the same thing as the day before. Hank just could not ride his bike. He yanked off his helmet. He flung it down.

Hank went inside and sank into a chair. He saw a photo of himself on the desk. He was a baby in a stroller.

Mom said, "I used to push you fast. You would yell, 'Zing, zoom!'"

Hank had loved his tricycle too. He could go fast on that thing. Hank felt like giving up. What was he going to do?

Hank talked to his brother Max. "Don't be afraid of the bike," said Max. "It is just a hunk of metal. You won't get hurt."

Max and Hank put on their safety pads. "Now do what I do," said Max. Hank watched his brother roll on the ground. Then Max crawled on his knees. Hank joined in the fun. They didn't bang their knees. The safety pads kept them safe.

"Don't think about falling," said Max. "Will you try again?"

Hank was ready to try. This time he would really ride. Now Hank felt as if he had wings!

Advanced Selection 14 **Vocabulary:** safety, tricycle

Small Group Time

Pacing Small Group Instruction

5 Day Plan

DAY 1	• Phonemic Awareness/ Phonics • Decodable Reader
DAY 2	• Phonemic Awareness/ Phonics • Decodable Reader
DAY 3	• Phonemic Awareness/ Phonics • Leveled Reader
DAY 4	• High-Frequency Words • Decodable Reader
DAY 5	• Phonics Review • Leveled Reader

3 or 4 Day Plan

DAY 1	• Phonemic Awareness/ Phonics • Decodable Reader
DAY 2	• Phonemic Awareness/ Phonics • Decodable Reader
DAY 3	• Phonemic Awareness/ Phonics • Leveled Reader
DAY 4	• High-Frequency Words • Decodable Reader

3 Day Plan: Eliminate the shaded box.

SI Strategic Intervention — DAY 1

Phonemic Awareness•Phonics

■ **Segment and Blend Phonemes** Reteach pp. 46–47 of the Teacher's Edition. Model segmenting and blending these words. Then have children practice segmenting and blending on their own.

sink /s/ /i/ ngk/   **hung** /h/ /u/ /ng/   **junk** /j/ /u/ /ngk/   **rang** /r/ /a/ /ng/

■ ◔ **Consonant Patterns *ng, nk*** Reteach p. 47a of the Teacher's Edition. Then have children spell *sank* using letter tiles. Monitor their work.

• Change the *nk* in *sank* to *ng*. What is the new word?

• Change the *s* in *sang* to *b*. What is the new word?

• Change the *ng* in *bang* to *nk*. What is the new word?

Decodable Practice Reader 14A

■ **Review** Review words with the sounds *ng* and *nk* and the high-frequency words *a, could, into, row, now, to*. Then have children blend and read these words from the story: *flying, drinking, happy, winked, honking.*

> **If...** children have difficulty with any of these words,
> **then...** reteach the word by modeling. Have children practice the words, with feedback from you, until they can read them independently.

Have children reread the text orally. To achieve optimal fluency, children should reread the text three or four times.

Decodable Practice Reader 14A

Objectives
• Decode words in context by applying common letter-sound correspondences, including: consonant digraphs including *ng*.
• Decode words with common spelling patterns.

 **SI** *Strategic Intervention*

DAY 2

Phonemic Awareness•Phonics

■ **Segment and Blend Phonemes** Reteach p. 50c of the Teacher's Edition. Model segmenting and blending these words. Then have children practice segmenting and blending on their own.

pigpen /p/ /i/ /g/ • /p/ /e/ /n/   **bedtime** /b/ /e/ /d/ • /t/ /ī/ /m/

lipstick /l/ /i/ /p/ • /s/ /t/ /i/ /k/

■ **Compound Words** Reteach p. 50d of the Teacher's Edition. Write the following compound words on the board. Have children identify the two smaller words contained in each and then blend the two smaller words to form the compound word. Have children use the base words to determine the meaning of the compound words.

anthill	sandbox	cupcake	bedtime	racetrack
homemade	sunrise	suntan	sandpaper	weekend

Decodable Practice Reader 14B

■ **Review** Review compound words and the high-frequency words *to, do, eats, the, for, day*. Then have children blend and read these words from the story: *checks, lunch, while, use, nice*.

> **If...** children have difficulty with any of these words.
> **then...** reteach the word by modeling. Have children practice the words, with feedback from you, until they can read them independently.

Have children reread the text orally. To achieve optimal fluency, children should reread the text three or four times.

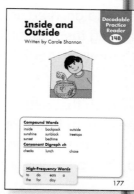

Decodable Practice Reader 14B

More Reading
Use Leveled Readers or other text at children's instructional level to develop fluency.

Objectives
• Use knowledge of the meaning of base words to identify common compound words.
• Use knowledge of the meaning of base words to read common compound words.

SI *Strategic Intervention*

Phonemic Awareness•Phonics

■ **Add Phonemes** Model adding a sound to the beginning of a word to make a new word. Say the word *ink* and have children repeat it. Now listen as I add the sound /th/ to the beginning of *ink*: /th/ *ink*. What is the new word? (think)

Have children add the initial sound shown to each word below to make a new word.

| /k/ link **clink** | /f/ lung **flung** | /d/ rank **drank** |

■ ◉ **Consonant Patterns *ng*, *nk* and Compound Words** Reteach p. 74e of the Teacher's Edition. Have children blend and read these additional words to help them practice the target phonics skills.

| ring | bathtub | trunk | sunshine | hang |

For a complete literacy instructional plan and additional practice with this week's target skills and strategies, see the **Leveled Reader Teaching Guide.**

Concept Literacy Leveled Reader

■ **Preview and Predict** Read the title and the author's name. Have children look at the cover and ask them to describe what they see. Help children activate their prior knowledge by asking them to look through the story and to use the pictures to predict things that might take place.

■ **Set a Purpose** Remind children that setting a purpose for reading can help them better understand what they read. Guide children to pay attention to the different things the boy in the story learns to read.

■ **Read** Provide corrective feedback as children read the story orally. During reading, ask them if they were able to confirm any of the predictions they made prior to the story.

If... children have difficulty reading the story individually,

then... read a sentence aloud as children point to each word. Then have the group reread the sentences as they continue pointing. Continue reading in this way until children read individually.

■ **Retell** Have children take turns retelling the story. Help them identify the things Jim learns to read by pointing to each picture and asking, What has Jim learned to read here?

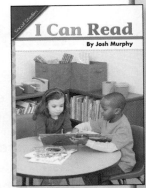

Concept Literacy

Objectives
• Recognize the change in a spoken word when a phoneme is added.
• Decode words with common spelling patterns.

   Go Digital! eReaders

Differentiated Instruction

 **DAY 4**

High-Frequency Words

■ **Review** Write *ever, sure, were, enough, every, any, own* on the board. Model saying each word. Then have children read each word, spell each word as you point to each letter, and have them say each word again. Allow time for children to practice reading these high-frequency words using the word cards.

Decodable Practice Reader 14C

■ **Review** Use the word lists to review the consonant patterns *ng, nk* and compound words.

> **If...** children have difficulty reading the story individually, **then...** read a sentence aloud as children point to each word. Then have the group reread the sentences as they continue pointing. Continue reading in this way until children read individually.

Check comprehension by having children retell the story including the characters, plot, and setting. Have children locate words in the story that have the consonant patterns *ng, nk* or that are compound words. List the words children identify. Then have children sort the words in a chart with columns labeled *ng, nk,* and *compound word*. Have children look at the compound word list. Have them identify the two base words that make up each compound word, and tell the meaning.

ng	nk	compound word
rang	drank	pancakes
things	sink	milkshakes
long	think	outside
hang	trunk	catfish
		inside

More Reading

Use Leveled Readers or other text at children's instructional level.

Decodable Practice Reader 14C

Objectives
• Decode words in context by applying common letter-sound correspondences, including: consonant digraphs including *ng*.
• Use knowledge of the meaning of base words to read common compound words.

More Reading

Use Leveled Readers or other text at children's instructional level.

Phonics Review

■ **Consonant Patterns *ng*, *nk* and Compound Words** Write these sentences on the board. Have children read them aloud as you track the print. Then call on individuals to blend and read the underlined words.

<u>Bring</u> a <u>backpack</u> to the <u>baseball</u> game.

<u>Frank</u> keeps a <u>pink</u> fish in a big <u>tank</u>.

I like to <u>drink</u> a <u>milkshake</u> on the <u>weekend</u>.

<u>Granddad</u> <u>sang</u> to me at <u>bedtime</u>.

For a complete literacy instructional plan and additional practice with this week's target skills and strategies, see the **Leveled Reader Teaching Guide.**

Below-Level Leveled Reader

Preview and Predict Read the title and the names of the author and illustrator. Have children look at the cover and ask them to describe what they see. Help children activate their prior knowledge by asking them to look through the story and to use the pictures to predict things that might take place.

Below-Level Reader

■ **Set a Purpose** Remind children that setting a purpose for reading can help them better understand what they read. Tell children to read to find out what one of the bluebirds in the story learns about singing.

■ **Read** Provide corrective feedback as children read the story orally. During reading, ask them if they were able to confirm any of the predictions they made prior to the story.

> **If...** children have difficulty reading the story individually,
> **then...** read each sentence aloud as children point to each word. Then have the group reread the sentences as they continue pointing.

■ ◉ **Compare and Contrast** Ask children to tell ways that Hank and Jan are alike and ways they are different. (Possible response: Alike: They are both bluebirds. Different: Hank is a boy and Jan is a girl.)

Objectives
- Make inferences about text.
- Establish purpose for reading selected texts.

OL On-Level

OL On-Level **DAY 1**

Phonics•Spelling

- 👁 **Consonant Patterns *ng, nk*** Write the following words on the board and have children practice reading words with consonant patterns *ng, nk*.

  swing   thank   shrink   stung

  Then have children identify whether the word has the /ng/ or /nk/ sound.

- **Words with *ng, nk*** Remind children that each spelling word ends with *ng* or *nk*. Clarify the pronunciation and meaning of each word. For example, say: A piece of paper is *blank* if nothing is written on it. Have children identify whether these words end with *ng* or *nk*: *sunk, bring, sang, rink, trunk, wing.*

Objectives
- Decode words in isolation by applying common letter-sound correspondences, including: consonant digraphs including *ng*.

OL On-Level **DAY 2**

Phonics•High-Frequency Words

- 👁 **Compound Words** Write the following words on the board and have children practice reading compound words. Then have children identify the two smaller words within each compound word and tell the meaning of each word.

  bedtime   campfire   sidewalk   pancake

- **High-Frequency Words** Hold up this week's High-Frequency Word Cards *(any, enough, ever, every, own, sure, were)* and review proper pronunciation. Continue holding the cards and have children chorally read each word. To help children demonstrate their understanding of the words, provide them with oral sentence frames such as: I am _____ my answer is right. (sure)

High-Frequency Word Cards for Grade 1
PEARSON

Objectives
- Use knowledge of the meaning of base words to read common compound words.
- Identify at least 100 high-frequency words from a commonly used list.

Pacing Small Group Instruction

20–30 min.

5 Day Plan

DAY 1	• Phonics • Spelling • Decodable Reader
DAY 2	• Phonics • High-Frequency Words • Decodable Reader
DAY 3	• Leveled Reader
DAY 4	• Conventions • Main Selection
DAY 5	• Phonics Review • Leveled Reader

3 or 4 Day Plan

DAY 1	• Phonics • Spelling • Decodable Reader
DAY 2	• Phonics • High-Frequency Words • Decodable Reader
DAY 3	• Leveled Reader
DAY 4	• Conventions • Main Selection

3 Day Plan: Eliminate the shaded box.

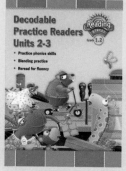

Decodable Practice Readers Units 2-3
- Practice phonics skills
- Blending practice
- Reread for fluency

Decodable Practice Readers

Ruby in Her Own Time **DI•27**

Small Group Time

DAY 3

For a complete literacy instructional plan and additional practice with this week's target skills and strategies, see the **Leveled Reader Teaching Guide.**

On-Level Leveled Reader

On-Level

■ **Preview and Predict** Read the title and the names of the author and illustrator. Have children look at the cover and ask them to describe in detail what they see. Help children preview the story by asking them to look through the story and to use the pictures to predict things that might take place.

■ 🔄 **Compare and Contrast** Before reading, remind children that setting a purpose for reading can help them better understand what they read. Guide children to pay attention to ways in which the baby in the story is like and different from most babies.

■ **Read** During reading, monitor children's comprehension by providing higher-order thinking questions. Ask:

• How is Mac like and different from babies you have seen?

• Is this a realistic story or a fantasy? How can you tell?

To help children gain a better understanding of the text, build upon their responses with a group discussion.

■ 🔄 **Inferring** Discuss these questions as a class.

• Why does the author say, "Mac was not just any boy"?

• Are Mac's parents surprised by what he can do? What do they say that shows this? ("Are you sure you are old enough?")

■ **Text to Text** Help children connect the story to *Ruby in Her Own Time*. Ask:

• How is Mac like and different from Ruby? (Possible response: Both are babies. Ruby is a duck who learns slowly. Mac is a human who learns fast.)

Objectives
• Make inferences about text.
• Establish purpose for reading selected texts.

 OL On-Level · DAY 4

Conventions

■ **Verbs That Add -s** Remind children that we add –s to the end of a verb to show what one person, animal, or thing does now: *Pat sings. The car stops.*

• Write this sentence on the board: *Rob walk on the grass.* Read the incorrect sentence aloud. What letter must we add to *walk* to make the sentence correct? (-*s*) Add *-s* to *walk* and read the corrected sentence aloud. Have children repeat the sentence after you.

Continue this process, changing the verb in the sentence to *run, hop, skip,* and *jump*. Have children tell you how to correct each sentence.

Objectives
• Understand and use verbs (present) in the context of reading, writing, and speaking.
• Speak in complete sentences with correct subject-verb agreement.

More Reading

Use Leveled Readers or other text at children's instructional level to develop fluency.

 OL On-Level · DAY 5

Phonics Review

■  **Consonant Patterns *ng, nk* and Compound Words** Have children practice blending and reading words that contain this week's target phonics skills. Write the following words on the board, and say and sound out each word with the children.

hillside	bang	dishpan	sling	blink
chunk	homework	thing	dunk	fireman

Then have children sort into separate groups words with /ng/, words with /nk/, and compound words.

Objectives
• Decode words in isolation by applying common letter-sound correspondences, including: consonant digraphs including *ng*.
• Use knowledge of the meaning of base words to read common compound words.

Small Group Time

20–30 min.

5 Day Plan

DAY 1	• Phonics • Advanced Selection
DAY 2	• Phonics • Comprehension • Main Selection
DAY 3	• Leveled Reader
DAY 4	• Comprehension • Paired Selection
DAY 5	• Fluency • Comprehension • Advanced Selection

A Advanced   DAY 1

Phonics•Advanced Selection

■ 🔊 **Consonant Patterns *ng*, *nk*** Have children practice with longer words containing consonant patterns *ng*, *nk*.

blinker	sprinkler	ankle	wrinkle	angle
thankful	triangle	anger	bunker	Thanksgiving

Have children write the words on cards and sort them by *ng* and *nk*. Then have them choose several words to use in sentences.

Advanced Selection 14

■ **Advanced Selection 14** Before reading, have children identify these story words: *safety* and *tricycle*. If they do not know these words, provide oral sentences with the words in context to help children determine their meaning. After reading, have children recall the two most important ideas of the story.

Objectives
• Decode words in isolation by applying common letter-sound correspondences, including: consonant digraphs including *ng*.

---

3 or 4 Day Plan

DAY 1	• Phonics • Advanced Selection
DAY 2	• Phonics • Comprehension • Main Selection
DAY 3	• Leveled Reader
DAY 4	• Comprehension • Paired Selection

3 Day Plan: Eliminate the shaded box.

A Advanced   DAY 2

Phonics•Comprehension

■ 🔊 **Compound Words** Have children practice reading longer compound words.

afternoon	scarecrow	thunderstorm	grasshopper	inchworm
tablecloth	sweatshirt	seashore	sailboat	daydream

Have children write the words and draw a line between the two smaller words. Show children how breaking up a compound word into its smaller words can help them read it.

Ruby in Her Own Time

■ **Comprehension** Have children silently read this week's main selection, *Ruby in Her Own Time*. Have them retell the story identifying characters, setting, and sequence of events. Discuss what makes *Ruby in Her Own Time* an animal fantasy. Point out that in real life animals do not speak like people.

Objectives
• Use knowledge of the meaning of base words to read common compound words.

A Advanced

DAY 3

More Reading

Use Leveled Readers or other text at children's instructional level.

For a complete literacy instructional plan and additional practice with this week's target skills and strategies, see the **Leveled Reader Teaching Guide.**

Advanced Leveled Reader

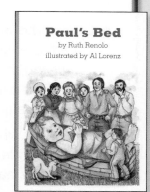

Paul's Bed
by Ruth Renolo
illustrated by Al Lorenz

Advanced Reader

■ **Activate Prior Knowledge** Read the title, the author's name, and illustrator's name. Have children look at the cover and describe in detail what they see. Remind them that the word *attempt* means "to try." Then activate the children's prior knowledge by asking them to tell about a problem they have attempted to solve.

■ **Compare and Contrast** Before reading, remind children that setting a purpose for reading can make a story more interesting. Guide children to notice how the baby in this story is like and different from real babies.

■ **Read** During reading, monitor children's comprehension by providing higher-order thinking questions. Ask:

• How are the things that Paul needs like and different from the things most babies need?

• How do Paul's beds change as the story moves along?

Build on children's answers to help them gain a better understanding of the text.

■ **Inferring** Have children discuss these questions with a partner.

• Did Paul's neighbors care about him? How can you tell?

• When Paul grew up, why did he have to build his own bed?

■ **Text to Self** Help children connect the story to their own lives. Ask:

• Have you ever gotten too big for something? Tell about it.

Objectives
• Make inferences about text.
• Establish purpose for reading selected texts.

Small Group Time

More Reading

Use Leveled Readers or other text at children's instructional level.

A Advanced **DAY 4**

Comprehension

- **Comprehension** Have children silently read this week's paired selection, "The Ugly Duckling." Have them retell the story identifying the characters, setting, and sequence of events. Then have them explain what caused the Ugly Duckling to look ugly to its brothers and sisters.

  Talk about what makes "The Ugly Duckling" a fairy tale. Be sure children understand that a fairy tale is a short fantasy story that sometimes has animal characters, and that it often begins with "Once upon a time" and ends with "lived happily ever after."

The Ugly Duckling

- **Text to Text** Have children tell about other fairy tales they know. Ask them to explain why the main character lives happily ever after.

Objectives
- Explain the function of recurring phrases in traditional fairy tales.
- Make inferences about text.

A Advanced **DAY 5**

Fluency•Comprehension

- **Fluency** Using the first few sentences of Advanced Selection 14, model reading with appropriate phrasing. Then have children read the selection to a partner as you listen to their reading. Provide corrective feedback as needed.

- **Comprehension** After they have finished reading the selection, have children retell what happened by stating the events in sequence. Then, on the back of the selection page, have them write three sentences about a time when they learned how to do something that seemed hard at first.

Advanced Selection 14

Objectives
- Read aloud grade-level appropriate text with fluency (appropriate phrasing).

Support for English Language Learners

The ELL lessons are organized by strands. Use them to scaffold the weekly lesson curriculum or during small-group time.

Concept Development

What do we learn as we grow and change?

■ **Activate Prior Knowledge** Write the Question of the Week and read it aloud. Underline the word *change* and have children say it with you. *Change* means that something is different. Display a picture of a baby. You were a baby once. In what ways did you grow and change? (grew bigger, got teeth, learned to walk and talk).

■ **Connect to New Concept** Have children turn to pages 44–45 in the Student Edition. Read the title aloud and have children track the print as you read it. Point to the pictures one at a time and use them to guide a discussion about how we grow and change. For example, point to the picture of the baby crawling. What is this baby doing? (crawling) Point to the picture of the baby walking. What is this baby doing? (walking) As we get older, we learn how to crawl and walk.

■ **Develop Concepts** Display ELL Poster 14 and have children identify the girl in each photo and how old she might be. (baby, toddler, preschooler, first-grader) How do people help the girl? Have children point to the girl getting help on the Poster. (people hold the baby's hands to help her walk, the girl's dad helps her learn to read) Use the leveled prompts below to assess understanding and build oral language. Point to pictures on the poster as you guide discussion.

Beginning Ask yes/no questions, such as, Is the girl in the first photo old enough to read? Is the girl in the last photo old enough to walk?

Intermediate Ask children questions that can be answered with simple sentences. What is the girl learning in the second photo? What can she do in the last photo? How does she change as she grows?

Advanced/Advanced High Have children answer the Question of the Week by giving specific examples from the poster and their own experiences.

■ **Review Concepts and Connect to Writing** Review children's understanding of the concept at the end of the week. Ask them to write in response to these questions: What is one way we change? What is one thing we learn as we grow? What English words did you learn this week? Write and display key ideas from the discussion.

Objectives
- Internalize new basic and academic language by using and reusing it in meaningful ways in speaking and writing activities that build concept and language attainment.
- Learn new language structures, expressions, and basic and academic vocabulary heard during classroom instruction and interactions.

Content Objectives
- Describe what we learn as we grow and change.

Language Objectives
- Use basic vocabulary for describing what we learn as we grow and change.

Daily Planner

DAY 1	• **Frontload Concepts** • **Preteach** Comprehension Skill, Vocabulary, Phonemic Awareness/Phonics, Conventions/Writing
DAY 2	• **Review** Concepts, Vocabulary, Comprehension Skill • **Frontload Main Selection** • **Practice** Phonemic Awareness/Phonics, Conventions/Writing
DAY 3	• **Review** Concepts, Comprehension Skill, Vocabulary, Conventions/Writing • **Reread Main Selection** • **Practice** Phonemic Awareness/Phonics
DAY 4	• **Review Concepts** • **Read ELL/ELD Readers** • **Practice** Phonemic Awareness/Phonics, Conventions/Writing
DAY 5	• **Review** Concepts, Vocabulary, Comprehension Skill, Phonemic Awareness/Phonics, Conventions/Writing • **Reread ELL/ELD Readers**

See the ELL Handbook for ELL Workshops with targeted instruction.

Use this week's Concept Talk Video to help children build background knowledge about animals. See the Concept Talk Video Routine (*ELL Handbook*, page 500) for suggestions.

Support for English Language Learners

Language Objectives

- Add phonemes.
- Identify and use consonant patterns *ng*, *nk*.
- Learn relationships between letters and the sounds they represent in English.
- Spell words with accuracy.

 Transfer Skills

Consonant Patterns

Although the digraph *ch* is a letter in the Spanish alphabet, the digraphs *sh*, *th*, *wh*, *ph*, *gh*, and *ng* have zero transfer in Spanish, Cantonese, Vietnamese, and Hmong. Provide additional practice in saying consonant digraphs and patterns.

Initial Consonant Blends

Some learners may pronounce words such as *stop* or *play* with a slight vowel sound before the first phoneme (like *estop*). This is a natural step on the path to pronunciation of the English word. Provide practice with words that begin with consonant blends.

ELL Teaching Routine

For more practice with consonant patterns, use the Sound-by-Sound Blending Routine (*ELL Handbook*, page 493).

Phonemic Awareness: Add Phonemes

■ **Preteach Adding Phonemes**

- Have children open to pp. 46–47. Point to the alligator family. What is the family doing? (eating) Say *eat* slowly. Help children hear that a word such as *eat* rhymes with a similar word by adding a new sound to the beginning. Write *meat* on the board. Listen as I say this rhyming word aloud: /m/ + eat = meat. If you say *up*, you can add the /k/ sound to the beginning to make *cup*.

- Say each of the words on the left and then the word on the right. Have children pronounce the new sound and then say the new word.

  | at | cat | (/k/) | oat | boat | (/b/) | lay | play | (/p/) |

- Have children point out other pictures whose names have the sound of /o/ at the beginning or the middle. Write the words and point to the letters that make the sound so children can associate the letters with the sounds they make. Have children write words themselves.

■ **Practice** Remind children that adding a new sound to the beginning of some words can make a new word. Say the word *and*. Have children repeat it. Explain that the word *and* can be changed into a few new words by adding different initial sounds.

| and | sand | (/s/) | and | band | (/b/) | and | grand | (/gr/) |

Phonics: Consonant Patterns *ng*, *nk*

■ **Preteach** Display Sound-Spelling Card 44. This is a swing. What sound do you hear at the end of *swing*? /ng/ Say it with me: /ng/. Point to *ng*. The sound /ng/ is spelled *ng*. Display Sound-Spelling Card 45. This is a skunk. What sound do you hear at the end of *skunk*? (/ngk/) Say it with me: /ngk/. Point to *nk*. The sound /ngk/ is spelled *nk*.

■ **Listen and Write** Distribute Write and Wipe Boards. Write the word *ring* on the board. Copy this word. As you write *ng*, say the sound to yourself. /ng/. Now say the sound aloud. (/ng/) Underline *ng* in *ring*. The letters *n* and *g* spell /ng/ in *ring*. Repeat the instruction for *nk* using the word *trunk*. The letters *n* and *k* spell /ngk/ in *trunk*. Focus on spelling. As you read words aloud, have children listen to the sound and spell correctly, either *ng* or *nk*.

Objectives

- Learn relationships between sounds and letters of the English language and decode (sound out) words using a combination of skills such as recognizing sound-letter relationships and identifying cognates, affixes, roots and base words.

 ELL *English Language Learners*

■ **Reteach and Practice** Say and write the word *sing*. Remind children that the letters *ng* make the sound /ng/. Say and write *bunk*. Remind children that the letters *nk* make the /ngk/ sound. Write and say the following words: *thing*, *bring*, *sank*, *bank*, and *wink*. Have children read the words with you as you point to each one. Have children raise a hand when they hear /ng/ and clap once when they hear /ngk/.

Beginning Identify /ng/ and /ngk/ words such as *bang*, *gang*, *song*, *wing*, *pink*, *wink*, and *rink*. Have children repeat the words. Write them on the board. Have children write them.

Intermediate Have children repeat the /ng/ and /ngk/ words. Ask children to copy the words. Have children underline the /ng/ sound and circle the letters that stand for the /ngk/ sounds in the words. Then have children write very brief sentences with the words.

Advanced/Advanced High Have children repeat and write the words. Have children underline the letters that stand for the /ng/ sound and circle the letters that stand for the /ngk/ sound in the words. Then have children write two short sentences with these or other words that end in *ng* or *nk*.

Phonics: Compound Words

■ **Preteach** Have children turn to Envision It! on page 50 of the Student Edition.

• The word for the picture is *football*. Point to the football to indicate the meaning. The word *football* is made up of two different words: *foot* and *ball*. A compound word is a word that is made up of two smaller words. The meaning of each smaller word helps you decide the meaning of the compound word. The word *football* means "a ball that you kick with your foot."

■ **Practice** Distribute Letter Tiles *a, e, i, o, b, l, p, t, s, n, d,* and *x* to pairs. Give each pairs two *p* and two *i* Letter Tiles.

• What two words are in the word *sandbox*? Spell the word *sandbox*.

• What two words are in the word *laptop*? Spell the word *laptop*.

• What two words are in the word *inside*? Spell the word *inside*.

Language Objectives
• Associate the consonant patterns *nk* and *ng* with their spellings.
• Read compound words.
• Distinguish sounds of English.

Catch Up
Compound words are words that are made up of two smaller words in the English language.

 Transfer Skills
Compound Words Speakers of Cantonese, Vietnamese, and Hmong, languages in which words consist of one syllable, may need extra explanation and practice with the concept of compound words.

Practice Page
ELL Handbook page 271 provides additional practice for this week's skill.

Objectives
• Distinguish sounds and intonation patterns of English with increasing ease.
• Spell familiar English words with increasing accuracy, and employ English spelling patterns and rules with increasing accuracy as more English is acquired.

Ruby in Her Own Time **DI•35**

Support for English Language Learners

Content Objective

- Monitor and adjust oral comprehension.

Language Objectives

- Discuss oral passages.
  Use contextual support.
- Use a graphic organizer to take notes.
- Ask for information.

ELL Teacher Tip

To help children fill out the Story Map, divide the story into sections for beginning, middle, and end. After each section is finished, fill out the appropriate section of the Story Map before continuing on to the next section of the story.

ELL English Language Learners

Listening Comprehension

Read Aloud

Little Cheep

Mother Hen's eggs hatched. She was so happy. She told her little chicks about living on the farm.

"The tasty bugs are in the dirt over there," she said. "We sleep in the barn." The littlest chick, Cheep, didn't want to eat bugs or sleep in the barn.

She went around the farm to find something else to do. She tried to act like a duck and splash in the pond. But she just sank in the water.

She tried to act like a cat and chase mice. But the cats started chasing her.

She decided to hop back to the farm. She saw chickens eating bugs. "I can do that!" Chick said. She ate and ate. "Being a chick isn't so bad after all," she thought. Then she went to the barn and took a nap.

Prepare for the Read Aloud The modified Read Aloud above prepares children for listening to the oral reading "Something Else to Do" on page 49b.

- **First Listening: Listen to Understand** Write the title of the Read Aloud on the board. This is about a little chicken who does not want to do the things that chickens do. What other things does she try to do? What happens in the end? Before reading, ask children to listen for new language they do not understand. Have children ask about any unfamiliar words during the reading. After reading, have children ask questions about the information in the story to be sure they understand what they have read.

- **Second Listening: Listen to Check Understanding** Using the Story Map A graphic organizer (*ELL Handbook*, page 506), work with children to tell what happened in the story. They should tell what happened at the beginning, middle, and end of the story. Review the completed maps together.

Objectives

- Use visual, contextual, and linguistic support to enhance and confirm understanding of increasingly complex and elaborated spoken language.
- Understand the general meaning, main points, and important details of spoken language ranging from situations in which topics, language, and contexts are familiar to unfamiliar.
- Demonstrate listening comprehension of increasingly complex spoken English by following directions, retelling or summarizing spoken messages, responding to questions and requests, collaborating with peers, and taking notes commensurate with content and grade-level needs.

Modeled Pronunciation Audio CD

High-Frequency Words

■ **Preteach** Distribute copies of this week's Word Cards (*ELL Handbook*, p. 143). Have children point to or hold up the corresponding card when you say a word in a sentence or make a gesture. When appropriate, use opposites to reinforce meaning.

- *Ever* tells of any time or all the time. Is she *ever* home?

- If you are *sure*, you feel no doubt about something.

- *Were* is the plural of *was*. **Point to yourself.** I was. **Motion to the whole class.** We were.

- If you have *enough* of something, you have as much or as many as you need. We have *enough* books for the whole class.

- *Every* means "each one " or "all." **Point to each child.** *every*

- *Any* means "some." **Show your empty hands.** I do not have *any* cookies.

- When you *own* something, it is yours to keep. **Hold something possessively.** own

■ **Practice** Briefly repeat each clue. Have children hold up and read each Word Card corresponding with the clue.

■ **Speaking/Writing with High-Frequency Words**

- **Teach/Model** Write the sentences on the board. Model filling in the missing word from the first sentence. 1. We each have our _____ book. (own) 2. He was _____ he knew the answer. (sure) 3. We _____ going to the store. (were) 4. I looked at _____ book in the room. (every) 5. Did you _____ see a red cat? (ever) 6. One minute is not _____ time to eat. (enough) 7. Did you eat _____ carrots? (any)

- **Practice** Give each pair of children a set of the Word Cards. Have them work together to find the correct word for each sentence you read.

Beginning/ Intermediate Read the sentences aloud, pausing for each missing word. Have children hold up the correct Word Card for each sentence. Then write each word.

Advanced/Advanced High Have children write the sentences from the board, adding the missing words. They can copy from the Word Cards.

Language Objectives
- Use accessible language to learn new and essential language.
- Use high-frequency English words.
- Understand details of spoken language.

Mini-Lesson: Listening
For extra practice with high-frequency words, turn to p. 51 of the Student Edition. Have children listen as you read the passage aloud to prepare children for reading on their own. Elicit important points from children by asking questions.

Objectives
- Use strategic learning techniques such as concept mapping, drawing, memorizing, comparing, contrasting, and reviewing to acquire basic and grade-level vocabulary.
- Understand the general meaning, main points, and important details of spoken language ranging form situations in which topics, language, and contexts are familiar to unfamiliar.

Support for English Language Learners

Content Objectives

- Identify ways things are the same.
- Identify ways things are different.

Language Objective

- Discuss how things are the same and different.

Cognates

Provide the cognates *comparar* (*compare*) and *contraste* (*contrast*) to children. Discuss the similarities in the spellings and pronunciations of the words.

Guide Comprehension
Compare and Contrast

■ **Preteach** Show two items to children, such as a blue and a red marker. This is a blue marker. This is a red marker. They are alike because they are both markers. They are different because one is blue and the other one is red. Explain to children that when we compare, we tell how two things are the same. When we contrast, we tell how the things are different.

■ **Practice** Have children turn to Envision It! on page EI•3 in the Student Edition. Discuss the picture with children. Have them name ways the two caps are the same. Then have them name ways the two caps are different.

■ **Reteach/Practice** Distribute copies of the Picture It! (*ELL Handbook*, p. 144). Have students look at the images. Tell them to listen as you read the story under each picture aloud. Have students listen for clue words.

Leveled LS Support

Beginning Reread the story aloud. Guide them as they move their finger along as you read each word. Ask two students to role play Ray and his father reading in the same room. Allow them to have fun with it, and choose their own books to use.

Intermediate Have students underline ways that Ray and his father are alike. Have them circle ways that they are different. (**Answers** Alike box: they both like to read; they both have many books. Different box: Ray likes books with pictures; Ray's dad likes books with words; Ray's dad sits. Ray lies on the floor.)

Advanced/Advanced High Ask students to point out what clue word helped them figure out that Ray and his father had something in common (*also*). Ask them to think of another clue word that could have worked (*too*).

MINI-LESSON

Academic Language

Tell children that there are words we can use to describe how two things are the same, or similar, such as *both*, *also*, and *too*.

Objectives

- Understand the general meaning, main points, and important details of spoken language ranging from situations in which topics, language, and contexts are familiar to unfamiliar.

 English Language Learners

Reading Comprehension
Ruby in Her Own Time

Student Edition pp. 52–53

■ **Frontloading**

• **Background Knowledge** Read the title aloud and discuss it. Point to the duck. This is Ruby. Discuss the meaning of the phrase "in her own time."

• **Preview** Guide children on a picture walk through the story, asking them to identify people, places, and actions. Reteach these words using visuals in the Student Edition: *nest* (page 54), *driving rain* (page 55), *hatch* (page 56), *feathers* (page 57), *swam* (page 63), *broad* (page 65) and *stretched* (page 69).

• **Predict** What do you think Ruby does in her own time?

Sheltered Reading Ask questions to guide children's comprehension:

• p. 58: Point to the blue egg. What was different about the fifth egg? (It didn't hatch.)

• p. 60: Point to the ducklings. What did the Rufus, Rory, Rosie, and Rebecca eat? (anything and everything)

• p. 67: Where did Rufus, Rory, Rosie, and Rebecca fly? (across the water, among the trees)

• p. 73: Point to the duckling. Who did Ruby bring back with her? (her babies)

■ **Fluency: Appropriate Phrasing** Remind children that reading with appropriate phrasing means to pause and stop in the right places as you read. Read p. 58, modeling phrasing. Point out the periods, commas, and question marks. Have pairs read p. 61. Have children read with appropriate phrasing as their partners listen and offer feedback. For more practice, use the Fluency: Paired Reading Routine (*ELL Handbook*, p. 496).

After Reading Help children retell the story using the pictures on the Retelling Cards. Ask questions that prompt children to summarize the important parts of the text. Then turn to p. 83 of the Student Edition. Ask children to share information and ideas. As children give information, have others summarize what they hear to check for listening comprehension.

Content Objectives
• Monitor and adjust comprehension.

• Make and adjust predictions.

Language Objectives
• Read grade-level text with appropriate phrasing.

• Summarize text using visual support.

• Understand details of spoken language.

• Demonstrate comprehension by following directions.

Audio Support
Prepare children for reading *Ruby in Her Own Time* by using the eSelection or the AudioText CD.

Mini-Lesson: Following Directions
Have students turn to p. 82 in the Student Edition. Read the prompt for Listening. Ask children to follow the directions given: share ideas, give everyone a turn, and listen to each other. As children do the activity, ask them to repeat the directions to you. Ask them what other directions would be helpful in talking about a book.

Objectives
• Use visual and contextual support and support from peers and teachers to read grade-appropriate content area text, enhance and confirm understanding, and develop vocabulary, grasp of language structures, and background knowledge needed to comprehend increasingly challenging language.
• Demonstrate English comprehension and expand reading skills by employing basic reading skills such as demonstrating understanding of supporting ideas and details in text and graphic sources, summarizing text and distinguishing main ideas from details commensurate with content area needs.

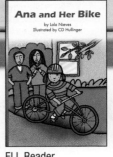
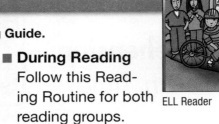

ELL Reader   ELD Reader

For additional leveled instruction, see the **ELL/ELD Reader Teaching Guide.**

Comprehension: *Ana and Her Bike*

- **Before Reading** Distribute copies of the ELL and ELD Readers, *Ana and Her Bike*, to children at their reading level.

  - **Preview** Read the title aloud with children and allow for them to look through the pages. This story is about a girl named Ana. She has a new bike. Activate prior knowledge about bike safety. The story in our book was about how things grow and change over time. This story is also about how things can grow and change over time. How does Ana change over time?

  - **Set a Purpose for Reading** Let's read to find out how Ana changes over time.

- **During Reading** Follow this Reading Routine for both reading groups.

  1. Read the entire Reader aloud slowly as children follow along and finger point.

  2. Reread the Reader one page at a time, having children echo read after you.

- **After Reading** Use the exercises on the inside back cover of *Ana and Her Bike* and invite children to share drawings and writing. In a whole-group discussion, ask children to list the steps Ana took to learn how to ride her bike. Encourage children to discuss what happened at the beginning, middle, and end of the story. Children can point to each step as they discuss them.

ELD Reader Beginning/Intermediate

- **pp. 2–3** Point to Ana. What does Ana wear on her head?

- **pp. 5–7** Point to Ana's mom and dad. Who helps Ana learn to ride her bike?

Writing Draw a picture of something you have learned how to do. Label your picture. Ask children to work in pairs and share their picture with the whole class.

ELL Reader Advanced/Advanced-High

- **p. 3** Point to the helmet. Why does Ana need a helmet?

- **p. 6** Point to Ana. When does Ana ride?

Study Guide Distribute copies of the ELL Reader Study Guide (*ELL Handbook*, page 148). Scaffold comprehension by reviewing how Ana learned to ride her bike. Review their responses together. (**Answers** See *ELL Handbook*, pp. 245–248.)

Objectives

- Understand the general meaning, main points, and important details of spoken language ranging from situations in which topics, language, and contexts are familiar to unfamiliar.

 eReaders

 English Language Learners

Conventions
Verbs that Add -s

■ **Preteach** Present examples of brief sentences with action verbs in present tense, including some that end in -s and some that do not, such as the following: *Kimi plays. Joe plays. They play. Alberto walks. Mary walks. We walk.* Display and read the sentences. Point out the -s at the end of certain verbs. Point out the subject of each such sentence, one person doing the action. Tell students that it is important that subjects and verbs agree when speaking in formal English. Continue using several different verbs.

■ **Practice** Have children repeat the sentences after you. Ask questions that solicit the use of verbs that add -s, and provide verbs such as *run*, *read*, and *play*. Remind children that when you spell these verbs, you don't change the spelling of the word. You simply add –s. Demonstrate with a sentence from the Student Edition, p. 50. Ask children how the verb in item one would be spelled if the sentence were only about Tom. (*Tom snacks on nuts*…)

■ **Reteach** Remind children that present tense verbs with the subjects *he*, *she*, and *it* add -s. Use examples, such as *She plays soccer* and *He works hard at school*. Mention or point to an apple and say, *An apple tastes good*. Repeat using different singular subjects, verbs, and sentences.

■ **Practice** Give children guided practice at their language proficiency level.

Beginning/Intermediate Give pairs of children two subjects. Ask children to say and write a sentence in the present tense for each subject. Monitor verbs ending in -s. Help children edit their sentences for correct subject-verb agreement.

Advanced/Advanced High Have children write three short sentences in the present tense for the pronouns *he*, *she*, and *it*. Then have children edit partners' sentences, making sure the pronouns agree with the verbs.

Content Objective
• Identify verbs that end in -s.

Language Objectives
• Use verbs that end in -s in sentences.

• Adapt spoken language appropriately for formal purposes.

• Write sentences with verbs that end in -s.

• Use a spelling rule to spell familiar words in English.

Transfer Skills
Verbs that Add -s Children of various language backgrounds may add -s to both the nouns and verbs in sentences: *The dogs runs.* Point out that in English, verbs add -s for singular subjects, not plural subjects.

Grammar Jammer
For more practice with verbs, use the Grammar Jammer for this target skill. See the Grammar Jammer Routine (*ELL Handbook*, page 501) for suggestions on using this learning tool.

Support for English Language Learners

Content Objectives
- Identify sentences that express a writer's preferences.
- Identify the characteristics of an animal fantasy.
- Express opinions about the story.

Language Objectives
- Write sentences that express preferences.
- Share feedback for editing and revising.

Mini-Lesson: Expressing Opinions

Tell children that giving comments about the story is expressing opinions. Opinions are our feelings about something. Turn to p. 76 in the Student Edition and have children express two opinions about things that Ruby does. Provide sentence frames: *I like when Ruby* _____. *I like Ruby because* _____. The word *like* is an opinion word.

ELL English Language Learners

Write Comments About a Story

■ **Introduce Terms** Explain to children that when they write comments about a story, they tell what they thought about the story. Comments can be opinions, or what you think about a story. Comments can also be about your preferences, or about how you are like a character in a story.

■ **Introduce Sentences that Express Preferences** Explain that good stories contain sentences that express a writer's preferences, or things that he or she likes to do. Write these sentences on the board:

> The bird likes to take her time. I like to take my time too.

Have children think of things that Ruby liked to do in *Ruby in Her Own Time*. Then have them describe two things Ruby does that they like to do. Reread the sentences on the board aloud to children.

■ **Model** Draw a two column chart on the board. Label them *Ruby, [Child's name]*. Engage children in comparing and contrasting Ruby to themselves.

Ruby	[Child's Name]
takes her own time	take my time

■ **Write** Write the following frames on the board: *Ruby likes to* _____. *I like to* _____. *Ruby likes to* _____. *But I like to* _____. Have children draw a two-column chart under the sentence frames and think of things that Ruby likes to do and then compare them with the things they like to do and record them in the chart. Then have children use their chart to fill in the sentence frames.

 Leveled Support

Beginning Supply the graphic organizer. Write the word *Ruby* in the first column. Think of one thing Ruby liked to do. Draw a picture of it. Have children tell about their pictures. Have children tell if they like to do what Ruby does. If not, have them tell something they do enjoy doing. Then have them draw a picture that tells about their preference.

Intermediate Guide children's writing. What things does Ruby like to do? What things do you like to do? Help children with their spelling.

Advanced/Advanced High Have children use their chart for prewriting. Then have them write their sentences that express their preferences.

Objectives
- Write using newly acquired basic vocabulary and content-based grade-level vocabulary.

Common Core Standards
Weekly Planning Guide

Selection: The Class Pet
Genre: Expository Text

Alignment of the Common Core Standards with This Week's Skills and Strategies

This Week's Common Core Standards for English Language Arts	Instructional Summary
Reading Standards for Informational Text	
Informational Text 1. Ask and answer questions about key details in a text.	The comprehension lesson helps children distinguish between **facts and opinions.** Then guided instruction and questions help them identify facts and opinions in the Listening Comprehension selection "The End of Summer" and the main selection *The Class Pet.* Children ask and answer questions as they **monitor and clarify** their understandings of content and word meaning.
Informational Text 3. Describe the connection between two individuals, events, ideas, or pieces of information in a text.	
Informational Text 4. Ask and answer questions to help determine or clarify the meaning of words and phrases in a text.	
Foundational Skills Standards	
Foundational Skills 3. Know and apply grade-level phonics and word analysis skills in decoding words.	The lesson helps children segment, blend, and read words with the **inflected ending -es** as well as *r*-controlled *or* and *ore.* In fluency activities, children focus on using **appropriate phrasing** to reread with expression.
Foundational Skills 3.f. Read words with inflectional endings.	
Foundational Skills 4.b. Read on-level text orally, with accuracy, appropriate rate, and expression on successive readings.	
Writing Standards	
Writing 2. Write informative/explanatory texts in which they name a topic, supply some facts about the topic, and provide some sense of closure.	For the lesson's Writing section, children **write a summary** of the expository reading selection. The teacher guides writing to help children provide information. For the Research and Inquiry project, children **choose a topic,** chart facts, and share information with peers.
Writing 8. With guidance and support from adults, recall information from experiences or gather information from provided sources to answer a question.	
Speaking and Listening Standards	
Speaking/Listening 3. Ask and answer questions about what a speaker says in order to gather additional information or clarify something that is not understood.	This lesson's listening and speaking activities focus on giving **descriptions** with many details and use of adjectives and strong verbs. Questions help children identify relevant details as they prepare their descriptions.
Speaking/Listening 4. Describe people, places, things, and events with relevant details, expressing ideas and feelings clearly.	
Language Standards	
Language 1.c. Use singular and plural nouns with matching verbs in basic sentences (e.g., *He hops; We hop*).	The Conventions section and the Writing Mini-Lesson focus on the forms of **present tense verbs.** The lesson explicitly teaches the **spelling** of words with the inflected ending -es and high-frequency words. The reading selection uses **conjunctions** to connect words and ideas. Children can use conjunctions in speaking and writing activities.
Language 1.g. Use frequently occurring conjunctions (e.g., *and, but, or, so, because*).	
Language 2.d. Use conventional spelling for words with common spelling patterns and for frequently occurring irregular words.	

Additional Support for a Common Core Standard This Week

Use the following instruction to supplement the teaching of one of this week's Common Core Standards.

Common Core Standard: Language 1.g.
Have children read page 97 of the selection *The Class Pet* aloud. Then write the first two sentences on the board.

- Circle the conjunctions *and* and *or* in the sentences. Tell children that *and* and *or* are conjunctions. They connect words, ideas, or parts of sentences. Identify the words connected by the conjunctions.
- Explain the meaning of *and* (also) and *or* (gives a choice).
- Have children find other sentences in the story with one of these conjunctions.
- Ask children to use the word *and* or the word *or* to complete these sentences: *Do you want grapes _____ an orange? We can walk to the park _____ play on the swings.*

ISBN-13: 978-0-328-64369-1 ISBN-10: 0-328-64369-6

Grade 1 • Unit 3 • Week 3
The Class Pet

Unit 3

THE BIG QUESTION
What is changing in our world?

- Introduce and explore this unit's weekly concepts through rich, structured conversations
- Develop complex content knowledge and vocabulary
- Expand on a single concept with engaging literature and nonfiction
- Build better readers in all content areas
- Align instruction to **Common Core Anchor Standards**

Week 1

A Place to Play
Question of the Week
How do places change?

connect to SOCIAL STUDIES

Concept Talk Guide children as they discuss questions such as:

- What are some ways your neighborhood has changed?

Writing Think about a place to play that you think is interesting. Now write a made-up story about children playing at that place.

Week 2

Ruby in Her Own Time
Question of the Week
What do we learn as we grow and change?

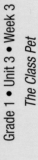
connect to SOCIAL STUDIES

Concept Talk Guide children as they discuss questions such as:

- What can you do now that you could not do when you were younger?

Writing Look at the pictures in *Ruby in Her Own Time*. Think about what Ruby does. Write sentences that tell two things Ruby does that you like.

You Are Here: Week 3

The Class Pet
Question of the Week
What can we learn about animals as they grow and change?

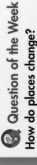

As children answer this unit's Big Question and this week's Question of the Week, they will address:

Reading 1. Read closely to determine what the text says explicitly and to make logical inferences from it; cite specific textual evidence when writing or speaking to support conclusions drawn from the text. **(Also Reading 3.)**

Concept Talk Guide children as they discuss questions such as:

- Think about different animals. How are the babies different from the adults?

As children answer this week's Concept Talk question, they will address:

Speaking/Listening 3. Evaluate a speaker's point of view, reasoning, and use of evidence and rhetoric.

The Class Pet
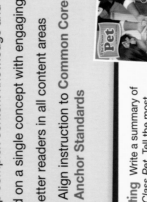
connect to SCIENCE

Writing Write a summary of *The Class Pet*. Tell the most important events and ideas.

As children write about this week's prompt, they will address:

Writing 2. Write informative/explanatory texts to examine and convey complex ideas and information clearly and accurately through the effective selection, organization, and analysis of content.

Listening and Speaking On page 116, children learn to use their senses when they describe something. By doing so, they address:

Speaking/Listening 4. Present information, findings, and supporting evidence such that listeners can follow the line of reasoning and the organization, development, and style are appropriate to task, purpose, and audience.

Week 6

Where Are My Animal Friends?
Question of the Week
What do animals do when the seasons change?

connect to SCIENCE

Concept Talk Guide children as they discuss questions such as:

- Why do you think squirrels gather and hide nuts in the fall?

Writing Think about Raccoon and Squirrel in *Where Are My Animal Friends?* What would they say if they could call Goose on a phone? Write a play scene showing what they would say.

Week 5

I'm a Caterpillar
Question of the Week
What changes can be seen in nature?

connect to SCIENCE

Concept Talk Guide children as they discuss questions such as:

- How do different kinds of animals change as they grow?

Writing Think of changes in nature. Plants and animals grow. Seasons change. Draw two pictures to show one way a plant or animal changes. Write captions about your pictures.

Week 4

Frog and Toad Together
Question of the Week
What changes happen in a garden?

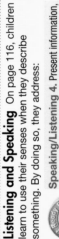
connect to SCIENCE

Concept Talk Guide children as they discuss questions such as:

- What do seeds look like when you first plant them? Then what happens?

Writing Think of actions Toad tried to help his garden grow. Write a list telling what Toad did that really helped the garden grow. In another list, tell his actions that did not help.

This Week's ELL Overview

ELL Handbook

- Maximize Literacy and Cognitive Engagement
- Research Into Practice
- Full Weekly Support for Every Selection

The Class Pet
  - Multi-Lingual Summaries in Five Languages
  - Selection-Specific Vocabulary Word Cards
  - Frontloading/Reteaching for Comprehension Skill Lessons
  - ELD and ELL Reader Study Guides

- Transfer Activities
- Professional Development

Daily Leveled ELL Notes

ELL notes appear throughout this week's instruction and ELL Support is on the DI pages of your Teacher's Edition. The following is a sample of an ELL note from this week.

English Language Learners

Beginning Write several plural *-es* words from *Boxes for Flo* on the board. Underline *-es* in each word. Say each word aloud, clapping your hands for each syllable of the word. Have children repeat each word, clapping their hands for each syllable.

Intermediate Have children read each sentence with an *-es* word. Have them use the pictures to help identify each *-es* word as a plural noun or a verb.

Advanced Have children find words from *Boxes for Flo* that mean "more than one." Ask them to use each word in a new sentence. Monitor pronunciation.

Advanced High Organize children into pairs. Have them brainstorm a list of plural *-es* words and write several basic sentences with the words.

ELL by Strand

The ELL lessons on this week's Support for English Language Learners pages are organized by strand. They offer additional scaffolding for the core curriculum. Leveled support notes on these pages address the different proficiency levels in your class. See pages DI•54–DI•63.

ELL Guy
Dr. Jim Cummins

The Three Pillars of ELL Instruction

ELL Strands	Activate Prior Knowledge	Access Content	Extend Language
Vocabulary p. DI•58	Preteach	Teach/Model	Practice
Reading Comprehension p. DI•59	Preteach	Reteach/Practice	Leveled Practice Activities
Phonics, Spelling, and Word Analysis pp. DI•55–DI•56	Preteach	Listen and Write	Leveled Practice Activities
Listening Comprehension p. DI•57	Prepare for the Read Aloud	First Listening	Second Listening
Conventions and Writing pp. DI•62–DI•63	Preteach/Introduce Terms	Practice/Model	Leveled Practice Activities/ Leveled Writing Activities
Concept Development p. DI•54	Preteach Concept	Develop Concepts	Review Concepts and Connect to Writing

This Week's Practice Stations Overview

Six Weekly Practice Stations with Leveled Activities can be found at the beginning of each week of instruction. For this week's Practice Stations, see pp. 84h–84i.

Small Group

Teacher-led

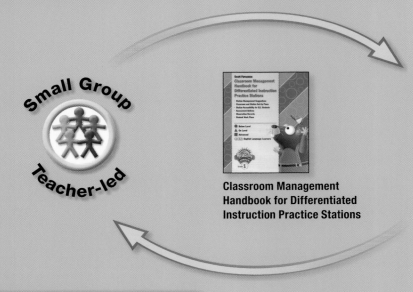

Classroom Management Handbook for Differentiated Instruction Practice Stations

Practice Stations

Daily Leveled Center Activities

 Below

 On-Level

 Advanced

ELL

Practice Stations Flip Charts

	Listen Up	Word Work	Words to Know 	Let's Write 	Read for Meaning 	Get Fluent
Objectives	• Identify words with consonant patterns *ng* and *nk*.	• Write words with *ng* and *nk*. • Write compound words.	• Identify high-frequency words *ever, sure, were, enough, every, any, own*.	• Write sentences using verbs that add *-s*.	• Compare and contrast characters in a story. • Compare and contrast using background knowledge.	• Read aloud with appropriate phrasing.
Materials	• *Listen Up* Flip Chart Activity 15	• *Word Work* Flip Chart Activity 15 • paper • pencils • crayons	• *Words to Know* Flip Chart Activity 15 • High-Frequency Word Cards for Unit 3, Week 2 • Letter Tiles • paper • pencils	• *Let's Write* Flip Chart Activity 15 • Unit 3 Student Book • paper • pencils	• *Read for Meaning* Flip Chart Activity 15 • Leveled Readers • T-charts • paper • pencils	• *Get Fluent* Flip Chart Activity 15 • Leveled Readers

This Week on Reading Street!

 Question of the Week

What can we learn about animals as they grow and change?

Changes

Daily Plan

Don't Wait Until Friday

Whole Group

- ◉ Ending -es; Plural -es
- ◉ Vowels: r-Controlled or, ore
- ◉ Fact and Opinion
- • Fluency
- • Vocabulary

MONITOR PROGRESS	Success Predictor			
Day 1 Check Word Reading	Day 2 Check Word Reading	Day 3 Check High-Frequency Words/Retelling	Day 4 Check Fluency	Day 5 Check Oral Vocabulary

Small Group

Teacher-Led

- • Reading Support
- • Skill Support
- • Fluency Practice

Practice Stations

Independent Activities

Customize Literacy More support for a Balanced Literacy approach, see CL•1–CL•47.

Customize Writing More support for a customized writing approach, see CW•1–CW•10.

Whole Group

- • Writing for Tests: Summary
- • Conventions: Verbs That Do Not Add -s

Assessment

- • Weekly Tests
- • Day 5 Assessment
- • Fresh Reads

You Are Here! Unit 3 Week 3

This Week's Reading Selections

Main Selection
Genre: **Expository Text**

Paired Selection

Decodable Practice Readers

Leveled Readers

ELL and ELD Readers

Resources on Reading Street!

	Build Concepts	Phonemic Awareness and Phonics	Vocabulary
Whole Group	 Student Edition pp. 84–85 Sing With Me	 Student Edition pp. 86–87 Sound-Spelling Cards	 Student Edition p. 89
Go Digital	• Concept Talk Video • Sing with Me Animations	• Interactive Sound-Spelling Cards • Decodable eReaders	• Vocabulary Activities • Journal Word Bank
Small Group and Independent Practice	 Practice Station Flip Chart Leveled Readers ELL and ELD Readers	 Practice Station Flip Chart Decodable Practice Readers	 Practice Station Flip Chart Student Edition p. 89
Go Digital	• eReaders	• Decodable eReaders • Letter Tile Drag and Drop	• Journal Word Bank • Vocabulary Activities
Customize Literacy	• Leveled Readers	• Decodable Practice Readers	• High-Frequency Word Cards
Go Digital	• Concept Talk Video • Big Question Video • eReaders	• Interactive Sound-Spelling Cards • Decodable eReaders	• Sing with Me Animations • Vocabulary Activities

Question of the Week

What can we learn about animals as they grow and change?

Comprehension

Student Edition
pp. 92–105

- Envision It! Animations
- eSelections

Fluency

Decodable
Practice
Readers

- eSelections
- eReaders

Conventions and Writing

Student Edition
pp. 108–109

- Grammar Jammer

Practice Station   Leveled   ELL and ELD
Flip Chart   Readers   Readers

Practice Station   Decodable
Flip Chart   Practice
                    Readers

Practice Station   Reader's and
Flip Chart   Writer's Notebook

- eReaders
- Story Sort

- Decodable eReaders

- Grammar Jammer

- Envision It! Skills and Strategies Handbooks
- Leveled Readers

- Leveled Readers

- Reader's and Writer's Notebook

- Envision It! Animations
- eReaders

- eReaders

- Grammar Jammer

You Are Here!
Unit 3
Week 3

Week 3

My 5-Day Planner for Reading Street!

Don't Wait Until Friday SUCCESS PREDICTOR

	Check Word Reading **Day 1** pages 84j–89	Check Word Reading **Day 2** pages 90a–105g
Get Ready to Read	**Concept Talk,** 84j–85 **Oral Vocabulary,** 85a–85b *features, mature, natural* **Phonemic Awareness,** 86–87 Segment and Blend Phonemes **Phonics,** 87a–88a ◉ Ending -*es*; Plural -*es* **READ Decodable Practice Reader 15A,** 88b–88c **Spelling,** 88d Pretest	**Concept Talk,** 90a–90b **Oral Vocabulary,** 90b *swoop, tumble* **Phonemic Awareness,** 90c Segment and Blend Phonemes **Phonics,** 90d–91a ◉ Vowels: *r*-Controlled *or, ore* **READ Decodable Practice Reader 15B,** 91b–91c **Review Phonics,** 91d Ending -*s, -es*; Plural-*s, -es* **Spelling,** 91e Practice
Read and Comprehend	**High-Frequency Words,** 89 Introduce *away, car, friends, house, our, school, very* **Listening Comprehension,** 89a–89b ◉ Fact and Opinion	**High-Frequency Words,** 91 Build Fluency *away, car, friends, house, our, school, very* **Story Words,** 92a Introduce *brown, fur, mouse, teaches* **Vocabulary,** 92a Descriptive Words **Build Background,** 92b **READ Main Selection—First Read,** 92c–105a *The Class Pet* **Genre,** 105b Expository Text
Language Arts	**Conventions,** 89c Verbs That Do Not Add -*s* **Writing for Tests,** 89d–89e Summary **Research and Inquiry,** 89f Identify and Focus Topic	**Conventions,** 105c Verbs That Do Not Add -*s* **Writing for Tests,** 105d–105e Summary: Write to a Prompt **Handwriting,** 105f Letter *R* and *r*; Letter Size **Research and Inquiry,** 105g Research Skill: Classifying/Categorizing

You Are Here! Unit 3 Week 3

Question of the Week

What can we learn about animals as they grow and change?

Check High-Frequency Words Check Retelling	Check Fluency	Check Oral Vocabulary
Day 3 pages 106a–109c	**Day 4** pages 110a–115f	**Day 5** pages 116a–117k
Concept Talk, 106a–106b **Oral Vocabulary,** 106b *crumple* **Phonemic Awareness,** 106c Add Phonemes **Phonics,** 106d–106e ◉ Ending *-es*; Plural *-es* ◉ Vowels: *r*-Controlled *or, ore* **Spelling,** 106f Dictation	**Concept Talk,** 110a–110b **Oral Vocabulary,** 110b *nibble, nudges, wriggle* **Phonological Awareness,** 110c `Review` **Phonics,** 110d Consonant Patterns *ng, nk;* Compound Words **READ Decodable Practice Reader 15C,** 110e–110f `Review` **Fluent Word Reading,** 110g **Spelling,** 110h Partner Review	**Concept Wrap Up,** 116a `Review` **Oral Vocabulary,** 116b **Phonemic Awareness,** 116c Add Final Phonemes `Review` **Phonics,** 116c ◉ Ending *-es*; Plural *-es* ◉ Vowels: *r*-Controlled *or, ore* **Spelling,** 116d Test
`Review` **High-Frequency Words,** 106g *away, car, friends, house, our, school, very* `Review` **Story Words,** 106g *brown, fur, mouse, teaches* **READ Main Selection—Second Read,** 92–105, 106h–107a **Fluency,** 107b Appropriate Phrasing	**Science in Reading,** 110i **READ Paired Selection,** 110–115a "Belling the Cat" **Fluency,** 115b Appropriate Phrasing	**Listening and Speaking,** 116–117 **Vocabulary,** 117a Descriptive Words **Fluency,** 117a Phrasing `Review` **Comprehension,** 117b ◉ Fact and Opinion `Review` **Vocabulary,** 117b High Frequency and Story Words **Genre,** 117c Fable **Assessment,** 117d–117f Monitor Progress
Conventions, 108a–109a Verbs That Do Not Add *-s* **Writing for Tests,** 108–109a Summary: Evaluation **Listening and Speaking,** 109b Give Descriptions **Research and Inquiry,** 109c Gather and Record Information	**Conventions,** 115c Verbs That Do Not Add *-s* **Writing for Tests,** 115d–115e Summary **Research and Inquiry,** 115f Review and Revise Topic	`Review` **Conventions,** 117g Verbs That Do Not Add *-s* **Writing for Tests,** 117h–117i Summary **Research and Inquiry,** 117j Communicate **Wrap Up Your Week,** 117k ❓ What can we learn about animals as they grow and change?

Week 3

Grouping Options for Differentiated Instruction
Turn the page for the small group time lesson plan.

Planning Small Group Time on **Reading Street!**

SMALL GROUP TIME RESOURCES

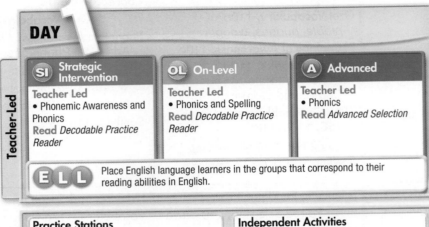

Look for this Small Group Time box each day to help meet the individual needs of all your children. Differentiated Instruction lessons appear on the DI pages at the end of each week.

DAY 1

Teacher-Led

SI Strategic Intervention	**OL** On-Level	**A** Advanced
Teacher Led • Phonemic Awareness and Phonics **Read** *Decodable Practice Reader*	**Teacher Led** • Phonics and Spelling **Read** *Decodable Practice Reader*	**Teacher Led** • Phonics **Read** *Advanced Selection*

ELL Place English language learners in the groups that correspond to their reading abilities in English.

Practice Stations
• Listen Up
• Word Work

Independent Activities
• *Reader's and Writer's Notebook*
• Concept Talk Video

ELL

ELL Reader
Advanced
Advanced-High

ELD Reader
Beginning
Intermediate

ELL Poster

You Are Here!
Unit 3
Week 3

Day 1

SI Strategic Intervention	**Phonemic Awareness and Phonics**, DI•43 **Read Decodable Practice Reader 15A**, DI•43
OL On-Level	**Phonics and Spelling**, DI•48 **Read Decodable Practice Reader 15A**, DI•48
A Advanced	**Phonics**, DI•51 **Read Advanced Selection**, DI•51
ELL English Language Learners	DI•54–DI•63 **Frontload Concept Preteach Skills Writing**

Reading Street Response to Intervention Kit

Reading Street Leveled Practice Stations Kit

Question of the Week

What can we learn about animals as they grow and change?

SI Strategic Intervention

OL On-Level

A Advanced

Below-Level Reader

Decodable Practice Readers

On-Level Reader

Advanced Reader

Concept Literacy Reader

Advanced Selection

Small Group Weekly Plan

Day 2	Day 3	Day 4	Day 5
Phonemic Awareness and Phonics, DI•44 **Read Decodable Practice Reader 15B**, DI•44	**Phonemic Awareness and Phonics**, DI•45 **Read Concept Literacy Leveled Reader**, DI•45	**High-Frequency Words**, DI•46 **Read Decodable Practice Reader 15C**, DI•46	**Phonics Review**, DI•47 **Read Below-Level Leveled Reader**, DI•47
Phonics and High-Frequency Words, DI•48 **Read Decodable Practice Reader 15B**, DI•48	**Read On-Level Leveled Reader**, DI•49	**Conventions**, DI•50 **Reread Main Selection**, DI•50	**Phonics Review**, DI•50 **Reread On-Leveled Reader**, DI•50
Phonics and Comprehension, DI•51 **Read Main Selection**, DI•51	**Read Advanced Leveled Reader**, DI•52	**Comprehension**, DI•53 **Read Paired Selection**, DI•53 **Reread Leveled Reader**, DI•53	**Fluency and Comprehension**, DI•53 **Reread Advanced Selection**, DI•32
DI•54–DI•63 **Review Concept** **Practice Skills** **Frontload Main Selection** **Writing**	DI•54–DI•63 **Review Concept** **Practice Skills** **Reread Main Selection** **Writing**	DI•54–DI•63 **Review Concept** **Practice Skills** **Read ELL or ELD Reader** **Writing**	DI•54–DI•63 **Review Concept** **Review Skills** **Writing**

Practice Stations for Everyone on Reading Street!

Listen Up!
Generate rhyming words.

Objectives
• Identify words with consonant patterns *ng* and *nk*.

Materials
• *Listen Up!* Flip Chart Activity 15

Differentiated Activities

⬤ Say the words *sing, bang, think,* and *junk*. Think of words that rhyme with these words. Say them to a partner. What is the ending sound in each word?

▲ Say the words *sing, bang, think,* and *junk*. Think of words that rhyme with these words. Say them to a partner. What is the ending sound in each word? Now think of other words with those ending sounds.

◼ Say the words *sing, bang, think,* and *junk*. Think of words that rhyme with these words. Say them to a partner. What is the ending sound in each word? Now think of other words with those ending sounds. Say more rhyming words.

Technology
• Interactive Sound-Spelling Cards

Word Work
Consonant patterns *ng, nk;* compound words

Objectives
• Write words with *ng* and *nk*.
• Write compound words.

Materials
• *Word Work* Flip Chart Activity 15
• paper
• pencils
• crayons

Differentiated Activities

⬤ Write this sentence at the bottom of a piece of drawing paper:
I hung up my pink bathrobe.
Now draw a picture to match the sentence. Underline the word with *ng,* the word with *nk,* and the compound word.

▲ Write a list of words with *ng,* words with *nk,* and compound words. Draw pictures of as many of the words as you can, and then label the pictures.

◼ Write a silly story about a pink skunk. Use as many *ng* and *nk* words as you can, along with some compound words. Underline the *ng* and *nk* words and compound words. Draw a picture to go with your story.

Technology
• Interactive Sound-Spelling Cards

Words To Know
Practice high-frequency words.

Objectives
• Identify high-frequency words *ever, sure, were, enough, every, any, own.*

Materials
• *Words to Know* Flip Chart Activity 15
• High-Frequency Word Cards for Unit 3, Week 2
• Letter Tiles
• paper
• pencils

Differentiated Activities

⬤ Use the Word Cards. Match the letters in each word with Letter Tiles.

▲ Look at the Word Cards. Write the words on your paper.

◼ Look at the Word Cards. Write two sentences using the words.

Technology
• Online Tested Vocabulary Activities

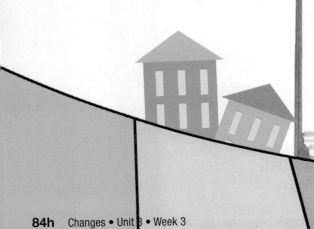

You Are Here!
Unit 3
Week 3

Use this week's materials from the
Reading Street Leveled Practice Stations
Kit to organize this week's stations.

Key

 Below-Level Activities

△ On-Level Activities

▢ Advanced Activities

Practice Station
Flip Chart

Let's Write!
Use verbs in writing.

Objectives
• Write sentences using verbs that add -s.

Materials
• *Let's Write!* Flip Chart Activity 15
• Unit 3 Student Book
• paper
• pencils

Differentiated Activities

⬤ Think about Ruby in *Ruby in Her Own Time.* Use this sentence frame to tell about what Ruby does: **Ruby _____ .** Be sure to add -s to the verb you use. Write as many sentences as you can to tell about what Ruby does.

△ Think about Ruby in *Ruby in Her Own Time.* Write about what Ruby does. Be sure to add -s to the verb you use. Write as many sentences as you can to tell about what Ruby does. Underline the verbs.

▢ Think about the ducks in *Ruby in Her Own Time.* Write about what each one does. Be sure to add -s to the verbs you use. Write as many sentences as you can to tell about what each duck does. Underline the verbs.

Read For Meaning
Compare and contrast.

Objectives
• Compare and contrast characters in a story.
• Compare and contrast using background knowledge.

Materials
• *Read for Meaning* Flip Chart Activity 15
• Leveled Readers
• T-charts
• paper
• pencils

Differentiated Activities

• To **compare,** find what is alike. To **contrast,** find what is different.

⬤ Read *Hank's Song.* Think about Hank and Jan. How are they alike? How are they different? Share your comparisons and contrasts with a partner.

△ Read *Mac Can Do It!* Think about what Mac is like and what a real baby is like. Use a T-chart to list comparisons in one column and contrasts in the other.

▢ Read *Paul's Bed.* Think about what Paul is like and what a real baby is like. Use a T-chart to list comparisons in one column and contrasts in the other.

Technology
• Leveled eReaders

Get Fluent
Practice fluent reading.

Objectives
• Read aloud with appropriate phrasing.

Materials
• *Get Fluent* Flip Chart Activity 15
• Leveled Readers

Differentiated Activities

⬤ Work with a partner. Take turns reading pages from *Hank's Song.* As you read, look at how words are grouped and read with appropriate phrasing. Punctuation can help you read with appropriate phrasing. Give your partner feedback.

△ Work with a partner. Take turns reading pages from *Mac Can Do It!* As you read, look at how words are grouped and read with appropriate phrasing. Punctuation can help you read with appropriate phrasing. Give your partner feedback.

▢ Work with a partner. Take turns reading pages from *Paul's Bed.* As you read, look at how words are grouped and read with appropriate phrasing. Punctuation can help you read with appropriate phrasing. Give your partner feedback.

Technology
• Reading Street Readers CD-ROM

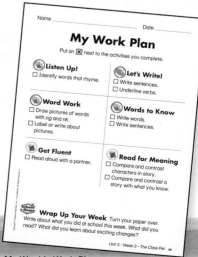

Name _____ Date _____

My Work Plan
Put an ☒ next to the activities you complete.

Listen Up!
☐ Identify words that rhyme.

Let's Write!
☐ Write sentences.
☐ Underline verbs.

Word Work
☐ Draw pictures of words with *ng* and *nk.*
☐ Label or write about pictures.

Words to Know
☐ Write words.
☐ Write sentences.

Get Fluent
☐ Read aloud with a partner.

Read for Meaning
☐ Compare and contrast characters in story.
☐ Compare and contrast a story with what you know.

Wrap Up Your Week Turn your paper over. Write about what you did at school this week. What did you read? What did you learn about exciting changes?

Unit 3 • Week 3 • *The Class Pet*

My Weekly Work Plan

Week 3

Objectives

- Introduce concepts: what we can learn about animals as they grow and change.
- Share information and ideas about the concept.

Today at a Glance

Oral Vocabulary
features, mature, natural

Phonemic Awareness
Segment and Blend Phonemes

Phonics and Spelling
⊙ Ending *-es*, Plural *-es*

Fluency
Oral Rereading

High-Frequency Words
away, car, friends, house, our, school, very

Comprehension
⊙ Fact and Opinion

Conventions
Verbs That Do Not Add *-s*

Writing
Writing for Tests: Summary

Research and Inquiry
Identify and Focus on Topic

Concept Talk

 Question of the Week

What can we learn about animals as they grow and change?

Introduce the concept

To build concepts and to focus children's attention, tell them that this week they will talk, sing, read, and write about what we can learn about animals as they grow and change. Write the Question of the Week and track the print as you read it.

ROUTINE — **Activate Prior Knowledge** — **Team Talk**

 Think Have children think for a minute about what we can learn about animals as they grow and change.

 Pair Have pairs of children discuss the question.

3 Share Have children share information and their ideas with the group. Remind them to ask questions to clarify information. Guide discussion and encourage elaboration with prompts such as: Think about different animals. How are the babies different from the adults?

Routines Flip Chart

Anchored Talk

Develop oral language

Have children turn to pages 84–85 in their Student Edition. Read the title and look at the photos. Use these questions to guide discussion and create the "What can we learn about animals as they grow and change?" concept map (shown on the next page).

- We know that animals' bodies change as they grow. Let's add *Their bodies change* to our map. How is the cow in the picture different from the calf? (The cow is bigger and has horns.) Most animals get bigger, so let's add *They get bigger,* and *Cows grow horns.*

- This frog looked very different when it was young. How has it changed? (It was a tadpole. The tadpole grew legs and became a frog.) Let's add *Tadpoles become frogs* to our map.

Oral Vocabulary

Let's Talk About

Growing and Changing
- Discuss animal life cycles.
- Discuss what we can learn about animals as they grow and change.

READING STREET ONLINE
CONCEPT TALK VIDEO
www.ReadingStreet.com

You've learned **1 5 8** Amazing Words so far this year!

84 | 85

Student Edition pp. 84–85

Amazing Words

You've learned **1 5 8** words so far.

You'll learn **0 0 9** words this week!

features	crumple
mature	nibble
natural	nudges
swoop	wriggle
tumble	

Writing on Demand

Develop Writing Fluency

Ask children to write about what they know about how animals change as they grow. Have them write for two or three minutes. Children should write as much as they can. Tell them to try to do their best writing. You may want to discuss what children wrote during writing conferences.

Connect to reading

Explain that this week, children will read about how a mouse changes as it grows. Animals don't just change in looks as they grow. They also change in what they eat and the things they can do. Let's add those things to our map, too.

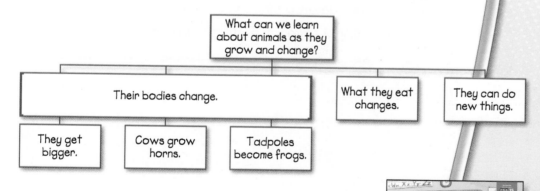

What can we learn about animals as they grow and change?
- Their bodies change.
  - They get bigger.
  - Cows grow horns.
  - Tadpoles become frogs.
- What they eat changes.
- They can do new things.

ELL English Language Learners

Listening Comprehension

English learners will benefit from additional visual support to understand the key terms in the concept map. Use the pictures on pp. 84–85 to scaffold understanding. For example, when talking about how animals change in appearance, point to and name each animal and its features as they are being discussed.

ELL Support Additional ELL support and modified instruction are provided in the *ELL Handbook* and in the ELL Support lessons on pp. DI•54–DI•63.

 **Preteach Concepts** Use the Day 1 instruction on ELL Poster 15 to assess and build background knowledge, develop concepts, and build oral vocabulary.

 Poster 15

Objectives
- Build oral vocabulary.
- Discuss the concept to develop oral language.
- Share information and ideas about the concept.

Oral Vocabulary
Amazing Words

Introduce Amazing Words

Display p. 15 of the *Sing with Me* Big Book. Tell children they are going to sing "My Puppy Buddy," which is about how a puppy changes as it gets older. Ask children to listen for the Amazing Words *features*, *mature*, and *natural* as you sing. Sing the song again and have children join you.

 Sing with Me Big Book

Sing with Me Big Book, p. 15

Teach Amazing Words

Amazing Words Oral Vocabulary Routine

1 **Introduce the Word** Relate the word *mature* to the song: The song says that the puppy gets bigger as he *matures*. Supply a child-friendly definition: When people or animals *mature*, they grow older and become adults. Have children say the word.

2 **Demonstrate** Provide examples to show meaning: As a baby bird *matures*, it grows feathers and learns to fly. Young boys and girls take many years to *mature* into adults.

3 **Apply** Have children demonstrate their understanding: In what ways have you *matured* since you were a baby?

See p. OV•3 to teach *features* and *natural*.

Routines Flip Chart

Check understanding of Amazing Words

Have children look at the picture on page 15. In what ways will this puppy look different when he has fully *matured*? (Possible response: When he has matured, his face, body, and legs will be longer. His fur will be less fluffy.)

Describe the puppy's *features*. (Possible response: His features are brown fur, a short tail, floppy ears, a black nose, and big black eyes.)

It's *natural* for dogs to dig holes. What else is it *natural* for them to do? (Possible response: It's natural for dogs to bark at strangers, chew bones, and chase squirrels.)

Have children demonstrate their understanding of the Amazing Words by completing these sentences orally.

Apply Amazing Words

One change that happens to children as they **mature** is _____.

One **feature** of a turtle is _____.

It's **natural** for a cat to _____.

Corrective feedback

If... children have difficulty using the Amazing Words, **then...** remind them of the definitions and provide opportunities for children to use the words in sentences.

Preteach Academic Vocabulary

Write the following on the board:

- fact and opinion
- expository text
- verbs that do not add -*s*

Have children share what they know about this week's Academic Vocabulary. Use children's responses to assess their prior knowledge. Preteach the Academic Vocabulary by providing a child-friendly description, explanation, or example that clarifies the meaning of each term. Then ask children to restate the meaning of the Academic Vocabulary in their own words.

Amazing Words

features	crumple
mature	nibble
natural	nudges
swoop	wriggle
tumble	

English Language Learners
Cognates The Spanish word for *natural* is identical in spelling to the English word. Pointing out this similarity may help Spanish-speaking children learn the word.

Objectives

- Segment and blend words with ending *-es.*
- Read words with ending *-es.*

Skills Trace

- **Ending *-es*; Plural *-es***
Introduce U3W3D1
Practice U3W3D3; U3W3D4
Reteach/Review U3W3D5;
U3W4D4
Assess/Test Weekly Test U3W3
Benchmark Test U3

KEY:
U=Unit   W=Week   D=Day

Student Edition pp. 86–87

Phonemic Awareness
Segment and Blend Phonemes

Introduce

Have children look at the picture on pages 86–87 of their Student Edition. What kind of flowers do you see in the picture? **(roses)** The word *roses* is made from a base word and an ending. The base word is *rose*. The ending is /əz/. What kind of seats do you see in the picture? **(benches)** *Benches* is also made from a base word and ending. The base word is *bench*. What ending do you hear? **(/əz/)**

Model

Listen to how I blend the two parts of *roses*: /rōz/, /əz/, *roses*. **Continue** modeling with *benches*.

Guide practice

Guide children as they segment and blend the base word and ending of these words from the picture: *fences, bushes, horses,* and *crunches.*

Corrective feedback

If... children make an error,
then... model by segmenting the parts of the word, and have them repeat the segmenting and blending of the word.

Phonics—Teach/Model
↻ Ending -es; Plural -es

Sound-Spelling
Card 139

Sound-Spelling
Card 124

ROUTINE

① Connect Write the words *digs* and *hats*. Ask children what they know about reading these words. (They have a base word, *dig* or *hat*, and the ending -*s*. You put the base word and ending together to read the word.) *Hat* is a noun. In a noun, an -*s* ending means "more than one." *Digs* is a verb. In a verb, an -*s* ending means that someone is doing something now. Tell children that today they will learn how to read words with the ending -*es*.

② Use Sound-Spelling Card Display Sound Spelling Card 139. For some base words, we use the ending -*es* instead of -*s*. Point to *peaches* and say the word. This word is made up of the base word *peach* and the ending -*es*. Have children say *peach* several times as you point to *peach*. Have children say -*es* several times as you point to -*es*. Then have children put the base word and ending together to say *peaches*. Repeat the process with Sound Spelling Card 124 and *tosses*.

③ Model Write *fixes*. *Fixes* is made from the base word *fix* and the ending -*es*.

When I come to a word that ends with -*es*, I look to see if it has a base word and an ending. I read the base word and the ending: *fix*, -*es*. Then I read the two parts together as one word: *fixes*.

④ Guide Practice Have children read *fixes* with you. Write the words below. Have the group read the words with you. Then help them identify the base word and ending in each.

| taxes | waxes | messes | dresses |
| kisses | fishes | flushes | pinches |

⑤ Review What do you know about reading these words? (They are made up of a base word and the ending -*es*. If the base word is a noun, -*es* means more than one. If the base word is a verb, -*es* means that someone is doing something now.)

Routines Flip Chart

Differentiated Instruction

Ⓐ Advanced
More Challenging Words
If children can easily read the Guide Practice words, have them read and identify the base word and ending of these words: *matches, finishes, stitches, watches,* and *crunches*.

Vocabulary Support

You may wish to explain the meaning of these words.

taxes money that people pay to support a government

waxes covers with a liquid that hardens to make a smooth surface

English Language Learners
Practice Plural Words In Spanish, plurals are formed by adding -*s* to words ending in a vowel (*madre/madres*) and -*es* to words ending in a consonant (*mes/meses*). Because of this, Spanish speakers may add -*es* to any words ending in a consonant. Give children additional oral practice adding plural endings to words ending in consonants other than *s, x, z, sh* or *ch*.

The Class Pet **87a**

Objectives
◎ Read words with ending *-es*.
• Decode words in context and isolation.

Check Word Reading
▪ SUCCESS PREDICTOR

Phonics—Build Fluency
◎ Ending *-es;* Plural *-es*

Model **Envision It!**	Have children turn to page 88 in their Student Edition. Look at the picture on this page. I see a picture of *peaches*. The word *peaches* is made up of a base word and an ending. When I say *peaches*, I hear the base word *peach* and the ending *-es*. I also see a girl who tosses a ball. When I say *tosses*, I hear the base word *toss* and the ending *-es*.

Student Edition p. 88

Guide practice	For each word in "Words I Can Blend," ask children to identify the base word and ending. Make sure that children pronounce each word part correctly. Then have them blend the two parts to say the complete word.
Corrective feedback	**If...** children have difficulty blending a word, **then...** model blending the word, and then ask children to blend it with you.

Blend and Read

Decode words in isolation

After children can successfully segment and blend the words, point to words in random order and ask children to read them naturally.

Decode words in context

Have children read each of the sentences. Have them identify words in the sentences that are made up of a base word and the ending -es.

Team Talk Pair children and have them take turns reading each of the sentences aloud.

On their own

Use Reader's and Writer's Notebook p. 345.

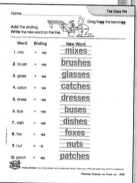

Reader's and Writer's Notebook, p. 345

Don't Wait Until Friday

MONITOR PROGRESS Check Word Reading ↻ Ending -es; Plural -es

Write the following words and have the class read them. Notice which words children miss during the group reading. Call on individuals to read some of the words.

foxes	rushes	fusses	classes	kisses	
dishes	mops	glasses	rocks	wishes ←	**Spiral Review** Row 2 contrasts -es plurals with -s plurals.
catches	kicks	mixes	yelling	rested ←	Row 3 contrasts ending -es with inflectional endings -ed, -ing, and -s.

If... children cannot blend words with ending -es at this point,

then... use the Small-Group Time Strategic Intervention lesson, p. DI•43, to reteach words with ending -es. Continue to monitor children's progress using other instructional opportunities during the week. See the Skills Trace on p. 86–87.

Day 1	Day 2	Day 3	Day 4	Day 5
Check Word Reading	Check Word Reading	Check High-Frequency Words/Retelling	Check Fluency	Check Oral Vocabulary

Success Predictor

Differentiated Instruction

SI Strategic Intervention

If children are having difficulty reading words with ending -es, write the words, and have children underline the ending and circle the base word. Tell them to cover up the ending and read the base word. Then have them uncover the ending and read the whole word.

ELL

English Language Learners

Plural Endings In Chinese, Hmong, and Vietnamese, nouns do not have a plural form. Children may need extra practice adding -s and -es to indicate plurality. Provide oral practice by pointing to one object such as a pen and having children name it, then pointing to two or more of that same object and having children use the plural form.

Word Reading

Success Predictor

Decodable Practice Reader 15A
Ending -es; Plural -es

Decode words in isolation

Have children turn to page 193. Have children decode each word.

Decodable Practice Reader 15A

Review High-frequency words

Review the previously taught words *where, the, out, to, some, into, a, down, her, for,* and *of.* Have children read each word as you point to it on the Word Wall.

Preview Decodable Reader

Have children read the title and preview the story. Tell them they will decode words that end in *-es* in this story.

Decode words in context

Pair children for reading and listen as they decode. One child begins. Children read the entire story, switching readers after each page. Partners reread the story. This time the other child begins.

Flo is packing boxes.
She packs dishes and dresses.
She packs sketches and brushes.

194

Where did the boxes go?
Flo rushes out to get some.

195

Bo pitches boxes into a bin.
When the top presses down,
it smashes them flat.

196

Flo wishes she had those boxes.
Will Bo save her some?
Grumpy Bo will not.

197

Decodable Practice Reader 15A

Flo fixes homemade lunches.
She gets Bo passes for buses.
That makes Bo happy.

198

Nice Bo saves bunches
of boxes for Flo.
Thanks, Bo.

199

Flo fetches all the boxes.
She dashes back to her packing.

200

Corrective feedback

If... children have difficulty decoding a word, **then...** refer them to the Sound-Spelling Cards to identify the sounds in the word. Then prompt them to blend the word.

- What is the new word?
- Is the new word a word you know?
- Does it make sense in the story?

Check decoding and comprehension

Have children retell the story to include characters, setting, and events. Then have children locate words that have an -es ending. List words that children name. Children should supply *boxes, dishes, dresses, sketches, brushes, rushes, pitches, presses, smashes, wishes, fixes, lunches, passes, buses, bunches, fetches,* and *dashes.*

Point out that the -es on the end of *boxes, dishes, dresses, sketches, brushes, lunches, bunches, passes,* and *buses* means "more than one." Explain that the words *rushes, pitches, presses, smashes, wishes, fixes, fetches,* and *dashes* are action words with the ending -es. Action words can have an -es ending and words that mean "more than one" can have an -es ending.

Reread for Fluency

Have children reread Decodable Practice Reader 15A to develop automaticity decoding words with the ending -es and the plural -es.

> **ROUTINE** **Oral Rereading**
>
> 1. **Read** Have children read the entire book orally.
> 2. **Reread** To achieve optimal fluency, children should reread the text three or four times.
> 3. **Corrective Feedback** Listen as children read. Provide corrective feedback regarding their fluency and decoding.

Routines Flip Chart

Differentiated Instruction

A Advanced

Extend Language Have children read the sentences that have words with the plural -es ending. Ask them to change the plural nouns to singular nouns and say each sentence aloud with the singular noun. For example, *She gets Hank passes for buses* becomes *She gets Hank a pass for a bus.*

English Language Learners

Ending -es; Plural -es

Beginning Write several plural -es words from *Boxes for Flo* on the board. Underline -es in each word. Say each word aloud, clapping your hands for each syllable of the word. Have students repeat each word, clapping their hands for each syllable.

Intermediate Have children read each sentence with an -es word. Have them use the pictures to help identify each -es word as a plural noun or a verb.

Advanced/Advanced High Have children find words from *Boxes for Flo* that mean "more than one." Ask them to use each word in a new sentence. Monitor pronunciation.

Spelling Pretest
Words with -es

Dictate spelling words

Dictate the spelling words and read the sentences. Have children write the words. If needed, segment the words for children, clarify the pronunciations, and give meanings of words. Have children check their pretests and correct misspelled words.

1.	fix	Could you **fix** my broken bike?
2.	fixes	Mr. Smith **fixes** cars.
3.	class*	My **class** walked down the hall.
4.	classes	All the **classes** lined up to go home.
5.	wish	I **wish** I could get a new puppy.
6.	wishes*	Tom **wishes** his tooth would fall out.
7.	kiss	I will **kiss** the baby.
8.	kisses	Mom **kisses** Megan good night.
9.	bus	The **bus** is late today.
10.	buses	**Buses** take people around the city.

*Words marked with asterisks come from the selection *The Class Pet*.

On their own

Use Let's Practice It! p. 142 on *Teacher's Resource DVD-ROM*.

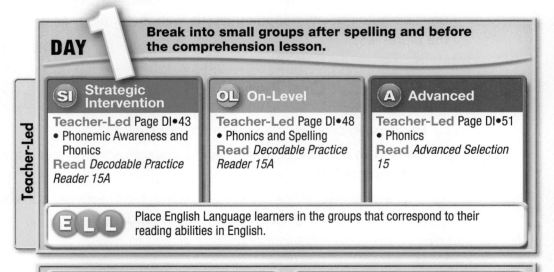

Let's Practice It! TR DVD•142

Small Group Time

DAY 1 Break into small groups after spelling and before the comprehension lesson.

Teacher-Led

SI Strategic Intervention	**OL On-Level**	**A Advanced**
Teacher-Led Page DI•43	Teacher-Led Page DI•48	Teacher-Led Page DI•51
• Phonemic Awareness and Phonics	• Phonics and Spelling	• Phonics
Read *Decodable Practice Reader 15A*	Read *Decodable Practice Reader 15A*	Read *Advanced Selection 15*

ELL Place English Language learners in the groups that correspond to their reading abilities in English.

Practice Stations	**Independent Activities**
• Listen Up	• Read independently/Reading Log on *Reader's and Writer's Notebook* p. RR4
• Word Work	• Concept Talk Video

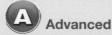

High-Frequency Words

Differentiated Instruction

A Advanced

Extend Spelling Challenge children who spell words correctly to spell more difficult words such as: *benches, sunglasses, crunches, flashes, taxes,* and *fizzes.*

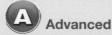
ROUTINE Nondecodable Words

Introduce

1 Say and Spell Look at p. 89. Some words we have to learn by remembering the letters rather than saying the sounds. We will say and spell the words to help learn them. Point to the first word. This word is *very.* The letters in *very* are v-e-r-y, *very.* Have children say and spell each word, first with you, and then without you.

2 Identify Familiar Letter-Sounds Point to the first letter in *very.* You know the sound for this letter. What is this letter and what is its sound? (*v,* /v/)

3 Demonstrate Meaning Tell me a sentence using the word *very.* Repeat this routine with the other Words I Can Read.

Routines Flip Chart

Phonics/Spelling Generalization

The spelling words consist of a base word, and then the base word with the ending *-es,* pronounced /əz/.

Read words in isolation

Have children read the words on p. 89 aloud. Add the words to the Word Wall.

Read words in context

Have children read the sentences aloud. Have them identify this week's High-Frequency Words in the sentences.

On their own

Use *Reader's and Writer's Notebook* p. 346.

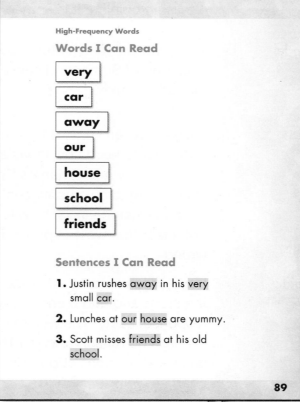

High-Frequency Words

Words I Can Read

very

car

away

our

house

school

friends

Sentences I Can Read

1. Justin rushes away in his very small car.

2. Lunches at our house are yummy.

3. Scott misses friends at his old school.

89

Student Edition p. 89

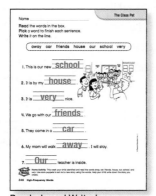

Reader's and Writer's
Notebook p. 346

ELL

English Language Learners
Survival Vocabulary Have children use the word *very* to describe something. Children might say, *My puppy is **very** silly.*

Frontload Read Aloud Use the modified Read Aloud in the *ELL Support* pages to prepare children to listen to "The End of Summer" on p. 89b.

Objectives
◎ Recognize fact and opinion in text.

Skills Trace
◎ **Fact and Opinion**
Introduce U3W3D1; U3W5D1
Practice U3W3D2; U3W3D3;
U3W3D4; U3W5D2; U3W5D3;
U3W5D4
Reteach/Review U3W3D5;
U3W5D5; U4W3D2
Assess/Test Weekly Tests
U3W3; U3W5
Benchmark Tests U3

KEY:
U=Unit   W=Week   D=Day

Listening Comprehension
🎯 Fact and Opinion

Introduce

Envision It!

When we read, it is important to know the difference between a fact and an opinion. A **fact** is a piece of information that we can prove is true. For example, it is a fact that the word *book* has four letters. An **opinion** is a person's belief, way of thinking, or judgment. You cannot call an opinion right or wrong. For example, I am stating my opinion if I say, "Grape jelly tastes better than strawberry jelly." Your opinion might be different.

Have children turn to pp. EI•4–EI•5 in their Student Editions. These pictures and sentences show an example of a fact and an opinion. **Discuss these questions using the pictures:**

• Which sentence tells a fact? How do you know? (*It is raining* tells a fact. A person can prove it is raining by looking out the window.)

• Which sentence tells an opinion? How do you know? (*Rainy days are fun* tells an opinion. It is someone's belief. It isn't right or wrong.)

Student Edition EI•4–EI•5

Model

Today we will read a story about bear cubs who love the summer. **Read "The End of Summer." Draw a T-chart or use Graphic Organizer 4 to model fact and opinion.**

Think Aloud

When I read, I look in the text for facts and opinions. This helps me learn new ideas as I read. When Squirrel says "summer lasts only a few months," he is stating a fact. I can prove it by observing or by reading a nonfiction book about seasons. Squirrel is telling his opinion when he says, "Fall is the best season!" This is Squirrel's belief, not a fact that we can prove. It is neither right nor wrong.

Guide practice

Have children name other facts and opinions from the story, and add them to the chart. (Possible response: *Fact:* "The weather is cool." *Opinion:* "There's no reason to cry!") Then have children state facts and opinions about winter. Add these to the chart as well.

On their own

Use *Reader's and Writer's Notebook* p. 347.

Reader's and Writer's
Notebook, p. 347

The End of Summer

It was the cubs' first summer, and they were enjoying summer's delightful activities. Each day they went swimming with Mama Bear, splashing and playing tag in the lake. They picked berries and had picnics under leafy, green trees.

One day the cubs were swimming while Mama Bear picked flowers. Squirrel came by, carrying a sack of nuts. "Hello, cubs!" he called. "Do you feel that cool nip in the air? The season will soon be over. Summer will end and fall will be here soon. I think fall is the best season!"

"What do you mean, summer will end?" asked the cubs. "Do you mean it will not be warm enough to swim and have picnics?"

"Well, yes," said Squirrel. "Don't you know that summer lasts only a few months? Then it is fall, and then it is . . ." But Squirrel didn't finish his sentence because the cubs began to cry and wail and call for their mother.

Mama Bear came running. "Why are you crying, dears?" she asked. "There's no reason to cry!"

"Squirrel just told us that summer will end," said the cubs. "We thought it would always be summer!"

"There, there, my dears," said Mama Bear. "It is true. I was waiting for the right time to tell you because you both love summer so much!"

"But what will happen when summer ends?" asked the cubs. "What will we do with our days?"

"Do not worry," said Mama Bear. "After summer is fall. The weather is cool. We can take brisk hikes and pick pumpkins. You can play in the colorful leaves that fall from trees. We will eat lots of food to get ready for our long sleep."

"That sounds like fun!" said the cubs. "But we will miss summer."

"Do not worry, dears," said Mama Bear. "Summer will be back next year and every year because that is nature's way."

"Hooray! Hooray!" said the cubs. "Summer will be back next year and fall will soon be here, and we will have fun in new ways!"

Academic Vocabulary

fact a piece of information that can be proved to be true

opinion someone's judgment, belief, or way of thinking

Objectives

- Use present tense verbs with correct subject-verb agreement when writing and speaking.
- Use inflectional endings to spell verbs correctly.

MINI-LESSON

5 Day Planner
Guide to Mini-Lessons

DAY 1	Read Like a Writer
DAY 2	Remembering What You've Read
DAY 3	Evaluation
DAY 4	Strong Conclusions
DAY 5	Proofread for Fragments

Conventions
Verbs That Do Not Add -s

Model

Explain that a **verb** is the action word in a sentence. It tells what someone or something does. *Goes, sits,* and *swims* are verbs. A verb in the **present tense** means the action is happening now.

Display Grammar Transparency 15. Read the instructions aloud. Model identifying the verb in each example. Then read the directions and model number 1.

Grammar Transparency 15
TR DVD

- The sentence tells what two people, Carl and Jan, are doing. I do not add *-s* to the verb.
- I will circle the verb *move*. This verb shows that more than one person is doing something.

Guide practice

Continue with items 2–5, having children identify the correct present tense form of the verb in each sentence.

Connect to oral language

Have the class complete these sentence frames orally using the same verb for each sentence pair.

> Pair 1: He _____ the dog. They _____ the dog.
>
> Pair 2: Sam _____ the milk. Tom and Ray _____ the milk.

On their own

Team Talk Pair children and have them talk about things they like to do with a friend. Then have them identify the present tense form of the verbs they use.

Writing for Tests
Summary

MINI-LESSON

Read Like a Writer

■ **Introduce** This week you will write a summary. A summary tells about something you have read. It tells only the most important information. A summary is short.

Genre	Summary
Trait	Conventions
Mode	Expository

Prompt: Write a summary of your favorite story.

Ruby in Her Own Time is my favorite story. Ruby takes longer to do things than her brothers and sisters. She eats later. She swims later. But she flies farthest first. She leaves home. Then she comes back. She brings her new family.

348 Writing Writing for Tests

Reader's and Writer's Notebook
p. 348

■ **Examine Model Text** Let's listen to a summary. Track the print as you read aloud the summary on *Reader's and Writer's Notebook* p. 348. Have children follow along.

■ **Key Features** Read the prompt aloud. Remind children that in tests they have to write about what the prompt asks. Point out that the summary identifies the story. Help children find and identify the story being summarized. What main things happen in the story? Help children underline the main events summarized.

This summary tells about another story. The writer tells the main points from the story.

The summary is short. It only tells the important information.

Write Guy
Jeff Anderson

Nice, Big, Long, Pointless, Listy, Adjective Strings

As children learn to write, many love to "improve" sentences with adjectives—big adjectives, little adjectives, many adjectives. We don't want to encourage strings of adjectives. On the other hand, this is a problem that can correct itself. Show a sample of a sentence with too many adjectives (not written by the child). Ask which *one* adjective might be unnecessary.

Daily Fix-It

1. My dad fickses buss.
   My dad <u>fixes buses</u>.

2. i have a vere friendly class.
   <u>I</u> have a <u>very</u> friendly class.

Discuss the Daily Fix-It corrections with children. Review sentence capitalization, the spelling of the plural *buses*, the *y* spelling of the long *e* sound, and the *x* spelling in *fixes*.

English Language Learners
Conventions To provide children with practice on verbs that do not add -*s*, use the modified grammar lessons in the *ELL Handbook*.

Writing for Tests
Summary, continued

Review key features

Review key features of a summary with children. You may want to post these key features in the classroom to allow children to refer to them as they work on their summaries.

Key Features of Summaries

- is about something you have read
- tells the most important information
- is short

Connect to familiar texts

Use examples from texts familiar to children. Point out that many books, videos, and DVDs have summaries on the back cover. These summaries are short and give important information about the book or movie.

Look ahead

Tell children that tomorrow they will write their own summaries.

ROUTINE Quick Write for Fluency **Team Talk**

1. **Talk** Read the following question aloud, and have children discuss answers with partners.

   What things do you need to tell in a summary?

2. **Write** Have children write short sentences to answer the question. Make sure their sentences include the correct verb form.

3. **Share** Partners can read their answers to one another.

Routines Flip Chart

Research and Inquiry
Identify and Focus Topic

Teach

Display and review the concept map about this week's question: *What can we learn about animals as they grow and change?* What are some things you would like to learn about animals? Ask children to share their ideas. Point out that they can learn about groups of animals, such as mammals, or individual animals, such as frogs.

Model

Think Aloud It has been so much fun learning about my dog as he grows and changes. I like learning about cats and horses, too. I know that dogs, cats, and horses are mammals. I think I'd like to know more about what makes a mammal a mammal. What do mammals have in common? How do they change as they grow?

Guide practice

Give children time to think of animals they would like to research. Record children's suggestions as a list.

Wrap Up Your Day

✔ **Phonics: Ending -es; Plural -es** Write *benches* and ask children to identify the base word (*bench*) and the ending (*-es*). What does the *-es* ending show? (There is more than one bench.)

✔ **Spelling: Words with -es** Have children name the spelling for each sound in *mashes.* Write the spelling as children write the letters in the air. Continue with *inches, misses,* and *sixes.*

✔ **Build Concepts** Ask children to recall what happened in the Read Aloud, "The End of Summer." What did you learn about animals in this story? (Bears take care of their cubs.)

✔ **Homework** Send home this week's Family Times Newsletter from Let's Practice It! pp. 137–138 on the *Teacher Resource DVD-ROM.*

Let's Practice It!
TR DVD•137–138

SI Strategic Intervention

Selecting a Topic If children have trouble coming up with a topic, show them an animal family tree. They can choose either individual animals (crocodiles) or animal groups (reptiles).

Preview DAY 2

Tell children that tomorrow they will read about what happens to mice as they grow and change.

Objectives

- Discuss the concept to develop oral language.
- Build oral vocabulary.

Today at a Glance

Oral Vocabulary
swoop, tumble

Phonemic Awareness
Segment and Blend Phonemes

Phonics and Spelling
◉ Ending -*es*, Plural -*es*
◉ *r*-Controlled *or*, *ore*

Fluency
Paired Reading

High-Frequency Words

Story Words
brown, fur, mouse, teaches

Comprehension
◉ Fact and Opinion
◉ Monitor and Clarify

Vocabulary
Descriptive Words

Conventions
Verbs That Do Not Add -*s*

Writing
Writing for Tests: Summary
Write to a Prompt

Handwriting
Letter *R* and *r* / Letter Size

Research and Inquiry
Research Skill: Classifying/
Categorizing

Concept Talk

 Question of the Week

What can we learn about animals as they grow and change?

Build concepts

To reinforce concepts and to focus children's attention, have children sing "My Puppy Buddy" from the *Sing with Me* Big Book. Do you think this puppy could dig holes when he was first born? Explain why or why not. (Possible response: No. He would have been too small and weak. He had to grow bigger and stronger before he could dig holes.)

🔘 Sing with Me Big Book Audio

Introduce Amazing Words

Display the Big Book *Mr. George Baker*. Read the title and identify the author. Explain that in the story, the author uses the words *tumble* and *swoop*. Have children listen as you read the story to find out what Harry and Mr. George see outdoors that tumbles and swoops.

Use the Oral Vocabulary routine on the next page to teach *tumble* and *swoop*.

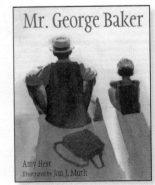

Big Book

ELL **Reinforce Vocabulary** Use the Day 2 instruction on ELL Poster 15 to reinforce meanings of high-frequency words.

ELL Poster 15

Oral Vocabulary
Amazing Words

Teach Amazing Words

Amazing Words — **Oral Vocabulary Routine**

① **Introduce the Word** Relate the word *tumble* to the book. Harry tells of watching leaves *tumble* from the trees. Supply a child-friendly definition. To *tumble* means to fall helplessly. Have children say the word.

② **Demonstrate** Provide examples to show meaning. You *tumble* to the ground when you trip. Cereal *tumbles* into a bowl when you pour it from a box.

③ **Apply** Have children demonstrate their understanding. What else might you see *tumble* to the ground outdoors?

See p. OV•3 to teach *swoop*.

Routines Flip Chart

Anchored Talk

Add to the concept map

Discuss how the behavior of animals changes as they grow older.

- In the song "My Puppy Buddy," as the puppy matures, he does new things. What new things does he do as he grows? (Possible response: He eats more food. He digs holes.) Let's add *They eat more* under *What they eat changes* and *Dogs can dig holes* under *They can do new things*.

- In yesterday's Read Aloud, "The End of Summer," the mother bear's job is to take care of her cubs. Will she always take care of them? Why or why not? (Possible response: No. When they get older, they will be able to take care of themselves.) Let's add this to our map, too.

Amazing Words

features	crumple
mature	nibble
natural	nudges
swoop	wriggle
tumble	

Differentiated Instruction

 Strategic Intervention

Amazing Words Since *swoop* and *tumble* both name falling motions, demonstrate the difference using hand gestures: a smooth, sweeping gesture for *swoop*, and hands circling each other downward for *tumble*. Have children imitate the gestures as they say the words.

ELL

English Language Learners

Consonant Blends Consonant blends are often challenging for learners of English because their home language may not combine consonant phonemes in similar ways. For example, Spanish-speakers may add the /e/ sound at the beginning of words with *s*-blends, saying *estop* or *esleep*. Have children practice pronouncing *swoop* and other *s*-blend words such as *score, slip, smoke, snail* and *stand*.

Media To have children derive meaning from a variety of media find an appropriate Website, CD-ROM, or DVD that provides an audio and video account of how animals grow and change. Have children listen to and derive meaning to build and reinforce concept and language attainment. To assess their concept and language attainment have them create a class book about animals growing and changing.

Objectives

- Segment and blend words with the /ôr/ sound.
- Associate the sound /ôr/ with *or* and *ore*.
- ◎ Blend and read words with /ôr/ spelled *or, ore*.

Skills Trace

◎ **Vowels:** *r-Controlled or, ore*
Introduce U3W3D2
Practice U3W3D3; U3W3D4
Reteach/Review U3W3D5; U3W4D4
Assess/Test Weekly Test U3W3
Benchmark Test U3

KEY:
U=Unit   W=Week   D=Day

Phonemic Awareness
Segment and Blend Phonemes

Model isolating sounds

Have children look at the picture on pages 86–87 in their Student Edition. Look at the man sweeping. He is doing one of his chores. The middle sound I hear in the word *chores* is /ôr/. The last sound I hear in *chores* is /z/. I see roses with thorns. Each thorn is sharp. The middle sound I hear in the word *thorn* is /ôr/. The last sound I hear in *thorn* is /n/.

Student Edition p. 86–87

Model segmenting and blending

Listen to the sounds in the word *chores*: /ch/ /ôr/ /z/. There are three sounds in *chores*. Let's blend those sounds to make a word: /ch/ /ôr/ /z/, *chores*. Continue modeling with *thorn*.

Guide practice

Guide children as they segment and blend these words from the picture: *horse, horn, doors, floor, cores, born*.

Corrective feedback

If... children make an error,
then... model by segmenting the word, and have them repeat the segmenting and blending of the word.

On their own

Have children segment and blend the following words.

/b/ /ôr/ /d/ **board**	/p/ /ôr/ /ch/ **porch**	/w/ /ôr/ /m/ **warm**
/f/ /ôr/ /t/ **fort**	/k/ /ôr/ /k/ **cork**	/t/ /ôr/ /n/ **torn**

Phonics—Teach/Model
 r-Controlled *or, ore*

Sound-Spelling Card 91

Sound-Spelling Card 93

ROUTINE Blending Strategy

1 Connect Write *spot*. You studied words like this already. What sound does *o* spell in this word? (/o/) Have children read the word aloud. Today you'll learn to read words with the /ôr/ sound.

2 Use Sound-Spelling Cards Display Card 91. The sound you hear at the beginning of *orchestra* is /ôr/. The sound /ôr/ can be spelled *or*. Have children say /ôr/ several times as you point to *or*. Follow the same procedure with Card 93 for the *ore* spelling of /ôr/.

3 Model Write *corn*. In this word, the letters *or* spell the sound /ôr/. This is how I blend this word. Segment and blend *corn*. Follow this procedure to model blending *more*.

4 Guide Practice Continue the process in step 3. This time have children blend with you.

for	sore	form	born	shore	snore
tore	worn	cord	north	thorn	storm

5 Review What do you know about reading these words? (The letters *or* or *ore* can spell the sound /ôr/.)

Routines Flip Chart

Differentiated Instruction

A Advanced

More Challenging Words If children can easily read the words in Guide Practice, write and read aloud these words: *seashore, important, ordinary, before, auditorium, laboratory, information.* Discuss the meaning of each word. Have partners make flash cards by copying each word onto an index card. Then have them turn the cards over and take turns picking a word. Tell them to read the word and use it in a sentence.

Vocabulary Support

You may wish to explain the meaning of these words.

cord a rope, or a covered wire that connects something to an electrical outlet

north the direction to the left of sunrise

English Language Learners

Visual Support Model isolating sounds while using the pictures on pp. 86–87 of the Student Edition as visual support. For example: /d/ /ôr/, *door*. Who can point to a door? Now let's say the sounds of *door* together: /d/ /ôr/, *door*.

Objectives

- Associate the sound /ôr/ with *or* and *ore*.
- Blend and read words with /ôr/ spelled *or* and *ore*.
- Read words in context and in isolation.

Check Word Reading
SUCCESS PREDICTOR

Phonics—Build Fluency
r-Controlled *or, ore*

Model

Envision It!

Have children turn to page 90 in their Student Edition. Look at the pictures on this page. The word in the first picture is *orchestra*. When I say *orchestra*, the first sound I hear is /ôr/. In *orchestra*, /ôr/ is spelled *or*. The word in the second picture is *score*. When I say *score*, the last sound I hear is also /ôr/. In *score*, /ôr/ is spelled *ore*.

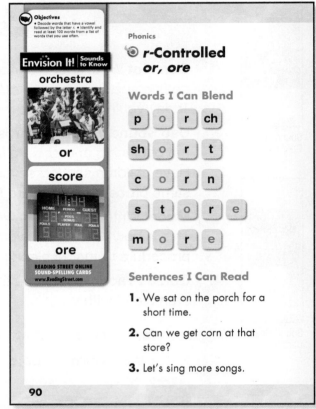

Student Edition p. 90

Guide practice

For each word in *Words I Can Blend*, ask for the sound of each letter or group of letters. Make sure children identify the correct sound for *or* and *ore*. Then have children blend the whole word.

Corrective feedback

If... children have difficulty blending a word,
then... model blending the word, and ask children to blend it with you.

Blend and Read

Decode words in isolation

After children can successfully segment and blend the words, ask them to read the words naturally.

Decode words in context

Have children read each of the sentences. Have them identify words in the sentences with /ôr/ spelled *or* or *ore*.

Team Talk Pair children and have them take turns reading each of the sentences aloud.

On their own

Use *Reader's and Writer's Notebook* p. 349.

Reader's and Writer's
Notebook, p. 349

Don't Wait Until Friday

MONITOR PROGRESS | Check Word Reading ↻ *r*-Controlled *or, ore*

Write the following words and have the class read them. Notice which children miss words during the group reading. Call on those individuals to read some of the words.

torn	chore	fork	port	storm
chop	porch	rock	corn	store
fort	hole	score	choke	thorn

Spiral Review
Row 2 contrasts *r*-controlled *or, ore* words with short *o* words.

Row 3 contrasts *r*-controlled *or, ore* words with long *o* words.

If... children cannot blend words with *r*-controlled *or, ore,*

then... use the Small Group Time Strategic Intervention lesson, p. DI•44, to reteach words with *r*-controlled *or, ore.* Continue to monitor children's progress using other instructional opportunities during the week. See the Skills Trace on p. 90c.

| Day 1 | Day 2 | Day 3 | Day 4 | Day 5 |
| Check Word Reading | Check Word Reading | Check High-Frequency Words/Retelling | Check Fluency | Check Oral Vocabulary |

Spelling Patterns

/ôr/ Spelled *or, ore* The /ôr/ sound may be spelled *or* or *ore*.

English Language Learners
Pronunciation In languages such as Spanish, Polish, Farsi, and Arabic, the /r/ sound is flapped or rolled, so speakers of these languages may have difficulty pronouncing *r*-controlled vowels, especially when *r* is followed by a final consonant. Have children practice saying words such as *port, torn, sort, cork, fork.*

Word Reading

Success Predictor

Objectives
- Apply knowledge of sound-spellings to decode unknown words when reading.
- Decode words in context and in isolation.
- Practice fluency with oral rereading.

Decodable Practice Reader 15B
Vowels: *r*-Controlled *or, ore*

Decodable Practice Reader 15B

Decode words in isolation

Have children turn to page 201. Have children decode each word.

Review High-frequency words

Review the previously taught words *from, the, I, who, are, a, water, of, to,* and *eat.* Have children read each word as you point to it on the Word Wall.

Preview Decodable Reader

Have children read the title and preview the story. Tell them they will read words that have the /ôr/ sound in the story.

Decode words in context

Pair children for reading, and listen as they decode. One child begins. Children read the entire story, switching readers after each page.

I wore my cap from the store.
I got my backpack.
We can go!

202

We are at a port.
I see ships in the water.
I take a photo of the ships.

203

Decodable Reader 15B

Dad and I see a ball game.
The score is six to five.
Who will win the trophy?

204

We drive to a big fort.
It has a big flag.

205

It is hot.
We can swim at the shore.
I can run or jump in the waves.

206

We go for a short walk.
We stop to eat clams and corn.
Dad has more clams than Mom.

207

We had fun.
But it is time to go!

208

Corrective feedback

If... children have difficulty decoding a word,

then... refer them to the Sound-Spelling Cards to identify the sounds in the word. Then prompt them to blend the word.

- What is the new word?
- Is the new word a word you know?
- Does it make sense in the story?

Check decoding and comprehension

Have children retell the story to include characters, setting, and events. Then have children locate /ôr/ words in the story. List words that children name. Children should supply *wore, port, score, fort, store, shore, or, for, short, corn,* and *more.* Ask children to say the words. Ask them how they know that these words have the sound /ôr/. (They have the letters *or* or *ore.*)

Reread for Fluency

Have children reread Decodable Practice Reader 15B to develop automaticity decoding words that have the /ôr/ sound.

 ROUTINE **Paired Reading**

 1 **Reread** To achieve optimal fluency, have partners reread the text three or four times.

2 **Corrective Feedback** Listen as children read. Provide corrective feedback regarding their fluency and decoding.

Routines Flip Chart

English Language Learners
Vowels: *r*-Controlled *or, ore*

Beginning Before reading, lead children through *At the Shore.* Point out /ôr/ words such as *wore, port,* and *fort.* Have children say them aloud.

Intermediate After reading, have children find words that are spelled with *or* or *ore.* Have children use the words in a sentence. For example, I *wore* a coat *for* the game. Monitor children's pronunciation.

Advanced/Advanced High Have children find words spelled with *or* and *ore* and sort them into groups of rhyming words.

Objectives

• Apply knowledge of letter-sound correspondences and words with endings -s, -es to decode words in context and in isolation.

• Spell words with ending -es.

Phonics Review

Ending -s, -es; Plural -s, -es

Review Sound-Spellings

Review words with endings -s and -es and plural -s and -es using Sound-Spelling Cards 124, 129, 139, and 141.

Decode words in isolation

Display these words. Have the class blend the words. Then point to the words in random order and ask children to decode them quickly.

passes	swings	misses	thanks
ropes	hushes	punches	dishes
talks	buzzes	games	foxes

Corrective feedback

Model blending decodable words and then ask children to blend them with you.

Decode words in context

Display these sentences. Have the class read the sentences.

Team Talk Have pairs take turns reading the sentences naturally.

Sam stacks five boxes.

He dashes back home to feed his cats.

Jill catches all three balls.

Spelling
Words with -es

Guide Practice

Tell children that you will segment the sounds in each spelling word. They should repeat the sounds in each word as they write the word. Check the spelling of each word before saying the next word.

1. /f//i//ks/ **fix**
2. /f//i//ks//ə//z/ **fixes**
3. /k//l//a//s/ **class**
4. /k//l//a//s//ə//z/ **classes**
5. /w//i//sh/ **wish**
6. /w//i//sh//ə//z/ **wishes**
7. /k//i//s/ **kiss**
8. /k//i//s//ə//z/ **kisses**
9. /b//u//s/ **bus**
10. /b//u//s//ə//z/ **buses**

On their own

Use *Reader's and Writer's Notebook* p. 350.

Small Group Time

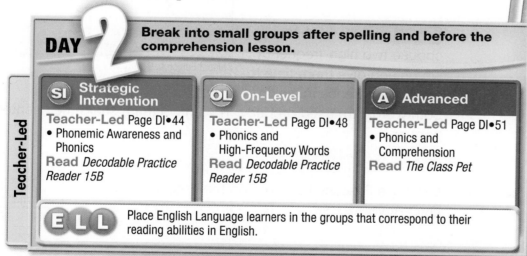

DAY 2 — Break into small groups after spelling and before the comprehension lesson.

Teacher-Led

SI Strategic Intervention
Teacher-Led Page DI•44
- Phonemic Awareness and Phonics
Read *Decodable Practice Reader 15B*

OL On-Level
Teacher-Led Page DI•48
- Phonics and High-Frequency Words
Read *Decodable Practice Reader 15B*

A Advanced
Teacher-Led Page DI•51
- Phonics and Comprehension
Read *The Class Pet*

ELL Place English Language learners in the groups that correspond to their reading abilities in English.

Practice Stations
- Listen Up
- Word Work

Independent Activities
- Read independently/Reading Log on *Reader's and Writer's Notebook* p. RR4
- AudioText of Main Selection

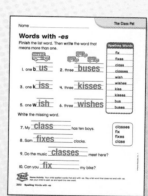

Reader's and Writer's Notebook, p. 350

English Language Learners

Plurals Children may need practice adding -es to show plural nouns. In Chinese, Hmong, and Korean, nouns do not have a plural form.

Objectives
- Learn story words: *brown, fur, mouse, teaches.*
- Review high-frequency words.
- Identify descriptive words.

High-Frequency Words
Build Fluency

Read words in isolation

Remind children that there are some words we learn by remembering the letters, rather than by saying the sounds. Then have them read each of the highlighted high-frequency words aloud.

Read words in context

Chorally read the "I Can Read!" passage along with the children. Then have them read the passage aloud to themselves. When they are finished, ask children to reread the high-frequency words.

Team Talk Have children choose two high-frequency words and give them time to create a sentence in which both words are used properly. Then have them share their sentence with a partner.

On their own

Use Let's Practice It! p. 141 on the *Teacher Resource DVD-ROM.*

I Can Read!

Flor and Jim are best friends at school. Jim must go away for three weeks. He brushes his teeth, packs his bag, and gets in the car.

Flor rushes to his house. "This will be very sad, Jim," said Flor. "Our school will not be the same."

"Come back in three weeks, Flor," said Jim. "We can meet on my porch."

You've learned
- Ending *-es;* Plural *-es*
- Vowels: *r*-Controlled *or, ore*

High-Frequency Words
very car away our
house school friends

91

Student Edition p. 91

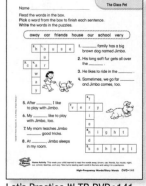

Let's Practice It! TR DVD•141

Story Words
The Class Pet

Introduce story words

Use Vocabulary Transparency 15 to introduce this week's story words. Read each sentence as you track the print. Frame each underlined word and explain its meaning.

brown — the color of soil or chocolate

fur — the hair that covers the bodies of some animals

mouse — a small, furry animal with a pointed snout and a thin, bare tail

teaches — gives information or explains how to do something

Have children read each sentence with you.

Vocabulary Transparency 15
TR DVD

Vocabulary
Descriptive Words

Model descriptive words for feelings

Explain that **descriptive words** can tell how a person feels. Start a list on the board, and label it *Feelings*.

 Think Aloud The word *happy* describes a feeling. People feel happy when they are with others they like or are doing things they enjoy. I'll put *happy* on our list.

Guide practice

Ask children to think of other words for feelings. Discuss the meaning of each word and add it to the list.

On their own

Have children choose a word from the list and draw a picture about a time when they felt that way. Have them share their pictures with the class and use the word in a sentence about the picture.

Differentiated Instruction

A Advanced

Descriptive Words Have children write sentences containing words for feelings by completing the following sentence frame: _____ *makes me* _____. Example: *My dog makes me happy.* Have children use as many different feeling words as they can.

Academic Vocabulary

descriptive words words that tell how something looks, sounds, smells, tastes, or feels

English Language Learners
Understand General Meaning Ask children to listen as you read aloud p. 91 in the Student Edition. After reading, have them restate the general ideas in the passage using the familiar language of the high-frequency words. Have them ask questions about any unfamiliar situations in the passage.

Multilingual Vocabulary Lists Children can apply knowledge of their home languages to acquire new English vocabulary by using the Multilingual Vocabulary List (*ELL Handbook* pp. 465–476).

Objectives
- Build background about caring for a pet.
- Preview and predict.
- Use key structure and elements of expository text to improve understanding of text.
- Set a purpose for reading text.

Build Background
The Class Pet

Background Building Audio

Have children listen to the CD. Tell them to listen to find out what gerbils and hamsters look like and what kinds of equipment and food are needed to take care of them.

 Background Building Audio

Discuss caring for pets

Team Talk Have children turn to a partner and use these questions for discussion:

- What kinds of equipment are needed to take care of pets that you know about?
- What do these pets need to eat and drink?
- What other special care do they need?

Organize information in a chart

Draw a chart with large squares. Ask children to share the information they discussed about pet care. Record their responses.

	Equipment	Food	Other Care
hamster	cage water bottle food dish	hamster mix water	keep cage clean
dog	food dish water dish	dog food water	give dog baths take for walks

Connect to selection

We've been discussing different kinds of pets. In the selection we are about to read, *The Class Pet,* a teacher brings a pet mouse to school. We'll learn about the features of mice, what they eat, and how they behave. We'll also learn how newborn baby mice change as they mature into adults.

Student Edition pp. 92–93

Double Day Read!

Main Selection—First Read
The Class Pet

Practice the skill

Fact and Opinion Remind children that a **fact** tells something that can be proved true by observing, checking in a book, or asking an expert. An **opinion** tells someone's idea or feeling about something. It can't be proved true or false.

Introduce the strategy

Monitor and Clarify Explain that good readers often ask themselves if they understand what they are reading. If something doesn't make sense, they try different ways to fix the problem. Have children turn to page EI•15 in their Student Edition.

Envision It! | Think Aloud

The girl is confused about what she has read. She rereads part of the book. She thinks about what it says and creates an image in her head. That helps her understand. As I read *The Class Pet*, I will create images if I need help understanding.

Student Edition EI•15

Introduce genre

Let's Read Together Expository text is writing that gives facts and information. As they read *The Class Pet,* ask children to look for facts about mice.

Preview and Predict

Have children read the title of the story. Read the name of the author, and have children describe what an author does. Have children activate prior knowledge by looking at the photos and predicting the kinds of information they will learn about mice.

Set a purpose

Good readers read for a purpose. Setting a purpose helps us to think and understand more as we read. Guide children to set a purpose for reading the selection.

Tell children that today they will read *The Class Pet* for the first time. Use the Day 2 Guide Comprehension notes to help children develop their comprehension of the selection.

Double Day Read!

First Read

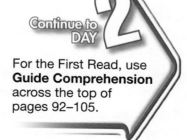
Continue to DAY 2

For the First Read, use **Guide Comprehension** across the top of pages 92–105.

 INTERACT with TEXT

Strategy Response Log

Genre Have children use p. RR27 in their *Reader's and Writer's Notebook* to identify the characteristics of expository text.

Academic Vocabulary

monitor and clarify a comprehension strategy by which readers actively think about whether or not they understand what they are reading and use appropriate strategies to make sense of difficult words, ideas, or passages

ELL

English Language Learners

Build Background Before children listen to the CD, build background and elicit prior knowledge. On the CD, a family will visit a pet shop to buy a hamster or a gerbil. What kinds of information do you think they will want to find out about each kind of animal before they buy one?

Frontload Main Selection Ask children what they already know about mice, using the picture on page 92. Then do a picture walk of the selection so children can see and talk about the appearance, eating habits, and behavior of mice, and how baby mice change as they mature.

Guide Comprehension
Skills and Strategies

DAY 2

Connect to Concept

Growing and Changing Look at the pictures on pages 92–93. How do you think this mouse has changed since it was first born? (Possible response: It has gotten bigger. It eats more. It can run and climb.)

Amazing Words

Have children continue discussing the concept using the Amazing Words *features, mature,* and *natural.*

The Class Pet
by Nichole L. Shields

Genre **Expository text** tells about real people, places, and animals. This selection is about how mice grow and change.

Question of the Week
What can we learn about animals as they grow and change?

92   93

Student Edition pp. 92–93

Extend Thinking
Think Critically

DAY 3

Higher-Order Thinking Skills

Evaluation Is it a good idea to use photos in *The Class Pet,* or would it have been better to use drawings as in *Ruby in Her Own Time?* Why? (Possible response: Photos are better because *The Class Pet* is about real mice.)

Analysis Is the author's main purpose in writing *The Class Pet* to have readers enjoy the cute mice or to teach about mice? Explain. (The purpose was to teach. Most of the text and photos give information about mice and how they live.)

Word Reading

High-Frequency Words Point out the words *school,* *house,* and *our.* Have children practice reading these words.

Skills

⊙ **Fact and Opinion** Read the first sentence on page 95. Which part tells an opinion? (the part that says Dory is cute) Why is this an opinion? (It tells how the author feels about Dory. Others may feel differently.) Which part tells a fact? (the part that says Dory is a tan mouse) Why is this a fact? (It can be proved true by observing.)

Miss Ford takes a glass box to school.

"This will be a house for our class pet," Miss Ford tells the class.

94

The pet is a cute tan mouse.
The class names it Dory.

Miss Ford teaches lessons on pets.
She uses Dory in these lessons.

95

Student Edition pp. 94–95

Higher-Order Thinking Skills

Synthesis We learned from our CD about the equipment needed to care for a hamster or gerbil. Which of those things are similar for a mouse? (cage, hanging water bottle, food dish, cage bedding, exercise wheel)

If... children have difficulty comparing the equipment and food needed for gerbils, hamsters, and mice,

then... help children recall the information they learned from the CD by asking questions such as, *What did the family find out about the equipment needed to feed hamsters and gerbils?*

Skills and Strategies, continued

DAY 2

Vocabulary

Story Words Have children locate the story word *brown* on page 96. Which mouse is almost completely brown? (the one next to the black mouse)

Strategies

Monitor and Clarify *Monitor and clarify* gives us ways to figure out things that aren't clear. On p. 97, how can we use this strategy to figure out what a pellet is? (We can reread the sentence that tells us a pellet is food. We can make a picture in our heads of a pellet.)

Dory is tan.

But mice can be black, white, <u>or</u> brown.

Mice can have stripes <u>or</u> spots too.

Mice need to eat and drink. Pet <u>stores</u> may sell seed <u>mixes</u> or hard pellets.

But mice will eat all <u>sorts</u> of things, such as <u>corn</u> and nuts.

96

97

Student Edition pp. 96–97

Think Critically, continued

DAY 3

Higher-Order Thinking Skills

Analysis How are the sentences and pictures arranged on page 96? (Each picture is near the sentence that tells about it.) Why is this helpful? (Possible response: If you don't understand the words in the sentence, the pictures can help you guess what they mean.)

Synthesis Reread the last sentence on page 97. What hint does this give you about why outdoor mice sometimes move into people's homes? (Corn and nuts are foods that people eat too. People have these and other foods that mice like in their homes.)

Word Reading

Decoding Have children check their reading of new words using these guidelines:

• Did I blend the sounds to read the word?

• Did I put the new word in the sentence to make sure it made sense?

• Did I look for word parts to help me understand the word?

Strategies

Monitor and Clarify Read the first sentence on page 99. The picture doesn't show a nest made of torn cloth and cotton, so how can you use what you know to make a picture in your head of what it might look like? (Possible response: I know what cloth and cotton look like, so I can make a picture in my head of little pieces of cloth and cotton piled together to make a soft nest.)

Mice use torn cloth and cotton to make nests. Mice that live outside use grass and branches.

Mice like to run and jump late at night. It is time for them to sleep when the sun rises.

98

99

Student Edition pp. 98–99

Higher-Order Thinking Skills

Evaluation Is it important for pet owners to make sure their pets have a chance to exercise? Why do you think so? (Possible response: Yes. Animals need exercise to stay strong. Also, most animals love to run and play and are not happy when they can't.)

If... children have difficulty judging whether exercise is important for animals,

then... ask them about their own experiences with dogs, cats, and other pets. Do the pets they know like to sit still all day? What active things do they like to do?

Skills and Strategies, continued

DAY 2

Vocabulary
Story Words Have children locate the story word *fur* on page 100. What part of a mouse is its fur? (the hair that covers its body)

Skills
Fact and Opinion Is the statement that newborn mice have no fur a fact or opinion? Why? (fact; can be proved true by observing) Is *Mice look awful without fur* a fact or opinion? Why? (opinion; tells what someone feels, but others, such as their mom, may think they look fine)

A mom can have lots of very small mice. Ten of them can be born at the same time. They nap in a nest.

When mice are born, they have no fur. These mice cannot see yet.

Student Edition pp. 100–101

Think Critically, continued

DAY 3

Higher-Level Thinking Skills
Analysis We've learned that very young mice cannot leave their nest. What information on page 100 explains why? (They have no fur to keep them warm, and they cannot see.)

Connect to Science
Eyes of Newborns Many animals are born before they are ready to see. Their brain must mature before their eyes can work. Eyes of mice first open about 14 days after birth. **Team Talk** Have partners discuss what any newborns they have seen can and cannot do.

Vocabulary

Descriptive Words for Feelings What word could you use to describe the way the baby mouse on page 102 might be feeling? (Possible response: *tired, sleepy*)

Strategies

Monitor and Clarify Read the first sentence on page 103. If this sentence did not make sense to you, how could you use the monitor and clarify strategy to figure out what the author meant? (Possible response: I could turn back and reread the part about mice not being able to see when they are first born.)

For a short time, small mice cannot eat seeds. They just sleep and drink milk. Time passes and small mice get fur.

More time passes and small mice can see. They can be away from the nest.

These mice can eat seeds and nuts like their mom.

102

103

Student Edition pp. 102–103

Review Compare and Contrast

Analysis How is the younger mouse on page 102 different from the older ones on page 103? (Possible response: The younger mouse can't see; the older ones can. The younger one can't leave the nest; the older ones can. The younger one just drinks milk; the older ones eat seeds and nuts. The younger one is just starting to get fur; the older ones have all their fur.)

If... children have difficulty describing differences between the younger and older mice,

then... break the question into smaller topics: *What is different about their eyes? Their fur? Do they eat the same food? Can both the younger and the older mice leave the nest?*

Skills and Strategies, continued

DAY 2

Vocabulary
Descriptive Words for Feelings
What word could you use to describe how the children on page 105 might be feeling? (Possible response: *excited, happy, glad, interested*)

Strategy Self-Check
Ask children to tell how they used the monitor and clarify strategy to figure out words and ideas as they read. Prompt with questions such as, *Which pictures helped you? What picture did you make in your head to understand something better? Which parts did you reread?*

Continue with DAY 2
Comprehension Check
p. 105a

Miss Ford tells the class that mice like friends. She tells the class that Dory wishes for one.

104

The next week, Miss Ford takes a box from her car. In it is a mouse. The class names it Cory. Dory and Cory become friends.

105

Student Edition pp. 104–105

Think Critically, continued

DAY 3

Higher-Order Thinking Skills
Analysis What new things might the children learn from having two mice instead of one? (Possible response: They will see how mice play together and get along with each other. They will see if different mice do things in different ways.)

Evaluation Is having a classroom pet a good way to learn about animals? Why do you think so? (Possible response: Yes. You can see and touch the animal. You can help take care of it. Your teacher can also explain things about the animal.)

Comprehension Check

Have children discuss each question with a partner. Ask several pairs to share their responses.

☑ **Expository text** How is *The Class Pet* different from a story about make-believe mice? (Possible response: *The Class Pet* gives facts and information about real mice. In a make-believe story, the mice would talk and do other things that real mice don't do.)

☑ **Confirm predictions** Which photos helped you predict what you would learn from *The Class Pet?* Explain. (Possible response: The photo of a mouse with food helped me predict that I would learn what mice eat; the photo of a mouse carrying grass helped me predict that I would learn how mice make nests.)

☑ **Main idea and details** Reread page 96. What is the main idea of this page? What is one detail that tells about the main idea? (Possible response: The main idea is that mice can be different colors. One detail is that mice can have stripes.)

☑ **Sequence** Describe how a mouse's body changes from the time it is born to the time it is full grown. Use words like *first, next, and then.* (Possible response: First, the mouse is very small and pink. It has no fur, and its eyes are closed. Next, it starts to grow fur, and its eyes open. Then, it looks like a grown mouse, only smaller. It keeps getting bigger until it is full grown.)

☑ **Connect text to world** Think of a baby animal that you know about from a book, TV, or real life. How is it different from a full-grown animal of its kind? (Possible response: A baby bird is very small and covered with soft fluff instead of smooth feathers. It can't fly, and it can't find its own food.)

Differentiated Instruction

 Strategic Intervention

Sequence If children have difficulty describing the sequence of changes in the appearance of mice, have them look back at the photos on pages 100–103. Draw children's attention to the changes in appearance at each stage in the life cycle of mice.

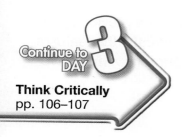

Continue to DAY 3

Think Critically
pp. 106–107

DAY 2 Read and Comprehend

Objectives

- Identify the features of expository text.
- Compare and contrast two texts.
- Correctly identify and use verbs that do not add -s.

Genre
Expository Text

Identify features of expository text

Compare and contrast *The Class Pet* and *Ruby in Her Own Time* to have children identify the features of expository text.

- Let's remember the story *Ruby in Her Own Time*. It's about a family of ducks. *The Class Pet* is about a class that has a pet mouse. How are these two readings similar? **(They are both about animals.)**

- *Ruby in Her Own Time* is an example of animal fantasy. What do we know about animal fantasy? **(The animals do things that they cannot do in real life.)** What do the ducks in the story do that real ducks can't do? **(They talk to each other.)**

- How are the animals in *The Class Pet* different from the animals in *Ruby in Her Own Time*? **(The mice in *The Class Pet* are real. They act just like real mice. The story is true.)**

Guide practice

Explain that the class will continue to compare and contrast *The Class Pet* and *Ruby in Her Own Time*. Use Graphic Organizer 28. Label the separate circles with the titles of the two selections. Label the intersection of the circles *Both*. Let's begin by writing what the two selections have in common. In the middle, I'll write *about animals*. Now let's talk about some differences. We already said that the animals in *Ruby in Her Own Time* are not real, but the animals in *The Class Pet* are real. I'll write that in the two circles. Continue listing similarities and differences. Have children study the finished Venn diagram. Discuss the differences between animal fantasy and expository text.

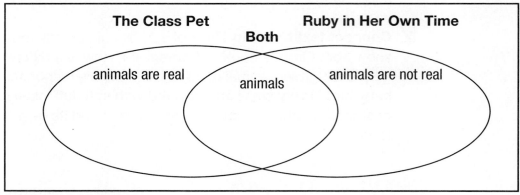

The Class Pet | Ruby in Her Own Time
Both
animals are real | animals | animals are not real

Graphic Organizer Flip Chart 28

On their own

Divide children into small groups and assign each group a previously read expository text from the Student Edition. Have them identify the features that tell the selection is about real people, animals, and/or events. Have them share their information with the class.

105b   Changes • Unit 3 • Week 3

Conventions
Verbs That Do Not Add -s

Model verbs that do not add -s

On the board, write *Erik rides his bike. Erik and his mother ride to school.* Point to each word as you read it. Ask children to identify which sentence is talking about more than one person. (the second) What is the verb in each sentence? (*rides, ride*) These verbs are in the present tense. What does that mean? (They are happening now.) We do not add *s* to a verb if it shows what more than one person does now. That's why the verb in the second sentence is *ride*.

Guide Practice

Write the following sentence frame:

> **Dory and Cory _____.**

Display page 105 of *The Class Pet*. Point to the sentence *Dory and Cory become friends.* What verb names what Dory and Cory are doing now? (*become*). Write *become friends* on the line and read the sentence aloud. Why is there no *-s* at the end of *become*? (There are two mice doing the action.)

Have children name additional verbs to complete the sentence frame, showing what Dory and Cory might do together.

Connect to oral language

Have the class complete these sentence frames orally using present tense verbs.

> 1. We _____ our stories.
>
> 2. The girls _____ at the park.
>
> 3. Maria _____ her food.

On their own

Use *Reader's and Writer's Notebook* p. 351.

Reader's and Writer's
Notebook, p. 351

Differentiated Instruction

SI Strategic Intervention

Present Tense Verbs If children have difficulty differentiating between verbs that add -s and verbs that do not add -s, have them chant sentences that alternate singular and plural subjects—for example, *She LIKES pizza. We LIKE pizza. She GOES home. We GO home. She SINGS songs. We SING songs. She PLAYS tag. We PLAY tag.*

Daily Fix-It

3. I kis my mom before I catch the buss.
I kis<u>s</u> my mom before I catch the bu<u>s</u>.

4. My fiends meet at the bus sop.
My f<u>r</u>iends meet at the bus s<u>t</u>op.

Discuss the Daily Fix-It corrections with children. Review the *s* and *ss* spellings of /s/ and the consonant blends *fr* and *st*.

English Language Learners

Conjugating Verbs Some English learners may conjugate present tense verbs in their first language by dropping the last two letters of the infinitive and adding one of several endings. These endings may be based not only on whether the subject is singular or plural, but also on whether it is formal or informal, masculine or feminine. Make sure that children understand the rules that apply for English.

Objectives
- Generate summary ideas.
- Recognize features of a summary.
- Include interesting details.

Writing for Tests
Summary

Introduce the prompt

Review with children the key features of a summary. Explain that today children will write their own summaries. Read aloud the writing prompt.

Writing Prompt

> Write a summary of *The Class Pet*. Tell the most important events and ideas.

MINI-LESSON

Remembering What You've Read

■ **Introduce** Explain that in test-taking situations, children still need to take time to plan their writing. When a prompt tells you to write a summary, you should take a minute to think about the story you will write about. Try to remember the most important information. Think about the ideas that you want to tell in your summary. Also, think about the order you want to tell them.

■ **Model** After I read the prompt, I think about *The Class Pet*. I try to tell myself the story. In *The Class Pet*, the teacher gets the class a pet mouse. The story tells things about mice and their babies. In the end, the teacher gets another mouse for the class. These are all important things I will include in my summary.

Discuss rubric

Have children look at the writing rubric on *Reader's and Writer's Notebook* p. 352. Have children listen as you read through the rubric. Explain that, when they write their summaries, children should try to do the things listed in the rubric. To narrow the evaluation, you might direct children's attention to one or two elements within the rubric, such as Conventions, this week's Writing Trait.

INTERACT with TEXT

Rubric
Summary
Top-Score Response

Focus/Ideas	A good summary tells important information.
Organization	A good summary tells the ideas in the correct order.
Voice	A good summary shows that you understand the ideas.
Word Choice	A good summary uses words that describe and show time order.
Sentences	A good summary uses complete sentences.
Conventions	A good summary uses subjects and verbs that go together.

Reader's and Writer's Notebook p. 352

Sample test

Have children get paper and pencils ready to take a writing test. Display the writing prompt for children, and give them time to write to the prompt. Remind children to allow themselves a few minutes after writing to reread what they've written and make changes or additions.

ROUTINE Quick Write for Fluency **Team Talk**

1. **Talk** Have children take two minutes to discuss three main events from *The Class Pet*.
2. **Write** Each child briefly writes the events in order.
3. **Share** Each child reads the sentences to the partner.

Routines Flip Chart

Differentiated Instruction

SI Strategic Intervention

Summarizing If children find it difficult to differentiate between important and unimportant details, help them make distinctions. Give children the following example: *The teacher gave the class a pet mouse. Dory is tan.* Explain that the first sentence is an important detail. The second sentence is not. It should not be included in a summary.

ELL

English Language Learners
Support Test Taking Tell children that as they prepare to write a summary, they should take time to recall the main events and ideas from the selection they will summarize. This will help them write cohesive, organized summaries.

Objectives
- Write with consistent letter size.
- Form the letters *R* and *r*.
- Classify and categorize items.

Handwriting
Letter *R* and *r*/Letter Size

Model letter formation

Display upper- and lower-case letters: *Rr*. Use the stroke instructions pictured below to model proper letter formation.

D'Nealian™   Ball and Stick

Model consistent letter size

Explain that when we write a word, all the letters in that word should be the right size. Write the word *snore*. When I write the letters in a word, I need to pay attention to how big or small they are. Write the word *snore* again, with some letters much too small and others much too big. Wow, that is difficult to read! By making my letters all the same size—not too small or too large—I make it easier for others to read and understand what I write.

Guide practice

Write the following words, one with letters that are too large, one with letters that are too small, and one with a mixture of tiny and huge letters.

for	explore	chore

Team Talk Have children work in pairs to discuss what is wrong with each word and how it needs to be fixed. Have them share with the class.

On their own

Use the *Reader's and Writer's Notebook* p. 353.

Reader's and Writer's Notebook, p. 353

Research and Inquiry
Research Skill: Classifying/ Categorizing

Teach

Tell children that to **classify and categorize** is to put things, such as pictures or words, into groups. For example, we can classify bodies of water as rivers, lakes, or oceans. Explain that classifying and categorizing helps us understand the world around us.

Model

Think Aloud Display Research Transparency 15. This is an example of words that we can classify and categorize. All of the words in the word box are names for animals. We can categorize animals as either wild or tame. Point to the word *shark*. Sharks live in the wild. People do not take them home as pets or farm animals. I will write the word *shark* in the **Wild Animals** sorting box.

Guide practice

Work with children to classify the remaining words in the word box. As they classify each animal, have a volunteer complete the following sentence, substituting the appropriate animal and adjective: A [hamster] is a [tame] animal because _____.

Academic Vocabulary

classify and categorize to put things, such as pictures or words, into groups

Research Transparency 15
TR DVD

Wrap Up Your Day

✔ **Vowels: *r*-Controlled *or, ore*** Write the words *core* and *form*. Have children tell which letters stand for the sound /ôr/. (*ore; or*)

✔ **High-Frequency Words** Point to these words on the Word Wall: *away, car, friends, house, our, school,* and *very*. Have children read each word and use it in a sentence.

✔ **Build Concepts** Monitor children's use of oral vocabulary as they summarize the Big Book, *Mr. George Baker*.

Preview DAY 3

Tell children that tomorrow they will reread *The Class Pet.*

Objectives
• Build oral vocabulary.
• Identify details in text.
• Share information and ideas about the concept.

Today at a Glance

Oral Vocabulary
crumple

Phonemic Awareness
Add Phonemes

Phonics and Spelling
◉ Ending *-es*, Plural *-es*
◉ *r*-Controlled *or, ore*

High-Frequency Words
away, car, friends, house, our, school, very

Story Words
brown, fur, mouse, teaches

Comprehension
Review Compare and Contrast

Fluency
Appropriate Phrasing

Conventions
Verbs That Do Not Add *-s*

Writing
Writing for Tests: Summary

Listening and Speaking
Give Descriptions

Research and Inquiry
Gather and Record Information

Concept Talk

 Question of the Week
What can we learn about animals as they grow and change?

Build concepts

To reinforce concepts and to focus children's attention, have children sing "My Puppy Buddy" from the *Sing with Me* Big Book. Why is it interesting to have a baby animal as a pet? (Possible response: It's interesting because you can see how your pet grows and does new things as it matures.)

 Sing with Me Big Book Audio

Monitor listening comprehension

Display the Big Book *Mr. George Baker*. As children listen to the story, have them think about whether or not Mr. George Baker likes going to school. Then read the book aloud.

• Do you think Mr. George Baker likes going to school? How can you tell? (Yes. He is always happy waiting for the bus. He dances with Mrs. Baker.)

• Why do you think he is happy to go? (He wants to learn to read. He knows he can do it.)

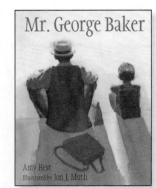
Big Book

ELL **Expand Vocabulary** Use the Day 3 instruction on ELL Poster 15 to help children expand vocabulary.

ELL Poster 15

Oral Vocabulary
Amazing Words

Amazing Words

features	crumple
mature	nibble
natural	nudges
swoop	wriggle
tumble	

Teach Amazing Words

Amazing Words — Oral Vocabulary Routine

1 **Introduce the Word** Relate the word *crumple* to the book. Harry says George's hat is *crumpled*, and so are his shoes. Supply a child-friendly definition: When you *crumple* something, you bend it out of shape and wrinkle it. Have children say the word.

2 **Demonstrate** Provide examples to show meaning. A car's front end may be *crumpled* after it is in an accident. Paper is *crumpled* when it is in a ball. A hat may look *crumpled* after you sit on it.

3 **Apply** Have children demonstrate their understanding. Show me how you would *crumple* something.

Routines Flip Chart

Anchored Talk

Add to the concept map

Use these questions to discuss how baby animals grow and change as you add to the concept map.

- We know that baby animals grow bigger. In *The Class Pet,* what else did we learn about how the bodies of baby mice change as they mature? (They grow fur. Their eyes open and they are able to see.) Let's add this information to our map.

- How does the food that baby mice eat change as they grow? (Newborn mice just drink milk. As they get older, they stop drinking milk and begin to eat nuts and seeds.) Let's add *Instead of milk, mice eat seeds and nuts.*

- What are some things older mice do that very young mice cannot do? (Possible responses: They build nests and have babies.) Let's add *Mice make nests and have babies.*

English Language Learners
Apply Vocabulary Pair the word *crumpled* with the antonym *smooth.* Using a variety of objects in the classroom that can be shown both smooth and crumpled such as a piece of newspaper, a bag, a sweater, and a scarf, display each object in both conditions and have children complete sentence frames like these: *The jacket is* (smooth). *The jacket is* (crumpled).

Objectives
- Add phonemes to create new words.
- Build words with -or, -ore.
- ◎ Read words with ending -es and /ôr/ spelled or, ore.

Phonemic Awareness
Add Phonemes

Model adding phonemes

Read together the last bulleted point on pp. 86–87 of the Student Edition. Today we are going to use this picture to help us add a sound to one word to make a new word. The directions tell us to add the sound /t/ to the end of the word *shore*. When I add /t/ to the end of *shore*, I make a new word: *short*. Now I will look for a picture of something *short* in the picture.

Student Edition p. 86–87

Guide practice

Help children add one sound to each word below to make a new word. Then have them point to the matching picture in their Student Edition.

/k/ ow (cow)	**she /p/** (sheep)	**/g/ oat** (goat)
bar /n/ (barn)	**row /z/** (rose)	**/m/ an** (man)

On their own

Have children add sounds to the following words to make new words.

store /m/ (storm)	**/ch/ or** (chore)	**core /d/** (cord)
/n/ ice (nice)	**say /f/** (safe)	**/f/ arm** (farm)

Team Talk Have partners think of beginning sounds they could add to *eat* to make new words and then ending sounds they could add to *see* to make new words. Ask children to share their words.

Phonics
Build Words

Model word building

Now we are going to build words with /ôr/ spelled *or* or *ore*. Write *horn* and blend it. Watch me change /h/ to /w/. Model blending the new word, *worn*.

Guide practice

Have children spell *worn* with letter tiles. Monitor children's work as they build words.

- Change the /w/ in *worn* to /t/. Say the new word together.

- Change the /n/ in *torn* to /e/. Say the new word together.

- Change the /t/ in *tore* to /m/. Say the new word together.

- Change the /m/ in *more* to /sh/. Say the new word together.

Corrective feedback

For corrective feedback, model the correct spelling and have children correct their tiles.

Fluent Word Reading

Model

Write *stork*. I know the sounds for *s, t, or,* and *k*. I blend them and read the word *stork*. Write *foxes*. I see *es* at the end, so I know this might be a base word with the *-es* ending. Do I see a base word? Yes, I see *fox*. I blend *fox* with *-es* and read *foxes*.

Guide practice

Write the words below. Say the sounds or word parts in your head for each spelling you see. When I point to the word, we'll read it together. Allow one second per sound previewing time for the first reading.

dashes	morning	fort	buses
fizzes	store	bunches	

On their own

Have children read the list above three or four times, until they can read one word per second.

Differentiated Instruction

Ⓐ **Advanced**
Build *or, ore* Words If children are able to build the words in the class activity easily and independently, have them use letter tiles to build these more difficult words with *or, ore*: force, forecast, forest, forty.

English Language Learners
Produce /ch/ and /sh/ Children whose first language is Spanish often have difficulty distinguishing and correctly pronouncing /ch/ and /sh/. Have children practice saying words pairs such as *dish/ditch, mash/match, wish/which, cash/catch*.

The Class Pet **106d**

Objectives

◎ Correctly pronounce words with the ending *-es* or the plural *-es*, and associate the sound /ôr/ with the spellings *or* or *ore*.

- Blend and read words with the ending *-es* or the plural *-es* and words with /ôr/ spelled *or* or *ore*.
- Decode words in context and isolation.
- Spell words with *-es*.

🔊 Blend and Read

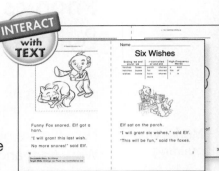

Reader's and Writer's Notebook pp. 355–356

Decode words in isolation

Have children turn to pages 355–356 in the *Reader's and Writer's Notebook* and find the first list of words. Each word in this list has the ending *-es*, the plural *-es*, or the sound /ôr/ spelled *or* or *ore*. Let's blend and read these words. Be sure that children identify the correct sounds in words that have the ending *-es*, the plural *-es*, or the sound /ôr/ spelled *or* or *ore*.

Next, have children read the high-frequency words.

Decode words in context

Chorally read the story along with the children. Have children identify words in the story that have the ending *-es*, the plural *-es*, or the sound /ôr/ spelled *or* or *ore*.

Team Talk Pair children and have them take turns reading the story aloud to each other. Monitor children as they read to check for proper pronunciation and appropriate pacing.

On their own

To further develop automaticity, have children take the story home to reread.

Spelling
Words with -*es*

Spell high-frequency words

Write *friends* and *very* and point them out on the Word Wall. Have children say and spell the words with you and then without you.

Dictation

Have children write these sentences. Say each sentence. Then repeat it slowly, one word at a time.

> 1. **The bus ride was very nice.**
> 2. **Dan wishes he had his kite.**
> 3. **We sang with my friends.**

Proofread and correct

Write each sentence, spelling words one at a time. Have children circle and rewrite any misspelled words.

On their own

Use *Reader's and Writer's Notebook* p. 357.

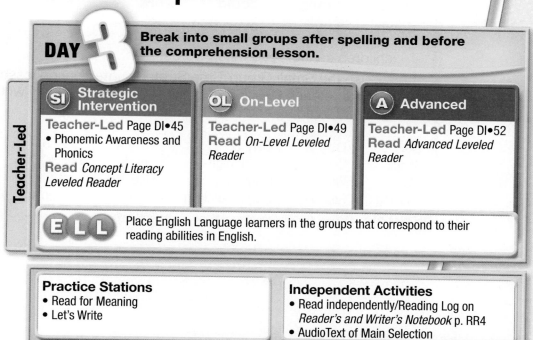

Reader's and Writer's Notebook p. 357

Spelling Words

Words with -*es*

1. fix
2. fixes
3. class
4. classes
5. wish
6. wishes
7. kiss
8. kisses
9. bus
10. buses

High-Frequency Words

11. friends   12. very

Small Group Time

DAY 3 Break into small groups after spelling and before the comprehension lesson.

Teacher-Led

SI Strategic Intervention
Teacher-Led Page DI•45
• Phonemic Awareness and Phonics
Read *Concept Literacy Leveled Reader*

OL On-Level
Teacher-Led Page DI•49
Read *On-Level Leveled Reader*

A Advanced
Teacher-Led Page DI•52
Read *Advanced Leveled Reader*

ELL Place English Language learners in the groups that correspond to their reading abilities in English.

Practice Stations
• Read for Meaning
• Let's Write

Independent Activities
• Read independently/Reading Log on *Reader's and Writer's Notebook* p. RR4
• AudioText of Main Selection

ELL

English Language Learners
Plurals Write these words on the board: *fox, fix, dash, bus, crush,* and *bunch.* Say each word aloud as you point to it. Ask children to repeat after you. Explain to children that when you add the ending -*es* to each of these words it becomes a plural, or more than one. Have children add the -*es* ending to the words and then ask them to say the new words aloud.

Objectives

- Read high-frequency words.
- Establish purpose for reading text.
- Review key features of expository text.

Check High-Frequency Words
SUCCESS PREDICTOR

High-Frequency and Story Words

Read words in isolation

Display and review this week's high-frequency words and story words. Have children read the words aloud.

Read words in context

Display the following sentence frames. Have children complete the sentences using high-frequency and story words. Have children read each completed sentence with you.

1. My mom *teaches* tenth grade at that _____. (school)
2. We like talking with *our* _____ on the phone. (friends)
3. His class has a *brown* _____ in a cage. (mouse)
4. Did she see a cat with *very* thick black _____? (fur)
5. Deb and Mike drove *away* in a red _____. (car)
6. My *friends* will meet me at my _____ next week. (house)

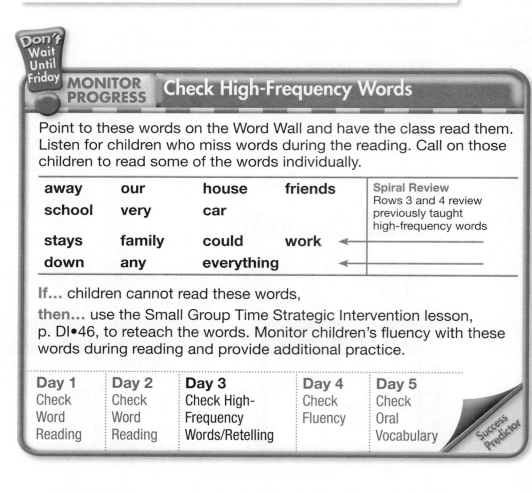

Don't Wait Until Friday

MONITOR PROGRESS | **Check High-Frequency Words**

Point to these words on the Word Wall and have the class read them. Listen for children who miss words during the reading. Call on those children to read some of the words individually.

away	our	house	friends	**Spiral Review**
school	very	car		Rows 3 and 4 review previously taught high-frequency words
stays	family	could	work ←	
down	any	everything	←	

If... children cannot read these words,

then... use the Small Group Time Strategic Intervention lesson, p. DI•46, to reteach the words. Monitor children's fluency with these words during reading and provide additional practice.

Day 1	Day 2	Day 3	Day 4	Day 5
Check Word Reading	Check Word Reading	Check High-Frequency Words/Retelling	Check Fluency	Check Oral Vocabulary

Success Predictor

Main Selection—Second Read
The Class Pet

Review
Compare and contrast

Recall this week's main selection, *The Class Pet.* Tell children that today they will read the story again. Remind children that when we tell how things are like each other, we **compare;** when we tell how things are different, we **contrast.** Seeing how things are alike and different helps us understand our reading. What is one way that newborn mice are like many other newborn animals? (Possible response: They are small and weak.) What is one way that newborn mice are different? (Possible response: Many other animals already have fur when they are born.)

Review
Genre: expository text

Let's Read Together Remind children that expository text gives facts and information. Have children recall some of the facts in *The Class Pet.* (Possible response: Mice can be different colors; they are most active late at night.)

Set a purpose

Remind children that good readers read for a purpose. Guide children to set a new purpose for reading *The Class Pet* today, perhaps to find out how mice keep themselves and their families safe and healthy.

Extend thinking

Tell children they will now read *The Class Pet* for the second time. Use the Day 3 Extend Thinking notes to encourage children to use higher-order thinking skills to go beyond the details of the selection.

For the Second Read, use **Extend Thinking** across the bottom of pages 92–105.

Second Read

Story Words

brown the color of soil and chocolate

fur the hair that covers the bodies of some animals

mouse a small, furry animal with a pointed snout and a thin, bare tail

teaches gives information or explains how to do something

Academic Vocabulary

compare to tell how things are alike
contrast to tell how things are different

ELL

English Language Learners
Vocabulary Prepare children for the sentence-frames activity and the second reading of *The Class Pet* by reviewing the meanings of the high-frequency and story words. Draw quick sketches for *car, house, mouse,* and *fur.* Use antonyms and pantomime for *away* and *very.* (Example: Walk *to* my desk. Walk *away* from my desk. I am a *little* tired. I am *very* tired.) Point to examples for *brown.* Use simple sentences and pantomime for *friends* and *teaches* (I play with my *friends.* She *teaches* me to speak English.) Pair *our* with *my* and use gestures: *my* chair, *our* flag.

High-Frequency Words

Success Predictor

Objectives

- Summarize a nonfiction selection.
- Identify fact and opinion.
- Monitor and clarify understanding.
- Write clear, coherent sentences.

Check Retelling

SUCCESS PREDICTOR

Objectives
- Read on your own for a period of time. • Say the main idea in your own words whether you heard it or read it. • Write short comments on stories, poems, and nonfiction articles that have information.

Envision It! Retell

READING STREET ONLINE
STORY SORT
www.ReadingStreet.com

106

Think Critically

1. Why is a mouse a good pet to have in a classroom?
   Text to World

2. Why do you think the author wanted to write about mice? Author's Purpose

3. What is one fact about what mice eat? Fact and Opinion

4. How do the pictures help you understand how baby mice change as they grow? What can you do if you still don't understand?
   Monitor and Clarify

5. **Look Back and Write**
   Look back at page 100. Why do you think the mother mouse keeps the baby mice in the nest? Write about it.
   TEST PRACTICE Extended Response

Meet the Author

Nichole L. Shields

Nichole L. Shields, an award-winning poet, never had a mouse as a class pet. In fact, her favorite mice are the cartoon characters she watched on television as a child!

Ms. Shields thinks it is important to learn about animals, and she wrote about mice to help teach children about how one kind of animal grows and changes.

Here are other books about how animals grow and change.

Use the Reading Log in the *Reader's and Writer's Notebook* to record your independent reading.

107

Student Edition pp. 106–107

Retelling

Envision It! Have children work in pairs, retelling the selection to one another. Remind children that their partners should include the topics, main ideas, and what they learned from the reading. Children should use the retelling strip in the Student Edition as they retell. Monitor children's retelling.

Scoring rubric

> **Top-Score Response** A top-score response makes connections beyond the text, elaborates on the topics, main ideas, and what children learned from the reading.

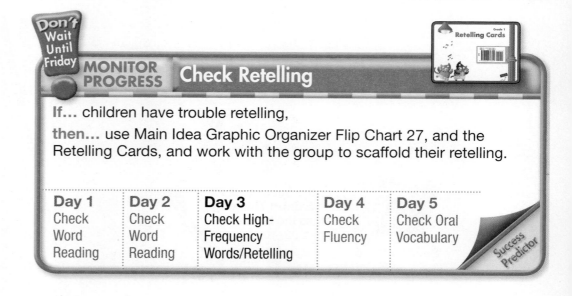

Don't Wait Until Friday

MONITOR PROGRESS | **Check Retelling**

Grade 1
Retelling Cards

If... children have trouble retelling,

then... use Main Idea Graphic Organizer Flip Chart 27, and the Retelling Cards, and work with the group to scaffold their retelling.

Day 1	Day 2	Day 3	Day 4	Day 5
Check Word Reading	Check Word Reading	Check High-Frequency Words/Retelling	Check Fluency	Check Oral Vocabulary

Success Predictor

Think Critically

Text to World

1. Possible response: A mouse can live in a small cage. It is not hard to take care of a mouse.

Author's Purpose

2. Possible response: The author wanted to write about mice because he or she thinks they are interesting.

Fact and Opinion

3. Possible response: Mice eat corn and nuts.

Monitor and Clarify

4. The pictures show mice at different ages, so you can see how they have changed at each age. If I still don't understand, I can read the words around the pictures.

5. **Look Back and Write** For writing fluency, assign a five-minute time limit. As children finish, encourage them to reread their response and proofread for errors.

Scoring rubric

> **Top-Score Response** A top-score response uses details from the text and the pictures to explain why the mother keeps the babies in the nest. For example:
>
> The mother mouse keeps the babies safe in the nest. They have no fur and can't see. They are weak. If they left the nest, they could get hurt.

Meet the author

Read aloud page 107 as children follow along. Ask children what authors do.

Read Independently

After children enter their independent reading into their Reading Logs, have them paraphrase a portion of the text they have just read. Tell children that when we paraphrase, we express the meaning of what we have read using our own words.

Differentiated Instruction

A Advanced

Look Back and Write Ask children who show proficiency with the writing prompt to write about how another kind of animal changes as it gets older.

 INTERACT with TEXT

Strategy Response Log

Monitor and Clarify Have children revisit the text and identify places where they had difficulty with comprehension. Have them use p. RR27 in their *Reader's and Writer's Notebook* to identify a fix-up strategy that helps them clarify their understanding.

Plan to Assess Retelling

☐ Week 1: Strategic Intervention

☐ Week 2: Advanced

☑ This week: Assess Strategic Intervention children.

☐ Week 4: On-Level

☐ Week 5: Strategic Intervention

☐ Week 6: Assess any children you have not yet checked during this unit.

Retelling

Success Predictor

DAY 3 Read and Comprehend

Objectives

- Read aloud fluently and attend to punctuation.
- Understand verbs in the context of reading and writing.
- Use verbs when speaking.
- Speak in complete sentences using correct subject-verb agreement.

Model Fluency
Appropriate Phrasing

Model fluent reading

Have children turn to Student Edition page 94. Point to the period at the end of the first sentence on page 94. When I read this page, I will watch for the marks at the ends of the sentences. A period tells me to stop. I will remember to stop after each period.

Guide practice

Have children read the pages with you. Then have them reread the pages as a group until they read with appropriate phrasing, paying attention to punctuation. Continue the same way with page 95.

Corrective feedback

If... children have difficulty reading with appropriate phrasing, attending to end punctuation,
then... prompt:

- Look at the end of each sentence. What does the end mark tell you about the way each sentence should be read?
- What does the end mark tell you about how your voice should sound?

Reread for Fluency

ROUTINE Choral Reading

1. **Select a Passage** For *The Class Pet,* use pp. 96–97.
2. **Model** First, have children track the print as you read.
3. **Guide Practice** Then have children read along with you.
4. **Corrective Feedback** Have the class read aloud without you. Monitor progress and provide feedback. For optimal fluency, children should reread three to four times.

Routines Flip Chart

Check comprehension

How is Dory like all other mice? How is she different? (Possible response: Dory and all the other mice have four legs and long tails. Dory is tan. The other mice are black, white, and brown. They have spots or stripes.)

Conventions
Verbs That Do Not Add -s

Use *The Class Pet* or one of this week's Decodable Practice Readers.

Review
Verbs that do not add -s

Remind children that we do not add -s to the end of a verb that shows what more than one person, animal, or thing does now: Sally and Tom *jump*. We *make* pancakes.

Daily Fix-It

5. I wich Kim was in my klass.
   I wi<u>sh</u> Kim was in my <u>c</u>lass.

6. My best freinds ride the bus
   My best fr<u>ie</u>nds ride the bus<u>.</u>

Guide practice

Write these sentences on the board and have children supply a verb for each sentence. Ask if any of these verbs will end with -s. (no)

Discuss the Daily Fix-It corrections with children. Review sentence punctuation, the *c* spelling of /k/, the *ie* spelling of /e/, and the *sh* spelling of /sh/.

> 1. The girls _____ basketball.
> 2. They _____ in the choir.
> 3. The babies _____ .

What verb tense are we using in these sentences? **(present tense)**

Team Talk Have children take turns saying sentences about what they do with members of their family now.

Connect to oral language

Have children complete these sentence frames orally with present tense verbs.

> 1. Martha and John _____ cake.
> 2. Tammy _____ gifts on her birthday.
> 3. They _____ in art class.

On their own

Use *Reader's and Writer's Notebook* p. 358.

Reader's and Writer's Notebook, p. 358

English Language Learners
Consonant Digraph *th* Listen carefully to children's sentence production. If children have difficulty with the sound /th/ in *Martha* or *birthday*, say the sentences, emphasizing /th/, and have children repeat slowly.

Objectives
- Evaluate sample test-writing practice.
- Understand focus in writing.

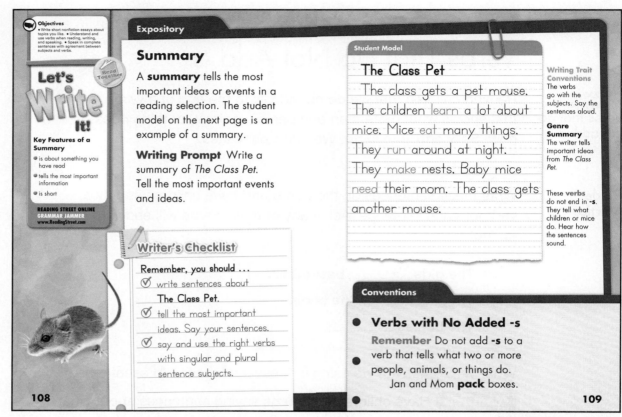

Objectives
• Write short nonfiction essays about topics you like. • Understand and use verbs when reading, writing, and speaking. • Speak in complete sentences with agreement between subjects and verbs.

Let's Write It!

Key Features of a Summary
- is about something you have read
- tells the most important information
- is short

READING STREET ONLINE
GRAMMAR JAMMER
www.ReadingStreet.com

Expository

Summary

A **summary** tells the most important ideas or events in a reading selection. The student model on the next page is an example of a summary.

Writing Prompt Write a summary of *The Class Pet*. Tell the most important events and ideas.

Writer's Checklist

Remember, you should . . .
- ☑ write sentences about **The Class Pet.**
- ☑ tell the most important ideas. Say your sentences.
- ☑ say and use the right verbs with singular and plural sentence subjects.

108

Student Model

The Class Pet

The class gets a pet mouse. The children learn a lot about mice. Mice eat many things. They run around at night. They make nests. Baby mice need their mom. The class gets another mouse.

Writing Trait Conventions The verbs go with the subjects. Say the sentences aloud.

Genre Summary The writer tells important ideas from *The Class Pet*.

These **verbs** do not end in **-s**. They tell what children or mice do. Hear how the sentences sound.

Conventions

- **Verbs with No Added -s**
  Remember Do not add **-s** to a verb that tells what two or more people, animals, or things do.
  Jan and Mom **pack** boxes.

109

Student Edition pp. 108–109

Let's Write It!
Summary

Teach

Use pages 108–109 in the Student Edition. Read aloud the Key Features of a Summary and the definition of a summary. Help children better understand the Writing Prompt by reading it aloud and discussing the Writer's Checklist with children.

Review the student model

Then read "The Class Pet" on page 109 to children. Point out the focus and organization of the writing—the writer tells the important events from the story in the correct order. Read aloud and briefly discuss the side notes about Genre, the Writing Trait, and Verbs with No Added -s to help children understand how an author writes a summary.

Connect to conventions

Read to children the Conventions note about Verbs with No Added -s. Point out verbs in the model paragraph (*learn, eat, run, make, need*).

Writing for Tests
Summary, continued

Differentiated Instruction

 Advanced

Evaluating Suggest that children submit written evaluations of their sample test writing. Children can rate each category and provide reasons for each rating.

MINI-LESSON

Evaluation

■ **Introduce** Use the rubric on *Reader's and Writer's Notebook* p. 352 to guide evaluation. We can use the rubric to evaluate our writing. We can look at our focus, our use of sentences, or our use of conventions. Let's look at the rubric for conventions. It says, *A good summary uses subjects and verbs that go together.* Let's read our sample tests and see if our subjects and verbs go together. I know that verbs that tell the action of more than one person, animal, or thing do not add -*s*. Verbs that tell the action of just one person, animal, or thing add -*s*. Let's look to make sure our verbs go with our subjects.

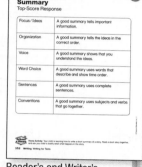

Reader's and Writer's Notebook p. 352

■ Explain that children should evaluate their writing in all six categories. Children should be reminded that their summary might receive good evaluations for each of the traits or evaluations that the child should try to improve. Explain that a low score just tells children where they need improvement and practice.

ROUTINE **Quick Write for Fluency** **Team Talk**

1. **Talk** Have partners talk for two minutes about their evaluations.
2. **Write** Each child writes a sentence about the evaluation process.
3. **Share** Partners read one another's sentences.

Routines Flip Chart

Objectives
- Give effective descriptions.
- Use adjectives when speaking.
- Use sensory language when giving descriptions.
- Listen attentively.
- Gather and record information for an inquiry project.

Listening and Speaking
Give Descriptions

Introduce giving descriptions

Tell children that people often give descriptions of something they have done, seen, heard, smelled, or felt. Giving descriptions helps people share information and make connections with each other.

- Good speakers use adjectives, such as *green* and *tall*, when they give descriptions.
- They use lots of details about how something looks, feels, sounds, tastes, and smells.
- Good listeners listen attentively when others give descriptions.

Model

Use the passage below to model giving a description.

Think Aloud I will never forget my first time riding in a hot air balloon. When I looked up, I could see the beautiful striped colors of the balloon. When I looked down, I saw orderly rows of tall, green corn in the fields below. The smell of hot flames was in the air. Every now and then, we heard a sudden poof and felt the balloon rise higher.

Guide practice

Briefly discuss things that children might want to describe. Make a list of ideas on the board. For one of the ideas, ask children the following questions:

1. What did you see?

2. What feelings did you have?

3. What did you hear?

4. What did you smell?

On their own

Have children take turns giving descriptions and listening to others' descriptions. Remind children to speak clearly and loudly and to listen attentively. Encourage speakers to use adjectives and lots of details. Have children speak in complete sentences with correct subject-verb agreement.

Research and Inquiry
Gather and Record Information

Teach

Tell children that today they will look through sources of information to find facts about a topic. Their goal is to find facts about several different animals.

Model

 Think Aloud Display the list of animals the class created on Day 1. Before we can find information, we have to decide what we're going to research. Our topic will be the animals we think are most interesting. We can gather information about our topic from a source like an encyclopedia or a textbook. As you gather information, remember to classify and categorize what you learn about animals.

Guide practice

Have children choose animals from the list. Then tell them to use reference works to locate information about the animals. Review using text features such as glossaries to find the information they need. Encourage children to find facts about animals at different stages of their lives—from birth to adulthood. Explain that they will use this information to make a chart classifying different animals.

Differentiated Instruction

A **Advanced**

Choosing a Topic Challenge children to choose a topic about a group of animals that they do not know very much about—for example, marsupials.

Wrap Up Your Day

✔ **Fact and Opinion** In *The Class Pet,* the author says, "The pet is a cute tan mouse." Which part of this sentence is fact? (The mouse is tan.) Which part is an opinion? (The mouse is cute.)

✔ **Monitor and Clarify** Remind children that they must ask themselves if they understand what they read. If they get confused, they must look for clues, such as pictures, that will clear up their confusion.

Preview DAY 4

Tell children that tomorrow they will read a fable about mice who try to solve a problem.

Objectives

- Discuss the concept to develop oral language.
- Build oral vocabulary.
- Identify details in text.

Today at a Glance

Oral Vocabulary
nibble, nudges, wriggle

Phonological Awareness
Segment and Blend Syllables

Phonics and Spelling
Review Consonant Patterns
ng, nk

Review Compound Words

High-Frequency Words
Review

Comprehension
Fables

Fluency
Appropriate Phrasing

Conventions
Verbs That Do Not Add *–s*

Writing
Writing for Tests: Summary
Write to a Prompt

Research and Inquiry
Review and Revise Topic

Concept Talk

Question of the Week

What can we learn about animals as they grow and change?

Build concepts

To reinforce concepts and to focus children's attention, have children sing "My Puppy Buddy" from the *Sing with Me* Big Book. The puppy in the song has a person to care for him. Who cares for baby animals that live outdoors in the natural world? (their mother or both parents) How? (They feed them and keep them safe until they can take care of themselves.)

 Sing with Me Big Book Audio

Review Genre: expository text

Have children tell the key features of expository text: it tells facts and information. Explain to children that today they will read about how another kind of pup—a seal pup—grows and changes in "Pup Grows Up," by Susan Yoder Ackerman.

Monitor listening comprehension

Recall how the newborn mice in *The Class Pet* changed as they matured. Have children listen to "Pup Grows Up" to find out if baby seals go through any of the same kinds of changes that baby mice do. Read the selection.

"Pup Grows Up"

ELL Produce Oral Language Use the Day 4 instruction on ELL Poster 15 to extend and enrich language.

ELL Poster 15

Oral Vocabulary
Amazing Words

Teach Amazing Words

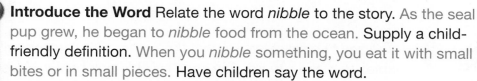

Amazing Words Oral Vocabulary Routine

1. **Introduce the Word** Relate the word *nibble* to the story. As the seal pup grew, he began to *nibble* food from the ocean. Supply a child-friendly definition. When you *nibble* something, you eat it with small bites or in small pieces. Have children say the word.

2. **Demonstrate** Provide examples to show meaning. At snack time we *nibbled* some corn chips. I can see that a mouse has *nibbled* at this bread.

3. **Apply** Have children demonstrate their understanding. What snacks do you like to *nibble* on during a movie?

See p. OV•3 to teach *nudges* and *wriggle*.

Routines Flip Chart

Anchored Talk

Add to the concept map

Discuss how baby animals grow and change.

- We've been learning how animals' bodies change as they grow up. We read in *The Class Pet* that baby mice grow fur. What will the baby seal in "Pup Grows Up" grow to help him stay warm in the water? **(a layer of fat)** Let's add this information to our map.

- What new skill is the baby seal learning? How? **(He is learning to hunt for food from the ocean by watching his mother.)** Where can we add this information to our map?

Amazing Words

features	crumple
mature	nibble
natural	nudges
swoop	wriggle
tumble	

Differentiated Instruction

SI **Strategic Intervention**
Have children act out *nibble, wriggle,* and *nudge* as they chant: *Nibble, nibble like a mouse! Wriggle, wriggle like a seal! Nudge, nudge, nudge!*

English Language Learners
Frontload Listening Before reading, review the pictures in *The Class Pet* to remind children about the kinds of changes that baby mice go through. If possible, translate the word *seal* for children and provide a picture of a seal.

Phonological Awareness
Segment and Blend Syllables

Model   This week we read about a mouse named Dory. Listen as I say the two syllables in *Dory*. **Slowly model the syllables: /dôr/ • /ē/. Now I will blend the two syllables together to say the name: /dôr/ • /ē/,** *Dory*.

Guide practice   I will say two syllables. Repeat them after me. Then we will blend the syllables to make a word. **Say each syllable pair below. Have children repeat them. Together, blend the syllables to form a word.**

Corrective feedback   If children make an error, model the correct response. Return to the word later in the practice.

> /tē/ • /chər/ (teacher)   /bā/ • /bēz/ (babies)   /les/ • /ən/ (lesson)
>
> /pel/ • /its/ (pellets)   /kot/ • /n/ (cotton)   /bran/ • /chəz/ (branches)

On their own   Say the two syllables in each word. Have children repeat the syllables and blend the word independently.

> /skėr/ • /ē/ (scurry)   /nib/ • /əl/ (nibble)   /par/ • /ənt/ (parent)
>
> /nā/ • /chər/ (nature)   /sī/ • /əns/ (science)   /wis/ • /kər/ (whisker)

Phonics Review

Consonant Patterns *ng, nk*; Compound Words

Review
Sound-spellings

To review last week's first phonics skill, write *hang* and *chunk*. You studied words like these last week. What do you know about the sound you hear when a word ends with *ng*? (The letters spell the sound /ng/.) What do you know about the sound you hear when a word ends with *nk*? (The letters spell the sound /ngk/.)

Corrective feedback

If children are unable to answer your questions about *ng* and *nk*, refer them to Sound-Spelling Cards 44 and 45.

Review
Compound words

To review last week's second phonics skill, write *cupcake.* You can read this word because it is a compound word. A compound word is made up of two or more smaller words. What are the two short words in this word? (*cup* and *cake*)

Guide practice

Draw a 3-column chart. I'm going to write some compound words. In your head, divide them into two smaller words. Then we will say each smaller word aloud, and I will write them in the chart. Write each word in the appropriate column. Have children identify words with /ng/ (*hang, king*) and /ngk/ (*link, sink*).

Compound Word	First Word	Second Word
hangout	hang	out
cufflink	cuff	link
kingfish	king	fish
sinkhole	sink	hole

On their own

Use *Let's Practice It!* pp. 139–140 on the *Teacher Resource DVD-ROM.*

Let's Practice It!
TR DVD•139

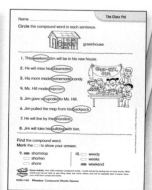

Let's Practice It!
TR DVD•140

Differentiated Instruction

 A Advanced

Compound Words If children can easily read the compound words, have them read these longer words: *paperclip, lady-bug, dressmaker, fingerprint, firecracker, grandparent.*

Academic Vocabulary

compound word a word made up of two or more short words

ELL

English Language Learners
Recognize Compound Words Children who speak languages in which words are monosyllabic, such as Cantonese, Hmong, and Vietnamese, may need extra help with reading, writing, and saying compound words. Have them practice with these words: *baseball, popcorn, desktop, pancake, campfire, pigpen, sandbox, bedtime.*

Decodable Practice Reader 15C
◉ Ending -es; Plural -es; Vowels r-Controlled /ôr/ or, ore

Decodable Practice Reader 15C

Decode words in isolation	Have children turn to page 209. Have children decode each word.
Review High-frequency words	Review the previously taught words *a, the, are,* and *to.* Have children read each word as you point to it on the Word Wall.
Preview	Have children read the title and preview the story. Tell them they will read some words that have the /ôr/ sound and those with the ending -es and the plural -es.
Decode words in context	Pair children for reading and listen as they decode. One child begins. Children read the entire story, switching readers after each page. Partners reread the story. This time the other child begins.

Decodable Practice Reader 15C

Corrective feedback

If... children have difficulty decoding a word, **then...** refer them to the Sound-Spelling Cards to identify the sounds in the word. Then prompt them to blend the word.

- What is the new word?
- Is the new word a word you know?
- Does it make sense in the story?

Check decoding and comprehension

Have children retell the story to include characters, setting, and events. Then point to the words in the story that have -*es* endings and those with the /ôr/ sound. Children should supply *tosses, catches, shore, short, glasses, dishes, boxes, store, more, for, or,* and *closes.*

Reread for Fluency

Have children reread Decodable Practice Reader 15C to develop automaticity decoding words that have the /ôr/ vowel sounds and those that are action words having -*es* endings and those that have the plural -*es* ending.

ROUTINE **Oral Rereading**

1. **Read** Have children read the entire book orally.
2. **Reread** To achieve optimal fluency, children should reread the text three or four times.
3. **Corrective Feedback** Listen as children read. Provide corrective feedback regarding their fluency and decoding.

Routines Flip Chart

ELL

English Language Learners
Decodable Reader

Beginning Have children preview the title of the reader. Point to the last word and spell it. Ask children what sound they think the letters *ore* spell. Say the word *shore* and have children repeat it. Tell children this word means "the place where the ocean meets the land."

Intermediate After reading, have children find words that are spelled with the -*es* ending and those spelled with *or* or *ore*. Have children use the words in a sentence. For example: *I wash the* dishes *at night. I went* for *a* short *walk.*

Advanced/Advanced High Have children tell words they know that rhyme with *short.*

Objectives

- Read words fluently in context and in isolation.
- Spell words with ending -es.
- Spell high-frequency words.

Fluent Word Reading
Spiral Review

Read words in isolation

Display these words. Tell children that they can blend some words on this list and others are Word Wall words.

Have children read the list three or four times until they can read at the rate of two to three seconds per word.

mule	own	stop	shady	when
rang	chomp	live	any	patches
sure	phone	just	weeds	blink
to	trees	your	sky	look

Word Reading

Corrective feedback

If... children have difficulty reading whole words,
then... have them use sound-by-sound blending for decodable words or have them say and spell high-frequency words.

If... children cannot read fluently at a rate of two to three seconds per word,
then... have pairs practice the list until they can read it fluently.

Read words in context

Display these sentences. Call on individuals to read a sentence. Then randomly point to review words and have children read them. To help you monitor word reading, high-frequency words are underlined and decodable words are italicized.

> *Can trees that <u>live</u> in shady patches get tall?*
>
> <u>Your</u> *phone just rang when Tom called.*
>
> *When I <u>look</u> up at <u>the</u> sky, sunshine makes me blink.*
>
> *Did that mule stop <u>to</u> chomp weeds?*

Sentence Reading

Corrective feedback

If... children are unable to read an underlined high-frequency word,
then... read the word for them and spell it, having them echo you.

If... children have difficulty reading an italicized decodable word,
then... guide them in using sound-by-sound blending.

Spelling
Words with -es

Partner Review

Supply pairs of children with index cards on which the spelling words have been written. Have one child read a word while the other writes it. Then have children switch roles. Have them use the cards to check their spelling and correct any misspelled words.

On their own

Use *Reader's and Writer's Notebook* p. 359.

Reader's and Writer's Notebook p. 359

Spiral Review

These activities review

• previously taught high-frequency words *sure, to, live, your, look, any, own.*

• consonant patterns: *ng, nk;* short *a; e; i; o; u;* long *u, u_e;* long vowels CVe; long *e, ee;* initial and final consonant blends; vowel sounds of *y;* syllable pattern CV; consonant digraphs *sh, th, wh, ch, tch, ph.*

Small Group Time

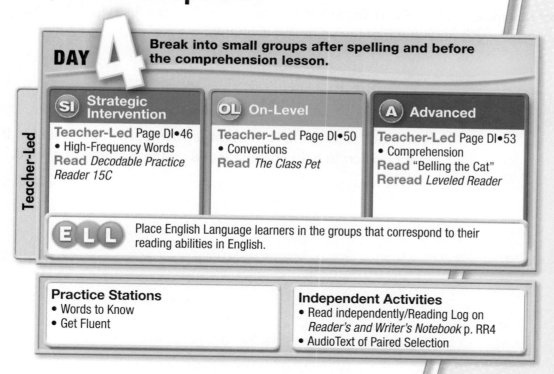

DAY 4 Break into small groups after spelling and before the comprehension lesson.

Teacher-Led

(SI) Strategic Intervention
Teacher-Led Page DI•46
• High-Frequency Words
Read *Decodable Practice Reader 15C*

(OL) On-Level
Teacher-Led Page DI•50
• Conventions
Read *The Class Pet*

(A) Advanced
Teacher-Led Page DI•53
• Comprehension
Read "Belling the Cat"
Reread *Leveled Reader*

E L L Place English Language learners in the groups that correspond to their reading abilities in English.

Practice Stations
• Words to Know
• Get Fluent

Independent Activities
• Read independently/Reading Log on *Reader's and Writer's Notebook* p. RR4
• AudioText of Paired Selection

E L L

English Language Learners
Fluent Word Reading Have children listen to a more fluent reader say the words. Then have them repeat the words.

Read Together

Science in Reading

Connecting meaning to personal experiences

Review with children that a fable is a story that has a moral, or lesson. Ask children to share real experiences from their own lives that taught them a lesson.

Preview and predict

Read the title and the first sentence of the selection. Have children look through the selection and predict what they might learn. (Possible response: They might learn that the problem is the cat.) Ask them what clue helped them make that prediction. (Possible response: the pictures)

Let's Think About

Genre

Fable Tell children that they will read a **fable**. Review the key features of a fable: it is a short story that teaches a lesson, or moral, and it often has animal characters that speak and act like people. Explain that this selection is a fable because it is a short story that teaches a lesson, or moral, and it has an animal character that talks and acts like a person.

Activate prior knowledge

Ask children to recall what they have already learned about mice. (Possible response: Mice like to run and jump late at night and sleep in the daytime. They like to eat seeds and nuts. They sleep in nests. They like to have friends.)

Set a purpose

Let's Read Together As children read, have them look for clues that indicate that the selection is a fable.

Let's Think About... Fable

As you read "Belling the Cat" together, use Let's Think About in the Student Edition to help children focus on the features of a fable.

Objectives
• Connect the meaning of a famous story or fable to your own experiences.

Science in Reading

Read Together

Genre
Fable
- A fable is a short story.
- A fable has made-up characters that are often animals.
- The characters in a fable try to solve a problem.
- A fable often teaches a moral, or lesson. The reader can usually connect the meaning of the fable to his or her own experiences.
- As you read "Belling the Cat," look for elements of a fable.
- If you come to a part you don't understand, remember to reread that part aloud to help you make sense of what you're reading.

Belling the Cat

a fable adapted from Aesop
illustrated by Viviana Garofoli

The mice had a problem. There was a new cat in the house. It slept by the kitchen table. It hid behind doors. It raced down the hall toward the mice.

They could see its eyes in the dark. They could hear it howl at night. They never felt safe!

Let's Think About...
What might make you think so far that this story is a fable? **Fable**

110

111

Student Edition pp. 110–111

Academic Vocabulary

moral the lesson or teaching of a fable or story

Guide Comprehension

Guide practice

Think Aloud The mice had a problem. They didn't feel safe because there was a new cat in the house. I can understand the problem better by using my own experiences to think of a time when a problem made me feel unsafe.

Let's Think About... Fable

Possible response: So far, I think this is a fable because it has made-up animal characters that are trying to solve a problem.

Objectives

- Use a personal experience to connect with the meaning of a well-known fable.
- Recognize structure and elements of a fable.
- Relate prior knowledge to new text.

The mice called a meeting. They had many ideas.

One little mouse pulled on his ear and said, "We need to hear that cat. Let's hang a bell on its neck."

What is the first step the mice take to solve their problem? **Fable**

How is this fable like an animal fantasy? **Fable**

112   113

Student Edition pp. 112–113

Guide Comprehension

Guide practice

Think Aloud

The first step the mice took was to have a meeting to come up with ideas. When I read about the mice's idea to put a bell on the cat, I wonder if it's a good idea, or not. I know from my experience that cats and mice are enemies. Cats catch mice!

Compare and contrast

Think Aloud

As I read *Belling the Cat*, I think about how the mice in the fable are different from real mice. I know that real mice can't talk, but made-up mice can.

Let's Think About... Fable

Possible response: This fable is like an animal fantasy because the animals act like people.

Academic Vocabulary

characters the people or animals in a fable or story

All the mice went along with the idea. They cheered and clapped. They danced and laughed.

Then a wise old mouse asked, "Who is going to bell the cat?"

Let's Think About...
What lesson do you think the mice will learn? **Fable**

Let's Think About...
Can you connect the moral of this fable to your own experiences? How? **Fable**

Moral: Some things are easier said than done.

Let's Think About...

Reading Across Texts How is Dory in *The Class Pet* different from the mice in "Belling the Cat"?

Writing Across Texts Think about Dory in *The Class Pet*. If she could talk, what would she say to the mice in "Belling the Cat"? Write the dialogue.

114

115

Student Edition pp. 114–115

Guide Comprehension

Guide practice

 Think Aloud

I wonder why the mouse characters in the fable clapped, cheered, danced, and laughed. I do those things when I'm happy. I think the mice are happy because they think their idea will work.

Predict

Think Aloud

When I read page 114, I ask myself if the mice will be able to hang a bell on the cat's neck. I think they might learn that it's not going to be easy.

Let's Think About... Fable

Possible response: The moral is "Some things are easier said than done." I say that I'm going to keep my room clean, but sometimes that's hard to do.

Guide Comprehension, continued

Confirm predictions Based on the text on page 114, what lesson do you think the mice will learn? Possible response: I think they will learn that it is hard to get the bell on the cat.

Connect to world What other idea might have worked to solve the problem? Possible response: Maybe the mice could have made friends with the cat.

Reading Across Texts How are the mice in *The Class Pet* different from the mice in *Belling the Cat*? The mice in *The Class Pet* are real mice. The mice in *Belling the Cat* are made-up characters. Real mice can't talk. Made-up mice can.

Writing Across Texts If Dory, in *The Class Pet,* could talk, what do you think she would say to the mice in *Belling the Cat*? Write the dialogue. Possible response: "We are going to put a bell around the cat's neck," said the mice. "The cat will eat you," said Dory. "You need a better idea."

Fluency
Appropriate Phrasing

Guide practice

- Have children turn to pages 98–99 in *The Class Pet.*
- Have children follow along as you read the pages with appropriate phrasing.
- Have children read the pages with you and then reread the pages as a group without you until they read with appropriate phrasing. To provide additional fluency practice, pair nonfluent readers with fluent readers.

ROUTINE **Paired Reading**

 Select a Passage For *The Class Pet,* use pp. 100–103.

 Model First, have children track the print as you read.

③ Guide Practice Then have children read along with you.

④ On Their Own For optimal fluency, have partners reread three or four times.

Routines Flip Chart

 MONITOR PROGRESS **Fluency WCPM**

As children reread, monitor their progress toward their individual fluency goals. Current Goal: 20–30 words correct per minute. End-of-Year Goal: 60 words correct per minute.

If... children cannot read fluently at a rate of 20–30 words correct per minute,

then... have children practice with text at their independent level.

Day 1	Day 2	Day 3	Day 4	Day 5
Check Word Reading	Check Word Reading	Check High-Frequency Words/Retelling	Check Fluency	Check Oral Vocabulary

Success Predictor

Differentiated Instruction

 Advanced

WCPM If children already read at 60 words correct per minute, allow them to read independently.

Fluency Assessment Plan

Do a formal fluency assessment with 8 to 10 children every week. Assess 4 to 5 children on Day 4 and 4 to 5 children on Day 5. Use the reproducible fluency passage, Teacher's Edition, page 117f.

Options for Oral Rereading

Use *The Class Pet* or one of this week's Decodable Practice Readers.

Objectives
- Use present tense verbs with correct subject-verb agreement when writing and speaking.
- Spell present tense verbs with correct inflectional endings.

Conventions
Verbs That Do Not Add -s

Test practice

Use *Reader's and Writer's Notebook* p. 360 to help children understand present tense verbs in test items. Recall that present tense verbs tell what two or more people, animals, or things do now: *run, open,* or *ask.* Model identifying a present tense verb in a sentence by writing this sentence on the board, reading it aloud, and underlining the present tense verb.

> **Mom and Felicia <u>open</u> their gifts.**

Then read the *Reader's and Writer's Notebook* p. 360 directions. Guide children as they mark the answer for number 1.

On their own

Use *Reader's and Writer's Notebook* p. 360.

Connect to oral language

After children mark the answers to numbers 1–6, review the correct choices aloud, and have children read each sentence, emphasizing the present tense verbs.

Reader's and Writer's
Notebook p. 360

Writing for Tests
Summary

MINI-LESSON

Strong Conclusion

■ Yesterday you used the rubric to evaluate your writing. Today you will write about another prompt.

■ Remind children that one of the key features of a summary is that it tells the main information from a story. Explain that children need to include strong conclusions in their summaries. When you end your summary, tell about the ending of your story. Use words such as *finally, in the end,* or *at last* to tell your readers you are at the end of your summary. Be sure to use strong words to tell the last events. That way your readers will remember your summary.

■ When I think about summarizing *The Class Pet,* I think about all the important information. I remember that, at the end, Dory and Cory become friends. I will write, *Finally, the mouse makes a new friend* in the conclusion of my summary.

Objectives
- Write a summary in response to a prompt.
- Review answers to inquiry questions.

Writing for Tests
Summary, continued

Write

Have children prepare their paper and pencils for writing. Display the writing prompt, and give children time to write to it. Remind children to think about the key features of summaries as they plan and write their responses.

> Write a summary of *Belling the Cat* or another story you have read. Tell the most important events.

Allow children a few minutes after writing to reread what they have written and make changes or additions.

ROUTINE   Quick Write for Fluency   [Team Talk]

1. **Talk** Have pairs discuss one thing they learned about growing and changing.

2. **Write** Have children write a short sentence describing what they learned.

3. **Share** Partners can read the sentences aloud to one another.

Routines Flip Chart

Research and Inquiry
Review and Revise Topic

Teach Tell children that the next step in the inquiry project is to review our topic to see if we have the information we set out to find. Or, did our answers lead to a different topic?

Model We wanted to find information about different animals. First, we listed animals we knew about. Then we picked the ones we thought were most interesting. Last, we gathered some information about our animals. Now I will look at the information I gathered. I will see if I found good facts about my animals. I will also think about how I can classify and categorize the information I found. If I did not find good information, I can always gather more.

Guide practice Have children look at the information they gathered during Day 3. Instruct them to work with a partner to choose the most interesting facts about their animals. If necessary, they can conduct more research to collect more facts. Finally, tell children that tomorrow they will organize all the information in order to share it with others.

On their own Use *Reader's and Writer's Notebook* p. 354.

Wrap Up Your Day

✔ **Phonics Review** List several nouns and verbs that take an -es ending. Have children read each base word, add -es, and blend the whole word.

✔ **Fluency** Write *Can we see that dog? Yes, we can!* Have children read the sentences three or four times until they can do so with appropriate phrasing.

Reader's and Writer's Notebook p. 354

Remind children that they heard about a baby harbor seal named Sandy. Tomorrow they will hear about Sandy again.

Objectives
- Review the concept: what we can learn about animals as they grow and change.
- Build oral vocabulary.
- Identify details in text.

Today at a Glance

Oral Vocabulary
Review

Phonics
◉ Review Ending -*es*, Plural -*es*
◉ Review *r*-Controlled *or, ore*

Comprehension
◉ Fact and Opinion

Story Words
Review

High-Frequency Words
Review

Conventions
Verbs That Do Not Add -*s*

Writing
Writing for Tests: Summary

Research and Inquiry
Communicate

Check Oral Vocabulary
SUCCESS PREDICTOR

Concept Wrap Up

Question of the Week
What can we learn about animals as they grow and change?

Review Concept

This week we have read and listened to selections about how baby animals grow and change. Today you will listen to find out what things a baby seal can do as soon as it is born, and what things it cannot do until it has matured a bit. **Read the story.**

"Pup Grows Up"

- What are some things the seal can do as soon as he is born? (He can cry, wriggle along the ground, swim, and hold his breath underwater.) What can't he do until he is more mature? (He can't eat fish, stay warm, or hunt on his own.)

Review Amazing Words

Orally review the meaning of this week's Amazing Words. Then display this week's concept map. Have children use Amazing Words such as *mature* and *features*, as well as the concept map, to answer the question "What can we learn about animals as they grow and change?"

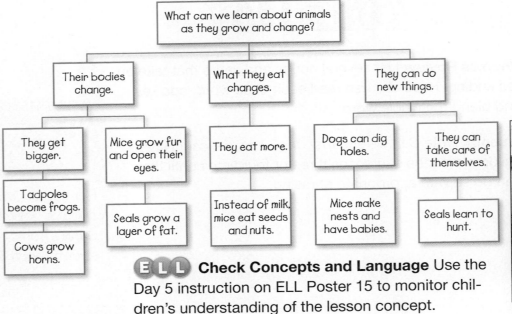

ELL Check Concepts and Language Use the Day 5 instruction on ELL Poster 15 to monitor children's understanding of the lesson concept.

ELL Poster 15

Oral Vocabulary
Amazing Ideas

Connect to the Big Question

Team Talk Pair children and have them discuss how the Question of the Week connects to this unit's Big Question, "What is changing in our world?" Tell children to use the concept map and what they've learned from this week's Anchored Talks and reading selections to form an Amazing Idea—a realization or "big idea" about **change**. Then ask each pair to share their Amazing Idea with the class.

Amazing Ideas might include these key concepts:

- As animals mature, their bodies grow and get new features.
- Animals are born with some skills and gain new ones as they grow.

It's Friday

MONITOR PROGRESS | **Check Oral Vocabulary**

Call on individuals to use this week's Amazing Words to talk about how baby animals grow and change. Prompt discussion with the questions below. Monitor children's ability to use the Amazing Words and note which words children are unable to use.

- **What *feature* of a newborn mouse looks *crumpled*?**
- **What do *mature* mice like to *nibble*?**
- **Why do seals have to *wriggle* to move on land?**
- **How do you suppose a mother seal *nudges* her baby?**
- **Why might a baby bird *tumble* from its nest?**
- **What *features* help owls *swoop* down and catch mice?**
- **Is it *natural* for dogs to learn to dance? Explain.**

If... children have difficulty using the Amazing Words,

then... reteach the unknown words using the Oral Vocabulary Routines, pp. 85a, 90b, 106b, 110b.

Day 1	Day 2	Day 3	Day 4	Day 5
Check Word Reading	Check Word Reading	Check High-Frequency Words/Retelling	Check Fluency	Check Oral Vocabulary

Success Predictor

Amazing Words

features	crumple
mature	nibble
natural	nudges
swoop	wriggle
tumble	

ELL

English Language Learners
Amazing Words Use pantomime or gesture to give children clues as you review the Amazing Words.

Objectives

◎ Review words with ending -es and plural -es.

◎ Review words with /ôr/ spelled or, ore.

• Add final sound to create a new word.

Assess

• Spell words with ending -es.

• Spell high-frequency words.

Phonemic Awareness
Add Final Phonemes

Review
Final phonemes

Have children add a final sound to each word below to make a new word. If children make an error, model the correct response. Return to the word later in the practice.

plan /t/ (plant)	**may /n/** (main)	**bee /k/** (beak)
fine /d/ (find)	**sir /ch/** (search)	**he /l/** (heel)
saw /ng/ (song)	**so /p/** (soap)	**to /b/** (tube)

Phonics
◑ Ending -es, Plural -es;
r-Controlled or, ore

Review
Target phonics skills

Write the following sentences on the board. Have children read each one, first quietly to themselves and then aloud as you track the print.

1. **Those foxes were born in this den.**

2. **That wave crashes on the shore.**

3. **Mom mixes corn with a big fork.**

4. **Ford tosses the ball and Hank catches it.**

(**Team Talk**) Have children discuss with a partner which words have the ending -es and which words have /ôr/ spelled or or ore. Then call on individuals to share with the class.

Spelling Test
Words with *-es*

Dictate spelling words

Say each word, read the sentence, repeat the word, and allow time for children to write the word.

1. **fix**	**Fix** that rip with a pin.
2. **fixes**	Mom **fixes** the car.
3. **class**	Our **class** has spelling every day.
4. **classes**	Six **classes** went on a trip.
5. **wish**	Peggy got her one **wish**.
6. **wishes**	You can make many **wishes**.
7. **kiss**	I **kiss** my cat.
8. **kisses**	Jan **kisses** her puppy on the nose.
9. **bus**	The **bus** will stop for me.
10. **buses**	I see five **buses** in line.

High-Frequency Words

11. **help**	My dad can **help** me.
12. **use**	Dot can **use** a map.

Small Group Time

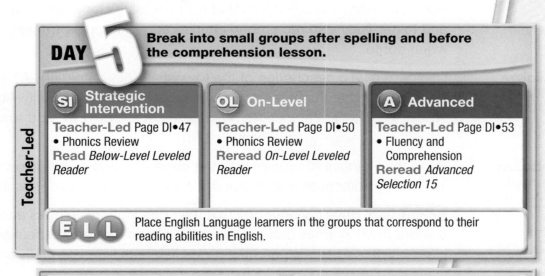

DAY 5

Break into small groups after spelling and before the comprehension lesson.

Teacher-Led

SI Strategic Intervention
Teacher-Led Page DI•47
• Phonics Review
Read *Below-Level Leveled Reader*

OL On-Level
Teacher-Led Page DI•50
• Phonics Review
Reread *On-Level Leveled Reader*

A Advanced
Teacher-Led Page DI•53
• Fluency and Comprehension
Reread *Advanced Selection 15*

ELL Place English Language learners in the groups that correspond to their reading abilities in English.

Practice Stations
• Words to Know
• Read for Meaning

Independent Activities
• Read independently/Reading Log on *Reader's and Writer's Notebook* p. RR4
• Concept Talk Video

Differentiated Instruction

 Strategic Intervention

Check Spelling Have children choose the correct spelling of each word from three random spellings.

A Advanced

Extend Spelling Practice with more words that form the plural by adding *-es*. Write the following words on the board and ask children to form the plural of each word: *bench, glass, crunch, flash, fizz,* and *tax.* Tell children that most of the time we form plurals by adding *s* to the end of a word. For example, the word *desk* becomes *desks* and the word *clock* becomes *clocks.* If a word ends in an *s, sh, ch, x,* or *z, -es* is added to form the plural of the word.

Objectives

◎ Give a description.
- Speak clearly and accurately.
- Listen attentively.
- Identify words that describe feelings.
- Read aloud fluently with appropriate phrasing.

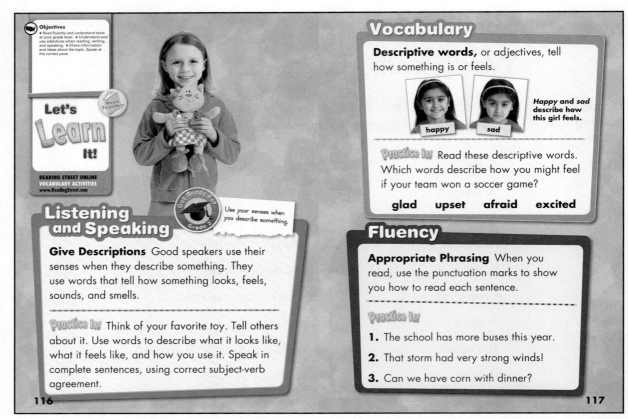

Student Edition pp. 116–117

Listening and Speaking
Give Descriptions

Teach

Have children turn to pages 116–117 of the Student Edition. Instruct them to look at the photo of the girl holding the toy cat. Remind children that good speakers use adjectives that tell how things look, feel, sound, smell, and taste. They also remember when to add -s to present-tense verbs and when not to.

Analyze model

Now let's give a description of the toy cat the girl is holding. What are some words that might tell how the toy cat looks and feels? (yellow, soft) *Yellow* and *soft* are adjectives. What adjectives could we add to describe the cat's clothing? (green, white, pink)

Introduce prompt

Read the Practice It! prompt with the class. Remind children to include interesting adjectives and to use the correct form of present tense verbs.

Team Talk Have children practice their descriptions in pairs and then present them in small groups. Remind children that good speakers speak clearly, with expression, and that good listeners listen carefully and politely.

Vocabulary
Descriptive Words for Feelings

Teach

Read and discuss the Vocabulary lesson on page 117 of the Student Edition. Use the model to remind children that adjectives can describe the way a person is feeling.

Model

Point to the first photo. This child is smiling. Which word describes how the child is feeling? (happy) Point to the other photo. This child is frowning. Which word describes how the child is feeling? (sad)

Guide practice

Read the instructions for the Vocabulary Practice It! Activity. Read the first word and have children repeat it after you.

The word *glad* describes the way we feel when something good happens. Winning a game is something good, so *glad* is a word I might use to describe how I felt when my team won.

On their own

Have partners talk about the feeling that each of the remaining words names and whether or not they would use the word to describe how they would feel after winning a soccer game.

Corrective feedback

Circulate around the room and listen as children discuss the words for feelings. Provide assistance as needed.

Fluency
Appropriate Phrasing

Teach

Read and discuss the Fluency instructions.

Read words in context

Give children a moment to look at the sentences. Then have them read each sentence three or four times until they can read each sentence with appropriate phrasing.

Differentiated Instruction

 Strategic Intervention

Pantomime Write the following words on cards: *happy, sad, excited, angry, surprised, tired, afraid.* Have children take turns picking cards and using gestures to act out the feeling.

Give Descriptions

To prepare themselves for skills needed in Grade 2, children should be able to give descriptions that include words appealing to at least two of the five senses. They should also be able to speak clearly and with appropriate phrasing and expression.

ELL

English Language Learners

Use Sentence Frames Provide this sentence frame to help children explore words for feelings: When _____, I feel _____.

Comprehension
 Fact and Opinion

Review fact and opinion

Remember that good readers pay attention to facts and opinions as they read. What do you call a statement that someone can prove? (a fact) What do you call a belief or judgment that is neither right nor wrong? (an opinion)

To check understanding of fact and opinion, read aloud the following paragraph and have children answer the questions that follow.

> I have always loved math. You get to use numbers in lots of fun ways. I like math because there is usually just one right answer. Four plus four always equals eight, no matter what. It's so easy! Lots of my friends like reading better than math. In reading, you work with words all day. I think that's too hard. The teacher asks a question about a story, and more than one answer can be right! I think I'll stick to math.

1. What is a fact in this paragraph? (Possible response: Four plus four always equals eight, no matter what.)

2. What is an opinion in this paragraph? (Possible response: It's so easy!)

Vocabulary
High-Frequency and Story Words

Review High-frequency words

Review this week's high-frequency words: *away, car, friends, house, our, school,* and *very*. Model making up a rhyme that includes a high-frequency word, for example: If you get into a car, you can drive it very far!

Team Talk Have children make up rhymes using the remaining high-frequency words.

Review Story words

Write the words *brown, fur, mouse,* and *teaches*. Read them aloud together. Then have children use two of the words in a single sentence.

Corrective feedback

If... children cannot tell what the story words mean,
then... review the definitions on page 92a.

Genre
Fable

Review
Review
Genre

Review with children that a fable is a short story that teaches a lesson, or moral. The characters in a fable are often animals that speak or act like people. The author wants readers to connect the moral of a fable to their own experience.

Teach

In *Belling the Cat,* some mice have a problem. There is a new cat in the house, and they are afraid the cat will eat them. They call a meeting to figure out what to do about the cat. One mouse has a great idea—to put a bell on the cat—but nobody wants to do it!

Model

 I know that in the story the mice come up with a way to solve their problem, but nobody wants to be the one to take the risk. This happens a lot in real life. I can *say* that I want my house to be perfectly clean, but do I always *do* the work? No, I don't.

Guide practice

Ask the following questions to guide children in describing a fable and determining its lesson, or moral.

- Who are the characters in this story, and what can they do that is different from real life? (The characters are mice, and they can talk and hold meetings.)

- What is the moral of *Belling the Cat*? How does it remind you of your own life? (Possible response: The moral is that some things are easier said than done. I always say I will practice piano every day, but it's much harder to actually do it!)

On their own

Do you think belling the cat is a good idea? Why or why not? (Possible response: I think it is a good idea. If the cat has a bell, the mice will always know when the cat is coming. Then the mice can run away.)

Differentiated Instruction

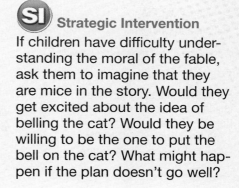 **Strategic Intervention**

If children have difficulty understanding the moral of the fable, ask them to imagine that they are mice in the story. Would they get excited about the idea of belling the cat? Would they be willing to be the one to put the bell on the cat? What might happen if the plan doesn't go well?

Academic Vocabulary

character one of the people or animals in a story

DAY 5 Wrap Up your Week

Assess

- ◎ Ending -es; Plural -es
- ◎ Vowels: r-Controlled or, ore
- • High-Frequency Words
- • Fluency: WCPM
- ◎ Fact and Opinion

Fluency Goals

Set individual fluency goals for children to enable them to reach the end-of-year goal.
- • Current Goal: 20-30 WCPM
- • End-of-Year Goal: 60 WCPM

Assessment
Monitor Progress

For a written assessment of endings -es and plural -es, vowels: r-Controlled or, ore, high-frequency words, and fact and opinion, use Weekly Test 15, pages 121–126.

Assess words in context

Sentence reading Use the following reproducible page to assess children's ability to read words in context. Call on children to read two sentences aloud. Start over with sentence one if necessary.

MONITOR PROGRESS | **Sentence Reading**

If... children have trouble reading endings -es and plural -es, vowels: r-Controlled or, ore,

then... use the Reteach Lessons on pp. 213–214 of *First Stop*.

If... children cannot read all the high-frequency words,

then... mark the missed words on a high-frequency word list and have the child practice reading the words with a fluent reader.

Success Predictor

Assess

Fluency Take a one-minute sample of children's oral reading. Have children read the fluency passage on page 117f.

Comprehension Have the child read the entire passage. (If the child has difficulty with the passage, you may read it aloud.) Then have the child identify facts and opinions in the passage.

MONITOR PROGRESS | **Fluency and Comprehension**

If... a child does not achieve the fluency goal on the timed reading,

then... copy the passage and send it home with the child for additional fluency practice, or have the child practice with a fluent reader.

If... a child cannot comprehend fact and opinion,

then... use the Reteach Lesson on p. 255 of *First Stop*.

Success Predictor

Monitor accuracy

Record scores Have children monitor their accuracy by recording their scores using the Sentence Reading Chart and by recording the number of words read correctly per minute on the Fluency Progress Chart in *First Stop*.

117d Changes • Unit 3 • Week 3

Name _____

Read the Sentences

1. Jan fixes very fine ham and eggs.

2. That house has swings on its porch.

3. Liz watches Miss Jones at school.

4. His friends set cake on dishes.

5. Dad is away for six weeks.

6. Our band wore tall black hats.

7. Cars and buses fill this lot.

8. We shop in this very big store.

MONITOR PROGRESS
- Fluency
- Ending *-es;* plural *-es*
- Vowels: *r*-controlled *or, ore*
- High-frequency words

Name _____

Read the Story

Morning Chores

Cole and Jess met on Vic's porch one morning. "Can 　　10
you play ball with us?" asked Cole. 　　17

"I have chores for this morning," said Vic. "I must 　　27
pick corn. I must sort my toys. I also have dishes to dry. 　　40
Next, I must stack boxes. Then I must pick up branches." 　　51

"We can help," said Jess. "We can help with all 　　61
those jobs, Vic. Then we can play ball." 　　69

Vic's mom watched Cole, Jess, and Vic as she fixed 　　79
lunch for them. "Vic is so lucky to have such fine pals," 　　91
she said. 　　93

In no time at all, no more jobs were left. Now they 　　105
could play ball. 　　108

MONITOR PROGRESS

• Check Fluency
• Fact and Opinion

Objectives
• Use present tense verbs with correct subject-verb agreement.
• Ask questions with correct subject-verb inversion.

Conventions
Verbs That Do Not Add -s

Review

Remind children that present tense verbs are verbs that tell what someone or something is doing now. Have them give examples of present tense verbs that agree with the subject *They*. (Possible responses: *cry, feel, find, walk, creep*)

Guide practice

Write the following questions. Have children write a verb that makes sense in each blank.

> 1. Do Amy and Sara _____ at the aquarium?
>
> 2. Do we _____ the bread?
>
> 3. Do they _____ their soccer game?

Connect to oral language

Display and read the following sentence frames. Have children work in pairs to name as many plural subjects as they can that could be used to complete each sentence. Then have children share their responses with the class.

> _____ ride bikes to the park.
>
> _____ sit on the bus together.
>
> _____ make balloon animals.

On their own

Use Let's Practice It! p. 143 on the *Teacher Resource DVD-ROM*.

Daily Fix-It

9. Dad say good-by.
   Dad say<u>s</u> good-by<u>e</u>.

10. Jan iz on her way?
    Jan i<u>s</u> on her way<u>.</u>

Discuss the Daily Fix-It corrections with children. Review sentence punctuation, the spelling of present tense verbs, the *s* spelling for /z/, and the *ye* spelling for /ī/.

Let's Practice It! TR DVD•143

Writing for Tests
Summary

Review Remind children that yesterday they learned more about summaries and wrote to another prompt. Today they will evaluate their writing from yesterday.

MINI-LESSON

Proofread for Fragments

■ **Teach** A sentence should make sense on its own. It must tell a complete thought. A sentence needs a subject and a verb. The subject tells who or what is doing something. The verb tells what that person, animal, or thing is doing. If your sentence is missing a subject or a verb, it is a fragment. You can fix a fragment by adding the missing part.

■ **Model** Write on the board: *Brings us lunch*. This is a fragment. It is missing the part that tells *who* brings lunch. We can fix this fragment by adding a word that tells *who. Dad brings us lunch.* Now it tells a complete thought.

■ Explain that, when they edit summaries, children should check each sentence, make sure it tells a complete thought, then add a subject or verb if one is missing.

Evaluate Now it is time to evaluate your summaries. Have children turn to their completed writing from yesterday's sample test. Explain that they will first evaluate their writing for conventions and focus. They should consider whether the summary includes all the main events from the story and whether all their subjects go with their verbs. Then have children consult the rubric in the *Reader's and Writer's Notebook* p. 352 to complete the evaluation of their writing.

ROUTINE
Quick Write for Fluency
Team Talk

1. **Talk** Have partners take one minute to tell what they learned about growing and changing in animals.

2. **Write** Each child writes a new short sentence about what they learned.

3. **Share** Partners trade sentences and read them aloud.

Routines Flip Chart

Teacher Note

Self-Evaluation Make copies of the Self-Evaluation form from the *Teacher Resource DVD-ROM,* and guide children as they use it.

Write Guy
Jeff Anderson

Adding Without Leaving Readers Hanging

A student might add worthwhile information but write a sentence fragment. I like to encourage the writer by welcoming the idea and yet helping students form solid sentences or add dependent parts in order to communicate. Children can recognize "sentences" that "leave the reader hanging" (that is, fragments). *Pacing back and forth.* That's not a complete sentence, but it may add a vivid image to a student's narrative. If it follows a sentence such as *I peeked out the window and saw Lee,* then a reader may wonder who is pacing back and forth. Let's help our young writers put images together. *I peeked out the window and saw Lee pacing back and forth.* That doesn't leave readers hanging. Kids can understand that.

English Language Learners
Support Editing Help children distinguish between sentences and fragments. Give children these questions to check for fragments: *Who is this about? What does she/he/it do?*

Objectives
- Review concept: people and animals changing as they grow.
- Organize information.
- Present results of an inquiry project.

Research and Inquiry
Communicate

Teach

Tell children that today they will create a T-chart that tells facts about their topic. Then they will share their charts with others.

Model

Think Aloud I wanted to know more about mammals. I found out that mammals drink their mother's milk and have hair all over their bodies. I can use these facts to classify animals into two groups: mammals and nonmammals. For example, I know that cats are covered in fur and drink their mother's milk. I think that means they are mammals. When I check a reference book, I find out that I am correct. I will put *cats* in the *Mammals* column of my chart.

Guide practice

Review children's topics and facts. Work with them to classify the information they have found.

On their own

Have children choose the facts they would like to include on their T-charts. Have children break themselves into groups based on the similarity of their topics. Then instruct them to read or present their charts to one another. Remind them how to be good speakers and listeners:

- Good speakers provide lots of details and use adjectives when they speak.
- Good listeners think about questions to ask the speaker when the speaker has finished.

Wrap Up Your Week!

Question of the Week

What can we learn about animals as they grow and change?

Think Aloud This week we explored how different animals grow and change. In *The Class Pet,* we read about the changes that baby mice go through as they mature into adult mice. In "Pup Grows Up," we learned what baby seals can do when they are first born, and what they must learn. Have children recall their Amazing Ideas about how different animals change as they grow. Then have children use these ideas to help them demonstrate their understanding of the Question of the Week.

Amazing Words

You've learned 009 words this week!

You've learned 167 words this year!

ELL

English Language Learners

Poster Preview Prepare children for next week by using Week 4, ELL Poster 16. Read the Poster Talk-Through to introduce the concept and vocabulary. Ask children to identify and describe objects and actions in the art.

Selection Summary Send home the summary of *Frog and Toad Together* in English and the child's home languages if available. Children can read the summary with family members.

Preview NEXT WEEK

Tell children that next week they will read about the changes that happen in a garden.

Weekly Assessment

Use pp. 121–126 of *Weekly Tests* to check:

✔ ◎ **Phonics** Ending *-es;* Plural *-es*

✔ ◎ **Phonics** Vowels: *r*-controlled *or, ore*

✔ ◎ **Comprehension Skill** Fact or Opinion

✔ **High-Frequency Words**

away	our
car	school
friends	very
house	

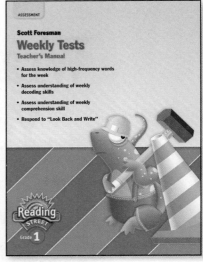

Weekly Tests

A
Advanced

OL
On-Level

SI
Strategic Intervention

Differentiated Assessment

Use pp.121–126 of *Fresh Reads for Fluency and Comprehension* to check:

✔ ◎ **Comprehension Skill** Fact and Opinion

✔ **Review** **Comprehension Skill** Compare and Contrast

✔ **Fluency** Words Correct Per Minute

Fresh Reads for Fluency and Comprehension

Managing Assessment

Use *Assessment Handbook* for:

✔ **Weekly Assessment Blackline Masters for Monitoring Progress**

✔ **Observation Checklists**

✔ **Record-Keeping Forms**

✔ **Portfolio Assessments**

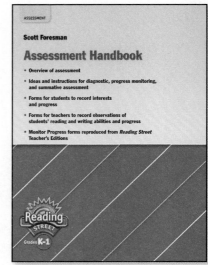

Assessment Handbook

What Moving Teaches You

Moving is hard. You leave your friends and switch schools.

At first, kids wish they didn't have to move, but not all wishes can come true. And moving teaches you good things. Here are some tips from kids who have moved.

Pat thinks it is hard to leave old friends at first. Then time passes. Pat says you will make new friends soon. Then you have more friends!

Jen misses her old house, but her new one has porches in the back and front. Also, she watches lots of frogs and turtles in the pond. She says your new house might have special things like benches under trees. The trees might have peaches.

Kara misses her old school, but she says her new one has better lunches. Kara likes her new computer classes. Are you like Kara?

Your family will use boxes to move dishes, glasses, books, and more. Imagine what you can do with the empty boxes! Andy made forts and buses with them. You can build a train that stretches across the yard. What else can you make with big boxes?

What is the most important moving tip? Try to be a friend to a new kid in your neighborhood!

Advanced Selection 15 **Vocabulary:** special, imagine

Small Group Time

Pacing Small Group Instruction

5 Day Plan

DAY 1	• Phonemic Awareness/ Phonics • Decodable Reader
DAY 2	• Phonemic Awareness/ Phonics • Decodable Reader
DAY 3	• Phonemic Awareness/ Phonics • Leveled Reader
DAY 4	• High-Frequency Words • Decodable Reader
DAY 5	• Phonics Review • Leveled Reader

3 or 4 Day Plan

DAY 1	• Phonemic Awareness/ Phonics • Decodable Reader
DAY 2	• Phonemic Awareness/ Phonics • Decodable Reader
DAY 3	• Phonemic Awareness/ Phonics • Leveled Reader
DAY 4	• High-Frequency Words • Decodable Reader

3 Day Plan: Eliminate the shaded box.

SI Strategic Intervention

Phonemic Awareness•Phonics

■ **Segment and Blend Phonemes** Reteach pp. 86–87 of the Teacher's Edition. Model segmenting and blending each base word and adding *-es* to it. Then have children practice segmenting, blending, and adding *-es* on their own.

flash /f/ /l/ a/ /sh/	**flashes** flash /əz/
mix /m/ /i/ /ks/	**mixes** mix /əz/
pass /p/ /a/ /s/	**passes** pass /əz/
lunch /l/ /u/ /n/ /ch/	**lunches** lunch /əz/

■ **Ending -es; Plural -es** Reteach p. 87a of the Teacher's Edition. Have children identify the base word and ending of each word below and then read the whole word.

pitches	**misses**	**boxes**	**dashes**	**matches**
wishes	**punches**	**itches**	**fusses**	**rushes**

Decodable Practice Reader 15A

■ **Review** Review words with ending *-es* and the high-frequency words *where, the, out, to, some, into, a, down, her, for, of*. Then have children blend and read these words from the story: *packing, grumpy, homemade, thank, those*.

> **If...** children have difficulty with any of these words,
> **then...** reteach the word by modeling. Have children practice the words, with feedback from you, until they can read them independently.

Have children reread the text orally. To achieve optimal fluency, children should reread the text three or four times.

Decodable Practice Reader 15A

Objectives
• Blend spoken phonemes to form one-two-syllable words, including consonant blends.
• Read base words with inflectional endings.

 SI Strategic Intervention

DAY **2**

Phonemic Awareness•Phonics

■ **Isolate Medial and Final Phonemes** Reteach p. 90c of the Teacher's Edition. Model segmenting and blending these words. Have children identify the middle and final sound in each word. Then have them practice segmenting and blending on their own.

George /j/ /ôr/ /j/   **cord** /k/ /ôr/ /d/   **more** /m/ /ôr/

■ 🔊 **r-Controlled or, ore** Reteach p. 90d of the Teacher's Edition. Then have children spell *born* using letter tiles. Monitor their work.

• Change the *b* in *born* to *c*. What is the new word?

    `c` `o` `r` `n`

• Change the *n* in *corn* to *k*. What is the new word?

    `c` `o` `r` `k`

• Change the *k* in *cork* to *e*. What is the new word?

    `c` `o` `r` `e`

Decodable Practice Reader 15B

■ **Review** Review words with the /ôr/ sound and the high-frequency words *from, the, are, a, water, of, to, eat*. Then have children blend and read these words from the story: *backpack, photo, who, trophy*.

> **If...** children have difficulty with any of these words,
> **then...** reteach the word by modeling. Have children practice the words, with feedback from you, until they can read them independently.

Have children reread the text orally. To achieve optimal fluency, children should reread the text three or four times.

Decodable Practice Reader 15B

More Reading
Use Leveled Readers or other text at children's instructional level to develop fluency.

Strategic Intervention

DAY **3**

Phonemic Awareness•Phonics

■ **Add Phonemes** Model adding a sound to the end of a word to make a new word. Say the word *for* and have children repeat it. Now listen as I add the sound /t/ to the end of *for*: *for* /t/. What is the new word? (fort)

Have children add the final sound shown to each word below to make a new word.

shore /t/ **short**	pour /ch/ **porch**	for /k/ **fork**

■ ◉ **Ending *-es*; Plural *-es*; and *r*-Controlled *or, ore*** Reteach p. 106e of the Teacher's Edition. Have children blend and read these additional words to help them practice the target phonics skills.

fort	**dresses**	**born**	**mashes**	**snore**	**patches**	**fixes**

For a complete literacy instructional plan and additional practice with this week's target skills and strategies, see the **Leveled Reader Teaching Guide.**

Concept Literacy Leveled Reader

■ **Preview and Predict** Read the title and the author's name. Have children look at the cover and ask them to describe what they see. Help children activate their prior knowledge by asking them to look through the selection and to use the photos to predict things they might learn about.

■ **Set a Purpose** Remind children that setting a purpose for reading can help them better understand what they read. Guide children to pay attention to the ways each baby animal is different from the adult animal.

■ **Read** Provide corrective feedback as children read the selection orally. During reading, ask them if they were able to confirm any of the predictions they made prior to reading.

If... children have difficulty reading the story individually,
then... read a sentence aloud as children point to each word. Then have the group reread the sentences as they continue pointing. Continue reading in this way until children read individually.

■ **Retell** Have children take turns retelling the selection. Help them recall what they learned about how animals change by asking, What kinds of animals did we see? How were the babies different from the adults?

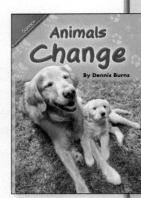

Concept Literacy

Objectives
• Use common syllabication patterns to decode words, including: *r*-controlled vowel sounds, including *or*.
• Read base words with inflectional endings.

DAY 4

More Reading
Use Leveled Readers or other text at children's instructional level.

High-Frequency Words

■ **Review** Write *away, car, friends, house, our, school, very* on the board. Model saying each word. Then have children read each word, spell each word as you point to each letter, and have them say each word again. Allow time for children to practice reading these high-frequency words using the word cards.

Decodable Practice Reader 15C

■ **Review** Use the word lists to review words with ending *-es* and words with the /ôr/ sound. Be sure children understand that *-es* can be a verb ending for verbs that tell about now, or a noun ending that means "more than one." Point out that the /ôr/ sound can be spelled *or* or *ore*. Then have children blend and read the words.

Decodable Practice Reader 15C

> **If...** children have difficulty reading the story individually,
> **then...** read a sentence aloud as children point to each word. Then have the group reread the sentences as they continue pointing. Continue reading in this way until children read individually.

Check comprehension by having children retell the story including the characters, plot, and setting. Have children locate words in the story that have the ending *-es* and the /ôr/ sound spelled *or* or *ore*. List the words children identify. Then have children sort the *-es* words into ending *-es* and plural *-es*.

Ending -es	More Than One -es
tosses	glasses
catches	dishes
	boxes

Small Group Time

DAY 5

Phonics Review

■ **Ending -es; Plural -es; and r-Controlled or, ore** Write these sentences on the board. Have children read them aloud as you track the print. Then call on individuals to blend and read the underlined words.

Go <u>north</u> to get to that pet <u>store</u>.

We packed <u>boxes</u> of <u>glasses</u> and <u>dishes</u>.

Mom <u>patches</u> all torn <u>dresses</u>.

<u>Mort</u> will <u>score</u> when he <u>tosses</u> the ball.

For a complete literacy instructional plan and additional practice with this week's target skills and strategies, see the **Leveled Reader Teaching Guide.**

Below-Level Leveled Reader

Preview and Predict Read the title and the names of the author and illustrator. Have children look at the cover and ask them to describe what they see. Help children activate their prior knowledge by asking them to look through the story and to use the pictures to predict things that might take place.

■ **Set a Purpose** Remind children that setting a purpose for reading can help them better understand what they read. Have children read to find out how Gus changes from the beginning to the end of the story.

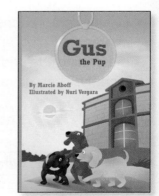

Below-Level Reader

■ **Read** Provide corrective feedback as children read the story orally. During reading, ask them if they were able to confirm any of the predictions they made prior to the story.

> **If...** children have difficulty reading the story individually,
> **then...** read each sentence aloud as children point to each word. Then have the group reread the sentences as they continue pointing.

■ 🔊 **Monitor and Clarify** Which pictures in the story helped you understand what you read? How did they help?

Objectives
• Use common syllabication patterns to decode words, including: r-controlled vowel sounds, including or.
• Establish purpose for reading selected texts.

On-Level

DAY 1

Phonics•Spelling

- ◉ **Ending -es; Plural -es** Write the following words on the board and have children practice reading them.

  crushes   switches   messes   foxes

  Then have children identify the base word and the ending of each word.

- **Words with -es** Remind children that some of the spelling words have the ending -es. Clarify the pronunciation and meaning of each word. For example, say: If I *wish* for something, I want it very much. Have children identify the base word and ending in each of these words: *fixes, classes, wishes, kisses, buses.*

Objectives
- Read words with inflectional endings.
- Spell base words with inflectional endings.

On-Level

DAY 2

Phonics•High-Frequency Words

- ◉ **r-Controlled *or, ore*** Write the following words on the board and have children practice reading words with the /ôr/ sound. Then have children identify the letters that spell the /ôr/ sound.

  chore   north   storm   bore

- **High-Frequency Words** Hold up this week's High-Frequency Word Cards (*away, car, friends, house, our, school, very*) and review proper pronunciation. Continue holding the cards and have children chorally read each word. To help children demonstrate their understanding of the words, provide them with oral sentence frames such as: I will miss you if you go _____. (away)

High-Frequency Word Cards for Grade 1
PEARSON

Objectives
- Use common syllabication patterns to decode words, including: r-controlled vowel sounds, including *or.*
- Read at least 100 high-frequency words from a commonly used list.

Pacing Small Group Instruction

20–30 min.

5 Day Plan

DAY 1	• Phonics • Spelling • Decodable Reader
DAY 2	• Phonics • High-Frequency Words • Decodable Reader
DAY 3	• Leveled Reader
DAY 4	• Conventions • Main Selection
DAY 5	• Phonics Review • Leveled Reader

3 or 4 Day Plan

DAY 1	• Phonics • Spelling • Decodable Reader
DAY 2	• Phonics • High-Frequency Words • Decodable Reader
DAY 3	• Leveled Reader
DAY 4	• Conventions • Main Selection

3 Day Plan: Eliminate the shaded box.

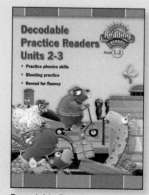
Decodable Practice Readers Units 2-3
• Practice phonics skills
• Blending practice
• Reread for fluency

Decodable Practice Reader

 **On-Level**

DAY 3

For a complete literacy instructional plan and additional practice with this week's target skills and strategies, see the **Leveled Reader Teaching Guide.**

On-Level Leveled Reader

On-Level

■ **Preview and Predict** Read the title and the names of the author and illustrator. Have children look at the cover and ask them to describe in detail what they see. Help children preview the selection by asking them to look through it and to use the illustrations to predict things they might learn about.

■ ◉ **Fact and Opinion** Before reading, remind children that setting a purpose for reading can help them better understand what they read. Tell children that this selection contains both facts and opinions. Review the difference. Have children read the selection to learn new facts about horses and to notice which sentences tell opinions rather than facts.

■ **Read** During reading, monitor children's comprehension by providing higher-order thinking questions. Ask:

• Is the last sentence on page 3 a fact or an opinion? Why? Is the first sentence on page 10 a fact or an opinion? Explain your answer.

• Do you think Lori and her mom take good care of their horses? Explain.

To help children gain a better understanding of the text, build upon their responses with a group discussion.

■ ◉ **Monitor and Clarify** Discuss with children how they used the monitor and clarify strategy during their reading. Ask these questions.

• What words did you get stuck on at first? How did you figure them out?

• Which pictures helped you understand what you read? Explain.

■ **Text to Text** Help children connect this selection to *The Class Pet*. Ask:

• In what ways is taking care of a horse like taking care of a pet mouse? In what ways is it different?

Objectives
• Monitor comprehension.
• Make inferences about text.

 OL On-Level **DAY 4**

Conventions

- **Verbs That Do Not Add -s** Remind children that when we tell what more than one person, animal, or thing does now, we do not add -s to the end of the verb: *The cats nap. My friends run.*

  - Write *The girls _____ at camp.* Which verb is correct in this sentence, *swim* or *swims*? (swim) Write *swim* in the blank and have children read the sentence aloud.

  Continue this process, using the verbs *hike, race, meet,* and *sing.* Have children determine the correct verb form and read the sentence aloud.

Objectives
- Understand and use verbs (present) in the context of reading, writing, and speaking.
- Speak in complete sentences with correct subject-verb agreement.

More Reading
Use Leveled Readers or other text at children's instructional level to develop fluency.

 OL On-Level **DAY 5**

Phonics Review

-  **Ending -es; Plural -es; and r-Controlled or, ore** Have children practice blending and reading words that contain this week's target phonics skills. Write the following words on the board, and say and sound out each word with the children.

| hisses | inches | thorn | waxes | porches |
| sore | stitches | rushes | more | hatches |

Then have children sort the words that have the ending -es, the plural -es, and the /ôr/ sound into different groups.

Objectives
- Use common syllabication patterns to decode words, including: r-controlled vowel sounds, including or.
- Read base words with inflectional endings.

Small Group Time

Pacing Small Group Instruction

20-30 mins.

5 Day Plan

DAY 1	• Phonics • Advanced Selection
DAY 2	• Phonics • Comprehension • Main Selection
DAY 3	• Leveled Reader
DAY 4	• Comprehension • Paired Selection
DAY 5	• Fluency • Comprehension • Advanced Selection

3 or 4 Day Plan

DAY 1	• Phonics • Advanced Selection
DAY 2	• Phonics • Comprehension • Main Selection
DAY 3	• Leveled Reader
DAY 4	• Comprehension • Paired Selection

3 Day Plan: Eliminate the shaded box.

A Advanced **DAY 1**

Phonics•Advanced Selection

■ 🔊 **Ending -es; Plural -es** Have children practice reading these words. Point out that final *y* changes to *i* before adding *-es*.

relaxes	babies	studies	dismisses	reaches
leashes	touches	finishes	bunnies	squishes

Discuss the meanings of unfamiliar words. Have children write each word, circle the ending, and write the base word. Then have them choose several words to use in sentences.

Advanced Selection 15

■ **Advanced Selection 15** Before reading, have children identify these story words: *special* and *imagine*. Provide oral sentences with the words in context. After reading, have children recall the two most important ideas of the story.

Objectives
• Read words with inflectional endings.

A Advanced **DAY 2**

Phonics•Comprehension

The Class Pet

■ 🔊 *r*-**Controlled *or, ore*** Have children practice reading longer words containing *r*-controlled *or, ore*.

seashore	orchestra	important	ordinary	before
storefront	auditorium	laboratory	portfolio	information

Discuss unfamiliar words. Have children write each word and circle the letters that spell /ôr/. Then have them use a few of the words in sentences.

■ **Comprehension** Have children silently read this week's main selection, *The Class Pet*. Have them retell the selection, recalling important facts and ideas. Discuss what makes *The Class Pet* expository text. Point out that it gives facts and information about real mice.

Objectives
• Use common syllabication patterns to decode words, including: *r*-controlled vowel sounds, including *or*.

For a complete literacy instructional plan and additional practice with this week's target skills and strategies, see the **Leveled Reader Teaching Guide.**

Advanced Leveled Reader

Advanced Reader

■ **Activate Prior Knowledge** Read the title, the author's name, and illustrator's name. Have children look at the cover and describe in detail what they see. Remind them that *mature* means "full-grown" or "to become more grown up." Then activate the children's prior knowledge by asking them to tell how a mature mouse is different from a baby mouse.

■ ◉ **Fact and Opinion** Before reading, remind children that setting a purpose for reading can make a story more interesting. Tell children that this story contains some facts and opinions. Review the difference. Have children read the story to learn facts about kittens and cats and to find opinions that the characters in the story state.

■ **Read** During reading, monitor children's comprehension by providing higher-order thinking questions. Ask:

• In what ways does Patches change during the story?

• Dad says that it's natural for cats to scratch. Is that a fact or an opinion? Explain. Britton's teacher says it would be fun to see Patches. Is that a fact or an opinion? Explain.

Build on children's answers to help them gain a better understanding of the text.

■ ◉ **Monitor and Clarify** Discuss with children how they used the monitor and clarify strategy during their reading. Ask these questions:

• What monitor and clarify strategy could you use if you did not know the meaning of the word *calico* on page 8? The word *shy* on page 10?

• What monitor and clarify strategy could you use if you did not understand why Dad and Britton took Patches to the vet?

■ **Text to World** Help children make connections to the story. Ask:

• In what ways is taking care of a kitten like taking care of a human baby?

Objectives
• Monitor comprehension.
• Make inferences about text.

Small Group Time

More Reading

Use Leveled Readers or other text at children's instructional level.

A Advanced **DAY 4**

Comprehension

Belling the Cat

■ **Comprehension** Have children silently read this week's paired selection, "Belling the Cat." Have them retell the story, identifying the characters and setting. Then have them why they think the author wrote this story.

Talk about what makes "Belling the Cat" a fable. Be sure children understand that a fable is a very short, made-up story that often has animals as characters and that teaches readers an important lesson, called a moral.

■ **Text to Text** Ask children to retell other fables they have read and the moral of each. If necessary, remind children that the stories "The Maid and the Milk Pail" and "The Fox and the Grapes" are fables they have read this year.

Objectives
- Explain the author's purpose in writing about the text.
- Restate the main idea, read.

A Advanced **DAY 5**

Fluency•Comprehension

Advanced Selection 15

■ **Fluency** Using the first few sentences of Advanced Selection 15, model reading with appropriate phrasing. Then have children read the selection to a partner as you listen to their reading. Provide corrective feedback as needed.

■ **Comprehension** After they have finished reading the selection, have children retell it by stating the most important ideas. Then, on the back of the selection page, have them write three sentences telling things they would like and not like about moving to a new home.

Objectives
- Read aloud grade-level appropriate text with fluency (appropriate phrasing).

The ELL lessons are organized by strands. Use them to scaffold the weekly lesson curriculum or during small-group time.

Concept Development

What can we learn about animals as they grow and change?

- **Preteach Concept** Write the Question of the Week on the board and read it aloud. Underline the word *animals* and have children say it with you. The word *animals* means living things like dogs, cows, and lions. What kinds of animals have you seen before in person? Make a list of the children's answers on the board.

- **Develop Concepts** Show this week's Concept Talk Video and ask children to name some of the changes in the video. (moving, learning a new language, meeting new people) What can be exciting about changes? During a second viewing, stop at appropriate places to talk about changes. Use the leveled prompts below to assess understanding and build oral language.

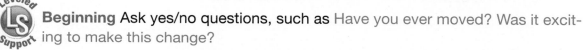

  Beginning Ask yes/no questions, such as Have you ever moved? Was it exciting to make this change?

  Intermediate Ask simple questions that could be answered in a word or two. What do you need to learn when you move to a new place? What changes have you had in your life?

  Advanced/Advanced-High Have children answer the Question of the Week by giving specific examples from the video and from their own experiences.

- **Review Concepts and Connect to Writing** Review children's understanding of the concept at the end of the week. Ask them to write in response to these questions: What changes do you see in animals as they grow up? What English words did you learn this week? Write and display key ideas from the discussion.

Content Objectives
- Describe how animals change as they grow.

Language Objectives
- Share information orally.
- Use basic vocabulary for describing animals.

Daily Planner

DAY 1	• **Frontload Concepts** • **Preteach** Comprehension Skill, Vocabulary, Phonemic Awareness/Phonics, Conventions/Writing
DAY 2	• **Review** Concepts, Vocabulary, Comprehension Skill • **Frontload Main Selection** • **Practice** Phonemic Awareness/Phonics, Conventions/Writing
DAY 3	• **Review** Concepts, Comprehension Skill, Vocabulary, Conventions/Writing • **Reread Main Selection** • **Practice** Phonemic Awareness/Phonics
DAY 4	• **Review Concepts** • **Read ELL/ELD Readers** • **Practice** Phonemic Awareness/Phonics, Conventions/Writing
DAY 5	• **Review** Concepts, Vocabulary, Comprehension Skill, Phonemic Awareness/Phonics, Conventions/Writing • **Reread ELL/ELD Readers**

*See the ELL Handbook for ELL Workshops with targeted instruction.

ELL Poster 15

Build concept understanding and oral vocabulary throughout the week by using the daily activities on ELL Poster 15.

Support for English Language Learners

Language Objectives

- Blend and segment phonemes.

 **Transfer Skills**

Because the /r/ sound is rolled or flapped in some languages, including Spanish, children who speak these languages originally may have trouble producing the /ôr/ sound.

ELL Teaching Routine

For more practice with plurals, use the Whole-Word Blending Routine (*ELL Handbook*, page 493).

Phonemic Awareness: Blend and Segment Phonemes

■ **Preteach the sound /ôr/**

- Have children open to pages 86–87. What animal is the man in the red shirt petting? (horse) Say the word *horse* slowly. I am going to say the sounds in *horse*. Listen for the middle sound: /h/ /ôr/ /s/. The middle sound I hear is /ôr/. Say /ôr/ with me. Say these words as you point to the corresponding pictures: *door*, *barn*, *core*, *four*. Have children repeat each word and give a thumbs up if they hear /ôr/.

- Have children point out other pictures whose names have the sound of /ôr/.

■ **Practice Producing Sounds of Newly Acquired Vocabulary** Listen again as I say all the sounds in *horse*. Stretch the sounds as you say them: /hhh/ /ôr ôr ôr/ /s s s/, *horse*. Now you try. Have children blend sounds to make these words.

/sh/ /ôr/ /t/, short	/m/ /ôr/, more
/k/ /ôr/ /n/, corn	/st/ /ôr/, store

Phonics: Ending *-es*; Plural *-es*

■ **Preteach** Display Sound-Spelling Card 139. These are peaches. What sound do you hear at the end of *peaches*? (/əz/) Say it with me: /əz/. Point to the *-es* at the end of *peaches*. The /əz/ sound in *peaches* is spelled *es*. Display Sound-Spelling Card 124. This word is *tosses*. What sound do you hear at the end of *tosses*? (/əz/) Say it with me: /əz/. Point to the *-es* at the end of *tosses*. The /əz/ sound in *tosses* is also spelled *es*. Have children practice producing the sound of /əz/ in other words with *-es*.

■ **Listen and Write** Distribute Write and Wipe Boards.

- Write the word *passes* on the board. Copy this word. As you write *es*, say the sound to yourself: /əz/. Now say the sound aloud. (/əz/) Underline *es* in *passes*. The letters *es* spells /əz/ in *passes*.

- Repeat the instructions using the words *dishes* and *fixes*.

For more practice pronouncing these sounds, use the Modeled Pronunciation Audio CD Routine (*ELL Handbook*, page 501).

Objectives

- Practice producing sounds of newly acquired vocabulary such as long and short vowels, silent letters, and consonant clusters to pronounce English words in a manner that is increasingly comprehensible.
- Learn relationships between sounds and letters of the English language and decode (sound out) words using a combination of skills such as recognizing sound-letter relationships and identifying cognates, affixes, roots and base words.

■ **Reteach and Practice** Write the following words on the board and have children read them aloud with you: *classes, dashes, catches, boxes, mixes.* Segment and blend each word with children. Point out the word endings. Now write *catch* and *box* on the board. Have children add the appropriate ending to each word.

Beginning/Intermediate Have children write the words. Then have them read the words aloud. Monitor for accurate pronunciation.

Advanced/Advanced-High Have children say the words aloud and then brainstorm a list of additional words that can end with *-es.*

Phonics: *r*-Controlled *or, ore*

■ **Preteach** Have children turn to Envision It! on page 90 of the Student Edition. The first picture shows an orchestra. Have children repeat the word after you. What sound do you hear at the beginning of *orchestra*? (/ôr/). What does the second picture show? (score) Have children repeat the word after you. What sound do you hear in the middle of *score*? (/ôr/) Notice that the /ôr/ sound is spelled differently in both words. How is /ôr/ spelled in *orchestra*? (or) How is /ôr/ spelled in *score?* (ore)

■ **Practice** Distribute Letter Tiles *c, e, h, m, p, o, r, s, and t* to pairs.

• Blend the sounds in *porch* and have pairs spell *porch* with their tiles: /p/ /ôr/ /ch/.

• Remove all of the letters that do not spell the /ôr/ sound.

• Add letters to spell *store*, /st/ /ôr/.

• Replace first letters with an /m/ to spell *more*, /m/ /ôr/.

• Have children write the new words they learned.

Language Objectives
• Identify the use of *-es* as final phoneme.
• Identify and produce the *r*-controlled *or, ore* sounds in words.

 Transfer Skills
Plural *-es* Other languages, including Spanish, also use *-es* as an ending for some plural words.

Practice Page
ELL Handbook page 314 provides additional practice for this week's skill.

Objectives
• Distinguish sounds and intonation patterns of English with increasing ease.
• Practice producing sounds of newly acquired vocabulary such as long and short vowels, silent letters, and consonant clusters to pronounce English words in a manner that is increasingly comprehensible.
• Learn relationships between sounds and letters of the English language to represent sounds when writing in English.
• Spell familiar English words with increasing accuracy, and employ English spelling patterns and rules with increasing accuracy as more English is acquired.

Support for English Language Learners

Content Objectives

- Monitor and adjust oral comprehension.

Language Objectives

- Discuss oral passages.
- Use a graphic organizer to take notes.

ELL Teacher Tip

You might have children act out the story to help improve their understanding.

ELL English Language Learners

Listening Comprehension

The Bears and Summer

The bear cubs were enjoying their first summer. They went swimming with Mama Bear in the lake. They played games in the water. They ate lunch under the green trees.

The cubs were swimming alone one day. Squirrel walked by. "Hello," he said to the young bears. "Summer is ending soon."

The news made the cubs cry for Mama Bear. "What's wrong?" Mama asked. She heard her cubs and came running.

"Squirrel said summer is going to end," the cubs said.

"Summer will end. Then fall will start. You can look at the leaves. You can eat a lot too. We have to get ready for our big sleep," said Mama Bear.

"That sounds fun. We will still miss summer," the cubs said.

"Summer will come back next year," said Mama Bear. The cubs cheered. They were happy. Summer would return. Fall would be fun too.

Prepare for the Read Aloud The modified Read Aloud above prepares children for listening to the oral reading "The End of Summer" on page 89b.

■ **First Listening: Listen to Understand** Write the title of the Read Aloud on the board. Are you sad when summer ends? I'm going to read a story about bears that are sad about the end of summer. Listen to hear what makes them feel better. After reading, ask children about the main characters and events. Who is sad about the end of summer? (the cubs) Who told them the news? (Squirrel) Why are they happy at the end? (Summer will be back and fall will be fun too.)

■ **Second Listening: Listen to Check Understanding** Using Story Map B (*ELL Handbook*, page 507), work with children to recall the characters and the events in the story. Ask questions to prompt answers as you fill in the graphic organizer.

Objectives

- Demonstrate listening comprehension of increasingly complex spoken English by following directions, retelling or summarizing spoken messages, responding to questions and requests, collaborating with peers, and taking notes commensurate with content and grade-level needs.

High-Frequency Words

■ **Preteach** Distribute copies of this week's Word Cards (*ELL Handbook*, p. 149). Have children point to or hold up corresponding cards when you say a word in a sentence or make a gesture. When appropriate, use opposites to reinforce meaning.

- Spread arms wide, pantomiming *very* big. An elephant is *very* big.
- Pantomime driving in a *car*. I am driving in a *car*.
- Walk away from the children. I am walking *away*.
- *Our* is the plural of *my*. Motion around the classroom. This is *our* classroom.
- Show a picture of a *house*. This is a *house*.
- Where are we? We are at *school* right now.
- A *friend* is someone you like and who likes you. Point to the children. You are my *friends*.

■ **Practice** Have children repeat the gesture and sentence after you say each word.

■ **Speaking/Writing with High-Frequency Words**

- **Teach/Model** Give each pair of children a set of Word Cards.
- **Practice** Have children use the cards to help them find the words in the classroom.

Beginning/Intermediate Have pairs of children look through books or at environmental print in the classroom to find the high-frequency words. Have them hold up the correct Word Card when they find a word. Read aloud to children the words or sentences they find.

Advanced/Advanced-High Have pairs write down the words or sentences they find and read them aloud.

Language Objectives
- Use accessible language to learn new and essential language.
- Internalize new basic language through speaking.
- Use high-frequency English words.
- Understand the general meaning of spoken English.

Cognates
For Spanish speakers, point out that the word for *car* is spelled *carro* in Spanish. Reinforce the concept that these languages share many words that are the same or similar.

Mini-Lesson: Listening
Use Student Edition p. 91 as practice for listening to understand the general meaning of spoken English. Read aloud as children follow along. Then ask questions to be sure students understand the passage, particularly with its use of high-frequency words.

Objectives
- Internalize new basic and academic language by using it and reusing it in meaningful ways in speaking and writing activities that build language attainment.

Support for English Language Learners

Content Objectives

- Identify facts in a text.
- Identify opinions in a text.

Language Objectives

- Use reasoning to distinguish fact and opinion.
- Write facts and opinions.
- Express opinions.

ELL English Language Learners

Guide Comprehension
Fact and Opinion

■ **Preteach** Model by sharing an example. A fact is a true statement. *We are at school* is a fact. An opinion is a belief. *School is always fun* is an opinion.

■ **Practice** Have children turn to Envision It! on page EI•4 and EI•5 in the Student Edition. Have children look at the two pictures. Ask children to identify which picture shows a fact and which shows an opinion. Ask children to explain the difference. Have children use the Envision pages as prompts for expressing their own opinions. Provide a frame: *I think _____ because _____.*

■ **Reteach/Practice** Distribute copies of the Picture It! (*ELL Handbook*, p. 150). Have students look at the picture while you read. Tell them to listen as you read aloud the story under the picture. (**Answers** *Facts:* My name is Sam. I do not like carrots. Carrots are vegetables. They grow in the dirt. My mom says they are tasty. Carrots have vitamins that help you see better. I still will not eat carrots! *Opinions:* Carrots taste like dirt. Good food is not orange.)

Beginning Ask students to look at the picture. Ask them what they think Sam's opinion is on carrots, based on the picture. Reread the story aloud.

Intermediate Have students underline the sentences that show Sam's opinion. Have them circle his mom's opinion.

Advanced/Advanced-High Have students tell you which facts explain why carrots are good for you. Then, ask whether there are any facts that explain what is bad about carrots (no, there are only opinions). After, ask which sentence explains a reason that carrots are good for you—but is based on opinion, rather than fact (My mom says they are tasty).

MINI-LESSON

Academic Language

Write several topics on the board, such as *sports*, *school*, *music*, and other topics children may be interested in. Go around the room and ask each student to express an opinion about a topic. Have children use the following sentence frame: *I think _____.* Encourage children to explain why they agree or disagree with their classmates' opinions.

Objectives

- Develop and expand repertoire of learning strategies such as reasoning inductively or deductively, looking for patterns in language, and analyzing sayings and expressions commensurate with grade-level learning expectations.
- Understand the general meaning, main points, and important details of spoken language ranging from situations in which topics, language, and contexts are familiar to unfamiliar.

 English Language Learners

Reading Comprehension
The Class Pet

Student Edition pp. 92–93

■ **Frontloading**

- **Background Knowledge** Read the title aloud and discuss it. What are some types of pets? What kind of pet do you want?

- **Preview** Guide children on a picture walk through the story, asking them to identify people, places, and actions. Reteach these words using visuals in the Student Edition: *seeds* (p. 97), *branches* (p. 99), *nest* (p. 101), and *friend* (p. 104).

- **Predict** What kind of pet do you think the children will get?

Sheltered Reading Ask questions such as the following to guide children's comprehension:

- p. 95: What type of pet does the class get? (a mouse named Dory)

- p. 97: What do mice eat? (seeds, pellets, corn, nuts)

- p. 100: How many mice can be born at one time? (ten)

- p. 105: What does Dory get at the end of the story? (a mouse friend named Cory) Would you like to have a mouse for a pet? Point to one of the pictures that shows why you would or would not like to have a mouse.

■ **Fluency: Appropriate Phrasing** Remind children that appropriate phrasing means paying attention to the periods, question marks, and exclamation points. Read page 95. Model reading with appropriate phrasing. Give students time to practice appropriate phrasing during silent reading. Then have children pair up and choose a passage from pages 96–100. Ask children to read the passage to their partners. The partners should give feedback for improvement. For more practice, use the Fluency: Choral Reading Routine (*ELL Handbook*, page 496).

After Reading Help children summarize the text with the Retelling Cards. Ask questions that prompt children to summarize the important parts of the text.

Content Objectives
- Monitor and adjust comprehension.
- Make and adjust predictions.

Language Objectives
- Read grade level text with appropriate phrasing.
- Summarize text using visual support.
- Speak using grade-level content vocabulary.

Audio Support
Prepare children for reading *The Class Pet* by using the eSelection or the AudioText CD. See the AudioText CD Routine (*ELL Handbook*, p. 500) for suggestions on using these learning tools.

Mini-Lesson: Speaking
Have children speak using content-area vocabulary, such as *pet*, *eat*, *drink*, and *born*. Have them use Student Edition p. 101 as a visual prompt for speaking. *(These babies were just born. They will need to eat and drink to grow. Then they can be class pets.)*

Objectives
- Demonstrate comprehension of increasingly complex English by participating in shared reading, retelling or summarizing material, responding to questions, and taking notes commensurate with content area and grade level needs.
- Read silently with increasing ease and comprehension for longer periods.

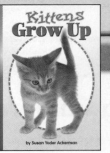

ELL Reader   ELD Reader

For additional leveled instruction, see the **ELL/ELD Reader Teaching Guide.**

Comprehension: *Kittens Grow Up*

■ **Before Reading** Distribute copies of the ELL and ELD Readers, *Kittens Grow Up*, to children at their reading level.

- **Preview** Read the title aloud with children: This is a story about kittens growing up. Activate prior knowledge. The story in our book was about mice growing up. This story is about growing up too. What happens when animals grow up? What happens when people grow up?

- **Set a Purpose for Reading** Let's find out what happens when kittens grow up.

■ **During Reading** Follow this Reading Routine for both reading groups.

1. Read the entire Reader aloud slowly as children follow along and finger point.

2. Reread the Reader one sentence at a time, having children echo read after you.

■ **After Reading** Use the exercises on the inside back cover of *Kittens Grow Up* and invite children to share drawings and writing. In a whole-group discussion, ask children how the kittens changed during the story. Ask children to point to pictures in the text that show the changes in the kittens.

ELD Reader Beginning/Intermediate

■ **pp. 3–6** What is life like for a kitten? Can you share some of the changes kittens make?

■ **pp. 7–8** What happened to the kitten? (It grew into a cat.)

Writing Draw a picture of a kitten doing something from the story. Have children work in pairs and share their pictures with the class. Have children discuss what is happening in their pictures.

ELL Reader Advanced/Advanced-High

■ **pp. 4–5** What happens when kittens fall down? (They try again.)

■ **p. 8** Why doesn't the mother cat need to wash the kitten anymore? (Because it has grown up)

Study Guide Distribute copies of the ELL Reader Study Guide (*ELL Handbook*, page 154). Scaffold comprehension by having children look back through the Reader for information in order to answer questions. Review their responses together. (**Answers** See *ELL Handbook*, pp. 245–248.)

Objectives
- Understand the general meaning, main points, and important details of spoken language ranging from situations in which topics, language, and contexts are familiar to unfamiliar.

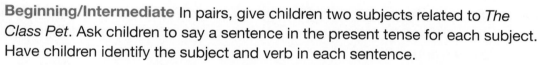 **English Language Learners**

Conventions
Verbs that Do Not Add -s

■ **Preteach** Have a boy read a book. He reads. Write *He reads* on the board. Pretend you are reading the book. I read. Write *I read* on the board. Remind children that when we use *I*, *we*, *you*, or *they*, the verb that follows does not end in *-s*. When we use *he*, *she*, or *it*, the verb does end in *-s*. Provide other example sentences using the verbs *dance* and *talk*.

■ **Practice** Leaf through the Student Edition to call attention to action pictures. Have children do the exercises below according to their language proficiency level.

 Leveled LS Support

Beginning/Intermediate In pairs, give children two subjects related to *The Class Pet*. Ask children to say a sentence in the present tense for each subject. Have children identify the subject and verb in each sentence.

Advanced/Advanced-High Have children write a sentence in the present tense for the subjects *I*, *you*, *we*, and *they* using *The Class Pet* as a guide. Tell children to underline the subject and verb in each sentence.

■ **Reteach**

• Write the following sentence frames on the board: *She _____. He _____. They _____.* Have children volunteer to act out verbs, such as *write*, *run*, *walk*, and *jump*. Have the rest of the class complete the appropriate sentence frame with the correct form of the verb.

• Have children use one of the verbs demonstrated in class to write two simple sentences. The first sentence should use *she*, *he*, or *it* as the subject. The second sentence should use *I*, *we*, or *they* as the subject. Have children share their sentences with partners and edit each other's writing.

■ **Practice** Create a chart on the board. In the first column, list the following verbs: *cook*, *ride*, *play*, and *drive*. Label the second column *He _____*. Label the third column *They _____*.

Beginning/Intermediate Have children copy the chart on their own paper. Work in pairs to write the appropriate form of the verb in each column. Have pairs take turns completing the chart on the board.

Advanced/Advanced-High Have children pair up. Have children complete the columns with sentences. Ask each pair to share their sentences with the rest of the class. Have classmates check for the appropriate verb tense.

Content Objectives
• Identify and use verbs that do not add *-s*.
• Correctly use verbs that do not add *-s* in sentences.

Language Objectives
• Speak using verbs that do not add *-s*.
• Write phrases and sentences using verbs that do not add *-s*.

Transfer Skills
In some languages, such as Spanish, the subject pronoun can be inflected in the verb ending. Have children practice English sentences with subject pronouns included.

Objectives
• Share information in cooperative learning interactions.
• Learn relationships between sounds and letters of the English language to represent sounds when writing in English.
• Spell familiar English words with increasing accuracy, and employ English spelling patterns and rules with increasing accuracy as more English is acquired.

Support for English Language Learners

Content Objectives

- Identify correct verbs to make subjects and verbs agree in sentences.

- Understand the definition of a summary.

- Expand reading skills by summarizing text.

- Understand when to use formal English.

Language Objectives

- Write a narrative summary of *The Class Pet*.

- Monitor sentences for subject-verb agreement.

- Explain with increasing specificity.

Mini-Lesson: Explaining

Have children explain with specificity and detail. Ask them to explain what mice are like when they are born. Then have them turn to p. 100 to add more details to their explanation. Ask questions: How many babies are born at a time? Where do they live? What do they look like?

Use Formal Language

Writing a summary is usually for formal purposes, like writing for a class or test. Summaries use formal English. Have children focus on writing complete sentences and using language for speaking to adults or in formal situations.

Write a Summary

- **Introduce Terms** Write the word *summary* on the board. Who has a favorite book they read recently? Choose a child who volunteers. Tell the class what happened in the book. Give the child a chance to describe what happened. If time permits, repeat the process with another child. What these children just told us was a summary of the books they read. A summary is a shorter version of a story. Tell children we use formal English in a summary.

- **Explain** Subject-Verb Agreement A sentence has a subject and a verb. If the sentence has a plural subject, you need to use a verb that is plural. Write *The girls walk home* on the board. What is the subject? (girls) What is the verb? (walk) Notice that the plural verb does not end with *-s*. Write *The boy walks home* on the board. What is the subject? (boy) What is the verb? (walks) In this sentence, the singular subject needs a singular verb. Notice that the singular verb does end with *-s*.

- **Model** Write the following sentences on the board: *The dog _____. The dogs _____. The child _____. The children _____. The class _____. The classes _____.* Fill in the blanks for the first pair of sentences. Remind children that plural verbs do not end in *-s* the way plural nouns do. Guide children in filling in the blanks for the other two pairs of sentences. Read each correct sentence aloud. Have children repeat the sentence.

- **Write** Have children look back through *The Class Pet*. Ask children to make a list of important things that happened in the story. Think about what things you might say if someone asked you to tell them about the story. Start children off by writing the following sentence on the board: *Miss Ford gave her class a pet*. Remind children to make sure their sentences have subjects and verbs that agree.

 Beginning Have children draw three pictures of things that happened in the story. Ask children to number the pictures in the right order. Have children copy a sentence from *The Class Pet* to illustrate each picture.

Intermediate Guide children's writing by asking questions: What happened next? What did you think was important in the story? Have children add three more sentences to the narrative list you started.

Advanced/Advanced-High Have children complete the list by adding three or more narrative sentences. Then have them write their sentences in paragraph form.

Objectives

- Monitor oral and written language production and employ self-corrective techniques or other resources.
- Demonstrate an increasing ability to distinguish between formal and informal English and an increasing knowledge of when to use each one commensurate with grade-level learning expectations.
- Write using newly acquired basic vocabulary and content-based grade-level vocabulary.

Customize Your Writing

Writing Forms and Patterns

- Instruction focuses on a different **product** each week.
- Mini-lessons and models help children learn key features and **organizational patterns**.

Grade 1 Products poetry, personal narrative, realistic story, play scene, letter, and so on

Grade 1 Organization Patterns beginning, middle, and end, main idea and details, sequence, and so on

Quick Writes for Fluency

- **Writing on Demand** Use the Quick Write routine for **writing on demand**.
- The Quick Write **prompt and routine** extend skills and strategies from daily writing lessons.

Writing Process ①②③④⑤

- Six **writing process** lessons provide structure to move children through the steps of the writing process.
- One-week and two-week pacing allows lessons to be used in **Writing Workshop**.

Steps of the Writing Process Plan and Prewrite, Draft, Revise, Edit, Publish and Present

Grade 1 Writing Process Products personal narrative, letter, expository article, realistic story, short report

Writing on

Reading STREET

MINI-LESSON

- Daily 10-minute mini-lessons focus instruction on the **traits** and **craft** of good writing.
- Instruction focuses on one writing trait and one writer's craft skill every week.

Traits focus/ideas, organization, voice, word choice, sentences, conventions

Craft drafting strategies, revising strategies, editing strategies

Read Like a Writer

- Use **mentor text** every week as a model to exemplify the traits of good writing.
- **Interact with text** every week to learn the key features of good writing.

Mentor Text Examine literature in the Student Edition.

INTERACT with TEXT Underline, circle, and highlight model text in the *Reader's and Writer's Notebook*.

Write Guy
Jeff Anderson

Need Writing Advice?

Writing instruction is all about creating effective writers. We don't want to crush the inner writer in a child by over-correcting and over-editing. What makes effective writing instruction? Children need to write, write, write! But is that enough? Probably not. All kinds of instruction and guidance go into making an effective writer.

The Write Guy offers advice on teacher and peer conferencing, focusing on writing traits, revising strategies, editing strategies, and much, much more.

Customize Your Writing

Sometimes you want to spend more time on writing—perhaps you do a **Writing Workshop**. This one- or two-week plan for the unit level writing projects can help.

1 Week Plan	Day 1	Day 2	Day 3	Day 4	Day 5
1 Plan and Prewrite	■	■			
2 Draft			■		
3 Revise				■	
4 Edit					■
5 Publish					■

2 Week Plan	Day 1	Day 2	Day 3	Day 4	Day 5	Day 6	Day 7	Day 8	Day 9	Day 10
1 Plan and Prewrite	■	■	■	■						
2 Draft					■	■	■			
3 Revise								■		
4 Edit									■	
5 Publish										■

Grade 1 Unit Writing Projects

Internet Guy
Don Leu

Unit Writing Project 1–21st Century Project

Unit 1 Trading Card

Unit 2 Pen Pal E-mail

Unit 3 Photo Essay

Unit 4 Story Exchange

Unit 5 E-Newsletter

Unit Writing Project 2–Writing Process

Unit 1 Personal Narrative

Unit 2 Letter

Unit 3 Expository Article

Unit 4 Realistic Story

Unit 5 Short Report

Photo Essay

Writing Project

Create a photo essay documenting changes in plant growth.

Purpose Learn to use a digital camera, including taking photographs, uploading the photographs to a computer, and inserting them into a document. Enhance formatting skills using word processing software.

Audience Class members, teacher, school, parents

Introduce genre and prompt

In this workshop we will take photographs with a digital camera to show how a seed grows and changes into a plant. We will write captions, or sentences that tell about the photographs. Then we will put the captions and photographs together to make a photo essay we can put on display.

Key Features of a Photo Essay

- displays a series of photographs that tell about a topic or event
- includes captions that tell about the photographs
- tells a story or a sequence of events

Teacher Tip

If children are not growing and photographing their own plants, help them use a search engine to find photographs of a seed growing into a plant. Be aware of school and district guidelines for Internet use, and direct children toward royalty-free image sites.

Objectives
- Understand and identify features of a photo essay.
- Learn the features and functions of a digital camera.

 Plan and Prewrite

MINI-LESSON

Read Like a Writer

■ **Examine Model Text** Let's look at an example of a photo essay. This is the kind of essay that you will create. Display 21st Century Transparency TC7. Read it aloud. Ask children to identify key features of a photo essay in the student model.

 A photo essay is a series of photographs that tells about a topic. This title tells me that this photo essay is about a bean seed and how it grows. The pictures show me what happened first, what happened next, and what happened last. Underneath each picture I see a caption. A caption is a sentence or title that tells about the picture. I can see and understand how a bean seed grows and changes.

21st Century Transparency
TC7, TR DVD

Customize Your Writing
Common Core Standards and 21st Century Writing

To excel in the 21st Century, students must:
- acquire new skills, tools, knowledge, and thinking skills
- develop these skills and habits that will serve them as lifelong learners
- engage technology to transform knowledge and skills into useful contributions within a wide array of learning and working communities

21st Century Writing and the Common Core Standards for English Language Arts

In this unit's 21st Century Writing Project, children will apply the five steps of process writing. The chart below provides instructional tips for guiding children through each step. Discuss these tips with children before they begin writing.

Process Writing Steps	Common Core Standards for English Language Arts	Tips for Unit 3 21st Century Writing
① Plan and Prewrite	Writing 2.	As children **plan** a photo essay, use the mini-lesson on page CW•5 to emphasize use of the words *first, next,* and *last.*
② Draft	Writing 2.	As children **draft** captions, use *21st Century Transparency TC7* to explain the purpose of captions.
③ Revise	Writing 5.; Language 1.j.	As children **revise,** have them whisper read their captions and decide if the sentences tell a complete idea. Use the *Revise Captions Mini-lesson* on page CW•8 for more suggestions.
④ Edit	Writing 5.; Language 2.	As children **edit,** use the Edit Captions Mini-lesson on page CW•9 to teach that sentences begin with a capital letter and end with a period.
⑤ Publish	Writing 6.	When children **publish** their photo essays, have them display their work. See *Options for Presenting* on page CW•10.

Integrating 21st Century Skills and the Common Core Standards College and Career Readiness Anchor Standards for Writing

The chart below shows the skills taught in this unit's 21st Century Writing Project and the College and Career Readiness Anchor Standards for Writing that correspond to these skills.

21st Century Skills in This Project	College and Career Readiness Anchor Standards for Writing
Using a Digital Camera pages CW•3–4	Writing 6. Use technology, including the Internet, to produce and publish writing and to interact and collaborate with others.
Inserting Photographs into Word Processing Documents pages CW•6	Writing 6. Use technology, including the Internet, to produce and publish writing and to interact and collaborate with others.
Drafting, Revising, and Editing Image Captions pages CW•5–7	Writing 5. Develop and strengthen writing as needed by planning, revising, editing, rewriting, or trying a new approach.
Formatting and Printing Documents pages CW•10	Writing 6. Use technology, including the Internet, to produce and publish writing and to interact and collaborate with others.

Writing Resources

Use the resources to the right to build writing skills during and after the teaching of Unit 3.

Writing Resources

Reader's and Writer's Notebook

Digital Resources
- Online Writing Transparencies

Teacher Resources DVD-ROM
- Reader's and Writer's Notebook
- Let's Practice It!
- Graphic Organizers
- Writing Transparencies

ISBN-13: 978-0-328-64369-1
ISBN-10: 0-328-64369-6

MINI-LESSON

Parts of a Digital Camera

■ A digital camera lets you take a photograph and upload the image to a computer. We will use a digital camera to take pictures that show how seeds grow and change.

■ Hold up the camera that children will be using. A digital camera has many parts. Turn the camera on and point to the camera lens. This is the *lens*. I point the lens toward the object I want to photograph. Point to the LCD screen on the digital camera. This screen shows what the lens is "seeing." I can see what the photograph will look like before I take it. Demonstrate how the camera frames an image by pointing the camera at different objects and allowing children to see the LCD screen. To take a photograph, I press the shutter button. Point to the button. When I press the shutter button, the image on the screen "freezes." Take a photograph of an object in the classroom and show the LCD display to children.

■ Have children take turns taking photographs around the classroom, school, or playground. Ensure that they are holding the camera properly, and make adjustments as needed.

Take Care of Your Digital Camera

✔ Handle the camera carefully and take care not to drop it or bang it on hard surfaces.

✔ Keep the lens and screen clean by keeping your fingers off them.

✔ Water can hurt the camera. Keep it from getting wet.

✔ Save the batteries. Turn the camera off when you are not using it.

Academic Vocabulary

Photo Essay A photo essay is a collection of photographs on one theme, accompanied by an explanation.

Differentiated Instruction

 Advanced
Write Instructions Have children write or dictate a list of instructions on how to use a digital camera. Post the instructions where the class can clearly read them.

 Strategic Intervention
Access Content To reinforce the purpose of captions, show children more examples of captions in magazines, newspapers, or books such as children's encyclopedias.

Technology Tip

Different models of digital cameras offer different features. Refer to the product manual in order to become familiar with the features before demonstrating the camera for children.

 Plan and Prewrite

Prepare the space	To prepare for this lesson, provide the materials and space necessary for children to plant seeds and observe them over a period of time. If possible, use clear plastic containers. Have children plant the seeds close to the side of the containers so they can see and photograph the growing roots.
Take the first photograph	Organize children into small groups of three or four. Have each group prepare and plant seeds in containers. Help children follow seed package instructions. Have children take photographs of their seeds in the containers before they are covered with dirt. Ensure that each group member takes his or her own photographs for his or her own photo essay. Remind them to keep the camera clean and free of dirt as they take their photographs.
Upload images	Assist children in uploading their images to the computer using devices such as a USB cable or memory card. Help them rename the files and keep them in a folder on the desktop. Repeat the process when the seedlings sprout and again when they have grown into small plants. Rename the image files after each step so that they can be easily identified later.

 Plan and Prewrite

MINI-LESSON

First, Next, and Last

■ A photo essay about an event shows what happens first, what happens next, and what happens last. We will put our photographs in order to show how a plant grows and changes.

■ Display 21st Century Transparency TC8. Let's practice putting pictures in order. Point to the first row. Which picture shows what happened first? (egg cracking) Which picture shows what happens next? (bird hatching from egg) Which picture shows what happened last? (baby bird fully hatched) Repeat the routine with the next two rows.

21st Century Transparency
TC8, TR DVD

Corrective feedback

If... children have difficulty identifying sequence,
then... ask them to picture in their mind what is happening. If the order in which things are happening does not make sense, ask them to try to figure out an order of events that *does* make sense.

Differentiated Instruction

 Advanced

Extend the Concept Have children take photographs of their small group while they are planting and tending their seeds. Have them use the photographs to create a photo essay about cooperation.

Teacher Tip

There are several varieties of plants that have hearty, quick-sprouting seeds. A few options for flowers are marigold, zinnia, and hyacinth bean vines. For edible plants try mung beans, lima beans, or wax beans.

Technology Tip

Many digital cameras require specific settings for indoor vs. outdoor photographs, and so on. To ensure success, adjust the camera settings to match the environment before children take photographs.

ELL

English Language Learners
Assess Content Use physical response to clarify meanings of the words *first, next,* and *last.* For example, model an activity with three steps such as reading a book saying, "*First,* I pick up the book. *Next,* I open the book. *Last,* I read the book."

Objectives

- Insert photographs into a word processing document.
- Draft captions for photographs.
- Use capiltalization and punctuation correctly.

Draft

Insert photographs

Now we will put our photographs into a word processing document so that we can add sentences that tell about them. We want our photo essays to make sense to our audience, so we must be careful to put our photographs in the correct order.

Display three photographs from the project on the projector: one of the newly planted seeds, one of the sprouting seedlings, and one of the plant. Which photograph do I want to put in the document first? (the seed right after it was planted) Model using the mouse to select the photograph and insert it into a word processing document. Which photograph do I want to put in the document next? (the sprout) Again, model inserting the photograph in the document. Repeat the process with the final photograph.

Assist children in using the mouse to select and insert their own photographs into a word processing document. Help them adjust formatting as needed.

2 Draft

Draft Captions

■ **Display 21st Century Transparency TC7 again.** This student wrote a caption below each picture. A caption is a title or group of words near a picture that tells what it shows. The words help the reader understand what is happening in the picture.

Think Aloud Point to the first caption and read it aloud:

The seed is in the soil.

This caption is a sentence. I know that it is a sentence because it tells a complete idea. Also, it begins with a capital letter and ends with a period. The sentence tells about the picture. It helps me understand what is happening in the picture.

21st Century Transparency
TC7, TR DVD

■ We will write captions for our photographs to help readers understand what happened to our seeds. We will write sentences for our captions. Remember to start each sentence with a capital letter and end with a period. **Have children draft one to two sentences for each photograph. Show children how to use the mouse to position the cursor below the appropriate photographs, or have them write captions in a different document and copy and paste the text when they are done.**

Academic Vocabulary

Caption A caption is a title or group of words near a picture that tells what the picture shows.

Differentiated Instruction

 Strategic Intervention

Support Drafting Have children who are not able to write independently work with partners. Children can create a sentence together and write it on a piece of paper before they type it into the document.

English Language Learners

Word Order English word order of subject-verb-object is different from that of some languages. For example, verbs in Spanish may appear before the subject. Model correct word order in English to help children understand the pattern.

Objectives
- Revise captions.
- Edit captions.

3 Revise

Revise Captions

■ Earlier we wrote drafts of sentences that tell about our photographs. Now we will revise our sentences. **Point to the caption below the second picture in the student model on 21st Century Transparency TC7. Read the caption aloud.**

The seed begins to change.

Think Aloud This is a good sentence. It begins with a capital letter and ends with a period. It tells a complete idea. It explains what is happening in the photograph. I want to add another sentence to explain how the seed is changing. I think it will help readers understand what is happening to the seed. **Write the following sentence below the caption:**

It grows roots.

Now readers can see how the seed is changing. My caption gives readers more information.

■ As children revise their captions, ask them to read their sentences in a whisper and consider the following questions:

✔ Do my sentences each tell a complete idea?

✔ Do my sentences clearly explain what is happening in the photograph?

✔ Do I need to add another word or sentence to help readers understand the photograph?

4 Edit

Edit the Draft

■ Write the following sentence on the board:

the seed will be a plant

What is wrong with this sentence? (It does not begin with a capital letter; it does not end with a period.) Make corrections as children identify the errors.

■ Now we will check our sentences for grammar and spelling errors. Display the following Editing Checklist on the board or on the projector and read it aloud to children:

Editing Checklist

✔ Did I spell words correctly?

✔ Do my sentences start with a capital letter?

✔ Do my sentences end with a period?

Format text After children have finished revising and editing their sentences, assist them in formatting their documents, adjusting margins and text-wrap as needed.

English Language Learners
Plural Nouns In some languages, including Chinese, Hmong, and Vietnamese, nouns do not have a plural form. Instead, the plural is indicated with an adjective. Help children practice plural nouns such as *seeds* and *roots* by adding -s.

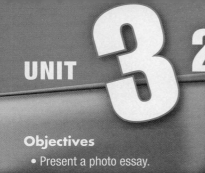

Objectives
• Present a photo essay.

 Publish and Present

Options for Presenting

Offer children two options for presenting their work:

Print copies of each child's photo essay and display them in the classroom or create a class book.	Host a classroom "garden day" and invite other classes to view the plants. Display the photo essays that accompany each plant near the container.

Publish photo essay

Now that we have revised and edited our drafts, we can publish our photo essays. Have children add a title to the top of their short essays and center the text. Assist them with moving the mouse and positioning the cursor as needed.

Print copies of the photo essays and put them on display in the classroom or create a class book. Children may also enjoy hosting a classroom "garden day" for other classes or family members to come and see their plants. Post the photo essays that accompany each plant near the container. Have children explain each photo essay to their guests.

Customize Literacy in Your Classroom

Table of Contents
for Customize Literacy

Customize Literacy is organized into different sections, each one designed to help you organize and carry out an effective literacy program. Each section contains strategies and support for teaching comprehension skills and strategies. *Customize Literacy* also shows how to use weekly text sets of readers in your literacy program.

Section 1: **Planning**..2–7

Section 2: **Instruction** 8–23

Section 3: **Matching Books and Readers** 24–41

Section 4: **Building Community** 42–47

Weekly Text Sets
to Customize Literacy

The following readers can be used to enhance your literacy instruction.

	Decodable Readers	Concept Literacy Reader	Below-Level Reader	On-Level Reader	Advanced Reader	ELD Reader	ELL Reader
Unit 3 WEEK 1	*Can Billy Fly?; Vi, Mo, and Me; We Go Fishing*	*Gardens Change*	*In My Room*	*Let's Build a Park!*	*A New Library*	*My Street*	*My Street*
Unit 3 WEEK 2	*Zing in a Tank; Inside and Outside; Pancakes*	*I Can Read*	*Hank's Song*	*Mac Can Do It!*	*Paul's Bed*	*Ana and Her Bike*	*Ana and Her Bike*
Unit 3 WEEK 3	*Boxes for Flo; At the Shore; Going to the Shore*	*Animals Change*	*Gus the Pup*	*Big Wishes and Her Baby*	*Britton Finds a Kitten*	*Kittens Grow Up*	*Kittens Grow Up*

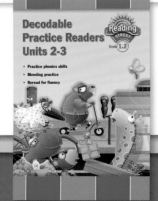
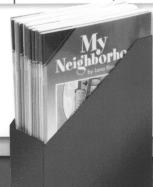

Customize Literacy in Your Classroom

Instruction in comprehension skills and strategies provides readers with avenues to understanding a text. Through teacher modeling and guided, collaborative, and independent practice, students become independent thinkers who employ a variety of skills and strategies to help them make meaning as they read.

Mini-Lessons for Comprehension Skills and Strategies

Envision It!

A Comprehension Handbook

Unit R	Character, Setting, Plot, Realism and Fantasy, Questioning, Monitor and Clarify, Background Knowledge
Unit 1	Character, Setting, Plot, Main Idea and Details, Cause and Effect, Summarize, Important Ideas, Story Structure
Unit 2	Sequence, Cause and Effect, Author's Purpose, Compare and Contrast, Predict and Set Purpose, Inferring
Unit 3	Sequence, Compare and Contrast, Fact and Opinion, Author's Purpose, Draw Conclusions, Visualize, Text Structure
Unit 4	Draw Conclusions, Theme, Facts and Details, Cause and Effect, Important Ideas, Questioning
Unit 5	Literary Elements, Draw Conclusions, Compare and Contrast, Main Idea and Details, Sequence, Theme, Monitor and Clarify, Summarize

Envision It! Visual Skills Handbook

Author's Purpose
Categorize and Classify
Cause and Effect
Compare and Contrast
Draw Conclusions
Fact and Opinion
Generalize
Graphic Sources
Literary Elements
Main Idea and Details
Sequence

Envision It! Visual Strategies Handbook

Background Knowledge
Important Ideas
Inferring
Monitor and Clarify
Predict and Set Purpose
Questioning
Story Structure
Summarize
Text Structure
Visualize

Anchor Chart Anchor charts are provided with each strategy lesson. These charts incorporate the language of strategic thinkers. They help students make their thinking visible and permanent and provide students with a means to clarify their thinking about how and when to use each strategy. As students gain more experience with a strategy, the chart may undergo revision.

See pages 107–128 in the *First Stop on Reading Street* Teacher's Edition for additional support as you customize literacy in your classroom.

Good Readers DRA2 users will find additional resources in the *First Stop on Reading Street* Teacher's Edition on pages 110–111.

Contents

Section 1 Planning — 2

Pacing Guide

Teaching Record Chart

Section 2 Instruction — 8

Comprehension Mini-Lessons
- Sequence
- Compare and Contrast
- Fact and Opinion
- Visualize (includes ANCHOR CHART)

Using Multiple Strategies

Glossary of Literacy Terms

Section 3 Matching Books and Readers — 24

Leveled Readers Skills Chart

What Good Readers Do

Conversation Starters: Asking Good Questions

Connecting Science and Social Studies

Section 4 Building Community — 42

Planning Teacher Study Groups

Trial Lessons

Books for Teachers

Section 1 Planning

Pacing Guide

This chart shows the instructional sequence from *Scott Foresman Reading Street* for Grade 1. You can use this pacing guide as is to ensure you are following a comprehensive scope and sequence. Or, you can adjust the sequence to match your calendar, curriculum map, or testing schedule.

Grade 1 READING

UNIT R

	Week 1	Week 2	Week 3	Week 4	Week 5	Week 6
Phonemic Awareness	Match Initial Phonemes	Match Initial Phonemes	Match Final Phonemes	Isolate Final Phonemes	Isolate Phonemes	Isolate Medial Phonemes
Phonics	/m/ spelled *m*, /s/ spelled *s, ss* /t/ spelled *t*, /a/ spelled *a*	/k/ spelled *c*, /p/ spelled *p*, /n/ spelled *n*	/f/ spelled *f, ff*, /b/ spelled *b*, /g/ spelled *g*, /i/ spelled *i*	/d/ spelled *d*, /l/ spelled *l, ll* /h/ spelled *h*, /o/ spelled *o*	/r/ spelled *r*, /w/ spelled *w*, /j/ spelled *j*, /k/ spelled *k*, /e/ spelled *e*	/v/ spelled *v*, /y/ spelled *y*, /u/ spelled *u*, /kw/ spelled *qu*, /z/, *z, zz*
High-Frequency Words	*I, see, a, green*	*we, like, the, one*	*do, look, you, was, yellow*	*are, have, they, that, two*	*he, is, to, with, three*	*where, here, for, me, go*
Comprehension Skill	Character	Setting	Plot	Realism/ Fantasy	Plot	Realism/ Fantasy
Comprehension Strategy	Questioning	Predict and Set Purpose	Story Structure	Questioning	Monitor and Clarify	Background Knowledge
Fluency	Oral Rereading	Oral Rereading	Oral Rereading, Paired Reading	Oral Rereading, Paired Reading	Oral Rereading, Paired Reading	Oral Rereading, Paired Reading

UNIT 1

	Week 1	Week 2
Phonemic Awareness	Blend and Segment Phonemes	Blend and Segment Phonemes
Phonics	Short *a* Final *ck*	Short *i* Final *x*
High-Frequency Words	*on, way, in, my, come*	*take, up, she, what*
Comprehension Skill	Character and Setting	Plot
Comprehension Strategy	Monitor and Clarify	Summarize
Fluency	Accuracy	Accuracy

UNIT 3

	Week 1	Week 2	Week 3	Week 4	Week 5	Week 6
Phonemic Awareness	Segment Phonemes	Blend and Segment Words	Add Phonemes	Blend and Segment Syllables	Isolate Medial and Final Phonemes	Add Phonemes
Phonics	Vowel Sounds of *y* Long Vowels (CV)	Final *ng, nk* Compound Words	Ending *-es*, Plural *-es* r-Controlled *or, ore*	Inflected *-ed, -ing* r-Controlled *ar*	r-Controlled *er, ir, ur* Contractions *'s, 've, 're*	Comparative Endings *dge/*j/
High-Frequency Words	*always, become, day, everything, nothing, stays, things*	*any, enough, ever, every, own, sure, were*	*away, car, friends, house, our, school, very*	*afraid, again, few, how, read, soon*	*done, know, push, visit, wait*	*before, does, good-bye, oh, right, won't*
Comprehension Skill	Sequence	Compare and Contrast	Fact and Opinion	Author's Purpose	Fact and Opinion	Draw Conclusions
Comprehension Strategy	Summarize	Inferring	Monitor and Clarify	Visualize	Text Structure	Background Knowledge
Fluency	Accuracy/ Rate	Phrasing	Phrasing	Expression/ Intonation	Expression/ Intonation	Expression/ Intonation

UNIT 4

	Week 1	Week 2
Phonemic Awareness	Substitute Initial Phonemes	Substitute Final Phonemes
Phonics	Long *a: ai, ay* Possessives	Long *e: ea* Inflected Endings
High-Frequency Words	*about, give, enjoy, would, worry, surprise*	*colors, drew, over, sign, draw, great, show*
Comprehension Skill	Draw Conclusions	Theme
Comprehension Strategy	Monitor and Clarify	Visualize
Fluency	Expression/ Intonation	Accuracy/ Rate

> Are you the adventurous type? Want to use some of your own ideas and materials in your teaching? But you worry you might be leaving out some critical instruction kids need? **Customize Literacy** can help.

	Week 3	Week 4	Week 5	Week 6
	Blend and Segment Phonemes	Blend and Segment Phonemes	Blend and Segment Phonemes	Blend and Segment Phonemes
	Short *o* -*s* Plurals	Inflected Endings -*s*, -*ing*	Short *e* Initial Blends	Short *u* Final Blends
	blue, little, get, from, help, use	*eat, her, this, too, four, five*	*saw, small, tree, your*	*home, into, many, them*
	Character and Setting	Main Idea and Details	Main Idea and Details	Cause and Effect
	Visualize	Important Ideas	Story Structure	Text Structure
	Rate	Accuracy/ Rate	Phrasing	Phrasing

UNIT 2

Week 1	Week 2	Week 3	Week 4	Week 5	Week 6
Blend and Segment Phonemes	Blend and Segment Phonemes	Distinguish Long/Short Sounds	Distinguish Long/Short Sounds	Distinguish Long/Short Sounds	Distinguish Long/Short Sounds
Digraphs *sh, th* Vowel Sound in *ball*	Long *a* (CVCe) *c*/s/ and *g*/j/	Long *i* (CVCe) Digraphs *wh, ch, tch, ph*	Long *o* (CVCe) Contractions *n't, 'm, 'll*	Long *u*, long *e* (CVCe) Inflected Endings -*ed*	Long *e: e, ee* Syllables VCCV
catch, good, no, put, want, said	*be, could, horse, old, paper, of*	*live, out, people, who, work*	*down, inside, now, there, together*	*around, find, food, grow, under, water*	*also, family, new, other, some, their*
Sequence	Cause and Effect	Author's Purpose	Sequence	Author's Purpose	Compare and Contrast
Predict and Set Purpose	Monitor and Clarify	Important Ideas	Inferring	Background Knowledge	Questioning
Accuracy/ Rate	Phrasing	Phrasing	Accuracy/ Rate	Phrasing	Accuracy/ Rate

	Week 3	Week 4	Week 5	Week 6
	Substitute Phonemes	Substitute Phonemes	Segment Syllables	Blend and Segment
	Long *o: oa, ow* Three-letter Blends	Long *i: ie, igh kn*/n/ and *wr*/r/	Compound Words Vowels *ew, ue, ui*	Suffixes -*ly*, -*ful* Vowels in *moon*
	found, once, wild, mouth, took	*above, laugh, touch, eight, moon*	*picture, room, thought, remember, stood*	*told, because, across, only, shoes, dance, opened*
	Facts and Details	Facts and Details	Theme	Cause and Effect
	Important Ideas	Questioning	Story Structure	Predict and Set Purpose
	Expression/ Intonation	Accuracy/ Rate/ Expression	Phrasing	Expression/ Intonation

UNIT 5

Week 1	Week 2	Week 3	Week 4	Week 5	Week 6
Delete Initial Phonemes	Blend and Segment Phonemes	Add Final Phonemes	Substitute Final Phonemes	Blend and Segment Phonemes	Delete Phonemes
Diphthongs *ow, ou* Syllables C + *le*	Vowel Patterns *ow, ou* Syllables V/CV, VC/V	Vowels in *foot* Inflected Endings	Diphthongs *oi, oy* Suffixes -*er*, -*or*	Syllable Patterns	Prefixes *un*-, *re*- Long Vowels *i, o*
along, behind, eyes, never, pulling, toward	*door, loved, should, wood*	*among, another, instead, none*	*against, goes, heavy, kinds, today*	*built, early, learn, science, through*	*answered, carry, different, poor*
Character, Setting, and Plot	Draw Conclusions	Compare and Contrast	Main Idea and Details	Sequence	Theme
Monitor and Clarify	Background Knowledge	Monitor and Clarify	Summarize	Text Structure	Inferring
Accuracy/ Rate/ Expression	Accuracy/ Rate/ Expression/ Phrasing	Expression/ Intonation	Phrasing	Expression/ Intonation	Phrasing

Pacing Guide

Grade 1 — LANGUAGE ARTS

UNIT R

	Week 1	Week 2	Week 3	Week 4	Week 5	Week 6
Speaking, Listening, and Viewing	Participate in a Discussion	Share Ideas	Follow, Restate, Give Instructions	Give Instructions	Ask Questions	Retell
Research and Study Skills	Parts of a Book	Parts of a Book	Signs	Map	Calendar	Library/ Media Center
Grammar	Nouns: People, Animals, and Things	Nouns: Places	Verbs	Simple Sentences	Adjectives	Sentences
Weekly Writing	Sentences	Sentences	Sentences	Sentences	Sentences	Sentences
Writing						

UNIT 1

	Week 1	Week 2
Speaking, Listening, and Viewing	Ask Questions	Share Information and Ideas
Research and Study Skills	Parts of a Book	Media Center/ Library Resources
Grammar	Sentences	Subjects
Weekly Writing	Story/Voice	Fantasy Story/ Conventions

UNIT 3

	Week 1	Week 2	Week 3	Week 4	Week 5	Week 6
Speaking, Listening, and Viewing	Relate an Experience	Share Information and Ideas	Give Descriptions	Present a Poem	Share Information and Ideas	Give Announce-ments
Research and Study Skills	Interview	Glossary	Classify and Categorize	Diagram	Technology: My Computer	Picture Graph
Grammar	Action Verbs	Verbs That Add -s	Verbs That Do Not Add -s	Verbs for Past and for Future	Am, Is, Are, Was, and Were	Contractions with Not
Weekly Writing	Realistic Story/ Organization	Comments About a Story/Voice	Summary/ Conventions	List/ Sentences	Captions and Pictures/ Focus/Ideas	Play Scene/ Sentences
Writing	Photo Writing/Expository Article					

UNIT 4

	Week 1	Week 2
Speaking, Listening, and Viewing	Give Descriptions	Share Information and Ideas
Research and Study Skills	Interview	Chart and Table
Grammar	Adjectives	Adjectives for Colors and Shapes
Weekly Writing	Letter/ Organization	Invitation/ Word Choice

Week 3	Week 4	Week 5	Week 6
Give Introductions	Share Information and Ideas	Give Descriptions	Give Directions
Picture Dictionary	Chart	List	Notes
Predicates	Declarative Sentences	Interrogative Sentences	Exclamatory Sentences
Short Poem/ Sentences	Personal Narrative/ Voice	Realistic Story/ Organization	Brief Composition, Focus/Ideas

Keyboarding/Personal Narrative

UNIT 2

Week 1	Week 2	Week 3	Week 4	Week 5	Week 6
Relate an Experience	Share Information and Ideas	Give Announcements	Informal Conversation	Share Information and Ideas	Follow Directions
Parts of a Book	Interview	Map	Periodicals/ Newsletters	Alphabetical Order	Picture Dictionary
Nouns	Proper Nouns	Special Titles	Days, Months, and Holidays	Singular and Plural Nouns	Nouns in Sentences
Friendly Letter/ Organizations	Poster; Brief Composition/ Sentence	Explanation/ Conventions	Poem/ Organization	Description/ Voice	Expository Paragraph/ Focus/Ideas

Electronic Pen Pals/Letter

UNIT 5

Week 3	Week 4	Week 5	Week 6
Present a Poem	Purposes of Media	Purposes of Media	Purposes of Media
Bar Graph	Glossary	Technology: Using E-mail	Alphabetical Order
Adjectives for Sizes	Adjectives for What Kind	Adjectives for How Many	Adjectives That Compare
Poem/ Focus/Ideas	Realistic Story/Voice	Thank-You Note/ Conventions	Directions/ Organization

Story Starters/Realistic Story

Week 1	Week 2	Week 3	Week 4	Week 5	Week 6
Techniques in Media	Share Information and Ideas	Techniques in Media	Respond to Media	Techniques in Media	Respond to Media
Reference Sources/ Take Notes	Dictionary	Text Features	Picture Graph	Technology: Web Page	Encyclopedia
Imperative Sentences	Pronouns	Using I and Me	Pronouns	Adverbs	Prepositions and Prepositional Phrases
Animal Fantasy/ Voice	Letter/Voice	Questions/ Word Choice	Persuasive Ad/Focus/ Ideas	Autobiography/ Sentences	Poem/ Conventions

E-Newsletter/Short Report

Teaching Record Chart

This chart shows the critical comprehension skills and strategies you need to cover. Check off each one as you provide instruction.

Reading/Comprehension	DATES OF INSTRUCTION		
Confirm predictions about what will happen next in text by "reading the part that tells."			
Ask relevant questions, seek clarification, and locate facts and details about stories and other texts.			
Establish purpose for reading selected texts and monitor comprehension, making corrections and adjustments when that understanding breaks down (e.g., identifying clues, using background knowledge, generating questions, re-reading a portion aloud).			
Connect the meaning of a well-known story or fable to personal experiences.			
Explain the function of recurring phrases (e.g., "Once upon a time" or "They lived happily ever after") in traditional folk and fairy tales.			
Respond to and use rhythm, rhyme, and alliteration in poetry.			
Describe the plot (problem and solution) and retell a story's beginning, middle, and end with attention to the sequence of events.			
Describe characters in a story and the reasons for their actions and feelings.			
Determine whether a story is true or a fantasy and explain why.			
Recognize sensory details in literary text.			

Tired of using slips of paper or stickies to make sure you teach everything you need to? Need an easier way to keep track of what you have taught, and what you still need to cover? **Customize Literacy** can help. 🙶

Reading/Comprehension	DATES OF INSTRUCTION		
Read independently for a sustained period of time.			
Identify the topic and explain the author's purpose in writing about the text.			
Restate the main idea, heard or read.			
Identify important facts or details in text, heard or read.			
Retell the order of events in a text by referring to the words and/or illustrations.			
Use text features (e.g., title, table of contents, illustrations) to locate specific information in text.			
Follow written multi-step directions with picture cues to assist with understanding.			
Explain the meaning of specific signs and symbols (e.g., map features).			
Establish purposes for reading selected texts based upon desired outcome to enhance comprehension.			
Ask literal questions of text.			
Monitor and adjust comprehension (e.g., using background knowledge, creating sensory images, re-reading a portion aloud).			
Make inferences about text using textual evidence to support understanding.			
Retell or act out important events in stories in logical order.			
Make connections to own experiences, to ideas in other texts, and to the larger community and discuss textual evidence.			

Student Edition 1.3, p. EI•7

Objectives:
- Identify what happens first, next, and last in a story.
- Identify sequence in nonfiction selections.

Sequence

What is it? **Sequence** means the order in which things happen. Sequence can also mean the steps we follow to make or do something. Identifying a sequence of events gives children a sense of story and helps them understand events and time relationships that are essential to comprehension. In Grade 1, children identify what happens first, next, and last in a story, and identify time relationships in nonfiction. Children understand that some words can signal sequence.

How Good Readers Use the Skill Children experience time relationships every day. Teachers can build on these experiences and help children connect them to reading. At first, children understand sequence as the order of what happens first, next, and last in a selection. Children can then move on to use clue words to decipher more complicated sequence relationships, such as flashbacks and simultaneous events.

Texts for Teaching

Student Edition
- *A Big Fish for Max,* 1.2, pages 20–33
- *The Big Circle,* 1.2, pages 112–127
- *A Place to Play,* 1.3, pages 20–33
- *Alexander Graham Bell: A Great Inventor,* 1.5, pages 174–193

Leveled Readers
- See pages 24–29 for a list of Leveled Readers.

Teach the Skill

Use the **Envision It!** lesson on 1.3, page EI•7 to visually review sequence.

Remind children that:
- events in a story happen in an order.
- words such as *first, then,* and *last* can help them figure out order.

Practice

Write the following sentences in random order on the board and have children put them in sequential order. Emphasize the words *first, next,* and *finally* to help children.

First the girl set out the spoons.
Next she put the soup in bowls.
Finally she ate dinner.

If... children have difficulty identifying sequence relationships, **then...** model using the words *first, next,* and *finally* with a familiar series of steps first in order and then out of order.

Apply

After children read a story, have them retell the events using the words *first, next,* and *finally.*

Writing

Children can write two things they do before school each day.

 Go Digital!   Leveled Reader Database   Envision It! Animations

Customize Literacy

Mini-Lesson 2

Teach the Skill
Use the **Envision It!** lesson on 1.3, page EI•7 to visually review sequence.

Remind children that:
- events in a story happen in an order.
- words such as *first, then,* and *last* can help figure out order.

Practice
Read aloud the following passage and have children listen for the events that happen in order. Ask them what happens first, next, and last.

Three pigs built three houses. First the wolf blew down the house made of straw. Then the wolf blew down the house made of sticks. Last the wolf tried to blow down the house made of bricks. He couldn't blow that house down. The pigs were safe.

If... children have difficulty identifying sequence relationships, **then...** chunk the text and have them point out clue words that identify events in each chunk.

Apply
As children read the assigned text, have them look for words that help them figure out order.

Writing
Children can write what happened first, next, and last in a familiar story.

Mini-Lesson 3

Teach the Skill
Use the **Envision It!** lesson on 1.3, page EI•7 to visually review sequence.

Remind children that:
- events in a story happen in an order.
- words such as *first, next,* and *last* can help children figure out order.

Practice
Explain that often things must be done in a certain order. Ask: What would I put on first, socks or shoes? Explain that putting on socks before shoes makes sense. Give a familiar task to groups of children, such as making a sandwich or planting a seed. The groups can work together to write what to do first, next, and last. Assist as necessary. Have the groups read the steps in order for the class.

If... children have difficulty identifying sequence relationships, **then...** provide a graphic organizer for additional practice.

Apply
As children read the assigned text, have them complete a sequence graphic organizer to order events in the selection.

Writing
Children can write how to do something familiar, such as play a game, in order.

Instruction

Compare and Contrast

Student Edition 1.3, p. EI•3

Compare and Contrast

What is it? **Comparing** and **contrasting** means finding likenesses and/or differences between two or more people, places, things, or ideas. At Grade 1, children use the terms *alike* and *different*. They compare and contrast stories, characters in stories, their experiences, objects, and so on. They use graphic organizers to show their ideas.

How Good Readers Use the Skill Comparing and contrasting are basic reasoning devices. We try to understand an unknown using the known—i.e., a likeness or difference. At first, students notice likenesses and differences. Older students begin to use clue words as signals for comparisons. They learn about similes and metaphors, which are literary comparisons. Students also learn that authors sometimes use comparison and contrast as a way to organize their writing.

Texts for Teaching

Student Edition
- *Honey Bees,* 1.2, pages 178–193
- *Ruby in Her Own Time,* 1.3, pages 52–73
- *Dot & Jabber and the Great Acorn Mystery,* 1.5, pages 98–119

Leveled Readers
- See pages 24–29 for a list of Leveled Readers.

Mini-Lesson 1

Teach the Skill

Use the **Envision It!** lesson on 1.3, page EI•3 to visually review compare and contrast.

Remind children that:
- *alike* means "the same or almost the same" and *different* means "not the same."
- they can makes groups by putting things that are alike together.

Practice

Show two objects to children, such as a pencil and a crayon. Ask: How are these things alike? How are these things different? Are there some things that are the same about these objects? Draw a Venn diagram (two overlapping circles) on the board with these labels: *Pencil, Both, Crayon.* Work together to list qualities that are unique to each and then list the qualities the two objects share.

If... students have difficulty identifying likenesses and differences of two objects,

then... give answer choices and have the student choose.

Apply

As children read on their own, have them think about how places and people they read about are alike and different.

Writing

Children can write a sentence about how the objects are the same or different.

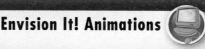

Mini-Lesson 2

Teach the Skill
Use the **Envision It!** lesson on 1.3, page EI•3 to visually review compare and contrast.

Remind children that:
- **alike** means "the same or almost the same" and **different** means "not the same."
- they can make groups by putting things that are alike together.
- characters, settings, and plots can be compared.

Practice
Model making comparisons in a story. Read a familiar story aloud. Then make a feature chart about two things in the story, such as two characters. Think aloud as you answer these questions: How are these two characters alike? How are they different? For example: These characters are the same age. They go to the same school. These are two ways these characters are alike. One character loves to build things. The other loves to play computer games. These are ways they are different. On the feature list, write ways the two are alike and different. Children work in pairs to create a feature list about themselves.
If... students have difficulty identifying likenesses,
then... have them select from choices.

Apply
As children read on their own, have them think about how places and people they read about are alike and different.

Writing
Have children write finish these sentences: *[name] and I are alike because we both _____ .*

Mini-Lesson 3

Teach the Skill
Use the **Envision It!** lesson on 1.3, page EI•3 to visually review compare and contrast.

Remind children that:
- **alike** means "the same or almost the same" and **different** means "not the same."
- they can make groups by putting things that are alike together.
- information in an article can be compared.

Practice
Use a familiar piece of nonfiction to show children that there are things to compare in informational selections too. Identify two or more things or ideas in the selection, such as how frogs and toads differ or how people lived in the past. Reread the selection together to locate likenesses and differences. Bring the group back together and record their ideas. For example, people in the past walked many places, today we drive or fly places. As children work, tell them that looking closely at what we read helps us understand it better.
If... children have difficulty finding likenesses,
then... model finding likenesses and have the children find another.

Apply
As children read on their own, have them think about how places and people they read about are alike and different.

Writing
Children can write sentences about how school and home are the same and different.

Envision It! Visual Skills Handbook
Fact and Opinion

Fact = It is raining.
Opinion = Rainy days are fun!

Fact and Opinion

Objectives:
- Define *fact* and *opinion*.
- Use clue words to identify statements as fact or opinion.
- Decide whether or not a fact can be checked.

What is it? A **statement of fact** tells something that can be proved true or false. A **statement of opinion** tells a person's ideas or feelings and cannot be proved true or false. At Grade 1, children are identifying statements of fact and opinion. They are determining whether or not a statement of fact can be checked.

Student Edition 1.3, pp. EI•4–EI•5

How Good Readers Use the Skill Children meet statements of facts and opinions throughout their day. We want to teach them how to distinguish the two and understand ways to check the veracity of factual statements and be able to judge statements of opinion thoughtfully. Evaluating statements of fact and statements of opinion boosts children's comprehension and helps them avoid being misled.

Texts for Teaching

Student Edition
- *The Class Pet,* 1.3, pages 92–105
- *I'm a Caterpillar,* 1.3, pages 158–173

Leveled Readers
- See pages 24–29 for a list of Leveled Readers.

Mini-Lesson 1

Teach the Skill
Use the **Envision It!** lesson on 1.3, pages EI•4–EI•5 to visually review fact and opinion with children.

Remind children that:
- a statement of **fact** tells something that can be proved true or false.
- a statement of **opinion** tells a person's ideas or feelings and cannot be proved true or false.

Practice
Write the following on the board and read them with children.
The Story of Ferdinand *was written by Munro Leaf.*
Everybody should read The Story of Ferdinand.
Ask: Which statement is a fact? How can you tell? Which is a statement of an opinion?
Talk with children about how a fact is a statement that can be proved to be true. (They could look at an actual book or they could check the Internet or ask a librarian.) Point out the word *should* in the second sentence and explain that opinions often contain judgment words such as *should, I think,* and *best.*
If... children have difficulty distinguishing statements of fact,
then... ask: *Could you check this information out? How?*

Apply
As children read, have them be alert for statements of fact and opinion.

Writing
Children can write an opinion about a favorite book.

Teach the Skill

Use the **Envision It!** lesson on 1.3, pages EI•4–EI•5 to visually review fact and opinion with children.

Remind children that:

- a statement of **fact** tells something that can be proved true or false.
- a statement of **opinion** tells a person's ideas or feelings and cannot be proved true or false.
- clue words and phrases, such as *I think, I believe, cute, best*, and so on, can signal an opinion.

Practice

Give children a familiar nonfiction selection and have partners read it together to identify statements of fact and opinion. Have them complete a chart, listing the statements they identify. Help children suggest how statements of fact can be checked.

Statement	Fact?	Opinion?
The temperature outside is 68°.	Yes. We could look at a thermometer.	No. We can prove it.

If... children have difficulty distinguishing opinions,
then... ask: *Can you prove this is the [cutest] or is that just what someone thinks?*

Apply

As children read, have them look for statements of fact and opinion.

Writing

Children can look at a photograph and write a statement of fact about it.

Instruction

Teach the Skill

Use the **Envision It!** lesson on 1.3, pages EI•4–EI•5 to visually review fact and opinion with children.

Remind children that:

- a statement of **fact** tells something that can be proved true or false.
- a statement of **opinion** tells a person's ideas or feelings and cannot be proved true or false.
- clue words and phrases, such as *best, in my opinion, I believe, I think,* and so on can signal an opinion.

Practice

Remind children that opinions often have judgment words or phrases: *should, must, best, I think, in my opinion.* Write these sentences on the board and talk about why they are opinions. *I think "Babe" is the best movie ever. Everyone must see it!* Let partners work together to write a paragraph that includes both statements of fact and opinion. Give pairs a topic—such as pets or sports—or let them choose one of their own. Have children complete a chart like the one for Mini-Lesson 2 to show their facts and opinions. Then have children share their paragraphs.

If... children have difficulty writing statements of fact and opinion,
then... give them a topic and sentence starters to complete, such as *The weather today is _____. I think this kind of weather _____.*

Apply

As children read, have them look for statements of fact and think about how they would check them out.

Writing

Children can write a few sentences that are facts and then add an opinion, underlining it.

Student Edition 1.3, p. EI•21

Objectives:
- Use personal experiences and details from the text to visualize.
- Create mental images to better comprehend what is read.

Texts for Teaching

Student Edition
- *The Big Blue Ox,* 1.1, pages 74–83
- *Frog and Toad Together: The Garden,* 1.3, pages 126–141
- *Cinderella,* 1.4, pages 60–77

Leveled Readers
- See pages 24–29 for a list of Leveled Readers.

Mini-Lesson

Understand the Strategy

Visualizing means creating pictures in the mind. These pictures are created by combining what readers already know with descriptive words in a text. Visualizing involves all the senses, not just sight.

Teach

Use the **Envision It!** lesson on 1.3, page EI•21 to introduce visualizing.

Tell children that authors use descriptive language to help us "place" events in a story, to understand characters, to picture events, and so on. We call this visualizing, and it means to see pictures in your mind. Use a piece of text that describes an event to model making pictures in your mind. Think aloud as you do. The chart below has some examples based on a passage about children in Iceland who rescue baby pufflings.

Details from Text	What I Visualize
• Thousands of puffins nest on rocky coasts of Iceland.	• I hear a lot of squawking. I think the ground is slippery with bird droppings.
• The baby birds need to get to the sea, but city lights confuse them. Some die.	• I feel the dampness of the sea. I can feel the rocky ground.
• Children come out at night to help the pufflings get to the water.	• I see little birds running crazily.
	• I see shadows made by moonlight.

Practice

Supply children with a text and have them work in pairs to visualize. Then bring the groups together and talk about the pictures they made in their minds as they read. Make sure children identify details from text that helped them visualize.

If... children have difficulty visualizing,

then... model, describing the pictures you form as you read.

Apply

Remind children to make pictures as they read, using what they already know and the details the author puts in the text.

Anchor Chart

Anchor charts help students make their thinking visible and permanent. With an anchor chart, the group can clarify their thinking about how to use a strategy. Display anchor charts so readers can use them as they read. Here is a sample chart for visualize.

Visualizing

1. Preview. Look at the pictures. Is this a story? Is it informational?

2. Read a little to see what it is all about.

3. Read to see how the author tells about places and people. Close your eyes and think. What pictures do you see?

4. Look for details. How do things smell? taste? feel? sound? look?

5. Make a chart or a web to write down details that help you make a picture.

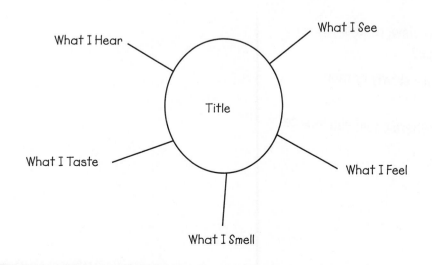

What I Hear

What I See

Title

What I Taste

What I Feel

What I Smell

Anchor Chart

Using Multiple Strategies

Good readers use multiple strategies as they read. You can encourage children to read strategically through good classroom questioning. Use questions such as these to help children apply strategies during reading.

Questioning

- Who or what is this question about?
- Where can you look to find the answer to this question?
- What do you want to know about _____?
- What questions to do you have about the _____ in this selection? Use the words *who, what, when, where, why,* and *how* to ask your questions.
- Do you have any questions after reading?

Graphic Organizers

- What kind of graphic organizer could you use to help you keep track of the information in this selection?

Monitor and Clarify

- Does the story or article make sense?
- What don't you understand about what you read?
- Do you need to reread, review, read on, or check a reference source?
- Do you need to read more slowly or more quickly?
- What is a _____? Where could you look to find out?

Predict and Set Purpose

- What do you think this story or article will be about? Why do you think as you do?
- What do you think you will learn from this selection?
- Do the text features help you predict what will happen?
- Based on what has happened so far, what do you think will happen next?
- Is this what you thought would happen?
- How does _____ change what you thought would happen?

Preview

- What do the photographs, illustrations, or graphic sources tell about the selection?
- What do you want to find out? What do you want to learn?

Background Knowledge

- What do you already know about _____?
- Have you read stories or articles by this author before?
- How is this selection like others that you have read?
- What does this remind you of?
- How does your background knowledge help you understand _____?
- Did the text match what you already knew? What new information did you learn?

Story Structure

- Who are the characters in this story? What is the setting?
- What is the problem in this story? How does the problem get solved?
- What is the point of this story?

Summarize

- What two or three important ideas have you read so far?
- How do the text features relate to the important ideas?
- Is there a graphic organizer that can help you organize the information before you summarize?

Text Structure

- How has the author organized the writing?
- What clues tell you that the text is structured _____?

Visualize

- When you read this, what do you picture in your mind?
- What do you hear, see, or smell?
- What do you think _____ looks like? Why do you think as you do?

> ❝ You know explicit strategy instruction is a must! But you also want students to use strategies every time they read. **Customize Literacy** shows you how to help them do this. ❞

Glossary of Literacy Terms

This glossary lists academic language terms that are related to literacy.
They are provided for your information and professional use.

A

alliteration	the repetition of a consonant sound in a group of words, especially in poetry
allusion	a word or phrase that refers to something else the reader already knows from history, experience, or reading
animal fantasy	a story about animals that talk and act like people
answer questions	a reading strategy in which readers use the text and prior knowledge to answer questions about what they are reading
antonym	a word that means the opposite of another word
ask questions	a reading strategy in which readers ask themselves questions about the text to help make sense of what they read
author's point of view	the author's opinion on the subject he or she is writing about
author's purpose	the reason the author wrote the text
autobiography	the story of a real person's life written by that person

B

background knowledge	the information and experience that a reader brings to a text
biography	the story of a real person's life written by another person

C

cause	why something happens
character	a person, an animal, or a personified object in a story
chronological order	events in a selection, presented in the order in which they occurred
classify and categorize	put things, such as pictures or words, into groups
climax	the point in a story at which conflict is confronted
compare	tell how things are the same
comprehension	understanding of text being read—the ultimate goal of reading
comprehension strategy	a conscious plan used by a reader to gain understanding of text Comprehension strategies may be used before, during, or after reading.
conclusion	a decision or opinion arrived at after thinking about facts and details and using prior knowledge
conflict	the problem or struggle in a story
context clue	the words, phrases, or sentences near an unknown word that give the reader clues to the word's meaning
contrast	tell how things are different

D

details	small pieces of information
dialect	form of a language spoken in a certain region or by a certain group of people that differs from the standard form of that language
dialogue	written conversation
diary	a day-to-day record of one's activities and thoughts
draw conclusions	arrive at decisions or opinions after thinking about facts and details and using prior knowledge

E

effect	what happens as the result of a cause
etymology	an explanation of the origin and history of a word and its meaning
exaggeration	a statement that makes something seem larger or greater than it actually is
expository text	text that contains facts and information, also called *informational text*

F

fable	a story, usually with animal characters, that is written to teach a moral, or lesson
fact	piece of information that can be proved to be true
fairy tale	a folk story with magical characters and events
fantasy	a story that could not really happen
fiction	writing that tells about imaginary people, things, and events
figurative language	the use of language that gives words a meaning beyond their usual definitions in order to add beauty or force
flashback	an interruption in the sequence of events of a narrative to include an event that happened earlier
folk tale	a story that has been passed down by word of mouth
foreshadowing	the use of hints or clues about what will happen later in a story

G

generalize	make a broad statement or rule after examining particular facts
graphic organizer	a drawing, chart, or web that illustrates concepts or shows how ideas relate to each other. Readers use graphic organizers to help them keep track of and understand important information and ideas as they read. Story maps, word webs, Venn diagrams, and KWL charts are graphic organizers.
graphic source	a chart, diagram, or map within a text that adds to readers' understanding of the text

H

historical fiction	realistic fiction that takes place in the past. It is an imaginary story based on historical events and characters.
humor	writing or speech that has a funny or amusing quality
hyperbole	an exaggerated statement not meant to be taken literally, such as *I'm so hungry I could eat a horse.*

I

idiom	a phrase whose meaning differs from the ordinary meaning of the words. *A stone's throw* is an idiom meaning "a short distance."
imagery	the use of language to create beautiful or forceful pictures in the reader's mind
inference	conclusion reached on the basis of evidence and reasoning
inform	give knowledge, facts, or news to someone
informational text	writing that contains facts and information, also called *expository text*
interview	a face-to-face conversation in which someone responds to questions
irony	a way of speaking or writing in which the ordinary meaning of the words is the opposite of what the speaker or writer is thinking; a contrast between what is expected and what actually happens

J

jargon	the language of a special group or profession

L

legend	a story coming down from the past about the great deeds of a hero. Although a legend may be based on historical people and events, it is not regarded as historically true.
literary elements	the characters, setting, plot, and theme of a narrative text

M

main idea	the big idea that tells what a paragraph or a selection is mainly about; the most important idea of a text
metacognition	an awareness of one's own thinking processes and the ability to monitor and direct them to a desired goal. Good readers use metacognition to monitor their reading and adjust their reading strategies.
metaphor	a comparison that does not use *like* or *as,* such as *a heart of stone*
meter	the pattern of beats or accents in poetry

monitor and clarify   a comprehension strategy by which readers actively think about understanding their reading and know when they understand and when they do not. Readers use appropriate strategies to make sense of difficult words, ideas, or passages.

mood   the atmosphere or feeling of a written work

moral   the lesson or teaching of a fable or story

motive   the reason a character in a narrative does or says something

mystery   a story about mysterious events that are not explained until the end, so as to keep the reader in suspense

myth   a story that attempts to explain something in nature

M

narrative   a story, made up or true, that someone tells or narrates

narrator   the character in a selection who tells the story

nonfiction   writing that tells about real things, real people, and real events

N

onomatopoeia   the use of words that sound like their meanings, such as *buzz* and *hum*

opinion   someone's judgment, belief, or way of thinking

oral vocabulary   the words needed for speaking and listening

outcome   the resolution of the conflict in a story

O

paraphrase   retell the meaning of a passage in one's own words

personification   a figure of speech in which human traits or actions are given to animals or inanimate objects, as in *The sunbeam danced on the waves.*

persuade   convince someone to do or to believe something

photo essay   a collection of photographs on one theme, accompanied by text

play   a story that is written to be acted out for an audience

plot   a series of related events at the beginning, middle, and end of a story; the action of a story

poem   an expressive, imaginative piece of writing often arranged in lines having rhythm and rhyme. In a poem, the patterns made by the sounds of the words have special importance.

pourquoi tale   a type of folk story that explains why things in nature came to be. *Pourquoi* is a French word meaning "why."

P

P

predict   tell what a selection might be about or what might happen in a text. Readers use text features and information to predict. They confirm or revise their predictions as they read.

preview   look over a text before reading it

prior knowledge   the information and experience that a reader brings to a text. Readers use prior knowledge to help them understand what they read.

prop   an item, such as an object, picture, or chart, used in a performance or presentation

R

reading vocabulary   the words we recognize or use in print

realistic fiction   a story about imaginary people and events that could happen in real life

repetition   the repeated use of some aspect of language

resolution   the point in a story where the conflict is resolved

rhyme   to end in the same sound(s)

rhythm   a pattern of strong beats in speech or writing, especially poetry

rising action   the buildup of conflicts and complications in a story

S

science fiction   a story based on science that often tells what life in the future might be like

semantic map   a graphic organizer, often a web, used to display words or concepts that are meaningfully related

sensory language   the use of words that help the reader understand how things look, sound, smell, taste, or feel

sequence   the order of events in a selection or the order of the steps in which something is completed

sequence words   clue words such as *first, next, then,* and *finally* that signal the order of events in a selection

setting   where and when a story takes place

simile   a comparison that uses *like* or *as,* as in *as busy as a bee*

speech   a public talk to a group of people made for a specific purpose

stanza   a group of lines in a poem

steps in a process   the order of the steps in which something is completed

story map	a graphic organizer used to record the literary elements and the sequence of events in a narrative text
story structure	how the characters, setting, and events of a story are organized into a plot
summarize	give the most important ideas of what was read. Readers summarize important information in the selection to keep track of what they are reading.
supporting detail	piece of information that tells about the main idea
symbolism	the use of one thing to suggest something else; often the use of something concrete to stand for an abstract idea

S

tall tale	a humorous story that uses exaggeration to describe impossible happenings
text structure	the organization of a piece of nonfiction writing. Text structures of informational text include cause/effect, chronological, compare/contrast, description, problem/solution, proposition/support, and ask/answer questions.
theme	the big idea or author's message in a story
think aloud	an instructional strategy in which a teacher verbalizes his or her thinking to model the process of comprehension or the application of a skill
tone	author's attitude toward the subject or toward the reader
topic	the subject of a discussion, conversation, or piece of text

T

Instruction

visualize	picture in one's mind what is happening in the text. Visualizing helps readers imagine the things they read about.

V

Leveled Readers Skills Chart

Scott Foresman Reading Street provides more than six hundred leveled readers. Each one is designed to:

- Practice critical skills and strategies
- Build fluency
- Build vocabulary and concepts
- Develop a lifelong love of reading

Grade 1

Title	Level*	DRA Level	Genre	Comprehension Strategy
Bix the Dog	A	1	Realistic Fiction	Summarize
Time for Dinner	B	2	Realistic Fiction	Important Ideas
Sam	B	2	Realistic Fiction	Monitor and Clarify
Mack and Zack	B	2	Realistic Fiction	Monitor and Clarify
The Sick Pets	B	2	Realistic Fiction	Summarize
On the Farm	B	2	Realistic Fiction	Visualize
At Your Vet	B	2	Realistic Fiction	Story Structure
Fun in the Sun	B	2	Expository Nonfiction	Text Structure
We Are a Family	B	2	Nonfiction	Predict and Set Purpose
Where They Live	C	3	Realistic Fiction	Visualize
Which Fox?	C	3	Realistic Fiction	Important Ideas
Which Animals Will We See?	C	3	Realistic Fiction	Text Structure
Let's Go to the Zoo	C	3	Nonfiction	Predict and Set Purpose
A Play	C	3	Realistic Fiction	Monitor and Clarify
A Class	C	3	Nonfiction	Monitor and Clarify
Here in My Neighborhood	C	3	Nonfiction	Important Ideas
Look at My Neighborhood	C	3	Realistic Fiction	Important Ideas
Look at Dinosaurs	C	3	Expository Nonfiction	Inferring
Around the Forest	C	3	Nonfiction	Background Knowledge
Learn About Worker Bees	C	3	Expository Nonfiction	Questioning
In My Room	C	3	Nonfiction	Summarize
Hank's Song	C	3	Fantasy	Inferring
Gus the Pup	C	3	Realistic Fiction	Monitor and Clarify
What Animals Can You See?	D	4	Expository Nonfiction	Text Structure
The Dinosaur Herds	D	4	Expository Nonfiction	Inferring
People Help the Forest	D	4	Expository Nonfiction	Background Knowledge
Honey	D	4	Nonfiction	Questioning
Let's Build a Park!	D	4	Fiction	Summarize
Mac Can Do It!	D	4	Fantasy	Inferring
The Seasons Change	D	4	Nonfiction	Visualize

* Suggested Guided Reading Level. Use your knowledge of students' abilities to adjust levels as needed.

The chart here and on the next few pages lists titles of leveled readers appropriate for students in Grade 1. Use the chart to find titles that meet your students' interest and instructional needs. The books in this list were leveled using the criteria suggested in *Matching Books to Readers: Using Leveled Books in Guided Reading, Grades K–3* by Irene C. Fountas and Gay Su Pinnell. For more on leveling, see the *Reading Street Leveled Readers Leveling Guide*.

Target Comprehension Skill	Additional Comprehension Instruction	Vocabulary
Plot	Sequence	High-Frequency Words
Main Idea and Details	Compare and Contrast	High-Frequency Words
Character and Setting	Draw Conclusions	High-Frequency Words
Character and Setting	Main Idea and Details	High-Frequency Words
Plot	Draw Conclusions	High-Frequency Words
Character and Setting	Plot	High-Frequency Words
Main Idea and Details	Theme	High-Frequency Words
Cause and Effect	Author's Purpose	High-Frequency Words
Sequence	Draw Conclusions	High-Frequency Words
Character and Setting	Theme and Plot	High-Frequency Words
Main Idea and Details	Compare and Contrast	High-Frequency Words
Cause and Effect	Setting and Plot	High-Frequency Words
Sequence	Compare and Contrast	High-Frequency Words
Cause and Effect	Main Idea and Details	High-Frequency Words
Cause and Effect	Author's Purpose	High-Frequency Words
Author's Purpose	Draw Conclusions	High-Frequency Words
Author's Purpose	Compare and Contrast	High-Frequency Words
Sequence	Cause and Effect	High-Frequency Words
Author's Purpose	Cause and Effect	High-Frequency Words
Compare and Contrast	Sequence	High-Frequency Words
Sequence	Author's Purpose	High-Frequency Words
Compare and Contrast	Realism and Fantasy	High-Frequency Words
Fact and Opinion	Cause and Effect	High-Frequency Words
Main Idea and Details	Compare and Contrast	High-Frequency Words
Sequence	Draw Conclusions	High-Frequency Words
Author's Purpose	Cause and Effect	High-Frequency Words
Compare and Contrast	Draw Conclusions	High-Frequency Words
Sequence	Author's Purpose	High-Frequency Words
Compare and Contrast	Realism and Fantasy	High-Frequency Words
Author's Purpose	Draw Conclusions	High-Frequency Words

Leveled Readers Skills Chart *Continued*

	Title	Level*	DRA Level	Genre	Comprehension Strategy
Grade 1	Animals Change and Grow	D	4	Nonfiction	Text Structure
	Ready for Winter?	D	4	Expository Nonfiction	Background Knowledge
	A Party for Pedro	D	4	Realistic Fiction	Monitor and Clarify
	Space Star	D	4	Realistic Fiction	Visualize
	Our Leaders	D	4	Nonfiction	Important Ideas
	Grandma's Farm	D	4	Realistic Fiction	Questioning
	A New Baby Brother	D	4	Realistic Fiction	Story Structure
	My Babysitter	D	4	Narrative Nonfiction	Predict and Set Purpose
	What Brown Saw	D	4	Animal Fantasy	Monitor and Clarify
	Fly Away Owl!	D	4	Realistic Fiction	Background Knowledge
	What a Detective Does	D	4	Realistic Fiction	Monitor and Clarify
	The Inclined Plane	D	4	Expository Nonfiction	Summarize
	Using the Telephone	D	4	Expository Nonfiction	Text Structure
	A Garden for All	D	4	Nonfiction	Inferring
	Big Wishes and Her Baby	E	6–8	Realistic Fiction	Monitor and Clarify
	Plans Change	E	6–8	Realistic Fiction	Visualize
	Let's Visit a Butterfly Greenhouse	E	6–8	Nonfiction	Text Structure
	Seasons Come and Go	E	6–8	Expository Nonfiction	Background Knowledge
	Special Days, Special Food	E	6–8	Expository Nonfiction	Monitor and Clarify
	The Art Show	F	10	Realistic Fiction	Visualize
	Treasures of Our Country	F	10	Nonfiction	Important Ideas
	A Visit to the Ranch	F	10	Realistic Fiction	Questioning
	My Little Brother Drew	F	10	Realistic Fiction	Story Structure
	The Story of the Kids Care Club	F	10	Expository Nonfiction	Predict and Set Purpose
	Squirrel and Bear	G	12	Animal Fantasy	Monitor and Clarify
	Puppy Raiser	G	12	Expository Nonfiction	Background Knowledge
	A Mighty Oak Tree	G	12	Expository Nonfiction	Monitor and Clarify
	Simple Machines at Work	G	12	Expository Nonfiction	Summarize
	Carlos Picks a Pet	H	14	Realistic Fiction	Monitor and Clarify
	That Cat Needs Help!	H	14	Realistic Fiction	Summarize

* Suggested Guided Reading Level. Use your knowledge of students' abilities to adjust levels as needed.

You know the theory behind leveled books: they let you match books with the interest and instructional levels of your students. You can find the right reader for every student with this chart. 💬

Target Comprehension Skill	Additional Comprehension Instruction	Vocabulary
Fact and Opinion	Sequence	High-Frequency Words
Draw Conclusions	Sequence	High-Frequency Words
Draw Conclusions	Author's Purpose	High-Frequency Words
Theme	Realism and Fantasy	High-Frequency Words
Facts and Details	Cause and Effect	High-Frequency Words
Facts and Details	Plot	High-Frequency Words
Theme	Realism and Fantasy	High-Frequency Words
Cause and Effect	Main Idea	High-Frequency Words
Character, Setting, and Plot	Realism and Fantasy	High-Frequency Words
Draw Conclusions	Cause and Effect	High-Frequency Words
Compare and Contrast	Cause and Effect	High-Frequency Words
Main Idea and Details	Cause and Effect	High-Frequency Words
Sequence	Author's Purpose	High-Frequency Words
Theme	Sequence	High-Frequency Words
Fact and Opinion	Setting	High-Frequency Words
Author's Purpose	Setting	High-Frequency Words
Fact and Opinion	Author's Purpose	High-Frequency Words
Draw Conclusions	Compare and Contrast	High-Frequency Words
Draw Conclusions	Author's Purpose	High-Frequency Words
Theme	Plot	High-Frequency Words
Facts and Details	Cause and Effect	High-Frequency Words
Facts and Details	Compare and Contrast	High-Frequency Words
Theme	Realism and Fantasy	High-Frequency Words
Cause and Effect	Author's Purpose	High-Frequency Words
Character, Setting and Plot	Realism and Fantasy	High-Frequency Words
Draw Conclusions	Main Idea	High-Frequency Words
Compare and Contrast	Draw Conclusions	High-Frequency Words
Main Idea and Details	Compare and Contrast	High-Frequency Words
Character and Setting	Compare and Contrast	Amazing Words
Plot	Sequence	Amazing Words

Matching Books & Readers

Leveled Readers Skills Chart Continued

Grade 1

Title	Level*	DRA Level	Genre	Comprehension Strategy
Loni's Town	H	14	Realistic Fiction	Visualize
Baby Animals in the Rain Forest	H	14	Expository Nonfiction	Important Ideas
Cary and Wildlife Shelter	H	14	Realistic Fiction	Story Structure
Around the World	H	14	Narrative Nonfiction	Text Structure
The Communication Story	H	14	Expository Nonfiction	Text Structure
Marla's Good Idea	H	14	Realistic Fiction	Inferring
Rules at School	I	16	Animal Fantasy	Predict and Set Purpose
School: Then and Now	I	16	Expository Nonfiction	Monitor and Clarify
Mom the Mayor	I	16	Realistic Fiction	Important Ideas
The Dinosaur Detectives	I	16	Expository Nonfiction	Inferring
All About Food Chains	I	16	Expository Nonfiction	Background Knowledge
Bees and Beekeepers	I	16	Expository Nonfiction	Questioning
A New Library	I	16	Narrative Nonfiction	Summarize
Paul's Bed	J	18	Traditional Tales	Inferring
Britton Finds a Kitten	J	18	Realistic Fiction	Monitor and Clarify
All About the Weather	J	18	Expository Nonfiction	Visualize
Learn About Butterflies	J	18	Expository Nonfiction	Text Structure
Monarchs Migrate South	J	18	Narrative Nonfiction	Background Knowledge
Cascarones Are for Fun	J	18	Expository Nonfiction	Monitor and Clarify
Jamie's Jumble of Junk	J	18	Realistic Fiction	Visualize
America's Home	K	20	Nonfiction	Important Ideas
Go West!	K	20	Legend	Questioning
Double Trouble Twins	K	20	Realistic Fiction	Story Structure
What Makes Buildings Special?	K	20	Expository Nonfiction	Predict and Set Purpose
Grasshopper and Ant	K	20	Fable	Monitor and Clarify
Ways to Be a Good Citizen	K	20	Expository Nonfiction	Background Knowledge
Great Scientists: Detectives at Work	L	24	Expository Nonfiction	Monitor and Clarify
Simple Machines in Compound Machines	L	24	Nonfiction	Summarize
Over the Years	L	24	Expository Nonfiction	Text Structure
Cody's Adventure	L	24	Realistic Fiction	Inferring

* Suggested Guided Reading Level. Use your knowledge of students' abilities to adjust levels as needed.

You know the theory behind leveled books: they let you match books with the interest and instructional levels of your students. You can find the right reader for every student with this chart. 99

Target Comprehension Skill	Additional Comprehension Instruction	Vocabulary
Character and Setting	Theme	Amazing Words
Main Idea and Details	Author's Purpose	Amazing Words
Main Idea and Details	Sequence	Amazing Words
Cause and Effect	Main Idea	Amazing Words
Sequence	Compare and Contrast	High-Frequency Words
Theme	Sequence	High-Frequency Words
Sequence	Character	Amazing Words
Cause and Effect	Draw Conclusions	Amazing Words
Author's Purpose	Cause and Effect	Amazing Words
Sequence	Draw Conclusions	Amazing Words
Author's Purpose	Cause and Effect	Amazing Words
Compare and Contrast	Main Idea	Amazing Words
Sequence	Author's Purpose	Amazing Words
Compare and Contrast	Character	Amazing Words
Fact and Opinion	Setting	Amazing Words
Author's Purpose	Plot	Amazing Words
Fact and Opinion	Cause and Effect	Amazing Words
Draw Conclusions	Author's Purpose	Amazing Words
Draw Conclusions	Sequence	Amazing Words
Theme	Character, Setting, Plot	Amazing Words
Facts and Details	Cause and Effect	Amazing Words
Facts and Details	Theme	Amazing Words
Theme	Realism and Fantasy	Amazing Words
Cause and Effect	Draw Conclusions	Amazing Words
Character, Setting and Plot	Cause and Effect	Amazing Words
Draw Conclusions	Compare and Contrast	Amazing Words
Compare and Contrast	Compare and Contrast	Amazing Words
Main Idea and Details	Cause and Effect	Amazing Words
Sequence	Draw Conclusions	Amazing Words
Theme	Sequence	Amazing Words

Matching Books & Readers

What Good Readers Do

You can use the characteristics and behaviors of good readers to help all your children read better. But what are these characteristics and behaviors? And how can you use them to foster good reading behaviors for all your children? Here are some helpful tips.

Good Readers enjoy reading! They have favorite books, authors, and genres. Good readers often have a preference about where and when they read. They talk about books and recommend their favorites.

Develop this behavior by giving children opportunities to respond in different ways to what they read. Get them talking about what they read, and why they like or dislike it.

This behavior is important because book sharing alerts you to children who are somewhat passive about reading or have limited literacy experiences. Book sharing also helps you when you select books for the class.

Good Readers read independently for longer periods of time.

Develop this behavior by taking note of the level of support children need during guided reading. Use this information to gauge independent reading time accordingly.

This behavior is important because children become better readers when they spend time reading many texts at their independent level.

Good Readers select books they can read.

Develop this behavior by providing a range of three or four texts appropriate for the child and then letting the child choose.

This behavior is important because children gain control over reading when they can choose from books they can read. This helps them become more independent in the classroom.

Good Readers use text features to help them preview and set purposes.

Develop this behavior by having children use the title and illustrations in fiction texts or the title, contents, headings, and other graphic features in nonfiction texts to make predictions about what they will be reading.

This behavior is important because previewing actually makes reading easier! Looking at features and sampling the text enables readers to predict and set expectations for reading.

❝ **Want to improve your students' performance by fostering good reading behaviors? Customize Literacy** can help. ❞

Good Readers predict and ask questions before and while they read.

Develop this behavior by asking questions. After reading a passage, ask children what they think will happen next in a fiction text. Have them ask a question they think will be answered in a nonfiction text and read on to see if it is.

This behavior is important because when children predict and ask questions as they read, they are engaged. They have a purpose for reading and a basis for monitoring their comprehension.

Good Readers read aloud at an appropriate reading rate with a high percent of accuracy.

Develop this behavior by timing children's oral reading to calculate their reading rates. You can also record children's miscues to determine a percent of accuracy. This will help identify problems.

This behavior is important because when children read fluently texts that are "just right," they find reading more enjoyable. A fluent reader is able to focus more on constructing meaning and is more likely to develop a positive attitude toward reading.

Good Readers read meaningful phrases aloud with appropriate expression.

Develop this behavior by giving children lots of opportunities to read orally. As they read, note children's phrasing, intonation, and attention to punctuation and give help as needed.

This behavior is important because reading fluently in longer, meaningful phrases supports comprehension and ease in reading longer, more complex texts.

CH-
QU-
ST-

Matching Books & Readers

Good Readers use effective strategies and sources of information to figure out unknown words.

Develop this behavior by teaching specific strategies for figuring out unknown words, such as sounding out clusters of letters, using context, reading on, and using references.

This behavior is important because when readers have a variety of strategies to use, they are more able to decode and self-correct quickly. Readers who do these things view themselves as good readers.

CH-
QU-
ST-

Good Readers construct meaning as they read and then share or demonstrate their understanding.

Develop this behavior by having children retell what they read or write a summary of what they read in their own words.

This behavior is important because the ability to retell or write a summary is essential for success in reading. It shows how well a child has constructed meaning.

Good Readers locate and use what is explicitly stated in a text.

Develop this behavior by asking questions that require children to go back into the text to find explicitly stated information.

This behavior is important because the ability to recall, locate, and use specific information stated in a text enables readers to respond to literal questions, as well as to support opinions and justify their responses.

 make connections.

Develop this behavior by asking questions to help children make connections: *What does this remind you of? Have you ever read or experienced anything like this?*

This behavior is important because making connections helps readers understand and appreciate a text. Making connections to self, the world, and other texts supports higher-level thinking.

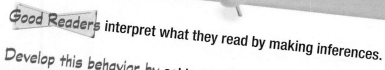 interpret what they read by making inferences.

Develop this behavior by asking questions to help children tell or write about what they think was implied in the text: *Why do you think that happened? What helped you come to that conclusion?*

This behavior is important because the ability to go beyond the literal meaning of a text enables readers to gain a deeper understanding. When children make inferences, they use background knowledge, their personal knowledge, and the text to grasp the meaning of what is implied by the author.

Good Readers determine importance and evaluate what they read.

Develop this behavior by always having children identify what they think is the most important message, event, or information in a text.

This behavior is important because readers must be able to sort out important from interesting information. The ability to establish and/or use criteria and provide support when making judgments is an important critical-thinking skill.

Good Readers support their responses using information from a text and/or their own background knowledge.

Develop this behavior by always asking children to give the reason(s) they identified an event, message, or ideas as most important.

This behavior is important because the ability to justify one's response is important for all learners. It enables others to know the basis for a decision and provides an opening for further discussion.

Matching Books & Readers

Conversation Starters

Asking Good Questions When children read interesting and thought-provoking books, they want to share! You can encourage children to think critically about what they read. Use questions such as the following to assess comprehension as well as evoke good class/group discussions.

Author's Purpose

- Who wrote this selection?

- Why did the author write this piece?

Cause and Effect

- What is one thing that happens in the story? Why did it happen?

- Is there one thing that causes several other things to happen?

Compare and Contrast

- What shows that the author is comparing people in this story?

- How are the characters and events in this story like and/or different from real people and events you know of?

Draw Conclusions

- Based on what you have read, seen, or experienced, what can you conclude about this event in the selection?

- This story seems to be a fantasy. Why might you conclude this?

- What can you decide about the characters?

Realism and Fantasy

- What clue word or words signal that this is a statement of opinion?

- What parts of this story could be make-believe? Why?

Graphic Sources

- This selection has many pictures. Which one or ones best help you understand the events or ideas in the selection? Why?

Literary Elements: Character, Setting, Plot, Theme

- Who are the main characters of the story? What are they like?

- Where does the story take place?

- What does the main character want at the beginning of the story?

- Retell the story, putting the things that happen in the right order.

- What is the big idea of the story? What lesson did you learn?

Sequence

- How is the sequence of events important in the text?

- Is the order of events important in this story? Why or why not?

Main Idea

- What is this selection mostly about?

- What details tell more about the main idea?

- What might be another good title for this selection?

Connecting Science and Social Studies

Scott Foresman Reading Street Leveled Readers are perfect for covering, supporting, or enriching science and social studies content. Using these books ensures that all children can access important concepts.

Grade 1 Leveled Readers

Science

Earth and Space Science

Nonfiction Books
- *All About the Weather*
- *The Communication Story*
- *Over the Years*
- *Ready for Winter?*
- *Using the Telephone*

Fiction Books
- *Cody's Adventure*
- *Marla's Good Idea*
- *What a Detective Does*

Life Science

Nonfiction Books
- *All About Food Chains*
- *Animals Change and Grow*
- *Around the Forest*
- *Around the World*
- *Baby Animals in the Rain Forest*
- *Bees and Beekeepers*
- *The Dinosaur Detectives*
- *The Dinosaur Herds*
- *Fun in the Sun*
- *Honey*
- *In My Room*
- *Learn About Butterflies*
- *Learn About Worker Bees*
- *Let's Go to the Zoo*
- *Let's Visit a Butterfly Greenhouse*
- *Look at Dinosaurs*
- *A Mighty Oak Tree*
- *Monarchs Migrate South*
- *People Help the Forest*
- *The Seasons Change*
- *Seasons Come and Go*
- *What Animals Can You See?*

Life Science

Fiction Books
- *Bix the Dog*
- *Britton Finds a Kitten*
- *Carlos Picks a Pet*
- *Cary and the Wildlife Shelter*
- *Mac Can Do It!*
- *Mack and Zack*
- *Plans Change*
- *Sam*
- *The Sick Pets*
- *Time for Dinner*
- *What Brown Saw*
- *Which Animals Will We See?*
- *Which Fox?*

Physical Science

Nonfiction Books
- *The Inclined Plane*
- *Simple Machines at Work*
- *Simple Machines in Compound Machines*

Grade 1 Leveled Readers

Social Studies

Citizenship

Nonfiction Books
- *A Class*
- *A Garden for All*
- *Great Scientists: Detectives at Work*
- *Here in My Neighborhood*
- *A New Library*
- *Puppy Raiser*
- *The Story of the Kids Care Club*
- *Ways to Be a Good Citizen*

Fiction Books
- *The Art Show*
- *At Your Vet*
- *Big Wishes and Her Baby*
- *Double Trouble Twins*
- *Fly Away Owl!*
- *Grasshopper and Ant*
- *Hank's Song*
- *Let's Build a Park!*
- *Look at My Neighborhood*
- *My Little Brother Drew*
- *On the Farm*
- *Paul's Bed*
- *A Play*
- *Rules at School*
- *Space Star*
- *Squirrel and Bear*
- *That Cat Needs Help!*

Culture

Nonfiction Books
- *Cascarones Are for Fun*
- *My Babysitter*
- *Special Days, Special Food*
- *We Are a Family*
- *What Makes Buildings Special?*

Fiction Books
- *Go West!*
- *Grandma's Farm*
- *Gus the Pup*
- *Jamie's Jumble of Junk*
- *A New Baby Brother*
- *A Party for Pedro*
- *A Visit to the Ranch*
- *Where They Live*

History

Nonfiction Books
- *School: Then and Now*
- *Treasures of Our Country*

Fiction Books
- *Loni's Town*

Government

Nonfiction Books
- *America's Home*
- *Our Leaders*

Fiction Books
- *Mom the Mayor*

Matching Books & Readers

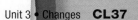

Connecting Science and Social Studies

Need more choices? Look back to Grade K.

Grade K Leveled Readers

Science

Earth and Space Science	Life Science	Physical Science
Fiction Books	**Nonfiction Books**	**Fiction Books**
• We Can Do It!	• A Winter Home	• Catch the Ball!
	• What Can You Do?	• The Best Club Hut
	• The Trip	
	• Pigs	
	• Frog's New Home	
	• A Small Trip	
	• Safe Places for Animals	
	Fiction Books	
	• A Walk in the Forest	
	• Looking for Animals	
	• Skip and Run	
	• Big Cats	
	• My Pal Fran	
	• Fun with Gram	
	• They Will Grow	
	• Sad and Glad	

Grade K Leveled Readers

Social Studies

Citizenship

Nonfiction Books
- *Fun for Us*
- *Nick Can Fix It*
- *The Box*

Fiction Books
- *Red and Blue*
- *Red and Legs*
- *Two or Three?*
- *Buds for Mom*
- *Ming on the Job*

Culture

Nonfiction Books
- *Homes*

Fiction Books
- *Max the Duck*
- *Five Bears*
- *My Walk in Antarctica*
- *The Bus Ride*
- *The Boat Ride*
- *Get On the Bus!*
- *Our Camping Trip*

History

Fiction Books
- *The Big Train*

Geography

Nonfiction Books
- *A Trip to Washington, D.C.*

Connecting Science and Social Studies

Need more choices? Look ahead to Grade 2.

Grade 2 Leveled Readers

Science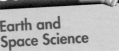

Earth and Space Science

Nonfiction Books
- *All About Astronauts*
- *An Astronaut Space Walk*
- *Desert Animals*
- *Hurricane!*
- *Deserts*
- *Look at Our Galaxy*

Fiction Books
- *Blizzard!*
- *Maggie's New Sidekick*
- *Rainbow Crow Brings Fire to Earth*
- *A Slice of Mud Pie*

Life Science

Nonfiction Books
- *Arachnid or Insect?*
- *Compost: Recycled Waste*
- *Farming Families*
- *How a Seed Grows*
- *How Can Animals Help?*
- *How Do Plants Grow?*
- *How to Grow Tomatoes*
- *Plants Grow Everywhere*
- *A Vet for All Animals*

Fiction Books
- *Annie Makes a Big Change*
- *Camping at Crescent Lake*
- *Growing Up*
- *Too Many Rabbit Holes*
- *Where Is Fish?*

Physical Science

Nonfiction Books
- *Many Types of Energy*
- *Sink or Float?*

Fiction Books
- *The Hummingbird*
- *Our School Science Fair*

Grade 2 Leveled Readers

Social Studies

Citizenship

Nonfiction Books

- *America's Birthday*
- *The Barn Raising*
- *Be Ready for an Emergency*
- *Everyone Can Make a Difference!*
- *Join an Adventure Club!*
- *Keeping Our Community Safe*
- *Protect the Earth*
- *The Rescue Dogs*
- *Service Workers*
- *Special Animal Helpers*
- *Using a Net*
- *What Can You Do?*
- *Working Dogs*

Fiction Books

- *Andrew's Mistake*
- *Camping with Pup*
- *Freda the Signmaker*
- *Hubert and Frankie*
- *Let's Work Together!*
- *Marty's Summer Job*
- *Sally and the Wild Puppy*
- *Stripes and Silver*
- *Too Many Frogs!*
- *Training Peanut*

Culture

Nonfiction Books

- *Celebrations and Family Traditions*
- *Living in Seoul*
- *Showing Good Manners*
- *Special Chinese Birthdays*
- *A World of Birthdays*

Fiction Books

- *Ana Is Shy*
- *The Camping Trip*
- *Country Friends, City Friends*
- *Dotty's Art*
- *The First People to Fly*
- *Glooskap and the First Summer: An Algonquin Tale*
- *Happy New Year!*
- *The International Food Fair*
- *Just Like Grandpa*
- *Living on a Ranch*
- *The New Kid in Bali*
- *Voting Day*

Economics

Nonfiction Books

- *Services and Goods*

Fiction Books

- *Country Mouse and City Mouse*
- *A Quiet Place*
- *Snakeskin Canyon*

History

Nonfiction Books

- *A Few Nifty Inventions*
- *The Hoover Dam*
- *Living in a Democracy*
- *Making Travel Fun*
- *Saint Bernards and Other Working Dogs*
- *Starting a New Life*
- *Women Play Baseball*

Fiction Books

- *At Home in the Wilderness*
- *A Class Play*
- *A Cowboy's Life*
- *Down on the Ranch*
- *Hank's Tortilla Factory*

Government

Nonfiction Books

- *Communicating Then and Now*
- *Let's Send a Letter!*

More Great Titles

Biography

- *American Revolution Heroes*
- *Baseball Heroes Make History*
- *Thomas Adams: Chewing Gum Inventor*
- *Three Great Ballplayers*

Matching Books & Readers

Planning Teacher Study Groups

Adventurous teachers often have good ideas for lessons. A teacher study group is a great way to share ideas and get feedback on the best way to connect content and students. Working with other teachers can provide you with the support and motivation you need to implement new teaching strategies. A teacher study group offers many opportunities to collaborate, support each other's work, share insights, and get feedback.

Think About It

A weekly or monthly teacher study group can help support you in developing your expertise in the classroom. You and a group of like-minded teachers can form your own study group. What can this group accomplish?

- Read and discuss professional articles by researchers in the field of education.
- Meet to share teaching tips, collaborate on multi-grade lessons, and share resources.
- Develop lessons to try out new teaching strategies. Meet to share experiences and discuss how to further improve your teaching approach.

Let's Meet!

Forming a study group is easy. Just follow these four steps:

1. **Decide on the size of the group.** A small group has the advantage of making each member feel accountable, but make sure that all people can make the same commitment!

2. **Choose teachers to invite to join your group.** Think about whom you want to invite. Should they all teach the same grade? Can you invite teachers from other schools? Remember that the more diverse the group, the more it benefits from new perspectives.

3. **Set goals for the group.** In order to succeed, know what you want the group to do. Meet to set goals. Rank goals in order of importance and refer often to the goals to keep the group on track.

4. **Make logistical decisions.** This is often the most difficult. Decide where and when you will meet. Consider an online meeting place where group members can post discussion questions and replies if people are not able to meet.

What Will We Study?
Use the goals you set to help determine what your group will study. Consider what materials are needed to reach your goals, and how long you think you will need to prepare for each meeting.

How Will It Work?
Think about how you structure groups in your classroom. Then use some of the same strategies.

- **Assign a group facilitator.** This person is responsible for guiding the meeting. This person comes prepared with discussion questions and leads the meeting. This could be a rotating responsibility dependent on experience with various topics. This person might be responsible for providing the materials.

- **Assign a recorder.** Have someone take notes during the meeting and record group decisions.

- **Use the jigsaw method.** Not everyone has time to be a facilitator. In this case, divide the text and assign each portion to a different person. Each person is responsible for leading the discussion on that particular part.

Meet Again
Make a commitment to meet for a minimum number of times. After that, the group can reevaluate and decide whether or not to continue.

> " Have some great teaching tips to share? Want to exchange ideas with your colleagues? Build your own professional community of teachers. **Customize Literacy** gets you started. "

Trial Lessons

Use your colleagues' experiences to help as you think about new ways to connect content and students. Use the following plan to create a mini-lesson. It should last twenty minutes. Get the support of your colleagues as you try something new and then reflect on what happened.

Be Creative! As you develop a plan for a mini-lesson, use these four words to guide planning: *purpose, text, resources,* and *routine.*

- **Purpose:** Decide on a skill or strategy to teach. Define your purpose for teaching the lesson.

- **Text:** Develop a list of the materials you could use. Ask your colleagues for suggestions.

- **Resources:** Make a list of the available resources, and consider how to use those resources most effectively. Consider using the leveled readers listed on pages CL24–CL29 and CL36–CL41 of Customize Literacy.

- **Routine:** Choose an instructional routine to structure your mini-lesson. See the mini-lessons in Customize Literacy for suggestions.

Try It! Try out your lesson! Consider audio- or videotaping the lesson for later review. You may wish to invite a colleague to sit in as you teach. Make notes on how the lesson went.

How Did It Go? Use the self-evaluation checklist on page CL45 as you reflect on your trial lesson. This provides a framework for later discussion.

Discuss, Reflect, Repeat Solicit feedback from your teacher study group. Explain the lesson and share your reflections. Ask for suggestions on ways to improve the lesson. Take some time to reflect on the feedback. Modify your lesson to reflect what you have learned. Then try teaching the lesson again.

Checklist for Teacher Self-Evaluation

How Well Did I ...	Very Well	Satisfactory	Not Very Well
Plan the lesson?			
Select the appropriate level of text?			
Introduce the lesson and explain its objectives?			
Review previously taught skills?			
Directly explain the new skills being taught?			
Model the new skills?			
Break the material down into small steps?			
Integrate guided practice into the lesson?			
Monitor guided practice for student understanding?			
Provide feedback on independent practice?			
Maintain an appropriate pace?			
Assess student understanding of the material?			
Stress the importance of applying the skill as they read?			
Maintain students' interest?			
Ask questions?			
Handle student questions and responses?			
Respond to the range of abilities?			

Building Community

Books for Teachers

Children aren't the only ones who need to read to grow. Here is a brief list of books that you may find useful to fill your reading teacher basket and learn new things.

A Professional Bibliography

Adams, M. J. "Alphabetic Anxiety and Explicit, Systematic Phonics Instruction: A Cognitive Science Perspective." *Handbook of Early Literacy Research.* The Guilford Press, 2001.

Adams, M. J. *Beginning to Read: Thinking and Learning About Print.* The MIT Press, 1990.

Afflerbach, P. "The Influence of Prior Knowledge and Text Genre on Readers' Prediction Strategies." *Journal of Reading Behavior,* vol. XXII, no. 2 (1990).

Armbruster, B. B., F. Lehr, and J. Osborn. *Put Reading First: The Research Building Blocks for Teaching Children to Read.* Partnership for Reading, Washington, D.C., 2001.

Bear, D. R., M. Invernizzi, S. Templeton, and F. Johnston. *Words Their Way.* Merrill Prentice Hall, 2004.

Beck, I., M. G. McKeown, and L. Kucan. *Bringing Words to Life: Robust Vocabulary Instruction.* The Guilford Press, 2002.

Biemiller, A. "Teaching Vocabulary in the Primary Grades: Vocabulary Instruction Needed." *Vocabulary Instruction Research to Practice.* The Guilford Press, 2004.

Blachowicz, C. and P. Fisher. "Vocabulary Instruction." *Handbook of Reading Research,* vol. III. Lawrence Erlbaum Associates, 2000.

Cunningham, P. M. and J. W. Cunningham. "What We Know About How to Teach Phonics." *What Research Says About Reading Instruction,* 3rd ed. International Reading Association, 2002.

Daniels, H. *Literature Circles.* 2nd ed. Stenhouse Publishers, 2002.

Dickson, S. V., D. C. Simmons, and E. J. Kame'enui. "Text Organization: Instructional and Curricular Basics and Implications." *What Reading Research Tells Us About Children with Diverse Learning Needs: Bases and Basics.* Lawrence Erlbaum Associates, 1998.

Diller, D. *Making the Most of Small Groups: Differentiation for All.* Stenhouse Publishers, 2007.

Duke, N. K., V. S. Bennett-Armistead, and E. M. Roberts. "Bridging the Gap Between Learning to Read and Reading to Learn." *Literacy and Young Children: Research-Based Practices.* The Guilford Press, 2003.

Duke, N. K. and C. Tower. "Nonfiction Texts for Young Readers." *The Texts in Elementary Classrooms.* Lawrence Erlbaum Associates, 2004.

Ehri, L. C. and S. R. Nunes. "The Role of Phonemic Awareness in Learning to Read." *What Research Has to Say About Reading Instruction.* 3rd ed. International Reading Association, 2002.

Fountas, I. C. and G. S. Pinnell. *Guided Reading: Good First Teaching for All Children.* Heinemann, 1996.

Fountas, I. C. and G. S. Pinnell. *Matching Books to Readers: Using Leveled Books in Guided Reading,* K-3. Heinemann, 1999.

Harvey, S. and A. Goudvis. *Strategies That Work: Teaching Comprehension to Enhance Understanding.* 2nd ed. Stenhouse Publishers, 2007.

Hiebert, E. H. and L. A. Martin. "The Texts of Beginning Reading Instruction." *Handbook of Early Literacy Research.* The Guilford Press, 2001.

Indrisano, R. and J. R. Paratore. *Learning to Write, Writing to Learn. Theory and Research in Practice.* International Reading Association, 2005.

Juel, C., G. Biancarosa, D. Coker, and R. Deffes. "Walking with Rosie: A Cautionary Tale of Early Reading Instruction." *Educational Leadership* (April 2003).

National Reading Panel. *Teaching Children to Read.* National Institute of Child Health and Human Development, 1999.

Pressley, M. *Reading Instruction That Works: The Case for Balanced Teaching,* 3rd ed. The Guilford Press, 2005.

Smith, S., D. C. Simmons, and E. J. Kame'enui. "Word Recognition: Research Bases." *What Reading Research Tells Us About Children with Diverse Learning Needs: Bases and Basics.* Lawrence Erlbaum Associates, 1998.

Snow, C., S. Burns, and P. Griffin, eds. *Preventing Reading Difficulties in Young Children.* National Academy Press, 1998.

Vaughn, S., P. G. Mathes, S. Linan-Thompson, and D. J. Francis. "Teaching English Language Learners at Risk for Reading Disabilities to Read: Putting Research into Practice." *Learning Disabilities Research & Practice,* vol. 20, issue 1 (February 2006).

WEEK 1

Oral Vocabulary for

Let's Learn
Amazing Words

Definitions, examples, and **applications** to use with the Oral Vocabulary in each lesson.

A Place to Play

Amazing Words Oral Vocabulary Routine

DAY 1

population

1. The *population* is the number of people who live in a place.

2. **Examples** The *population* of a town is the number of people who live in the town. All the people who live in a country make up the *population* of the country. The *population* of our class is the number of children in our class.

3. **Apply To The Instruction** Which of these is likely to have a larger *population,* a big city or a small town? Why?

public

1. Something that is *public* is for all people.

2. **Examples** *Public* property belongs to everyone. The *public* library is open to everyone in the community. A *public* school is free for everyone to attend. A place that belongs to one person or group is private, not *public.*

3. **Apply To The Instruction** Name a public place in our community. Tell what people do there.

DAY 2

shuffle

1. Shuffle means "to walk slowly and drag your feet."

2. **Examples** The tired man *shuffles* his feet. Does your mom ever tell you not to *shuffle* your feet?

3. **Apply To The Instruction** Show me how to *shuffle* your feet.

DAY 4

spindly

1. Something *spindly* is very long and thin.

2. **Examples** The dog wobbled on its *spindly* legs. Without enough water and light, the plant became *spindly.*

3. **Apply To The Instruction** If something is *spindly,* is it tall and thin or short and fat?

Ruby in Her Own Time

Amazing Words Oral Vocabulary Routine

DAY 1

attempt

1. When you *attempt* something, you try to do it.
2. **Examples** A baby will crawl before *attempting* to walk. The soccer player *attempts* to score a goal every game. I *attempted* to call you on the phone, but no one answered.
3. **Apply To The Instruction** What is something you will *attempt* to do in school this year?

time line

1. A *time line* is the amount of time it takes to do something. It can also be a chart that shows the order of events.
2. **Examples** My brother had a *time line* for learning to play the trumpet. We studied a *time line* about George Washington's life.
3. **Apply To The Instruction** What important things would you include in a *time line* of your life?

DAY 2

flatter

1. When you *flatter* someone, you praise that person too much to please him or her.
2. **Examples** The boy *flattered* his teacher when he told her that she was the best teacher in the world. You can *flatter* your mother by telling her that no one cooks as well as she does.
3. **Apply To The Instruction** Do you think people will like you better if you *flatter* them? Explain your answer.

DAY 4

lovely

1. If something is *lovely,* it is very pretty.
2. **Examples** The flowers in the garden are *lovely.* Mother looked *lovely* in her new dress. Grandma was wearing a *lovely* necklace.
3. **Apply To The Instruction** Name a word that means the opposite of *lovely.* Name a word that means almost the same as *lovely.*

The Class Pet

Let's Learn Amazing Words

Definitions, examples, and **applications** to use with the Oral Vocabulary in each lesson.

Amazing Words Oral Vocabulary Routine

DAY 1

features

1. *Features* are parts or details that stand out.
2. **Examples** We talk about people's or animals' *features* to tell what they look like. A skinny tail and a long nose are *features* of a mouse. One of the woman's outstanding *features* was her long red hair.
3. **Apply To The Instruction** Describe the *features* of your best friend.

natural

1. Something *natural* grows on its own in nature and is not made by people.
2. **Examples** *Natural* gas comes from the earth. The wild flowers were a *natural* beauty. These *natural* forests have been here for hundreds of years.
3. **Apply To The Instruction** Tell about something *natural* you have read about or seen on TV.

DAY 2

swoop

1. To *swoop* is to come down fast on something.
2. **Examples** The owl *swoops* to catch the mouse. The eagle is waiting to *swoop* down on the rabbit. Dad *swooped* the baby up out of the crib.
3. **Apply To The Instruction** Show me how you would *swoop* to catch something before it hit the ground.

DAY 4

nudges

1. *Nudges* means "to touch or push gently."
2. **Examples** The dog *nudges* me with her nose when she wants to be petted. My brother *nudged* me to wake me up during the movie. You might *nudge* someone to get that person to move.
3. **Apply To The Instruction** Demonstrate with a volunteer how to *nudge* someone.

wriggle

1. When you *wriggle,* you twist and move back and forth.
2. **Examples** The baby *wriggled* in her highchair because she wanted to play on the floor. The worm *wriggles* through the dirt. If you can't sit still, you might *wriggle* in your seat.
3. **Apply To The Instruction** Show me what it looks like to *wriggle.*

UNIT 3

Acknowledgments

Teacher's Edition

KWL Strategy: The KWL Interactive Reading Strategy was developed and is used by permission of Donna Ogle, National-Louis University, Skokie, Illinois, co-author of *Reading Today and Tomorrow,* Holt, Rinehart & Winston Publishers, 1988. (See also the *Reading Teacher,* February 1986, pp. 564–570.)

Understanding by Design Quotes: Wiggins, G. & McTighe, J. (2005). *Understanding by Design.* Alexandria, VA: Association for Supervision and Curriculum Development.

Illustrations

Cover Daniel Moreton

Running Header Steven Mach

Photographs

Every effort has been made to secure permission and provide appropriate credit for photographic material. The publisher deeply regrets any omission and pledges to correct errors called to its attention in subsequent editions.

Unless otherwise acknowledged, all photographs are the property of Pearson Education, Inc.

Student Edition

Acknowledgments

Text
Grateful acknowledgment is made to the following for copyrighted material:

Page 52: From *Ruby in Her Own Time* by Jonathan Emmett, illustrated by Rebecca Harry. Text copyright © 2003 by Jonathan Emmett, illustrations copyright © 2003 by Rebecca Harry. Reprinted by permission of Scholastic, Inc. Also from *Ruby Flew Too!* written by Jonathan Emmett and illustrated by Rebecca Harry (Copyright © 2004 Macmillan Publishers Ltd., London, UK), reprinted by permission of Macmillan Publishers Ltd.

Page 126: "The Garden" by Arnold Lobel from FROG AND TOAD TOGETHER. Text Copyright © 1971, 1972 by Arnold Lobel. Used by permission of HarperCollins Publishers.

Page 158: From "I'm a Caterpillar" by Jean Marzollo, illustrated by Judith Moffat. A Hello Science Reader! Scholastic Inc./Cartwheel Books. Text copyright © 1997 by Jean Marzollo, illustrations copyright © 1997 by Judith Moffat. Used by permission.

Page 212: "This Tooth" by Lee Bennett Hopkins. Copyright © 1970 by Lee Bennett Hopkins. First appeared in *ME!*, published by Seabury Press. Reprinted by permission of Curtis Brown, Ltd. All rights reserved.

Page 213: "Tommy" by Gwendolyn Brooks. Reprinted by Consent of Brooks Permissions.

Page 214: From "I'm a Caterpillar" by Jean Marzollo, illustrated by Judith Moffat. A Hello Science Reader! Scholastic Inc./Cartwheel Books. Text copyright © 1997 by Jean Marzollo, illustrations copyright © 1997 by Judith Moffat. Used by permission.

Note: Every effort has been made to locate the copyright owner of material reproduced on this component. Omissions brought to our attention will be corrected in subsequent editions.

Illustrations
E34, E35 Mary Anne Lloyd
14 Nathan Hale
20-36 Marisara Cocca-Leffler
39-41 Nan Brooks
46 Steve Simpson
70-81 Paul Eric Roca
94 Dani Jones
110-115 Viviana Garofoli
116 Erwin Haya
150 Orlando Ramírez
184 Ron Lieser
190-204 Scott Gustafson
212, 213 David Diaz

Photographs
Every effort has been made to secure permission and provide appropriate credit for photographic material. The publisher deeply regrets any omission and pledges to correct errors called to its attention in subsequent editions.

Unless otherwise acknowledged, all photographs are the property of Pearson Education, Inc.

Photo locators denoted as follows: Top (T), Center (C), Bottom (B), Left (L), Right (R), Background (Bkgd)

12 ©Joseph Sohm/Visions of America/Corbis, ©Rudy Sulgan/Corbis
42 (T) ©Don Mason/Brand X/Corbis
43 (B) ©Larry Williams/Corbis, (C) ©Photomorgana/Corbis
45 (T) ©Janette Beckman/Corbis, (B) ©Rana Faure/Getty Images
82 ©Leon M. Stone/Nature Picture Library, ©Rolf Nussbaumer/Nature Picture Library
83 ©Rolf Nussbaumer/Nature Picture Library, Radius Images/Jupiter Images
96 (CL) ©De Meester/ARCO/Nature Picture Library, (BL) ©DK Images, (TL) Emilio Suetak/©iStockphoto
97 (B) Stephen Hayward/©DK Images
99 (R) Jane Burton/©DK Images
100 (B) ©Jane Burton/Nature Picture Library
101 (B) ©Jose B. Ruiz/Nature Picture Library, (C) Kim Taylor/©DK Images
102 (B) ©Barrie Watts/©DK Images
103 (B) ©Jane Burton/Nature Picture Library
118 ©Max Spreewald/Getty Images
119 ©Robert Harding Picture Library Ltd./Alamy Images
146 (B) Dave King/DK Images
147 (CL) ©D. Boone/Corbis, (BL) William Taufic/Corbis
150 Digital Vision
151 ©Eric Baccega/Nature Picture Library, ©Ross Hoddinott/Nature Picture Library
182 (B) ©George McCarthy/Corbis

Student Edition p. 230

Teacher Notes

Teacher Notes

Teacher Notes

3

Teacher Notes

Teacher Notes

Teacher Notes

Teacher Notes

Teacher Resources

Looking for Teacher Resources and other important information?

In the **First Stop** on Reading Street

- Dear First Grade Teacher
- Research into Practice on Reading Street
- Guide to Reading Street
- Assessment on Reading Street
- Customize Writing on Reading Street
- Differentiate Instruction on Reading Street

- ELL on Reading Street
- Customize Literacy on Reading Street
- Digital Products on Reading Street
- Teacher Resources for Grade 1
- Index

Teacher Resources

Looking for Teacher Resources and other important information?

In the **First Stop** on Reading Street

- **Dear First Grade Teacher**
- **Research into Practice on Reading Street**
- **Guide to Reading Street**
- **Assessment on Reading Street**
- **Customize Writing on Reading Street**
- **Differentiate Instruction on Reading Street**

- **ELL on Reading Street**
- **Customize Literacy on Reading Street**
- **Digital Products on Reading Street**
- **Teacher Resources for Grade 1**
- **Index**